D1602174

Cases on Branding Strategies and Product Development:

Successes and Pitfalls

Sarmistha Sarma
Institute of Innovation in Technology and Management, Guru Gobind Singh Indraprashtha University, India

Sukhvinder Singh
Institute of Innovation in Technology and Management, Guru Gobind Singh Indraprashtha University, India

A volume in the Advances in Marketing, Customer Relationship Management, and E-Services (AMCRMES) Book Series

An Imprint of IGI Global

Managing Director:	Lindsay Johnston
Managing Editor:	Austin DeMarco
Director of Intellectual Property & Contracts:	Jan Travers
Acquisitions Editor:	Kayla Wolfe
Production Editor:	Christina Henning
Typesetter:	Amanda Smith
Cover Design:	Jason Mull

Published in the United States of America by
    Business Science Reference (an imprint of IGI Global)
    701 E. Chocolate Avenue
    Hershey PA 17033
    Tel: 717-533-8845
    Fax: 717-533-8661
    E-mail: cust@igi-global.com
    Web site: http://www.igi-global.com

Library of Congress Cataloging-in-Publication Data
Cases on branding strategies and product development : successes and pitfalls
/ Sarmistha Sarma and Sukhvinder Singh, editors.
    pages cm
 Includes bibliographical references and index.
 ISBN 978-1-4666-7393-9 (hardcover) -- ISBN 978-1-4666-7394-6 (ebook) -- ISBN 978-1-4666-7396-0 (print & perpetual access) 1. Product management--Case studies. 2. Brand name products--Case studies. 3. Branding (Marketing)--Case studies. 4. Brand choice--Case studies. I. Sarma, Sarmistha. II. Singh, Sukhvinder.
 HF5415.15.C33 2015
 658.8'27--dc23
                      2014040322

This book is published in the IGI Global book series Advances in Marketing, Customer Relationship Management, and E-Services (AMCRMES) (ISSN: 2327-5502; eISSN: 2327-5529)

British Cataloguing in Publication Data
A Cataloguing in Publication record for this book is available from the British Library.

For electronic access to this publication, please contact: eresources@igi-global.com.

Advances in Marketing, Customer Relationship Management, and E–Services (AMCRMES) Book Series

ISSN: 2327-5502
EISSN: 2327-5529

MISSION

Business processes, services, and communications are important factors in the management of good customer relationship, which is the foundation of any well organized business. Technology continues to play a vital role in the organization and automation of business processes for marketing, sales, and customer service. These features aid in the attraction of new clients and maintaining existing relationships.

The **Advances in Marketing, Customer Relationship Management, and E-Services (AMCRMES) Book Series** addresses success factors for customer relationship management, marketing, and electronic services and its performance outcomes. This collection of reference source covers aspects of consumer behavior and marketing business strategies aiming towards researchers, scholars, and practitioners in the fields of marketing management.

COVERAGE

- Mobile services
- Web Mining and Marketing
- Customer Retention
- Text Mining and Marketing
- Customer Relationship Management
- E-Service Innovation
- Online Community Management and Behavior
- Ethical Considerations in E-Marketing
- Telemarketing
- Relationship Marketing

IGI Global is currently accepting manuscripts for publication within this series. To submit a proposal for a volume in this series, please contact our Acquisition Editors at Acquisitions@igi-global.com or visit: http://www.igi-global.com/publish/.

Titles in this Series

For a list of additional titles in this series, please visit: www.igi-global.com

Cases on Branding Strategies and Product Development Successes and Pitfalls
Sarmistha Sarma (Institute of Innovation in Technology and Management, Guru Gobind Singh Indraprashtha University, India) and Sukhvinder Singh (Institute of Innovation in Technology and Management, Guru Gobind Singh Indraprashtha University, India)
Information Science Reference • copyright 2015 • 382pp • H/C (ISBN: 9781466673939) • US $195.00 (our price)

Handbook of Research on Managing and Influencing Consumer Behavior
Hans-Ruediger Kaufmann (University of Nicosia, Cyprus & International Business School at Vilnius University, Lithuania)
Business Science Reference • copyright 2015 • 728pp • H/C (ISBN: 9781466665477) • US $355.00 (our price)

Computer-Mediated Marketing Strategies Social Media and Online Brand Communities
Gordon Bowen (Regent's University, UK) and Wilson Ozuem (University of Gloucestershire, UK)
Business Science Reference • copyright 2015 • 313pp • H/C (ISBN: 9781466665958) • US $195.00 (our price)

Market Research Methodologies Multi-Method and Qualitative Approaches
Amandeep Takhar-Lail (University of Bedfordshire, UK) and Ali Ghorbani (Payame Noor University, Iran)
Business Science Reference • copyright 2015 • 300pp • H/C (ISBN: 9781466663718) • US $215.00 (our price)

Handbook of Research on Effective Marketing in Contemporary Globalism
Bryan Christiansen (PryMarke, LLC, USA) Salih Yıldız (Gümüşhane University, Turkey) and Emel Yıldız (Gümüşhane University, Turkey)
Business Science Reference • copyright 2014 • 463pp • H/C (ISBN: 9781466662209) • US $325.00 (our price)

Strategic Marketing in Fragile Economic Conditions
Irene Samanta (Graduate Technological Education Institute of Piraeus, Greece)
Business Science Reference • copyright 2014 • 300pp • H/C (ISBN: 9781466662322) • US $200.00 (our price)

DISSEMINATOR OF KNOWLEDGE

www.igi-global.com

701 E. Chocolate Ave., Hershey, PA 17033
Order online at www.igi-global.com or call 717-533-8845 x100
To place a standing order for titles released in this series,
contact: cust@igi-global.com
Mon-Fri 8:00 am - 5:00 pm (est) or fax 24 hours a day 717-533-8661

Table of Contents

Foreword xvi

Preface xviii

Acknowledgment xxvi

Learn Branding through Case Studies xxvii

Chapter 1
A Case-Based Identification of Internal and External Issues for Branding
Strategies...1
   Abu Sayeed Mondal, Swami Vivekananda Institute of Science and
      Technology, India
   Dilip Roy, University of Burdwan, India

Chapter 2
Promoting Bucovina's Tourism Brand...24
   Alexandru-Mircea Nedelea, Ştefan cel Mare University of Suceava,
      Romania

Chapter 3
Branding and Brand Management: Case of Amul..47
   Anupam Sharma, Thapar University Patiala, India

Chapter 4
Service Branding through Quality Practices in Public and Private
Telecommunication Organization 79
   Archana Krishnan, University of Delhi, India

Chapter 5
The Importance of Supply Chain Management in Positioning and Creating
Brands of Agro-Based Products..103
    Aroop Mukherjee, Universiti Putra Malaysia, Malaysia
    Nitty Hirawaty Kamarulzaman, Universiti Putra Malaysia, Malaysia

Chapter 6
Building and Development of Dairy "Dana" Brand..132
    Boris Milović, Sava Kovacevic Vrbas, Serbia

Chapter 7
Simply Food: The Crossroads in Front of a New-Born Food Brand.................165
    Hakim A. Meshreki, American University in Cairo (AUC), Egypt
    Maha Mourad, American University in Cairo (AUC), Egypt

Chapter 8
Branding and New Product Development: A Case of Glemma........................178
    Dennis Damen, Glemma, The Netherlands & Fontys University of
        Applied Sciences, The Netherlands
    Miao Wang, Fontys University of Applied Sciences, The Netherlands
    Tim Wijnhoven, Glemma, The Netherlands & Fontys University of
        Applied Sciences, The Netherlands

Chapter 9
Factors Influencing the Buying Behavior of Female Consumers with
Reference to Top Three Brands of Make-Up Cosmetics in Pune City..............194
    Mukta Srivastava, Allana Institute of Management Sciences, India

Chapter 10
A Case Study on Pitfalls in Branding of Boroline...239
    R. Padma, Jain University, India
    Pawan Sharma, Jain University, India

Chapter 11
Managing Brand Portfolio in a Crisis: The Case of a Pharmaceutical
Company in Egypt 254
    Rafic Nadi, American University in Cairo, Egypt
    Ahmed Tolba, American University in Cairo, Egypt

Chapter 12
Ariika Bean Bags: A Successful Brand Capable of International
Expansion?...277
    Rania Hussein, The American University in Cairo, Egypt
    Hend Mostafa, The American University in Cairo, Egypt

Chapter 13
Semiotics of Brand Building: Case of the Muthoot Group...............................298
    Sudio Sudarśan, Hult International Management School, USA

Chapter 14
Sensory Branding: Branding with Senses..327
    Surabhi Mukherjee Chakravarty, CMR – Institute of Management
    Studies, Bangalore, India & Alliance University, India

Conclusion 366

Compilation of References 391

About the Contributors 408

Index 415

Detailed Table of Contents

Foreword xvi

Preface xviii

Acknowledgment xxvi

Learn Branding through Case Studies xxvii

Chapter 1
A Case-Based Identification of Internal and External Issues for Branding
Strategies...1
> *Abu Sayeed Mondal, Swami Vivekananda Institute of Science and*
> *Technology, India*
> *Dilip Roy, University of Burdwan, India*

In this chapter, the authors offer a strategic platform to pinpoint the variables for developing branding strategies. The case elicits the internal and external aspects of a brand. These two aspects are considered to be the starting point of the strategic roadmap to reach success. A detailed discussion on the brand's internal and external aspects has been made with the help of a successful case. However, the authors go beyond the identification of internal and external aspects of brands and suggest a scheme for arriving at branding strategies. Basically, these two aspects of brands have been matched and a four-cell strategic guideline has been developed. The authors call this four-cell strategic guideline C4 strategy matrix, wherein four types of branding strategies (Continuity, Caution, Change, and Correction) are available.

Chapter 2

Promoting Bucovina's Tourism Brand...24
Alexandru-Mircea Nedelea, Ştefan cel Mare University of Suceava, Romania

In this chapter there is a presentation of Bucovina as an attractive tourism region of Romania, more and more appreciated by native and foreign tourists, having characteristics which distinguish it from the other Romanian tourism regions, namely the monasteries pertaining to UNESCO heritage. Nevertheless, the tourism in Bucovina can be oriented in many directions: historical and religious tourism, sports tourism, balneary tourism, and recreational tourism. The multitude of tourism forms that can be practiced in Bucovina must become well known; the possible visitors need to know that they can practice other forms of tourism besides the religious one, and this is why it is necessary to create the tourism brand of Bucovina. The promotion program of the brand of Bucovina must consider two main objectives: the presentation of the tourist sites and the deliverance of a good service quality.

Chapter 3

Branding and Brand Management: Case of Amul 47
Anupam Sharma, Thapar University Patiala, India

In the appearance of globalization and liberalization, both brand and branding have become essential parts of every competitive business firm. To become part of the competitive and ever-changing business world and to maintain the existing business image, business organizations have been continuously focusing upon introducing innovative branding practices and strategies. This chapter focuses on brand and branding strategies of Indian brand name dairy cooperative, AMUL, in western India (Gujarat Cooperative Milk Marketing Federation [GCMMF]), which has developed a successful model for doing business in the large, emerging Indian economy. Amul has been primarily accountable, through its inventive practices, and adaptive to market changes, for India's becoming the world's largest producer of milk. This chapter draws various lessons from the experiences of AMUL that would be useful to business organizations globally.

Chapter 4

Service Branding through Quality Practices in Public and Private
Telecommunication Organization 79
Archana Krishnan, University of Delhi, India

This chapter focuses on comparative analysis of service branding of two telecommunication organisations—one in the public and one in the private sector— through the implementation of quality initiatives. This case was designed after extensive interviews with senior managers to understand the practical issues and challenges involved in improvement of service branding of an organisation through the implementation of quality initiatives, such as benchmarking, leadership, service orientation, continuous improvement, and knowledge management, and their subsequent impact on organisation culture and organisation effectiveness. Even though the public sector organisation has taken several measures to improve service branding through quality in its services, it is engulfed in its own internal issues as compared to the private sector organisation. The real life scenarios of both the organisations presented in the case could facilitate young managers to address the challenges involved in improving the service branding of the organisation through the implementation of quality practices in the future.

Chapter 5
The Importance of Supply Chain Management in Positioning and Creating Brands of Agro-Based Products..103
Aroop Mukherjee, Universiti Putra Malaysia, Malaysia
Nitty Hirawaty Kamarulzaman, Universiti Putra Malaysia, Malaysia

This case aims to provide information on the importance of supply chain management in creating and positioning of brands of products by companies. Supply chain management entails configuration, collaboration, and coordination. The company that uses only costing for creating brands without resource availability exposes its supply chain to an insufferable risk. Consequently, the company hoping to create its brand in the world market needs to be more resilient in the supply chain process and resources. A strategic and holistic approach to supply chain in collaboration with different companies will help to identify the different strategies, which can be more resilient and efficient supply chain. Supply chain management acts as branding tool and is vital for conveying branded goods to the market in optimal time and cost. The creation of a brand name is linked to management strategies, but persistence and character are possible solely by using supply chain efficiently.

Chapter 6
Building and Development of Dairy "Dana" Brand 132
Boris Milović, Sava Kovacevic Vrbas, Serbia

For success it is not enough to have the best and highest quality product, best price, the best distribution network, and excellent promotion; the most important thing is how the consumer values it. The market for dairy products in Serbia is dominated by products that were perceived as average and ordinary, consumed simply to meet basic nutritional needs. Agricultural company Sava Kovacevic had great products, but not brands. Development of brand "Dana" is focused on that specific benefits found to provide consumers a brand as well as a range of values that a new brand represents. The very brand strategy is developed after a detailed analysis of the product, consumers for which it is intended (their lifestyles, habits, attitudes, etc.), competition and market conditions, market position of competing brands, and their communication with customers and the general public. Therefore, brand image of the product is built along with its unique position in the market.

Chapter 7
Simply Food: The Crossroads in Front of a New-Born Food Brand.................165
    Hakim A. Meshreki, American University in Cairo (AUC), Egypt
    Maha Mourad, American University in Cairo (AUC), Egypt

Simply food is the first food brand that was launched in September 2013 by "Orange International" company. Simply food's aim is to provide a high quality food round the corner for young students and business professionals who are seeking a high quality meal during their lunch break or their evening outing. Simply Food team has many prospects to work upon in terms of the management of the stores in addition to expansion and creation of other simply brands. Issues facing management are which simply sub-brands to launch that would be integrated into the simply brand and how to expand simply stores in Egypt and the region. Furthermore, what is the proper marketing strategy given the limited budget available that would help strengthening the simply brand? What is the proper regional expansion strategy that would enable the simply brand to the fast food destination for customers in the region?

Chapter 8
Branding and New Product Development: A Case of Glemma.........................178
    Dennis Damen, Glemma, The Netherlands & Fontys University of
        Applied Sciences, The Netherlands
    Miao Wang, Fontys University of Applied Sciences, The Netherlands
    Tim Wijnhoven, Glemma, The Netherlands & Fontys University of
        Applied Sciences, The Netherlands

The Glemma case explains brand management of a young startup company located in Eindhoven, The Netherlands. The case describes background, the current status, and present challenge of Glemma. Since the company is still in a very early stage, the management system is not mature yet. Hence, the Glemma case falls into the new product development category in the book. In addition, Glemma was a Web design company in the beginning; they released a universal reservation system on June 2013. Therefore, branding here is not only for Glemma itself but also for the new product they developed. The Glemma team has tried many times with various different approaches. In the early stage, the team really focused on brand image. They took on enormous projects just to deliver a professional image to customers. However, they did not reach their goal. A nice website didn't bring them any customers. Along with their experience, they figured out that brand experience is more important than brand image.

Chapter 9
Factors Influencing the Buying Behavior of Female Consumers with
Reference to Top Three Brands of Make-Up Cosmetics in Pune City 194
Mukta Srivastava, Allana Institute of Management Sciences, India

Customers are the end beneficiary of all the marketing activities. No matter what type of cosmetics a company is making (natural or chemical), what type of company it is (national or international), it has to satisfy the needs of the customers. No marketer can ever be successful until and unless it is able to understand the buying behavior of the end users. Hence, the current study addresses issues, such as, 'what factors are influencing the buying behavior of female consumers with reference to make-up cosmetics?' Has there been a relationship existing between the demographical factors and other influencing factors? How female consumers make decisions for buying a particular brand of make-up cosmetics and what factors affect the decision?

Chapter 10
A Case Study on Pitfalls in Branding of Boroline 239
R. Padma, Jain University, India
Pawan Sharma, Jain University, India

The Indian FMCG sector is the fourth largest sector in the economy with a total market size in excess of US$ 13.1 billion. The FMCG market is set to treble from US$ 11.6 billion in 2003 to US$ 33.4 billion in 2015. Skin care products are one of the key constituents of the FMCG sector. One of the major products under skin care products are antiseptic creams. In India, the market size of the antiseptic cream markets is approximately US$ 2.94 billion. The major players in the antiseptic cream industry are Betadine Cream, Boroline, Boroplus, Vicco Turmeric Cream, etc. With the growing market and many players, it becomes essential for every organization to retain the brand that it has set in the market. And every organization wants to take advantage the market and one such organization is Boroline.

Chapter 11
Managing Brand Portfolio in a Crisis: The Case of a Pharmaceutical
Company in Egypt 254
Rafic Nadi, American University in Cairo, Egypt
Ahmed Tolba, American University in Cairo, Egypt

Branding in pharmaceutical markets is more challenging than any other market due to the enormous regulations and restrictions from governmental bodies like MOH, Ministry of Health. This case tackles a real challenge that one of the leading pharmaceutical companies in Egypt is facing. Since the company has a well-established brand that has been in the market for more than 30 years, this brand has strong brand equity and is well known by consumers, end users. In the past 5 years with the devaluation of the Egyptian currency, the price of the active ingredients increased. Accordingly, the gross margin of the brand was highly affected, to the extent that it reflects losses in the net operating income. In any other market, it might be an option to increase the price and enhance the gross margin, but in the pharmaceutical industry, companies are price takers and only MOH has the right to set the price.

Chapter 12
Ariika Bean Bags: A Successful Brand Capable of International
Expansion?...277
> *Rania Hussein, The American University in Cairo, Egypt*
> *Hend Mostafa, The American University in Cairo, Egypt*

This case deals with Ariika, which produces a large variety of bean bags that have innovative designs. The company focuses on quality and aims at becoming the first branded bean bag in Egypt with high quality and reasonable prices. Over the years, Ariika was able to build a strong customer base, sell its products online, and maintain strong relationships with large retailers. The success of Ariika in the Egyptian market encouraged Attallah, the owner, to consider his next move. The key problems discussed in the case are, Should the company capitalize on possible opportunities by immediately expanding beyond Egypt? If they decide to expand abroad, how should the company strategically expand: in the two countries at the same time, sequentially one at a time, or only in one of them? Should they rely on simple exports or consider foreign direct investment?

Chapter 13
Semiotics of Brand Building: Case of the Muthoot Group...............................298
> *Sudio Sudarśan, Hult International Management School, USA*

Most theories in brand management, evolved from 20th century economics, rely on a convenient assumption of how consumers should make purchase decisions. In contradistinction, this chapter demonstrates a semiological tradition in the context of brand management using a 128-year-old brand, Muthoot Group, to expound upon the ways consumers prevalently perceive brands, which then drive their purchase decisions. Just as in marketing, where the focus changed from "economic exchange" to "social exchange," in brand management the focus needs to change from "symbols" to the way people use semiotic resources to produce both communicative artifacts and events to interpret them, which is also a form of semiotic production. Since social semiotics is not a self-contained field, the chapter historically plots the brand-building voyage of Muthoot Group, applying semiotic concepts and methods to establish a model of brand and extend the scientific understanding of differentiation, loyalty, and advocacy.

Chapter 14
Sensory Branding: Branding with Senses...327
Surabhi Mukherjee Chakravarty, CMR – Institute of Management
Studies, Bangalore, India & Alliance University, India

This chapter presents sensorial branding approaches in practice and theory. Senses play a vital role in human life. We understand almost everything in life through senses. Sensory branding is an approach through which marketers create better experience of brands. Our senses are our link to memory, which can tap right into emotion. Using senses and their effect on understanding the consumer paves the way for an enriching experience of brand, discriminating their personality, creating a core competence, more interest, preference, and customer loyalty. Sensory branding is the marketing strategy that is investigating the emotional relationships between consumer and the brand through senses. Two cases presented in the chapter are on Starbucks and Apple Inc., which highlight their sensorial strategies for stimulating consumers' relationships and fostering a lasting emotional connection that retains brand loyalty.

Conclusion 366

Compilation of References 391

About the Contributors 408

Index 415

Foreword

The brand experience has become the buzzword in marketing worldwide today. When I wrote my first books on this topic, *Experiential Marketing* in 1999 and *Customer Experience Management* in 2003, the movement on brand experiences was just starting; now it is in full swing.

But branding is more than just an experience. There are brand strategy issues, brand valuation issues, brand architecture and extensions issues, and internal, organizational branding. Branding requires analytics and creativity, as I wrote in my book *Big Think Strategy*.

Most importantly, branding requires a customer orientation. Customers decide on which brands will ultimately make it and be successful in business and become brand icons. Thus, the key goal of branding is loyalty and customer happiness, as I wrote in *Happy Customers Everywhere*.

As you can see, my own thinking on branding has covered many of the key topics. I wrote about such topics by presenting management frameworks. But what managers also need are great case examples.

Here is such a book with great practical cases. The efforts of the editors in compiling the cases is laudable and I congratulate Dr. Sarmistha Sarma and Mr. Sukhvinder Singh of India for their work. The book covers many issues related to the concept of branding. And it includes cases from many nations, like India, Egypt, Pakistan, Romania, and other markets.

The authors of the cases have brought together the various issues of branding in this useful collection of case studies. The book, *Cases on Branding Strategies and Product Development: Success and Pitfall*, will definitely add value to the existing body of knowledge in the branding literature.

Bernd Schmitt
Columbia University, USA & Institute on Asian Consumer Insight (ACI),
  Singapore

Bernd Schmitt, *PhD, is widely recognized for his major contributions to branding, marketing, and management through his unique focus on creativity, innovation, and the customer experience. He has authored or co-authored 8 books, which have been translated into more than 20 languages, including Experiential Marketing (1999), Customer Experience Management (2003), Big Think Strategy (2007), and Happy Customers Everywhere (2012). He is Robert D. Calkins Professor of International Business at Columbia Business School in New York, where he also directs the Center on Global Brand Leadership. Schmitt has been profiled on CNNfn's Business Unusual and has appeared on BBC, CNBC, CNBC-Asia, CNN, NHK, and on The Daily Show with Jon Stewart. He has contributed articles to The New York Times, the Asian Wall Street Journal, and the Financial Times. He is CEO of The EX Group, a consulting firm focusing on innovation and customer experience.*

Preface

OVERVIEW

The concept of branding has existed through time immemorial. Etymologically, the term *brand* is derived from the French word *brander*, which means "to burn." It was used by the farmers as a means to mark their livestock to distinguish them from one another. Various researches have concluded that the key to creating brand is the ability of the organization to choose the right name, logo, symbol, or any other distinguishing characteristic that sets to identify the product and make it unique when compared to others. These brand elements are the differentiators that make and mar a brand. The complex business environment demands that every organization builds a strong brand that facilitates a consumer to arrive at the right choice. A strong brand must deliver its promise of quality every time the consumer uses it, and this leads to strengthening of the brand position, which is consolidated with every passing year.

Organizations use various branding strategies. For example, Samsung uses its name for all its products while Procter and Gamble uses different brand names for different products. There are many beautiful stories associated with the naming of legendary brands of our times. The story of the christening of Apple Computers goes:

In the biography of Steve Jobs, Jobs told Walter Isaacson that he was "on one of my fruitarian diets" and had just come back from an apple farm, and thought the name sounded "fun, spirited and not intimidating" (Isaacson, 2011). Writing in his 2006 book *iWoz: Computer Geek to Cult Icon*, Apple's co-founder Steve Wozniak explains it this way: "It was a couple of weeks later when we came up with a name for the partnership. I remember I was driving Steve Jobs back from the airport along Highway 85. Steve was coming back from a visit to Oregon to a place he called an 'apple orchard.' It was actually some kind of commune. Steve suggested a name Apple Computer. The first comment out of my mouth was, 'What about Apple Records?' This was (and still is) the Beatles-owned record label. We both tried to come up with technical-sounding names that were better, but we couldn't think of any good ones. Apple was so much better, better than any other name we could think of" (Wozniak, 2006).

His concerns turned out to be justified. Apple Computer, Inc. was sued by Apple Records over trademark violations in 1989. In a 2006 interview with an MIT newspaper, Wozniak was asked again about the rationale behind the Apple name. Wozniak confirmed that it was Job's creation, and that he came up with the name after spending a few months working on an apple orchard. "After trying to think of better and more technical names, both Jobs and I realized that Apple was a good fit," he told the newspaper (Raja, 2006).

A book titled *Apple Confidential 2.0: The Definitive History of the World's Most Colorful Company* says that both Wozniak and Jobs tried out alternative brand names such as Executex and Matrix Electronics, but they didn't like anything as much as Apple Computer (Linzmayer, 1999).

Not only the names but the logo, jingles, and symbols of brands are based on people, places, or just abstract images.

PRESENT STATUS OF BRANDING RESEARCH

Brand management as a subject of research has not been a matter of concern to the companies in the world. Even for companies that had an understanding of the advantages of having a strong brand, brand management *per se* was not a matter of concern. In the United States of America there was the Robinson Patman Act (formerly the Clayton Act) that created some legal hindrances for companies to price similar products differently. Consequently, branded products could not be distinguished from the non-branded products.

In the year 1956, Wendell R. Smith founded the concept of segmentation, heralding a milestone in the marketing theories. He explained that in a heterogeneous market there are consumers with varied demand and the market itself is made up of smaller homogenous segments. The theories of segmentation were further extended by Daniel Yankelovich who was of the opinion that apart from income, education, demographic variables of age, life cycle, and social status, there are many more variables that can form the basis of segmentation of a market. Daniel proposed new concepts like the buying behavior, motives, values, consumer patterns, and aesthetic preferences. In the 1950s, Ross Cunningham discussed the concept of brand loyalty which evoked a lot of controversy in the academic circles; by then, companies had started investing in branding. Yet, there was little empirical evidence that branding efforts indeed have an effect on the increase in sales potential of a product. For many years, there was uncertainty on how companies could enforce the presence of their products as strong brands. This challenge was addressed by Marquardt et al. (1965) as a part of a research when they investigated this issue with respect to products of daily use. The findings of this study revealed that the consumers desired demystifies and simplifies the concepts of creation, execution, and the management of successful brands. The cases give us an insight into branding from the perspective of the consumer as well as the brand manager. The objective of this book is to explore the concept of branding and brand management. However, the concept of branding is comprehensive; therefore, only some of the critical aspects have been covered in the cases. The cases have explained the concept of branding, defined the concept, discussed brand equity, identified brand elements, brand awareness, etc. Brand is not a newly emerged concept; it has been in existence through the ages. The concept of branding emerged when people began to exchange their goods in order to buy what they did not have and then the idea of brand emerged. At that time, the artisans used trademarks in order to specify their unique products.

Today, the concept of brand is different and the significance of the same has increased many fold. Because there are many communication channels, people have the chance of getting exposed to lot of information. Therefore, the expectations of the people have increased. The world has become one market where there is tough competition among the brands to survive and flourish. We can well conclude that we are living in a branded culture and brands are the most important modes of communication in the modern media environment (Danesi, 2006). In the given conditions, the role and relevance of a book on branding cases becomes critical to the dissemination of knowledge about the concept of branding and in adding value to the existing body of literature available on the subject.

ORGANIZATION OF THE BOOK

Chapter 1, "A Scheme for Arriving at Branding Strategies with Case-Based Identification of Internal and External Issues," offers a strategic platform to pinpoint the variables for developing branding strategies. The case will elicit the internal and external aspects of a brand. These two aspects are considered to be the starting point of the strategic roadmap to reach success. The case is authored by Dr. Abu Sayeed Mondal and Prof. Dilip Roy. Mr. Abu Sayeed Mondal is an Assistant Professor at Department of Business Administration at Swami Vivekananda Institute of Science and Technology in Kolkata, India. Prof. Dilip Roy is a fellow of Indian Institute of Management, Calcutta (IIM-C) and a former professor of Department of Business Administration, The University of Burdwan.

Chapter 2, "Promoting Bucovina's Tourism Brand," is about promoting a tourism destination named Bucavina in Romania. The case deals with complex concept of place branding and the theoretical extrapolation of the branding concept with respect to a place of tourist destination. The author of the case is Prof. Alexandru Nedelea, an Associate Professor of Marketing at the University Stefan cel Mare of Suceava, Romania.

Chapter 3, "Branding and Brand Management: Case of Amul," focuses on brand and branding strategies of Indian brand name dairy cooperative, AMUL, in western India (Gujarat Cooperative Milk Marketing Federation [GCMMF]), which has developed a successful model for doing business in a large, emerging Indian economy. The author of the case is Dr. Anupam Sharma. She is working with Thapar University India.

Chapter 4, "Service Branding through Quality Practices in Public and Private Telecommunication Organization," focuses on comparative analysis of service branding of two telecommunication organizations—one each in the public and one in the private sector—through the implementation of quality initiatives. The author of the case is Ms. Archana Krishnan. She is a Senior Research Fellow at Faculty of Management Studies (FMS), University of Delhi, India.

Chapter 5, "The Importance of Supply Chain Management in Positioning and Creating Brands of Agro-Based Products," provides information on the importance of supply-chain management in creating and positioning brands of products by companies. Supply-chain management entails configuration, collaboration, and co-ordination of business processes. The company, which uses only costing for creating brands without resource availability, exposes its supply chain to an insufferable risk. The case is authored by Mr. Aroop Mukherjee and Dr. Nitty Hirawaty Kamarulza-man. Mr. Aroop Mukherjee is a PhD Scholar in the Department of Agribusiness and Information Systems, Universiti Putra Malaysia. Nitty Hirawaty Kamarulzaman is a senior lecturer in the Department of Agribusiness and Information Systems, Universiti Putra Malaysia.

Chapter 6, "Building and Development of Dairy 'Dana' Brand," deals with the development and the brand building of dairy products in Serbia. The market for dairy products in Serbia is dominated by products that were perceived as average and ordinary, consumed simply to meet basic nutritional needs. Agricultural company, Sava Kovacevic, had great products, but not brands. Development of brand "Dana" is focused on that specific benefits found to provide consumer a brand as well as a range of values that a new brand represents. The case is authored by Boris Milović, Associate Professor, Faculty of Sport, Belgrade, and CFO at Sava Kovacevic Vrbas, Serbia.

Chapter 7, "Simply Food: The Crossroads in Front of a New-Born Food Brand," deals with the branding of a food chain named Simply Foods, a brand launched by Orange International Company. The authors of the case are Dr. Hakim Meshreki and Dr. Maha Mourad. Dr. Hakim Meshreki is a visiting Assistant Professor of Marketing at the American University in Cairo, Egypt. Dr. Maha Mourad is an Associate Professor of Marketing at the Department of Management and Director of El-Khazindar Business Research and Case Center, School of Business, at the American University in Cairo (AUC), Egypt.

Chapter 8, "Branding and New Product Development: A Case of Glemma," deals with the branding and product development process of a techno-start-up company in The Netherlands. The authors of the case are Mr. Dennis Damen, Mr. Tim Wijnhoven of Glemma Netherlands, and Ms. Miao Wang, graduate student of International Business Management Studies at the Fontys University of Applied Sciences, The Netherlands.

Chapter 9, "Factors Influencing the Buying Behavior of Female Consumers with Reference to Top Three Brands of Make-Up Cosmetics in Pune City," analyses the role of branding of cosmetic against the buying behavior of consumers. The case is authored by Ms. Mukta Srivastava. She is Recognized Post Graduate Teacher of University of Pune, India.

Chapter 10, "A Case Study on Pitfalls in Branding of Boroline," analyses the pitfalls in branding of an age-old Indian brand of antiseptic cream called "Boroline." The case is authored by Mr. Pawan Kumar and Ms. R. Padma. Both of the authors are Assistant Professors at Jain Group of Institution, Bangalore, India.

Chapter 11, "Managing Brand Portfolio in a Crisis: The Case of a Pharmaceutical Company in Egypt," tackles a real challenge that one of the leading pharmaceutical companies in Egypt is facing. The company has a well-established brand that has been in the market for more than 30 years; this brand has strong brand equity and is well known by consumers and end users. The case is authored by Mr. Rafic Khalil and Dr. Ahmed Tolba. Mr. Rafic Nadi is an MBA student, Major Marketing, at the American University in Cairo. Dr. Ahmed Tolba is Chair and Associate Professor of Marketing, School of Business, at the American University in Cairo. He is also the founder of El-Khazindar Business Research and Case Center (KCC), the first center in the Middle East and North Africa region that focuses on developing world-class refereed case studies.

Chapter 12, "Ariika Bean Bags: A Successful Brand Capable of International Expansion?" deals with the brand expansion strategy followed by Ariika Bean Bags, a popular company in Egypt. The case is authored by Dr. Rania Hussein and a group of her students. She is an Assistant Professor of Marketing at the School of Business at the American University in Cairo. The student co-authors of the case are Mina Iskandar, Amin Atwa, John Hanna, Reem El Sisy, and Mrs. Hend Mostafa.

Chapter 13, "Semiotics of Brand Building: Case of the Muthoot Group," deals with a semiological tradition in the context of brand management using a 127-year-old brand, Muthoot Group. It explores the ways consumers prevalently perceive brands which then drive their purchase decisions. The case is authored by Prof. Sudio Sudarśan. He is a consumer behaviorist, brand strategist, and professor of Brand Management at Hult International Management School, United States of America.

Chapter 14, "Sensory Branding: Branding with Senses," analyses the branding process done through the senses and its implications on product choices. The case is authored by Ms. Surabhi Mukherjee Chakravarty. She is Faculty in Department of Management and Commerce, CMR Institute of Management Studies (CMRIMS), Bangalore, India.

Sarmistha Sarma
Institute of Innovation in Technology and Management, Guru Gobind Singh
    Indraprashtha University, India
Sukhvinder Singh
Institute of Innovation in Technology and Management, Guru Gobind Singh
    Indraprashtha University, India

REFERENCES

Danesi, M. (2006). *Brands*. Abingdon, UK: Routledge.

Isaacson, W. (2011). *Steve Jobs*. New York: Simon & Schuster.

Linzmayer, O. (1999). *Apple confidential 2.0: The definitive history of the world's most colorful company*. No Starch Press.

Marquardt, R., Makens, J., & Larzelere, H. (1965). Measuring the utility added by branding and grading. *JMR, Journal of Marketing Research*, *2*(1), 45–50.

Raja, K. (2006). Wozniak describes techno childhood; endorses autobiography. *The Tech, 126*(42).

Simon, C. J., & Sullivan, M. W. (1993). The measurement and determinants of brand equity: A financial approach. *Marketing Science*, *1*, 12.

Wozniak, S. (2006). iWoz: Computer geek to cult icon. New York: W.W. Norton and Co.

2.   *The brand identity as applied to a single or an extended family of good(s) or service(s) should also be taken into consideration. The brand identity is a program, which integrates all visual and verbal elements of a brand.*

3.   *The ongoing perception by the audiences, consumer, or public, of the brand is also significant. The target audience, which is a specific group of consumers for a brand, should be selected carefully and their perception should be investigated continuously.*

Further there are some more opinions by experts about brands:

A brand is a name, term, sign, symbol or design or combination of them, intended to identify the goods and service of one seller or group of sellers and to differentiate them from those of competition – (Keller, 2003).

In the ever increasing consumer markets of present times, brands provide the elements of differentiation between the offerings made by the companies. The distinction is critical as it can be a determinant of the success or the failure of a company. This is the reason that makes the management of brands critical for any company. Every brand differs from the other in terms of the logo trademark, design and the packaging of the same. Brands are also found to have symbolic values that enable the people to choose the best product according to their respective needs. Brand names represent many things to the consumer along with representing the functional prowess of the product offering. Besides it represents the customers' convenient summary like their feelings, knowledge and experiences with the brand. Moreover customers do not spend much time to find out about the product. When customer considers about the purchase they evaluate the product immediately by reconstructed product from memory and cued by the brand name (Hansen et al., 2003).

While trying to define the relationship between customers and brands we arrive at the term "brand equity". The term brand equity is largely debated in the accounting and the marketing literature. It has highlighted the importance of having a long term focus with the concept of brand management. The term brand equity has earned multiple meanings. The accountants have defined it differently from the marketers. (Fieldwick 1996) in many classified approaches:

1.   The total value of a brand as a separable asset when it is sold, or included on a balance sheet;

2.   A measure of the strength of consumers' attachment to a brand;

3.   A description of the associations and beliefs the consumer has about the brand.

The first approach is the one that is often called the brand valuation or brand value that is often adopted by the accountants.

The second is the measurement of the consumers' level of attachment to a brand while the third is the brand image.

The marketers on the other hand tend to define the term brand on the basis of the strength of the brand. Brand description and brand strength are often referred to as the "consumer brand equity" in order to differentiate it from the meaning in terms of asset valuation. A popular definition of brand equity in marketing terms is given by (Cravens, 1990) "Brand equity is a set of brand assets and liabilities linked to a brand, its name and symbol that add to or subtract from the value provided by a product or service to a firm and/or to that firm's customers."

Brand equity is therefore a set of assets and liabilities linked to a brand, its name and symbol that add to or subtract from the value provided by a product or service to a firm and / or to that firm's customers. For assets or liabilities to underlie brand equity they must be linked to the name and / or symbol of the brand. If the brand name or symbol should change, some or all of the assets or liabilities could be affected and even lost, although some might be shifted to a new name and symbol.

The success of a product, a service, a person or even a country is based on its beings perceived as unique. Every successful product or service or idea has a unique place in the mind of the consumer. These products and services have been able to distinctly differentiate themselves from the rest of the competitors. Branding is much more than marketing. In a way, it creates a memorable marketing experience on the part of the consumer. The promise of a successful branding programme is the display of oneself as distinctly different from the competition. Branding creates a perception that the product is unique. The distinction can be a function, form, ease of use, price or prestige, but the consumer believes that there is something different in the product. There can be tangible as well as intangible factors that affect the brand of an organization. Simply put, brand is the image of an organization perceived by the outside world. In the following paragraphs we shall try to understand the distinguishing elements of branding created by some of the popular companies of our times.

CASES OF SUCCESS AND PITFALLS IN BRANDING

The process of branding for products was created to protect them from failing in the market. A look at the history of branding in the 18th century suggests that brand identities were created to protect the products from being diluted in the minds of the consumers. The makers of brands created a human element in order to position the products. Before industrial revolution the buyers were dependent on the shopkeepers for the decision about purchase choices but, the brand identities began to create trust on themselves for being the buying choice of the consumer. Branding helped to save the mass produced products from failing. Brands have transformed the landscape of business and helped to develop global companies like McDonald's, Nike, Coca-Cola etc. Every strong brand has a history that has helped it grow and sustain the cut-throat competition in the marketplace. Here are some popular stories that go behind the making of these successful brands.

Coca Cola

Coca Cola derives its strength from its robust marketing framework that today encompasses many variants of the brand .The capabilities of company as against that of competition particularly that of Pepsi lie in its marketing strategy. It is rightly called the 'vision brand'. The marketing of Coke is outstanding and the communication mix is concocted to suite the tastes of target market. The Unique Selling Points of Coke are highlighted in its mission statements which say:

- To refresh the world.
- To inspire moments of optimism and happiness.
- To create value and make a difference.

Of late Coca Cola has gradually started moving from 'Creative Excellence' to 'Content Excellence'. The marketing strategy for Coke is designed keeping in mind the cultural dynamics of the place where it is sold.

As already mentioned it is present in almost every corner of the world, its marketing is designed keeping in mind the cultural nuances of the place. Coke is therefore a vehicle for promotion of events. It is a regular at the Olympic where it has had its presence since 1928, it has also had its presence at the FIFA World Cup apart from sponsoring other sporting events at the national level. The strength of Coca Cola rests on its marketing prowess conforming to all the 4 Ps of marketing mix elements. Product is unique, Price is competitive standing at $ 1.95 for the smallest bottle, Place mix is handled by its global availability with the concentrated formula supplied by the Coca Cola Company and bottled by various bottling units often franchised, and Promotion is one of the best balances of integrated marketing communication.

Another area of strength perceived for Coca Cola is the huge surge in revenue across three geographic segments. These are Latin America, East Asia and South Asia. Besides the company has record earnings from Bottling Investments. This growth in revenue has led to increase in top line growth or Coca Cola.

Google

Google was founded by Larry Page (Larry) and Sergey Brin (Sergey). They graduated in computer science from Stanford University in 1995.Both the friends began to work at extending their summer project on search engine in the year 1996. They were able to develop a technology that was capable of retrieving large body of information from data available in the internet. They called this search engine 'BackRub' due to its ability to analyse back links in given websites. By 1997 BackRub had gained great popularity due to its ability to provide solutions to massive problems. Larry and Sergey wanted more investment in this concept for which they approached many people including David Filo (Filo), the founder of Yahoo. Although Filo complemented on their technology he did not enter in any agreement. The owners of many other portal refused to invest in their technology. The CEO of one such portal told them, "As long as we are 80% as good as our competitors that is good enough. Our users do not really care about search" (www.google.com).

Finally help came from Andy Bechtolsheim (Andy), one of the co-founders of Sun Microsystems. Andy was impressed with their concept and handed over a check of $100,000 in favor of Google Inc., an organization that did not yet exist. The name Google was derived from the word Googol, which denotes the number one followed by a hundred zeros (www.google.com).

Pepsi

Pepsi is a household name now, but it wasn't always. The drink was originally called Brad's Drink after founder Caleb Bradham and the soda fountain in his drugstore. Brad's Drink was very popular with customers and included, among other ingredients, pepsin (a digestive enzyme) and cola nuts. Right before the end of the 19th century, the beverage was renamed Pepsi Cola and the names stuck all these years.

Pepsi-Cola is one of the most famous soft drinks consumed worldwide. Manufactured and marketed by PepsiCo, it was first developed and produced in the early 1890's by Caleb Bradham, a pharmacist in New Bern, North Carolina labeled as "Brad's drink". In 1898, Bradham renamed his drink into "Pepsi-Cola".

On June 16, 1903, the title Pepsi-Cola was trademarked and had since remained unchanged. But one aspect of Pepsi-Cola that witnessed many transformations over the years is the Pepsi logo. The Pepsi logo is one of the most famous and recognized logo design in the world.

In 1898, Bradham used a scribbled logo script as the first Pepsi logo to brand the product. When his business got established and people started enjoying his drink, Bradham decided to modify the Pepsi logo into a more customized version of the previous logo script. Thus, in 1905, a modified script logo was introduced, followed by a second change in Pepsi logo in 1906 with the inclusion of the slogan, "The Original Pure Food Drink", in it.

During the 1933's sugar crisis, Loft, Inc. bought Pepsi-Cola. As part of their marketing strategy, Pepsi-Cola doubled the quantity of its drink from six-ounce package size to twelve-ounces for 10 cents. Thus, the slogan "Refreshing & Healthful" was added to the Pepsi logo, which was printed on the bottle. When the price for the twelve-ounce bottle dropped to 5 cents, Pepsi-Cola reverted back to the old logo design.

In 1940, Walter Mack, the CEO of Pepsi-Cola, adopted the idea of 12-oz. embossed bottle with "Pepsi-Cola" baked into the glass. He further developed the idea of introducing the new bottle design with crown, labeled with the Pepsi logo. In 1941, the Pepsi bottle crown colors were changed to red, white and blue, along with the Pepsi logo, to commemorate the war efforts of the country.

By 1943, the Pepsi logo adopted a "bottle cap" look that included the slogan, "Bigger Drink, Better Taste". Later, in 1962, the Pepsi logo was replaced with two bulls-eye marks encircling "Pepsi", and then again in 1973, into a boxed Pepsi logo with minor typeface changes.

In 1991, Pepsi commemorated the evolution of its scripted Pepsi logo by featuring a logo design with an italic capital typeface. Later at the company's 100 years celebration in 1998, Pepsi-Cola unveiled a new logo that symbolized the brand's innovation and global recognition. The new Pepsi logo consists of a three-dimensional globe against an ice blue background, with the inclusion of the previously designed Pepsi typeface. It has been the official Pepsi logo of PepsiCo, till date.

Over the past century, the Pepsi logo has been evolved into remarkable designs with significant modifications. All in all, Pepsi logo is an exemplary piece of creativity and innovation. No doubt, it is one of the most recognized logos, ever.

Adidas

The moment we think of sports apparel the name of Adidas comes instantly into our mind. The Company's name is a combination of the founder's nickname and last name Adolf "Adi" Dassler. His brother, Rudolf "Rudi" Dassler, founded his own shoe company called, Ruda, which later was renamed Puma. It is indeed intriguing to analyse the success of the brand in the minds of the consumer. Experts are of the opinion that the identity of the brand has a lot to do with the success of the same. Those famous three stripes have inspired every sportsman and made Adidas the international face of sports gear and apparels. The brand identity of Adidas has an intriguing history described as under:

The Three Stripes

The evolution of Adidas logo and its popularity as an imagery has an interesting history. Adi Dassler had a unique idea in mind. He thought about a logo design that could give its brand a unique look so that it retains longer in the memory of the people. He then came up with those iconic three stripes. In 1967, the first official logo looked like this: The three stripes went well with the masses and complemented the slogan of the company: "The Brand with the 3 Stripes." Even Adi Dassler would not have known then that the three stripes would gain such massive recognition.

The Trefoil

It was not until 1972 that the Adi Dassler designed another and the most iconic one of the Adidas logos: The Trefoil. As the company spread its business in apparel and leisure industry, Adi Dassler realized the need for a more apt logo design that could demonstrate industrial diversity of his company. Adi Dassler did some creativity with the overall design and transformed the original "three-striped" logo into the "trefoil". The idea made sense to the diversity of the brand and the new logo became an instant hit with the masses.

The Triangle

In 1990, Adidas did one more makeover with the logo design. Creative director Peter Moore had an interesting idea in mind. He proposed that the three stripes should be slanted like a triangle. Adi Dassler liked the idea and approved it. The first version of the logo was visible on the equipment products of the company. Finally in 1997, the logo became the corporate symbol of the Adidas Company, while the classic Trefoil made exclusive for the traditional products. The Interesting Fact: The three slanted stripes of Adidas logo implicitly suggest a meaningful message to the audience. The triangular shape is symbolic of mountain which stands for the challenges to be overcome. It goes with the type of product line of the Adidas that mainly sells the shoes for the athletes.

Volkswagen

The legend behind naming of Volkswagen goes that Hitler proposed to build a cheap car that almost anyone could afford. He gave it the name "KdF Wagen," which we know as the Volkswagen. KdF was the abbreviation for "Kraft durch Freude" (Strength through Joy), a subsidiary of the Deutsche Arbeitsfront (German Labor Front), headed by Robert Ley. This chapter on the beginnings of the Volkswagen is taken from a book celebrating the achievements of "Kraft durch Freude." As it turned out, not many people got their cars until after the war. As the chapter notes, the first deliveries were planned for early 1940, at which point the factory had been turned over to war production (Arbeitsfront, 1938).

Nation Branding (Switzerland)

Founded in 2000 by the Swiss Federal Council and parliament, Presence Switzerland is an organization that has been charged with the strengthening of Switzerland's image abroad. In the Swiss Federal Council website it is said that in today's global society countries vie with each other for the world's attention, for people, for foreign investment and capital. Where people go for their holidays, where companies invest, where universities select scientists for their research activities, or where major conferences are held - all these decisions affect the prosperity of a country. And they are made by people. Their decisions are influenced to a greater or lesser extent by the image created in their minds by the country concerned. The way a country is perceived abroad is central in such decisions. A country therefore cannot allow itself to be indifferent to its image abroad. This is not only true for the political scene but especially for foreign opinion-makers, the opinion 'multipliers' of society. This is where the concept of nation branding comes in. Nation branding is a process by which a country creates a fair and balanced image of itself for a particular purpose. It is intended to ensure that its image is not dominated by events from the past, but corresponds with current reality and is oriented to the future. Nation branding is successful if a country has a clear identity and is heard in this age of information overkill. If this can be achieved the country will stand out above others, and the images it generates in peoples' minds become sharper and closer to reality" (www.presence.ch).

Starbucks

The Company has been able to transform coffee into a phenomenal brand. When people think of Starbucks, many images come to mind, the logo, and the coffee mug. These are brand qualities created by Starbucks to distinguish themselves from other coffee companies. Starbucks has created a consistent experience in every store, every ad, every employee and every cup of coffee they serve. Today, when people think coffee, they often think Starbucks. Not only does this translate into sales, it validates the company's most valuable asset: the Starbucks brand.

Designed by Terry Heckler of Heckler Associates, the iconic mermaid that beckons coffee drinkers was based on a classic 15th century Norse woodcut of the mythical siren. The hardy yet feminine look was perfect for the Pacific Northwest local. Evoking the local lumber industry's history in the area coupled with an inviting face, the logo was a perfect fit

However, the finely crafted corporate identity soon faced challenges. How do you place a bare breasted siren on the side of a truck? Modify! Eventually, the siren's hair was lowered to cover the bare-chested icon. Then the suggestive pose of the mermaid, posed a unique branding challenge during Starbucks rapid expansion. What had seemed a clever and folksy design in Seattle was considered risqué in other parts of the country? Modify Again! Soon, the offending pose was slightly altered, and then eventually the pose completely obscured.

Evolution of New Redesigned Starbucks Logo

The current Starbucks logo that the world knows today now focuses on the warm and inviting face of the mermaid, rather than her body. The iconic cigar band outline remains, framing one of the most famous corporate identities in the world. The story of the Heckler Associates modification and re imagination of each subsequent logo design is necessary for anyone interested in logos and branding.

Nike

The name "Nike" was taken from the Greek and means "goddess of victory." The logo represents the wing of the Greek Goddess. In the world of brands, Nike is definitely a victor. Nikes uses a simple logo, a great slogan and a list of superstars including Michael Jordan, LeBron James, Andre Agassi, Shane Warne, Maria Sharapova, and Venus and Serena Williams to promote their sales. The Nike "swoosh" logo was created in 1971 by Carolyn Davidson, a graphic design student at Portland State University. Davidson was asked for ideas by Phil Knight, the owner of Blue Ribbon Sports (BRS), a company she was freelancing for. Davidson took the job and developed an earlier concept of the now famous swoosh logo charging only $2.00 per hour for work. She was paid approximately $35.00 for the logo. Years later, in 1983, in a show of appreciation, Knight gifted Davidson with a gold Swoosh ring and an envelope filled with Nike stock. Introduced in the late 1980s, the "JUST DO IT" slogan became an instant success and remains a popular branded slogan some twenty plus years later. There are many companies that sell quality athletic shoes and a major component behind Nike's success is not their products, but their successful branding strategies.

Nike advertising is one of the most effective emotional branding examples in the marketing world today. Nike brand strategy is to build a powerful brand – so powerful that it inspires fervent customer loyalty from people literally all over the world. This is because Nike advertising uses the emotional branding technique of

Cosmopolitan Yogurt

One of the most popular brands that tried to extend to a different line of product but failed miserable was the Cosmopolitan Yogurt. Cosmopolitan is the world's largest selling women's magazine. It launched its own brand of yogurt under the name of 'Cosmopolitan Yogurt'. It was an effort to capitalize on the brand value of Cosmopolitan, yet the product failed and it was out of the shelves in 18 months. Cosmopolitan however has success with other crossovers. For example it is now the second best bed linen brand in the United Kingdom. Jane Wentworth a senior brand consultant said that it was obvious for Cosmopolitan yogurts to fail as any brand extension has to be credible for the mother brand.

Colgate Kitchen Entrees

Among the many strange brand extension efforts by various companies here was one by Colgate when it decided to use its name on a range of food products called Colgate's kitchen Entrees. The range never took off well and remained confined to the United States. The consumers did not seem to correlate with Colgate's name with a kitchen ware. Thus the brand failed miserable.

Pond's Toothpaste

Pond is one of the most popular face cream in the global market. But when the same brand name was brought out as toothpaste it failed to generate market interest. In a test conducted in a certain market the people were not able to distinguish between Colgate and Ponds toothpaste. Although Pond's had earlier successfully extended to the soaps category but the success of these was attributed to the fact that the fragrance of the cream was found in the soaps as well which enabled the consumers to link the same.

Frito-Lay Lemonade

Frito Lay a prominent brand of salty snacks in the global market tried to extend their brand identity by launching Lemonade. The company might have thought that a Frito Lay Lemonade might be a good option to quench the thirst created by a salty Frito Lay Chips. But the consumers failed to correlate the product with the other products of Frito Lay. Moving to an unrelated category of product was a mistake on the part of the company as this led to Brand Schizophrenia which bewildered the consumers and devalued the core brand.

McDonald's: The McLibel Trial

McDonald's is perhaps one of the biggest brands of our time. McDonald's itself claims that its chain of fast food restaurants represents the 'most successful food service organization in the world.' McDonald caters to approximately 40 million people every day across the globe. Indeed a phenomenal number of customers. The success of McDonald brand has been put forward in the words of Des Dearlove and Stuart Crainer as under:

"Henry Ford mastered mass product production; McDonald's has mastered mass service production. It has done so through strict adherence to simple beliefs. Quality, cleanliness and uniformity are the basis of the McDonald's brand. [. . .] A McDonald's restaurant in Nairobi, Kenya looks much the same as one in Warsaw, Poland or Battle Creek, Michigan. [. . .] In effect, the very uniformity of the brand is the crucial differentiating factor."

However the company has to face a turbulent time which hit the brand value hard. It was in the 1990s that the London's Greenpeace campaign was launched against the company. The libel case involved two activists Helen Steel and Dave Morris. The trial turned out to be the longest in the English history of corporate litigation continuing up to 313 days in court. As the trial progressed the media interest grew and the general public became involved in the proceedings. The verdict finally came in the year 1997 and McDonald emerged victorious with the judge absolving the charges of food poisoning, cancer and third world poverty on McDonald. Despite of being a winner in the court room McDonald was not able to undo the damage of the long trial.

Pan Am

Pan American World Airways popularly called Pan Am was one of the most famous airline brands. It held the pride position of being one of the best in the world for a long period of 60 years. It was till the year 1988 that the company was at its best. Then in the year 1988 there was as a disaster when the Pan Am Plane on its way from London to New York disappeared from the radar. It was later discovered that a bomb went off mid air killing all the 270 people. The ghastly nature of the tragedy tarnished the image of the airline which could never be recovered. Finally, after three years of the tragedy the company had to shut down due to bankruptcy.

Snow Brand Milk Products

Snow Brand dairy foods were a premier milk product company of Japan. The brand faced a bizarre case of food contamination that led to 14,800 people falling ill. The company was asked to recall all its products by Osaka state authorities. But the company partially recalled until it was forced to recall all the products. The health authorities made it public that the company was forced to recall leading to a negative public opinion about the company. Besides, the company withheld a lot of information about the exact nature of the incident. As a result of the incident, sales for the company took a nosedive and Snow Brand's president, Tetsuro Ishikawa, closed eight of his factories. Before the food poisoning, Snow Brand had a market share of 45 percent. This dropped to under 10 percent and the brand has still to recover back to its pre-2000 levels.

Thus these examples of brand failures remind us that branding is something that goes beyond the quantitative evidence available about the market. Empirical data hardly satisfy the branding ideologies. There are a number of vague constructs at play in creating brands like that of perception and belief. Both perception and belief of the consumer get built and are based on psychologically attributed to attitude, personality etc. The marketer needs to understand these attributed to fit the needs of the consumer with the brand offerings. If the gap in the need and the availability is met by the given product/service offering the consumer will readily take the brand and if it falls short of the expectations then the consumer will just not let it enter the periphery of his product choices. Thus it is important to understand the elements of branding discussed in the following paragraphs.

BRANDING CHALLENGES

The markets are inundated with new brands every day. New brands have been launched in sector such as telecom, retail, automobile Fast Moving Consumer Goods (FMCG), apparels and many more. There are approximately three brands launched in a day, but only 5% of these brands are seen to survive. The world has become one market and in order to succeed in any market in any part of the world, marketers have to face competition from the global players. Brand managers face many sleepless nights due to this tough competition. Brands need to thrive globally in order to survive locally. Brand managers have to face many challenges in order to see that their product succeeds. Brand managers need to understand the challenges well in order to make effective brand decisions. Some of the strongest challenges in building brands in today's market scenario are as follows:

- Consumers are aware of the various product choices and they have a greater understanding of the brand available in the market. Also, the consumers of today are educated and intelligent. There is information overload and internet has brought about wealth of information in the click of a mouse.

- There is massive brand proliferation. A number of brands are vying for the customer's attention which has lead to increased competition and greater difficulty in differentiation of the products. Globalization has fostered the proliferation of brands all over the globe.
- Increasing power of trade has significantly impacted the process of brand creation. There are a number of powerful retailers and wholesalers, therefore organizations are engaged in many below the line activities in order to motivate the retailers and wholesalers to sell their brands.
- Fragmentation of communication channel is another major challenge faced by the brand managers. There is increase in the number of television channels, radio channels and magazines which has led to target audience being distributed across the channels. This has added to greater issues and hindrances for the marketers as the advertisement budget has to be spread across a number of communication media.
- In order to differentiate in the market as against the competitor products and brands companies have to invest in a lot of marketing support. To be the choice of the customer, the brand needs to be outstanding in the market place. A brand is created over a period of time and requires consistent delivery of the brand promise.

OVERCOMING THE BRAND CHALLENGE

With the maturing of markets only companies can overcome the challenges of branding effectively. Companies strive to create brand equity and sustained customer loyalty. Brand equity and brand loyalty are two very different concepts often misinterpreted as same. Brand loyalty is a result of brand equity.

Brand Equity

Brand Equity is defined in terms of "the marketing effects uniquely attributable to the brand-for example, when certain outcomes result from the marketing of a product or service because of its brand name that would not occur if the same product or service did not have that name" (Keller, 2003). The need for understanding the concept of brand equity arises due to the need for measuring the financial worth of a brand and for improving the marketing productivity.

It was in 1980s that companies started putting a value in their balance sheets for the brands that they had acquired. Reckitt and Colman bought the Airwick Brand and added a value for this brand on the balance sheet; similarly, Grand Metropolitan bought the Smirnoff Brand and put up the value in the balance sheet. The moves by these companies started the tern among their counterparts in recognizing brands as financial assets in a company. The history of evaluating brand equity dates back to 1988 when Rank Hovis McDougall (RHM), a United Kingdom based flour miller valued the portfolio of his brands as against a hostile takeover bid by Australian firm-Goodman Fielder Wattie and included the value of the brands in the account books. This move was a defensive strategy to display the power of the brands to the bidding company, yet it helped in offsetting the takeover bid. It also helped in proving that brands can be evaluated and a financial worth attached to them. In 1989, the London Stock Exchange endorsed this concept of brand valuation as used by RHM, by providing the impetus for major branded goods companies to recognize the value of the brands as intangible assets in their balance sheets.

Brand Loyalty

Brand Loyalty is often associated with customer loyalty. The market is cluttered with many brands. A change in the market share has a significant financial implication; it is the brand loyalty that helps to ensure sales in a business scenario of acute competition. Brand loyalty is a measure of how attached the customer is to a brand. It tells one how attached a consumer is to a brand and also how likely a consumer is to shift to a newly launched brand which is in some way upgraded. Statistics proves that brand loyalty is given importance by not only marketers but also the consumers. Just 25% of US consumers consider brand loyalty as something that impacts their buying behavior (Ernst & Young, 2012), 78% of consumers are not loyal to a particular brand (Nielsen, 2014). A repeat customer spends 67% more than a new one (BIA/Kelsey, 2014) while 61% of Americans switch brands due to price (Nielsen, 2014).Female consumers (68%) are more loyal to brands than males (55%) (Analytic Partners, 2013) and 70% of customers cite poor customer service as a reason for not buying from a brand (McKinsey, 2006). A Totally Satisfied Customer contributes 2.6 times as much revenue as a Somewhat Satisfied Customer (InfoQuest, 2014) and 51% of U.S. consumers switched service providers in the past year due to poor customer service (Accenture, 2013). 85% of consumers say companies could have recognized & rewarded them for doing business with them (Accenture,2013) and 82% of small business owners said that loyal customers were the main way they grow their business (Constant Contact, 2014). It is found that 94% of customers who have a low-effort service experience will buy from that same company again (CEB, 2014).

LESSONS LEARNED FROM THE CASE STUDIES

Branding is therefore a topic of strategic significance for survival in the present market. In the various chapters of the book we shall try to understand the concept with the help of cases of successful branding and also that of failures in branding. The rational for building a strong brand is to get an identifier against the competitors. Learning from cases can be a help to the decision makers in arriving at strategic brand building decisions and to the academicians in understanding the elements of branding practices. Valuable lessons on branding have been learnt from the cases in the following chapters. For global branding success it is recommended that organizations need to standardize the essence of brands across the various markets that they are playing. After identifying the essence of a brand it becomes easier to execute the global brand image and also to leverage the values of the brand.

Companies also need to focus on the brand planning process with accountable people in place to ensure that the brand planning is executed on a global scale. The brand planning process should focus on the strengths of the brand to develop sustainable brand advantage. Global brand strategies should be translated into country specific strategies in order to reinforce the brand identity consistently in all the markets. Building of coherent brand architecture is a must for success branding practice. While moving from local to global markets, companies can acquire other brands through corporate alliances. International branding is done through an evolutionary process that results from a number of decisions taken over a period of time. A top down approach is often advocated in which the global brand strategy is delineated from that of the country specific branding strategy.

The various cases in the book are from different countries across the globe. It is seen that organizations need to explore opportunities beyond the geographical boundaries for further growth and profitability of the brands. There are advantages of economies of scale, increasing the brand life etc. Brands are created over a period of time. Therefore the brand managers have to nurture them in order to have the benefits trickle down for a longer period of time. There are challenges in developing brands of long life yet, all the rewards are worth the efforts. It will not be wrong to tell that some of the world's best known brands are those that have withstood the test of time. For example, Twinings was Established in 1706 by tea merchant Thomas Twining, the brand holds the world's oldest continually-used commercial logo created in 1787.Thomas Twining also opened Britain's first known tea room at No. 216 Strand, London in 1706, a shop that is still operational today. In 1964, the tea manufacturing company was bought by the Associated British Foods, and is now one of the most sough-after tea brands in the world. Similarly, Cadbury, the second largest confectionary brand in the world (after Wrigley's) was established in Birmingham in 1824 by John Cadbury, a merchant who sold tea, coffee and hot of the class discussion. This helps in improving the oral communication skills an extremely important aspect of executive function.

- **Social Skills:** The case study method involves the development of the social skills as the participants should display the ability to win over others in spite of accepting and accommodating the views of the others.

CASE METHOD IN BRAND MANAGEMENT

The case method is all the more important for courses like marketing management and brand management which draws inputs from diverse subjects like economics, behavioral sciences, finance etc. The decisions required in this area require skills of integration of multiple subject areas. Understanding of multiple subjects may be difficult in the beginning as the student is exposed to one subject at a time. The course on brand management is therefore taught across the globe with the help of case study method. However, paucity of relevant cases hinders the understanding of the subject in the right perspective.

TYPES OF CASES

A case study is a vivid description of a business situation that is faced by an organization. The format of a case study varies considerably. However every case must have a reasonably sufficient amount of factual data. Cases can be of various lengths from a few paragraphs to many pages. It is a misconception that cases can be considered complex on the basis of the length of the same. The reality is that even short cases can have a lot to analyze on the part of the student. In the given case study book there are cases of 5000 words to 11000 words approximately. A case study has to be an accurate description of a real business situation or a fictitious one (Easton, 1988). At times cases are disguised and the name of the real subject under discussion is withheld. These disguises however do not have a significant impact on the case per se. However, if the data significant to the case is missing than the results might be damaging to the very idea of the case. Therefore most of the authors of case studies prefer to use real life situations in business as cases. It demands enormous amount of experience as a case writer and analyst to draw a fictitious case. In this case study book all the cases are from the real business world and the authors are experts in case writing from various countries. This would give the student an insight into the cultural aspects in branding when reading each of the cases. Branding cases are generally historical cases or problem oriented (Issue based) cases. Historical cases are those that deal with those decisions have already been taken by an organization.

The summary of the cases are often found in great detail which describe the impact and the ramifications of certain decisions of the organization into the present state of brand. Historical cases are suited for stimulating discussions among the managers within the organizations and the outside stakeholders by helping them to understand the events the causes of the same and the consequences of the actions taken.

Issue based cases are those that give us a summary of the problems and the opportunity that was faced by the organization while being faced with a certain business situation. These cases however do not describe the manager's decisions. The summary of such cases gives a description of the actions taken the analysis of the actions etc. Issue based cases are better suited for the developing decision making skills among the managers.

Again cases can be made up of both primary as well as secondary data. The secondary data used in cases are drawn from the already published materials. Primary data based cases on the other hand have the required data drawn from the organizations. The present book has cases that have used both the primary as well as the secondary data.

The cases can be "dead" or "live" or somewhere in between. In the former type all the information is presented to the students at the beginning of the analysis (Easton, 1988). On the other hand a live case is one in which information is injected over a period of time. This enables the student to develop their knowledge about the organization. The other method is the piecemeal injection of information by the instructor to the class from time to time. Live cases are more interesting as the cases unfold as they are being solved. In this book we have a number of live cases that have sufficient support materials for the instructor to use in the class.

METHODS OF USING CASES

Cases may be used as a pedagogical tool as shown in Figure 1.

In a case study based course there are two methods that can be typically be followed. One of them is the open classroom discussion. In this the course instructor leads the class discussion and then he gives a few leading questions for which the entire class has to think of justifiable solution by brainstorming into the subject. In the next method, the students either individually or in groups are called to make a formal presentation of their analysis and the recommendations. While one of the students is presenting, the other students are trying to seek clarifications in the subjects discussed along with their observations of the same. The case study may be presented as an assignment, with the student required to write an analysis and recommendations. This may be done as a take-home assignment or as part of an examination, requiring immediate response. Now which method of case study dis-

Figure 1. Methods of using cases
Geoff Easton, (1988).

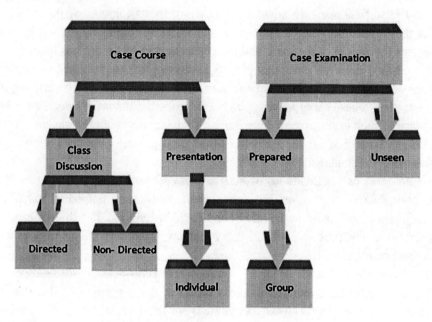

cussion to follow in the class is purely the discretion of the course instructor? However the skills required to control the class are higher in case of the former method. There is another method also used by some instructors in case study classes i.e. the use of roleplay.

Role play is a popular tool in management pedagogy. The case study may be presented either in whole or in part as a role play. For example, the students may be given 'parts' as people in the case and asked to present their 'character's' concerns

Table 1. Teacher and student roles in regular case class

When	Teacher	Student or Participant
Before Class	Assigns case and often readings. Prepares for Class. May consult Colleagues.	Receives case and assignment. Prepares individually. Discusses case in small groups.
During Class	Deals with readings. Leads Case discussion.	Raises questions regarding readings. Participates in discussions.
After Class	Evaluates and records student's participation. Evaluates material and updates teaching notes.	Compares personal analysis with colleague analysis. Reviews class discussion for major concepts learned.

Source: Michiel R. Leenders, Louis A., Mauffatte-Launders and James Erskine, Writing cases, (Ivey Publishing 4th Ed.).

and point of view. Discussion and analysis would proceed either through the role play or at the conclusion, as a class review. In this two or more students are assigned role of one or the other key executive in the case (Jaunch et al., 1988). The limitation of this method lies in the format of the case that might not have identified the key players and their respective thought process. The students may only be presented with part of the information and be required to ask particular questions to extract the rest of the data needed and provide their analysis and recommendations. The instructor or other students may serve as 'actors' to present the information and answer questions.

ROLE OF STUDENTS

Students play a pivotal role in the success of a case study method of teaching. The pedagogical significance of case study cannot be complete without the preparation by the students. Inadequate preparation ion the part of the students might yield absolutely no returns on the part of learning through case study. Therefore there are certain steps needed by the students to prepare for the case Jaunch et.al (1988):

1. Reading the case to familiarize with the facts of the same.
2. Identifying the key issues and problems on which the executive or the decision maker should be focusing their attention.
3. Identifying alternative courses of action.
4. Evaluating each of the alternative solutions of the actions developed.
5. Selecting one of the alternative solution.
6. Observing the solution from the point of view of implementing it.

A student might require more than one reading, preferably three readings are recommended to give a clear picture of the case. In the first reading the students get familiar with the details of the organization like the nature of the business, the problems faced by the organization.

The second reading is to critically examine and identify the problems and the issues that the organization is facing. Sometimes the problems are not very easily identifiable and the issues discussed in the case may be obscure. Many a times sub-issues are also present that need to identifies. While reading, the student should mark the places where he might see problems. Finally, the student would be able to recognize the problem in totality. There he has to think of the alternative solutions or the courses of action that might possibly be taken.

The novelty of the solution is the key to solving a case well. Creative and ingenuity is demanded from the students while they prescribe their solution for the case. Then there is the stage of evaluation of the alternatives. Here the student has to read the third and the final time to identify the alternative solutions along with the criteria of evaluation to be used for evaluating various alternatives on a comparative basis.

Once the student has taken the best course of action he has to look at it from the point of view of implementation and how the various tasks of implementation would be carried out . It exposes any weaknesses that might have been overlooked earlier. The students however have to prepare extensively for the historical cases may be on somewhat different lines. In such cases the event in question has already taken place and the learning outcome is derived from the evaluation of the process with which the decisions have been arrived at. This is why the historical cases are long and are often divided into two or more parts. The first one elaborating the premise in which the decisions have been taken while the following parts describe how effective the decisions have been. By reading the first part of the historical case the student should draw a flow chart of the decision process. Then they should determine the deficiencies in the analysis and describe the problems that may arise out of the decisions. The students might be given some lead questions by the instructor to enable the student to structure the ideas of the subject.

REQUIREMENTS OF CLASSROOM DISCUSSION

On discussing the cases in a classroom along with the peer group and the teacher there is a need to take efforts in understanding the management concepts involved in the case. In short optimum learning is to be desired from the case discussion. Here are some things to be noted in discussing cases in classrooms.

1.   There is a need to avoid rehashing the rehashing the case. The use of data is significant to help in arriving solution to the case.
2.   One must avoid the desire to participate for the sake of participating. Listening to the deliberations of the others can also be of great help to the learner. The view of various participants helps in understanding the nuances of the case. It is required that the students make relevant points at the right time concisely by accepting the views of the others.The process of the classroom discussion is facilitated when the students bring their analysis in written forms. This also helps in sharpening the listening skills students. If the students come unprepared then a lot of time in the class gets wasted when all the students start speaking as well as doing the analysis of the case at the same time. This is why the instructor is required to give the case studies in advance.
3.   There is a need to carefully take the assumptions which are realistic in nature and not absurd. A student should be careful not to get attached to a particular

problem or to commit to a solution or a strategy in advance and then start looking for information in the case to justify the same. Instead one must spend a good amount of time in identifying the problem as clearly as possible. The rational method of approaching a problem is by keeping aside opinions and personal biases.

PROBLEMS IN LEARNING BY CASE STUDY METHOD

After the discussions in the preceding sections, we can conclude that the case method of learning different from the other methods of teaching learning like lecture, seminar or tutorial. The list of additional skills developed with the help of case study method of learning is exhaustive. After a lecture a student has a feeling that he has indeed gain substantial knowledge. Many a times, a student is left to figure out what is the additional knowledge he has acquired after finishing the case discussion. It is more so in the case of subjects like brand management that has a lot of unstructured decision situations. The student may also express concerns over what concepts they have learnt. This happens because of the fact that improvements in higher level of learning created by the case study method are difficult to measure. For a student it is difficult to measure what progress he has made. Only when he is faced with such a business situation that bears similarity with the case study situation the student realized how much he knows to be confident of dealing with the same.

A good case will have all the relevant information relating to the issues being discussed in the case and the decisions that are to be taken, on which the case writer wants the students to focus their attention. The students might complain at times that the case contains too much information. This might be another perception created largely due to the instructor using the case with limited purpose in mind. In rare case it might be due to the fact that lack is perceptual due to the instructor using a case to demonstrate the points intended by the case writer. Such problems may be overcome by making suitable assumptions while doing the analysis or making decisions.

Another frequently occurring complaint may be due to the fact that the case might have too much of irrelevant information in it. This might also only be a perceptual condition with the instructor using the case with restricted purpose in mind and not being able to determine the purpose set by the writer of the case. Besides, the students might find the look at the matter as irrelevant due to their lack of appreciation of some of the issues dealt with in the case. The extra information in a case does not damage the case in any way except that it consumes a lot of extra time of the students. This problem can be taken care of by the instructor by selecting the cases that have the relevance to the topics discussed in class and that the instructor can also decide to discuss limited topics from a given case.

and psychological attributes. Pitcher (1985) holds that brand is a consumer's idea of a product. According to Keeble (1991), "a brand becomes a brand as soon as it comes in contact with the consumers." Gardner and Levy's (1955) definition, which provides a synthesis between identity and image, is:

A brand name is more than the label employed to differentiate among the manufacturers of a product. It is a complex symbol that represents a variety of ideas and attributes. It tells the consumers many things, not only by the way it sounds (its literal meaning if it has one), but, more important via the body of associations it has built up and acquired as public object over a period of time.

The definition of brand should incorporate the concept of added value which strikes a difference between brand and product (Jones, 1986). Jones (1986) defines brand as a "product that provides functional benefits plus added values that some consumers value enough to buy." The concept of added value finds an important place in the definition provided by de Chernatony and McDonald (1994):

Brands are an identifiable product, service, person or place augmented in such a way that the buyer or user perceives relevant unique added values which match their needs more closely.

A brand is not a name, logo, sign, symbol, advertisement, or spokesperson. A brand is not everything that an organization wants people, especially its target markets, to feel and believe about its products and services (Van deen Heever, 2000). A brand is a mixture of tangible and intangible attributes, symbolized in a trademark, which if properly managed, creates influence and generates value (Duncan, 2005).

Keller (2003) offers an account of the various roles played by brands. The roles played by the brand from consumer's point of view are summarized in the following points:

- Identification of source of product,
- Assignment of responsibility to product maker,
- Risk reducer,
- Search cost reducer,
- Establishes bond with the maker of a product,
- Serves as symbolic devise, and
- Signal of quality. (Source: Keller, 2003).

According to Davis (2002), the role of strong brands from company perspectives are considered in the following points:

- Generation of repeat business due to brand loyalty.
- Brand-based price premiums offer higher margins for the company.
- Strong brands endow credibility to the new products introduced in the market.
- Makes company less vulnerable to competitive actions because of strong brand's valued and sustainable point of differentiation.
- Brand strength enables company attract the best employees and keeping its satisfied employees.
- Strong brand facilitates greater shareholder and stakeholder returns.

BRANDING: A HISTORICAL OVERVIEW

The practice of branding is as old as human civilization. In ancient market place people used branding using symbols, signs, posters, pictorial symbols and trademarks. It was started ever since people owned cattle or created goods to be engaged in exchange. At the core of all branding activities there was human desire to be of someone consequence, to create a personal or social identity, to represent ownership, to stand out and to possess a good reputation. Branding was started as a sign to mean what an object is and then gradually took the form of naming it (Bastos & Levy, 2012). To ensure the ownership of cattle and sheep, they were branded with paint or pine tar and even with hot irons. Craftsmen used imprinted trademarks on the goods to denote the creator or the origin. Humans were branded too. Slaves were marked for assigning their ownership. For denouncing the criminals with disgrace, they were branded.

In primitive times the river side civilizations (Babylon, Egypt, and Greece) largely formed the major markets for trading and selling of goods. The goods were arrived at the riverside markets on ship. There were barkers who persuaded customers to buy with their barked out sales pitches describing spices, rugs, wines and other items. In Egypt information related to goods were written on papyrus papers which were posted on the walls and trees. Wall writings to advertise the goods were also in vogue. Writing on the walls in ancient city of Pompeii bore witness to this fact. To reach the illiterate mass pictorial signs were hung by the merchants and the store fronts were painted with colors. The same practices were prevalent in ancient Greece and Rome. In china at that time trade fairs were held. In the trade fairs the hawkers pitched displayed items. Branding was transformed from denotation to connotations implying something more than a name (Bastos & Levy, 2012). Negative connotations attached with branding started losing ground with the positive and commercial aspects taking upper hand.

At the outset of the Middle Ages commerce fell significantly with the collapse of the Roman Empire. Craftsmen took the back seat. Common mass were mostly illiterate except the clergy and a few rare people. At that time town criers played the major role of spreading information about goods and services. In the thirteenth century, the Magna Carta, the end of feudalism and trade between east and west brought betterment to the lives of people living in town. It was followed by the revival of crafts and emergence of the middle class. There was formation of craft guilds to control trade. The guild made the proprietary marks compulsory. Hand written handbills were distributed to advertise and woe customers. The merchants hung signs to help customers identify them and their type of business.

In China different forms of early branding and advertising were used with printed wrappers, banners, painted lanterns, painted pictures, and signboards, as well as printed advertisements. The Chinese did much progress in printing technology which, along with their great interests in painting, enabled them to devise these early methods of branding.

Invention of printing press by Johannes Gutenberg in 1448 in Germany ushered in a new era in branding and advertisement. The usage of this invention rapidly spread across Europe. From then it became very easy to reach public with printed information about the products and services and the popularity of advertising rose. By the late fifteen tenth century, the first English handbill announcing the availability of a book came into existence. The streets of London found its walls posted with huge numbers of printed advertisements promoting hawking goods. The first advertisement in the newspaper appeared in 1625 in England. The first known newspaper advertisement in America appeared in Boston Newsletter in 1704. The advertisements were restricted to the one section of the newspapers. These advertisements were mere the simple announcements about products and services and many newspapers repeated a single line copy of the advertisements several times to grab the attention of the customers. All these marked the advent of modern branding practices.

DEVELOPMENT OF BRANDING CONCEPTS VIS-À-VIS INDUSTRIAL DEVELOPMENT

Although the initiation of modern business practices dates back to 1820-30, the period from 1820-1900 was a land mark era in the history of management. This period was noted for unprecedented creative turbulence. Breakthroughs in the field of science and technology and economic unification due to construction of roads, rails and canals led towards a rapid industrial movement. The result was the evolution of modern business firms. This period was known as era of initiation or Industrial Revolution. Development of production technology and organization technology were the pre-occupations of the entrepreneurs. Not much time was spent for looking into the detailed operational aspect of the enterprises. Not much thought was devoted to branding. However, branding started evolving as a part of business activity. The product offering under brand names was introduced. The consumers started liking packaged branded goods. The practice of buying commodities out of barrels was fast losing ground. People wanted to buy readymade clothing, shoes and sealed goods for improved freshness. Branding involved helping consumers identify the products of their choices. For this purpose the manufactures sought to create visual identities. Manufacturers introduced labels, boxes and wrappers. Branding was aided by early form of advertising which aimed at disseminating information about goods to consumers. This period may well be called identification oriented branding era.

From 1900 onwards business houses started the consolidation effort to capitalize on the momentum of growth achieved in the previous era. In the previous era the business firms relied on the external technological environment and became successful. During this period, focus shifted to internal organizational environment to improve upon the production technology. The idea was to gain in proficiency in production by progressively reducing the average cost of production. Availability of cheap labor further provided the impetus to this effort. The market size was huge due to less number of competitors and demand was massive. The goods produced in bulk to meet this huge demand enabled the manufactures to enjoy the advantage of economies of scale. As result, the product was offered at the lowest possible price to the consumers who were primarily price-oriented. This phenomenon further pulled the demand in the market place. Thus, high volume and low price became the magic mantra of management. This continued till 1930's and the period is known as era of mass production. In mass production era basic products were offered to the consumers. Branding embraced the task of endorsing the basic commodity like products. Marketing became just an extension of production activity. Low priced branded products dominated the consumer economy created as a result of industrial growth. Through branding attempt was made to create identification systems for the manufacturers. Branding helped corporations achieve a visual image in the wake of minimum environmental challenges and little political interferences in business. However, branding did not restrict itself into the designing of logo or trade mark. Advertising agencies were evolved with the discovery new media types like radio and television. The manufacturers started sponsoring the radio programs to promote their brands. "Overblown" copy writing styles and melodramatic taglines were in vogue. This period of branding may be called generic branding era.

From 1930's another significant change was felt in the external business environment. Unlike the previous era, consumers started moving away from the low priced standard items. They were no longer satisfied with basic performance of these products. They demanded something more than that. Increasing number of affluent class of consumers pushed this trend. They were gradually getting interested in the high quality products without paying heed to the price of the same. Competition sneaked in the market. So, the concept of product differentiation was introduced to address this issue. It made the business firms adopt marketing orientation. The managers started paying more attention to the external environmental challenges..Thus, a shift towards an extroverted perspective took place. New problem-solving approaches were developed. New types of organizational structures were devised. The managers formed a different attitude to arrest the uncertainty of business dynamics. This period is known as mass marketing era which continued till the last of 19350's. In this era, branding started attracting serious thoughts. It happened especially due to focus of business shifted from production to product. There was pressing need to make the consumers aware of the differentiated quality of the product. This task was achieved through creating images of brands' promised benefits to consumers. Initially images of brand's functional benefits (to satisfy the "utilitarian" needs of the consumers) were depicted; later on symbolic benefits (to satisfy the psychological and social needs of the consumers) were stressed upon. Thus, creating brand image became be all and end all of branding. The literature on branding started emerging rapidly and increased focus to brand image signaled the departure from viewing brands as merely from identifiers to viewing them in terms of images (Gardner & Levy 1955; Oxenfeldt & Swann 1964; White 1959). These images were the perceptions about the brands created by the firms (Park et al. 1986) to secure competitive advantages and their standing in the market place (Welcker, 1949). Communicating brand image became necessary for the firms to help consumers to both differentiate a brand from its competitors (DiMingo, 1988; Reynolds and Gutman, 1984) and identify the needs that a brand promised to satisfy (Roth, 1995).

During the late 1950's academic research on branding threw light on the fact that it became difficult for the consumers to differentiate brands at the time of purchase considering functional benefits that a brand promised to offer. Gardener and Levy (1955) pointed out that the consumers could not discern the differences among brands as, more or less, all the brands in the product category made similar claims of superiority. The researchers argued that the firms must satisfy the symbolic needs created as a result of the consumers' desire for self-enhancement, social position, group membership, ego-identification (Park et. al, 1986). Advertising professionals and marketing practitioners went beyond this and they started embedding human characteristics to the bands to create symbolic brand image. In 1958 Martineau used the word 'brand personality' to denote non-material dimensions that contributed to a store's special image. To advertising agencies the popular copy strategies were creation of brand image through projection of brand personality. This was how image-oriented branding era prevailed in the mass marketing era. The branding concepts that ruled the image-oriented branding era were- brand image and brand personality.

During the mid 1960's organizations were found establishing style and speed of progress. A new industrial era- the Age of Discontinuity- began. This period was marked by unforeseen environmental turbulence coupled with changes in business dynamics and business boundaries. Technological and political changes also contributed to create an environment of "discrete changes" (Roy, 2006). Organizations became information dependent to deal with the extreme uncertainty in the business environment. Shortening of product life cycle proved to be the new success mantra. Product line extension emerged as the strategic options for the many firms. Branding turned into a complex job due to brand proliferation. Noise level in the market place rose in an unprecedented way. Chaos reigned supreme as a result of marketers' attempt to reach consumers' minds with the messages of large portfolio of products and brands. Advertising failed to do the job as compared to the previous eras (Trout and Ries, 1972). In Trout & Ries' (1972) own words the state-of-affairs were brought to light:

Today's marketplace is no longer responsive to strategies that worked in the past. There are just too many products, too many companies and too much marketing noise. We have become an over communicated society.

Al Ries and Jack Trout advocated a new approach to branding what they called brand positioning. This concept evolved as an epoch making discovery in the field of branding. Positioning involved the act of making the brands secure a distinctive place in the minds of the target market through creation of value proposition for the consumers and clarification of brand's essence. According to Al Ries and Jack Trout (1982):

Positioning starts with a product. A piece of merchandise, a service, a company, an institution or even a person... But Positioning is not what you do to a product. Positioning is what you do to the mind of the prospect. That is, you position the product in the mind of the prospect.

The idea behind the positioning concept was not to change the mind of the prospect, as traditional advertising used to do through creation of brand image; rather the mission was to be in the mind itself. Thus, positioning stood out as the key concept in the communication- oriented branding era which lasted till the late 1990's.

During the mid of 1980's, researcher like Kapferer (1986) added a new perspective to communication-oriented branding. He argued that effective communication of brand should ensure sending out messages and their receiving at the consumers' end. He propounded the brand identity concept based on the communication model

Smith (2001) show that successful extension is dependent on consumers' perception of fit between a new extension and parent brand. Consumers' evaluation of brand extension is largely affected by the positively evaluated symbolic brand associations (Reddy, Holak, and Bhat 1994; Park, Milberg and Lawson 1991). Consumer knowledge of the parent and extension categories also influences extension success (Moreau et al, 2001). Roy and Banerjee (2007) proposes CARE (credibility building, alteration, relationship building and expansion) –in strategies for integration of brand identity and brand image to cement a lasting bond of the brand with its consumers. The studies of Choi and Winterich (2013) investigate how moral identity of brand affects out-group brand attitudes of the consumers.

GENERATING FRESH INSIGHTS TO BRANDING STRATEGIES

In Search of a Starting Point

Branding brings benefits for the organization enabling the marketers to strategically address its products and markets. As a result, in most of the product categories marketing programs have largely become brand based. The major task that preoccupies the marketers is to develop branding strategies to triumph in the market place. Strategic thinking in terms of brand extension, brand revitalization, brand positioning and brand repositioning has surely empowered the brand managers. On the other hand, the concept of brand identity proves to be the password to unlock the mystery of branding. Although we talk of importance of branding strategies to be the key to success, conceiving strategies is not always easy on the part of the marketers. What could be the starting point of formulating branding strategies is also a baffling question.

C_4 Strategy Matrix: A Road Map to Branding Strategies

In various strategic approaches available in the literature, strategies have been developed through a matching process of the organization's internal factors and the factors external to it. Here, drawing an analogy with the strategic approach we would propose an approach involving a matching process of the brand's internal and external elements- internal effort and external realization. Internal effort signifies branding efforts to ensure brand's specific mode of communication, its adjustments to the external environment and its physical appearance. External realization is the brand's external effect realized by the consumers. The two dimensions – internal effort and external realization- vary from low to high and their interplay gives rise to four branding strategies- continuity, caution, change and correction.

Figure 1. C$_4$ strategy matrix

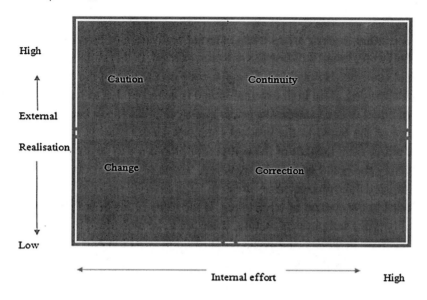

Details of the Branding Strategies

Continuity

When high degree of internal effort of branding has high external realization, continuity is the most suitable strategic choice. In this situation what brand is and how brand communicates are properly understood and perceived by the consumers in a highly favorable way. Here, brand requires investment in communication to maintain its strong strategic position. Since brand's embedded personality traits and physical qualities generate favorable external realization, brand should keep up the communication with these aspects as the main theme of communication. If the choice of brand name alludes to the brand's specific physicality and personality type and has significant contribution to creative strategy, highlighting of the same brand name should be considered. Personality and appearance of brand's creator may also play significant role in the brand theme. Communication should be maintained supporting this creator brand relationship. Sometimes type of product that brand endorses exhibits what the brand actually is or wants to be. If this is operating, communication should continue supporting that product or those product features should be made visible. No alteration in logo and visual symbol is desirable

Caution

Need for caution strategy arises when external realization of brand is high, even if internal effort for brand building has not been exerted. In this situation brand enjoys a favorable competitive position. Complacency on the part of the brand managers should be avoided. Here high external image is achieved due to functional performance of brand or due to attractive price- quality relationship or because of pioneer advantage of the brand in the product category. Under caution strategy possible areas of attack from the side of the competitor brands are to be ascertained. Means of protecting the brand need to be explored. Scope of further brand building is to be investigated through consumer research. High external realization of brand must be included in the content of advertising. If the users of the brand possess specific personality types and physical stature, these are to be embedded in the brand. Further investment in advertising is also a feasible proposition and it could serve as defense shield of the brand.

Change

This situation represents weakest strategic position of the brand. Here internal effort for brand building is not properly made. In view of the low internal effort and low external situation, this position poses a real problem to the brand managers. Failure in implementation of the caution strategy may lead to this situation also. Change strategy means discrete alteration in branding activities. There are two alternatives to the brand mangers. Management can drop the idea of brand building under the same creative strategy, because low external realization nullifies further allocation of resources. Otherwise, brand can be revived through change of brand name, total change in visual symbols or logos or packaging. Total change in either physique or personality or in both can be done. Selective promotion can be undertaken to make the brand turn around.

Correction

High internal effort and low external realization calls for correction strategy. When consumers do not perceive the brand building effort in a favorable way, this situation arises. The consequence of failure of development strategy can be this situation. It is also notable that if continuity strategy fails to retain the strong position of the brand, brand enters in this position. Under this strategy bottle necks in theme of the brand is to be eliminated. If there exists an abstract concept in communication aspect and physicality of the brand, that is to be simplified. Clarity of the content of advertising needs to be improved. Media plan of the brand is to be reengineered.

THE CASE OF SHAHNAZ HERBALS

Shahnaz Herbals was founded in 1970 by Shahnaz Hussain in her house in Delhi, India. The company was initially formed to offer beauty treatments to Indian women and later started offering its own beauty products. At the time of inception of Shahnaz Herbals Indian beauty and beauty service industry services were unorganized and fragmented. Basic beauty products like cold cream, shampoo, hair oil and toilet soap were available in the market for the consumers. People used to associate cosmetics with makeup items largely. All these products were chemical based. Shahnaz offered alternative methods of beauty services and alternative products- herbal method and herbal cosmetics- before the big companies in India could capture the markets with their existing cosmetics based products on which a good number of consumers were getting dependent to look good. Within three decades Shahnaz Herbals, with an estimated global worth of $ 500 million, had more than 350 products and 400 franchise salons operating in 138 countries across the world. The company, according to an FMCG analyst, registered annual turnover of Rs 650 crore. Shahnaz Herbals compete in India with the formidable skincare players like L'Oreal, Clarin's and BodyShop in Rs 5000 crore Indian beauty Industry which is expected, as per ASSOCHAM, to be Rs 10000 crore by 2014. The mid-to-upper market positioned aurvedic brand received tremendous popularity in Indian and international markets. Shahnaz herbals were the first Asian beauty products company to sell its products through reputed global stores like Bloomingdale's (New York), Galleries Lafayette (Paris), Seibu (Japan), Harrods, Selfridges (London) and La Rinaeccente(Milan).

The success of the company owes much to the Shanaz Hussain's branding which seems like an enigma to branding gurus and practitioners. "You (Husain) violate every norm that we teach of setting aside a part of your budget for advertising and publicity. It is not only her franchise-based enterprise but also her marketing strategies that are truly unique" said Dr Samuel Hayes, finance guru and Harvard Business School professor, about Shahnaz's branding. The 3 Cs – creator, creation and communication – particularly shape the realm of it. 'Creator' stands for Shahnaz Husain, creation denotes the brands and 'communication' is the iconoclastic approaches of the 'creator' making the 'creation' interact with the consumers.

Unlike the top international cosmetic brands which invest whopping amount in advertising, Shahnaz Husain did not advertise till the year 2008. Her brand's promise to offer customized and an alternative solution to the consumers were communicated through word-of-mouth publicity. "Advertising is a paid form of publicity; I have never relied on it" said Shahnaz.

Shahnaz Hussain brands are by far the best representatives of Shahnaz Hussain herself. She has put in all her experience, expertise, and rigorous training of ten years in chemistry and cosmetology in the various leading beauty schools of the west including L'Oréal and Schwarzkopf in her brands. Shahnaz becomes a prolific writer of beauty columns in reputed newspapers and magazines vouching for the benefits of the herbal cosmetics and cautioning against the use of chemical based products. She arranges seminars and conferences for this purpose on a regular basis. It has become a regular practice for her to reply personally to letters seeking beauty solutions. Mostly her brands carry her names and photographs to make consumers choose the brands counting on her expertise and experience. In Shahnaz's own words, "If it bears my name, it catches on." Shahnaz is also seen inaugurating her salons in various cities across the world wearing embroidered, self -designed clothes and with Louis Vuitton bag in her hands. In a word, Shahnaz Hussain is the real figurehead shaping the mode of communication of what the brand actually is.

For Shahnaz Hussain selling her beauty products and treatments is selling 5000 year old Indian civilization in a jar. In the startup years, she used to sell her own formulations in bottles bought from the local markets and she labeled them herself. One of her early creation is Shagrin which she formulated with the recipe of rice, rose petals, herbs and sandalwood oil. She has taken much care in packaging of her brands. She herself has visited khurja (a place in India known for pottery design going back centuries) for examining the pottery design and choosing jars for packaging for her products. The product ranges are based on specific extracts and accordingly they have been named like flower power, neem, oxygen, pearl concepts, 24 carat gold, and diamond collection etc. The physical appearances of the brands signify the natural ingredients of these products.

In 1980 Shahnaz Herbals went international with the participation of the festival of India in London. The huge customer acceptance of Shahnaz Hussain brands in Selfridges, London broke the stores cosmetic sales record for the sales of worth £2700 in two hours. The company broke another record in 2010 at Selfridges, London by selling the products of worth £4334 in a single transaction to an individual customer. In Galeries Lafayette (in Paris), the world's most prestigious cosmetic store, all the consignments were sold out during the India festival.

Shahnaz adopted franchise-based marketing strategies which enabled the brand Shahnaz Hussain to become the household names in India.The first Shahnaz Herbal franchise clinic was started in Kolkata in 1979. Shahnaz Hussain products are primarily sold through the franchise saloons. When a new salon is launched, it is done first in the international markets. In these salons clients are recommended products after diagnosis and clinical analysis of the skin and scalp condition.

The branding addressed the trend of rapid growth of male grooming products in the market. The company became one of the earliest players in the male hair and skin care market. Shahnaz Hussain brand was extended to the male segment with the launch of Shahnaz Herbal Salon for men in 1993.

The company plans to expand its operations in the markets across the globe through international branding, cementing the global franchise distribution channel and ensuring distribution of the brands in the unrepresented new markets by appointing distributors. It aims to improve its presence in major countries like USA, Canada, Kazakhstan and Kuwait, Bahrain, Oman, Australia, Singapore, Malaysia, South East Asia, New Zealand and other CIS countries including Russia, Belarus and Latvia by 2015.

CASE ANALYSIS

The close look at the above case enables us to identify two basic aspects of brand- one is the internal aspect and the other one is the internal aspect. From the above case it is evident how Shahnaz Hussain has played a pivotal role in making the brand effectively communicate with the consumers and making the consumers understand what the brand actually is. She truly defines the credo of the brand; she devises the momentum to reach success. Accordingly the brand is physically built. These two aspects can be considered under the internal aspect of a brand and this internal aspect is achieved through organization's internal brand building efforts.

One of the key external aspects of Shahnaz Hussain brands is consumers' projected image. Consumer's projected image is how the consumers want to be seen themselves after using the brand. This aspect unfolds the consumers' desire to move from being to becoming. In this case, consumers' projected image can be well understood by the brands' evoked image of the persons for whom beauty is an achievable reality, thanks to the Shahnaz Hussain brands. This aspect also gets integrated with the internal expects of the brands and contribute to brands' external effects. The brands' innovative products, which are the results of prolonged research and development activities, appeal to the consumers. Shahnaz Hussain's introduction of clinical system with client card- diagnosis and clinical analysis of the skin and scalp condition before recommending the products and individual consultations and treatments, is favorably perceived by the consumers. Shahnaz Hussain brands become the choice of women and men of India and foreign countries.

Her inauguration of salons, giving free consultation and pioneering of herbal products attracted media coverage and did publicity for her brands. Large pool of satisfied customer base and positive word of mouth has provided an impetus to Shahnaz Hussain brands. Uncompromising quality and alternative herbal based products behind the brands to potentially harmful chemical based ones win the minds of the many consumers. They are made more skin conscious, when they are aware of Shahnaz Hussain brands or interact with it. They also develop uncompromising attitude towards themselves at the time of making purchase decisions. The consumers' skin consciousness and uncompromising attitude toward themselves form the consumer's self-portrayal. Consumer's projected image and consumer's self portrayal, as mentioned above, are purely the consumer centric issues. These two issues form the external realization of the brand. Thus, the above case helps us derive two basic issues – internal effort and external realization- on which the branding strategies can be developed.

CONCLUSION

In this above case we have examined that there is high degree of internal effort for brand building both from communication and physicality perspectives. At the same time the high internal effort is accordingly realized by the consumers of the Shanaz Hussain brands. As per the C_4 strategy matrix when internal effort is high and external realization is also high, the recommended strategy is continuity strategy. The courses of action to be taken under continuity strategy are that investment in communication to maintain the strong position of the brand and advertising campaign is to be undertaken in selected media incorporating contribution of Shahnaz Hussain as brand's creator. Under the same creative strategy physical attributes of the brand are to be highlighted without any alteration in logo or visual symbols.

REFERENCES

Aaker, D. (1991). *Managing brand equity: Capitalizing on the value of a brand name*. New York: The Free Press.

Aaker, D. A. (1991). *Managing brand equity*. New York: Free Press.

Aaker, D. A. (1992). Managing the most important asset: Brand equity. *Strategy and Leadership*, *20*(5), 56–59. doi:10.1108/eb054384

Aaker, D. A., & Keller, K. L. (1990). Consumer evaluations of brand extensions. *Journal of Marketing*, *54*(1), 27–41. doi:10.2307/1252171

Aaker, J. L. (1999). The malleable self: The role of self-expression in persuasion. *JMR, Journal of Marketing Research*, *36*(2), 45–57. doi:10.2307/3151914

Alessandri, S. W., & Alessandri, T. (2004). Promoting and protecting corporate identity: The importance of organizational and industry context. *Corporate Reputation Review*, *7*(3), 252–268. doi:10.1057/palgrave.crr.1540224

Ambler, T. (1992). *Need-to-know-marketing*. London: Century Business.

American Marketing Association. (1960). *Marketing definitions: A glossary of marketing terms*. Chicago: IL AMA.

Ries, A., & Trout, J. (1982). *Positioning: The battle for your mind*. New York: Warner Books.

Arnold, D. (1992). *The handbook of brand management*. The Economist Books.

Aaker, D. A. (1991). Foreword. In *Managing brand equity* (p. ix). New York: The Free Press.

Azoulay, A., & Kapferer, J.-N. (2003). Do brand personality scales really measure brand personality? *Journal of Brand Management, 11*(2), 143–155. doi:10.1057/palgrave.bm.2540162

Bastos, W., & Levy, S. J. (2012). A history of the concept of branding: Practice and theory. *Journal of Historical Research in Marketing, 4*(3), 347–368. doi:10.1108/17557501211252934

Batra, R., Mayers, J. G., & Aaker, D. A. (2006). *Advertising management*. Delhi: Pearson Education.

Brown, G. (1992). *People, brands and advertising*. Warwick, UK: Millward Brown International.

Buzzell, R. D., & Gale, B. T. (1987). *The PIMS principle- Linking strategy to performance*. New York: Free Press.

Chernatony, L. D., & Riley, F. D. (1998). Defining a "brand": Beyond the literature with the experts' interpretations. *Journal of Marketing Management, 14*(5), 417–443. doi:10.1362/026725798784867798

Choi, W. J., & Winterich, K. P. (2013). Can brands move in from outside? How moral identity enhances out-group brand attitudes. *Journal of Marketing, 77*(2), 96–111. doi:10.1509/jm.11.0544

Cobb-Walgren, C. J., Ruble, C. A., & Donthu, N. (1995). Brand equity, brand preference, and purchase intent. *Journal of Advertising, 24*(3), 25–40. doi:10.1080/00913367.1995.10673481

Crainer, S. (1995). *The real power of brands: Making brands work for competitive advantage*. London: Pitman Publishing.

Czellar, S. (2003). Consumer attitude toward brand extensions: An integrative model and research propositions. *International Journal of Research in Marketing, 20*(1), 97–115.

Daniels, C. (2013). *Shahnaz Husain: The free spirit of an entrepreneur*. Retrieved February 17, 2014 http://news.in.msn.com/her_courage/shahnaz-husain-the-free-spirit-of-an-entrepreneur

Davis, S. (2002). Brand asset management: How businesses can profit from the power of brand. *Journal of Consumer Marketing*, *19*(4), 351–358. doi:10.1108/07363760210433654

de Chernatony, L., & McDonald, M. (1994). *Creating powerful brands*. Oxford, UK: Butterworth-Heinemann.

Dibb, S., Simkin, L., Pride, W. M., & Ferrell, O. C. (1994). *Marketing: Concepts and strategies* (2nd ed.). Boston: Houghton Mifflin.

Dibb, S., Simkin, L., Pride, W. M., & Ferrell, O. C. (1997). *Marketing: Concepts and strategies* (3rd ed.). Boston: Houghton Mifflin.

DiMingo, E. (1988). The fine art of positioning. *The Journal of Business Strategy*, *9*(2), 34–38. doi:10.1108/eb039211 PMID:10303386

Duncan, T. (2005). *Advertising & IMC*. New York: McGraw-Hill.

Fieldwick, P. (1996). What is brand equity anyway, and how do you measure it? *Journal of the Market Research Society*, *38*(2), 85–104.

Flock, E. (2009). *If it bears my name: It catches on*. Retrieved February 19, 2014 http://forbesindia.com/printcontent/4702

Gardner, B. B., & Levy, S. J. (1955). The product and the brand. *Harvard Business Review*, *33*, 33–39.

Hammer, M. (1997). Beyond the end of management. In *Rethinking the future*. London: Nicholas Barely Publishing.

Jenster, P. V., Hayes, H. M., & Smith, D. E. (2005). *Managing business marketing and sales- An international perspective*. Copenhagen Business School Press.

Jones, J. P. (1986). *What's in a name?* Aldershot, UK: Gower.

Joyce, T. (1963). Techniques of brand image measurement. In *New developments in research* (pp. 45–63). London: Market Research Society.

Kapferer, J.-N. (1986), "Beyond positioning, retailer's identity," paper presented at Esomar Seminar, 4-6 June, Brussels.

Kapferer, J.-N. (1992). *Strategic brand management*. London: Kogan Page.

Kapferer, J.-N. (2000). *Strategic brand management*. New Delhi: Kogan Page India.

Kapferer, J.-N. (2005). *Strategic brand management*. London, UK: Kogan Page.

Keeble, G. (1991). Creativity and the brand. In *Understanding brands by 10 people who do* (pp. 167–182). London: Kogan Page.

Keller, K. L. (1993). Conceptualizing, measuring, and managing customer-based brand equity. *Journal of Marketing, 57*(1), 1–22. doi:10.2307/1252054

Keller, K. L. (1993). Conceptualizing, measuring and managing customer- based brand equity. *Journal of Marketing, 57*(1), 1–22. doi:10.2307/1252054

Keller, K. L. (2001). *Building customer based brand equity: A blue print for creating strong brands*. Cambridge, MA: Marketing Science Institute.

Keller, K. L. (2003). *Strategic brand management: Building, measuring, and managing brand equity* (2nd ed.). Upper Saddle River, NJ: Prentice Hall.

Kerin, R., & Sethuraman, R. (1998). Exploring the brand value shareholder value nexus for consumer goods companies. *Journal of the Academy of Marketing Science, 26*(4), 260–274. doi:10.1177/0092070398264001

Klink, R. R., & Smith, D. C. (2001). Threats to external validity of brand extension research. *JMR, Journal of Marketing Research, 38*(3), 326–335. doi:10.1509/jmkr.38.3.326.18864

Kotler, P. (2000). *Marketing management*. Upper Saddle River, NJ: Prentice Hall.

Kotler, P., Armstrong, G., Saunders, J., & Wong, V. (1996). *Principles of marketing*. Hemel Hempstead, UK: Prentice Hall Europe.

Kotler, P., & Keller, K. L. (2006). *Marketing management*. New Delhi: Prentice Hall of India Private Limited.

Levy, S. J. (1999). *Brands, consumers, symbols and research: Sydney J. Levy on marketing*. Thousand Oaks, CA: Sage publications.

Martineau, P. (1958). The personality of a retail store. *Harvard Business Review, 36*, 47–55.

Martineau, P. (1959). Sharper focus for the corporate image. *Harvard Business Review, 36*(1), 49–58.

McWilliam, G. (1993). A tale of two gurus: Aaker and Kapferer on brands. *International Journal of Research in Marketing, 10*, 105–111.

Moreau, P., Lehmann, D. R., & Markman, A. B. (2001). Entrenched knowledge structures and consumer response to new products. *JMR, Journal of Marketing Research, 38*(1), 14–29. doi:10.1509/jmkr.38.1.14.18836

Ohnemus, L., & Jenster, P. V. (2009). Corporate brand thrust and financial performance. *International Studies of Management & Organization, 7*(4), 84–107.

Olins, W. (1989). *Corporate identity: Making business strategy visible through design.* London: Thames and Hudson.

Olins, W. (1990). *The Wolff Olins guide to corporate identity.* Ashgate Publishing.

Oxenfeldt, A. R., & Swann, C. (1964). *Management of the advertising function.* Belmont, CA: Wadsworth.

Park, C. W., Jaworski, B. J., & Maclnnis, D. J. (1986). Strategic brand concept-image management. *Journal of Marketing, 50*(4), 135–145. doi:10.2307/1251291

Park, C. W., Milberg, S., & Lawson, R. (1991). Evaluation of brand extensions: The role of product feature similarity and brand concept consistency. *The Journal of Consumer Research, 18*(2), 185–193. doi:10.1086/209251

Pitcher, A. E. (1985). The role of branding in International advertising. *International Journal of Advertising, 4,* 241–246.

Raturi, P. (2013). *An interview with Shahnaz Husain: You can be what you will yourself to be.* Academic Press.

Reddy, S. K., Holak, S. L., & Bhat, S. (1994). To extend or not to extend: Success determinants of line extensions. *JMR, Journal of Marketing Research, 31*(2), 243–262. doi:10.2307/3152197

Reynolds, T. J., & Gutman, J. (1984). Advertising as image management. *Journal of Advertising Research, 24,* 27–38.

Roth, M. S. (1995). The effects of culture and socioeconomics on the performance of global brand image strategies. *JMR, Journal of Marketing Research, 32*(2), 163–175. doi:10.2307/3152045

Roy, D. (2006). *Discourses on strategic management.* New Delhi: Asian Books Private Ltd.

Roy, D., & Banerjee, S. (2007). CARE-ing strategy for integration of brand identity with brand image. *International Journal of Commerce and Management, 17*(1), 140–148.

Schultz, M., & Hatch, M. J. (2003). The cycles of corporate branding: The case of the LEGO company. *California Management Review, 46*(1), 6–26. doi:10.2307/41166229

Simon, C. J., & Sullivan, M. W. (1993). The measurement and determinants of brand equity: A financial approach. *Marketing Science, 12*(1), 28–52. doi:10.1287/mksc.12.1.28

Trout, J., & Ries, A. (n.d.). Positioning cuts through chaos in marketplace. *Advertising Age*.

Van den Heever, J. (2000). *Brands and branding in South Africa*. Johannesburg, South Africa: Affinity.

Watkins, T. (1986). *The economics of the brand*. McGraw Hill Book Company.

Welcker, J. W. (1949). The community relations problem of industrial companies. *Harvard Business Review, 49*(6), 771–780.

White, I. S. (1959). The functions of advertising in our culture. *Journal of Marketing, 23*(1), 8–14. doi:10.2307/1249358

KEY TERMS AND DEFINITIONS

Brand Identity: The way a brand attempts to identify itself or its product.

Brand Positioning: The act of making the brands secure a distinctive place in the minds of the target market through creation of value proposition for the consumers and clarification of brand's essence.

Brand: A name, term, design, symbol, or any other feature that identifies the seller's good or services as distinct from those of other sellers.

Branding: The process of endowing product and services with the power of a brand.

C$_4$ Strategy Matrix: A four-cell decision matrix involving the interplay of internal effort and external realization of a brand to conceive four types of branding strategies -continuity, caution, change and correction.

External Realization: The way the target audience perceives the internal effort of a brand.

Internal Effort: A set of practices to ensure brand's specific mode of communication and the way it adjusts to its external environment with a particular physical appearance.

Chapter 2
Promoting Bucovina's Tourism Brand

Alexandru-Mircea Nedelea
Ştefan cel Mare University of Suceava, Romania

ABSTRACT

In this chapter there is a presentation of Bucovina as an attractive tourism region of Romania, more and more appreciated by native and foreign tourists, having characteristics which distinguish it from the other Romanian tourism regions, namely the monasteries pertaining to UNESCO heritage. Nevertheless, the tourism in Bucovina can be oriented in many directions: historical and religious tourism, sports tourism, balneary tourism, and recreational tourism. The multitude of tourism forms that can be practiced in Bucovina must become well known; the possible visitors need to know that they can practice other forms of tourism besides the religious one, and this is why it is necessary to create the tourism brand of Bucovina. The promotion program of the brand of Bucovina must consider two main objectives: the presentation of the tourist sites and the deliverance of a good service quality.

THE TOURISM IN BUCOVINA

In the north-eastern part of Romania, at the border with Ukraine, there stretches the Upper Land of Moldavia, the historical-geographic region of Suceava, also called Bucovina. The region occupies a significant place in the country's economy, being the second as surface, with a population of approximately 700.000 inhabitants. Suceava is the capital of the county, situated at some important commercial crossroads, which connects Central and Northern Europe with the Black Sea.

DOI: 10.4018/978-1-4666-7393-9.ch002

Bucovina is one of the most important Romanian tourism brands. Filled with a rich and long Romanian tradition and having cultural foundations of international importance, Bucovina wants to come again into tourists' attention as a purely ecological tourism region, as it was called by Mr. Peter Zimmer, an expert of the German company IBD/GTZ (Integrated service of consultancy for economics in Romania - the Society for Technical Cooperation), one of the initiators and promoters of the Bucovina Tourism Association. The multitude of tourism forms which can be practiced in Bucovina must become well-known, the possible visitors knowing the fact that they can practice also other forms of tourism beside the religious one, and this is why it is necessary to create the tourism brand of Bucovina. But, the tourism in Bucovina can be oriented towards many directions: historical and religious tourism, sports tourism, balneary tourism and recreational tourism.

Religious built heritage is a particular strength for Bucovina. Today's traveller is mainly interested in the tourist circuits, which includes the famous monasteries, Arbore, Humor, Moldovita, Sucevita, Suceava, Patrauti, Probota, and Voronet, with their painted frescoes on the exterior walls.

As a general approach of the reality, we consider that it is necessary to create a customized unitary offer of Bucovina. This must include adequate tourism programs, which should allow to tourists to remain 6 nights in the region. Such an offer should involve combined proposals, a diversity of hunting and fishing programs, hiking, horse rides, mountain-bike, sheep-fold visits, mountain-climbing, paragliding, etc. In order to make easier to conceive some unitary tourism programs for Bucovina, it is necessary to have an efficient communication between the representatives of the tourism agencies and the receiving structures (hotels, villas, bed and breakfast, etc.).

The value and the density of the historical monuments, such as churches (beginning with Volovat, Solca, Horodnic, Bogdana from Radauti) and monasteries (Putna, Voronet, Sucevita, Arbore, Moldovita, Humor, Slatina, Dragomirna, Sf. Ioan cel Nou, Risca, Rarau), some of them unique in the whole world, ranked and listed in the "Protected Universal Heritage" by UNESCO in 1972, situates the county - as often stated by authorized persons - on the first position in the country, in what the cultural and historical resources are concerned.

According to the Austrian art critic Josef Strzygowski (1913) 'Above all that can be seen in Moldavia, there are the strange churches that, through the polychromy of their facades, can be compared to the San Marco Church in Venice, or the Dome in Orvieto' (...). 'Art and spiritual life of Bucovina would become one of the sights of Europe.'(...) 'There is no other country in the world to offer something like that.'

Regarding the natural tourism resources, Bucovina's potential situates this region on the 10th position. As a consequence, Bucovina represents an attractive tourism region, of international concern, by its cultural, historical, secular and religious heritage, and based on its natural conditions, of great landscape value. The exceptional tourism potential of the region allows a pronounced development of the tourism, a sector which can be considered as a significant source of economic growth in the following years.

Bucovina, a province situated in the North-Eastern Romanian, is well-known for the beauty of its landscapes, for the wealth of its traditions and, especially, for its painted monasteries. These masterpieces of art of Byzantine influence are poofs of the glory of the Moldavian civilization during the XVth and the XVIth centuries. The value and the beauty of these "pearls" of Bucovina are known and recognized all over the world. The recognition of this reality is represented by the fact that the above mentioned monasteries are part of the UNESCO heritage.

The main attraction of Bucovina is represented by these monumental places of worship, thanks to the lively colors of the frescoes placed on the walls of the churches. They picture biblical scenes and other religious scenes and are made in a manner similar to the one of the comic books, and namely on segments. They used to have the role to stir the locals' imagination and to educate them in an orthodox spirit. What others were capable to attain a few hundreds of years ago, represents a special attraction for the nowadays tourists. A monastery can be "sold" a thousand times by the tourism agencies without losing its value, but quite the opposite.

Amongst the tourism activities which must be developed and promoted, we count:

- **The Thematic Programs:** (Hiking), encouraged by the existence of many marked roads, amongst we mention the old "Tatars' road ," up to the commune of Carlibaba and the other one towards the Moldovita Monastery. These road-maps can be crossed by foot or by horses that the locals can make available for the tourists. Also, of a special charm are the mountain roads to Rarau and Giumalau massifs. From the municipality of Vatra Dornei it is the possibility to go hiking, on foot or using 4x4 vehicles, for the mountains: Calimani, Ineu, Rodna and Obcina Mestecanisului.
- **The Riding Programs:** Horse riding can be practiced especially at the herd from the town of Radauti and Lucina. Visitors are able to test the value of the pure-bred horses in the riding hall of the enclosure. On the hippodromes near the stock-farm, equine contests are organized.
- The programs like "At home at the popular craftsmen" consisting of visits paid to the popular craftsmen workshops (some of them having the opportunity to provide accommodation to the tourists).

Bucovina is known for its folk costumes, furniture, pottery, tapestries and carpets. Every detail of these handicrafts reflects the historical and cultural heritage of the region, while providing unique keepsakes that can be handed down from generation to generation.

Bucovina represents a tourism destination within Romania's tourism macro-product. Thus, for the foreign tourists who perform a 10 day journey in our country, the Bucovina area has assigned, usually, a number of 2 days.

Internationally, within the well-known tourism destinations, there are tourism programs of 12 days in which the tourists have no time to be bored. A tourism product which takes place during a period of 10 days in Bucovina could not be possible for now, because the foreign tourist is a dynamic lover of tight schedules. He wants to "mark" as many tourism objectives, attractions and activities as possible in his tourism agenda (the tour-operators in the USA are promoting within their offers the program named "Europe in only 5 days").

Usually, in Bucovina, tourists are visiting two monasteries, afterwards they grow tired and go ahead to visit other tourism attractions (to admire, for instance, the Maramures gate). In this situation, we can identify the promotion within the same tourism product (circuit-type), of two or many complementary tourism destinations as a marketing strategy in the hospitality industry. In this case, we talk about Bucovina and Maramures or Neamt.

An attraction like the monasteries of Bucovina must represent only the main reason for which the tourists should be drawn to Romania, and, once they get here, they should be directed towards other tourism objectives.

Same as at the national level, the incoming activity is poorly developed in Bucovina. Most of the Romanian tourism agencies undertake mostly an outgoing activity, considered to be, by the local operators, as more profitable.

Bucovina has beautiful landscapes, and, thanks to its cultural, historical and religious objectives, it is one of the most precious places in Romania, highly valued by the domestic tourists, but also by international tourists.

Because in Romania, at the present moment, the demand for internal tourism is decreasing and will continue to decrease until the economic situation of the population will improve, the marketing efforts must be oriented to draw to Bucovina as many tourists as possible, from the developed countries. The number of foreign tourists and of staying overnight is smaller compared to the accommodation possibilities and the region's tourism potential. In reality, not only the number of foreign tourists which are visiting the region is the one that counts, but the profit resulted. The tourists from the neighboring countries are coming and will continue to come to Bucovina, especially for that small border traffic (according to some opinions, they are not considered as tourists, even if they are recorded in the customs statistics).

Normally, tourists come to Bucovina in organized groups, within some circuits which are conceived, distributed and promoted by the tour-operator agencies from Bucharest. Suceava represents, unfortunately, only a transit area. As a consequence, it is necessary to conceive some marketing strategies which should aim to keep the tourists in that area for at least one more day. In order to fulfill this objective, it is necessary to elaborate a coherent marketing strategy at the level of entire tourist region of Bucovina. For this purpose, it is necessary that all those involved and interested in the tourism development in the region to collaborate, in order to establish the content of the tourism programs which will be promoted under the brand of Bucovina.

The regional touristic promotion associations have the role to reunite all existent forces on the local level interested in promoting the touristic potential of the respective area.

Among the objectives of the Tourism Marketing Information Center Bucovina (www.tourisminbucovina.ro) and Bucovina Tourism Association we can mention:

- Conceiving a strategy regarding the promotion and the tourism development in Bucovina;
- Creating a data base with the touristic objectives and accommodation units of Bucovina;
- Developing tourism marketing strategies to grow the Bucovina touristic product quality;
- Organization of conferences, workshops and seminars about Bucovina brand;
- Tourism market studies regarding the hospitality industry in the area;
- Promoting the cooperation with the local and central administration;
- Promoting the cooperation and an efficient communication between the governmental institutions;
- Editing promotional materials;
- Taking part in internal and international tourism fairs.

BRAND AND TOURISM BRANDING

Branding is today often considered as a key priority for many companies in order to stay competitive on the market (Aaker & Joachimsthaler, 2000; Kapferer,2008).

Branding can be defined as the way in which the organization managing their brand and requires a long-term participation of both skills and resources (Kapferer, 2008).

An organization can use branding in order to identify and differentiate it selves from competitors', it is a way to ensure quality and honesty, identify the ownership and to hold the producer responsible for their actions (Daye, 2006; Kapferer, 2008)

Branding is also an essential component in the process of building a strong brand image and to create brand awareness, moreover it may increase marketing communication effectiveness, improve perceptions of product performance and create customer loyalty (Hoeffler &Keller, 2003;Keller, 2009).

A section of branding which refer to branding a country is defined as place branding (Moilanenand Rainisto, 2009; Anholt 2003; Kavaritzis, 2004; Kotler, Haider &Reid, 1993).

According to Kavaratzis (2005) there are several terms of place branding which all are similar to each other. A synonym for place branding is country and nation branding and the concept is also closely related to destination branding and city branding, where destination branding touch branding of a destination towards the tourism sector, and city branding relates to branding of one single city(Kavaritzis, 2004)

As place branding has the opportunity to enhance economic development, it has become a growing activity in governments around the world(Papadopoulos, 2004). The concept refers to different efforts taken by a country, regional or city government to marketing a country towards the rest of the world (Fetcherin, 2010; Aronczyk, 2008). In addition, it also tends to produce national solidarity and repair a bad reputation. Place branding could therefore be to great use, especially for less developed countries since it could lead to development and economic growth. (Anholt, 2003)

The tourism industry have become a key factor for economic growth in several developing countries (Sinclair, 1998). This statement is confirmed by the World Trade Organization (WTO, 2013.04.11)who see the travel and tourism industry as the world's biggest economic sector which contribute with trillions of dollars to the global economy each year(WTO, 2013.04.11).

According to World Trade Tourism Council about 260 million jobs around the world are created through the tourism sector (WTTC, 2013.02.25). These jobs are vital for people, in particular in developing countries, as they lead to wealth not only for the employee but also for the bigger community as they generates exports and stimulate capital investments (WTTC, 2013.02.25; Sinclair, 1998)

Every place is considered to have an image, whether they choose to manage it or not (Gilmore, 2002; Papadopoulos and Heslop, 2002; Fan, 2006; Anholt, 2003). A place which is not involved in the process of branding, tend to be positioned anyway, based on other parties opinions (Gilmore, 2002), and as images often are founded on individuals' personal opinions and previous knowledge, it does not necessary have to be correct information (Anholt, 2007).

Govers, Go and Kumar (2011) and Gilmore (2002) agree with this and argue that the current reality of a country widely can differ from a consumer's image. It could therefore be considered as devastating for a country not to manage their image (Anholt, 2007; Govers, Go & Kumar, 2011; Gilmore, 2002).

Extensive research in the area of branding has been done, but still, there is limited knowledge in the area of place branding (Fan, 2006; Kotler & Gertner, 2002). Hanna & Rowley (2011) argue that literature and researches of the area up to today do not offer a holistic view of the whole process, but rather individual parts, which can be seen as critical as Jansen (2008) argues that branding of a country includes multiple layers of the country.

Brand identity is important within the area of brand management (Kapferer, 2008) and should focus on differentiate the company among its competitors in a long-term perspective (Ghodeswar, 2008; Kapferer, 2008). De Chernatony (2010) and Harris and De Chernatony (2001) discuss the culture within the organization as being an important part of the brand identity process. Furthermore, a country's identity has to be developed from the people living in the country and their assumptions, values and beliefs (Papadopoulos & Heslop, 2002).

According to Kapferer (2008) the identity displays the features, which is based on the roots and heritage of the brand. The identity of a brand is the arrangement of components such as words, ideas, images and associations. These elements all together shape the customers' perception of a brand. (Upshaw, 1995) The foundation in brand identity is an understanding of the organization's customers and competitors as well as the market (Aaker & Joachimsthaler 2000; Kapferer 2008). Brand identity needs to fit the business strategy, it also has to reflect the company's willingness to deliver what the customers expects from the brand. (Ghodeswar, 2008) If a company lacks in communicating its core values to the target group it can turn out to be unsuccessful, even though the company might have a great offer and management. (Nandan, 2004).In order to manage the brand identity, the organization should identify the core values of the brand and make sure that the values are in line with the values of the people working within the organization (Harris & De Chernatony, 2001; Hatch & Schultz, 2008). According to Hanna and Rowley (2011), the brand identity is the core of the brand building process.

It is the result of the evaluation of the brand experience and it affect the brand architecture relationships. This means that stakeholder's interests are essential aspects when improving the brand identity further. Moreover, it is the differentiated features unique for one place and gives a structure on how to conduct one united brand. (Hanna & Rowley, 2011)

A strong brand architecture provides a proper structure and control when managing the brand into new markets (Douglas, Craig & Nijssen, 2001; Sanchez, 2004). Brand architecture is the structure of the organization, which manage the brand's portfolio and defines the different roles of the brands and the relationships between the different brands. Place brands often consist of one central brand supported by many sub-brands. These sub-brands can in a country be different companies and organizations, both private and public, such as tourist businesses, plants and community services (Hanna & Rowley, 2011). According to Aaker & Joachimsthaler (2000) there are different ways in how the many sub-brands of companies and organizations within a brand are connected to the central brand. If they are tight connected to each other the success of one sub-brand can enhance the other sub-brands, while a negative outcome on one sub-brand also affects the others. On the other hand, if the sub-brands are not tight connected they do not affect each other in the same way, either positive or negative. (Aaker & Joachimsthaler, 2000).According to Lagergren (1998), marketing communication is how a company or organization communicates with the market, where the communication can be seen as an exchange of ideas and experiences. The communication of a brand is an important component for the brand management, especially because of the meaning making and its structured functions (Duncan & Moriarty, 1998). As the marketplace today can be complex, marketing communications can help brands to stand out from the crowd and enhance their competitive advantages. Marketing communications makes it possible for marketers to inform, influence and remind the customers. (Keller, 2001) Customers and other stakeholders are involved in and influence the brand message, brand communication is therefore a key aspect when it comes to building relationship with its stakeholders (Duncan and Moriarty, 1998). Everything sends a brand message, and therefore, brand message needs to be consistent in order to create positive associations. It is also essential to have all the stakeholders in mind, and to strive for the brand communication being interactive.(Duncan & Moriarty, 1998)

Bucovina tourism can be oriented towards more directions: historical and religious tourism, sports tourism. The value and intensity of the historical monuments place Bucovina (Suceava county) on the first place from the point of view of cultural and historical resources.

Creating a Bucovina touristic brand must take into account the fact that it is necessary that this product be a complete one which includes: the cultural attraction visiting (monasteries, museums, churches, citadels etc.), sports tourism (hunting and fishing, mountain-biking, trekking, river-rafting) relaxation tourism, rural tourism which is included in more optional programs.

The brand represents that positive emotional and symbolic connection, caused by words, images, sounds and symbols in relation to a country or certain region of that country, which eases the choice and increases the satisfaction of the potential visitor.

The concept of tourism product appears as being connected to the offer of the tourism agencies, as well as of some tourism areas, as for instance Bucovina, Maramures, Delta. These have become real tourism brands of Romania.

The regional associations of tourism promotion, the tourism information centers and the tourism promotion offices of Romania, together with the factors of decision from the Public administration–especially the Ministry of Tourism, should create strategies of conceiving, structuring and promotion of Romania's important tourism brands.

In view of creating and promoting the brand of a tourism destination, it is necessary to have cooperation and coordination between the organizations performing at the national and international level, as well as the efforts made for promotion by the tourism operators at the regional and local level.

Creating a tourism brand for an area involves science, art and technique, to which much creativity is added.

A complex system of connections is being weaved around a brand which contributes to the communication of the values created. The brand is being construed starting from a logo and a slogan, but its power comes from all means of communication and promotion: directly, by audio-video spots, ad prints, online banners, posters, catalogs, direct correspondence.

In what the tourism brand is concerned, it represents that element of image which identifies the tourism products or services for a certain region; it gives the feeling of pride to the region locals, of recognition and satisfaction amongst the consumers.

The brand identity is based on components like:

- **Brand Culture:** Represents a characteristics system based on people's cultural aspects (traditions, events, gastronomy) and country (historical sites, monuments, archaeological sites, churches), implying, basically, the important aspects of the tourism destination.
- **The Name of the Brand:** In many cases, is the original name of the tourism destination.
- **The Logo of the Brand (Or the Symbol):** Constitutes a representative image, attractive and ease to remember, a fundamental element in order to define a destination. This kind of logos can be represented by an attractive panorama, a famous monument or a tradition.
- **The Slogan of the Brand:** An association of words which has the role to draw the attention of the possible tourists. The intention is to set the tourism product in the mind of the consumers in a memorable way.

Even if hundreds of thousands of dollars are invested in tourism brand communication campaigns, the consumers are the ones who get to decide if it rises to their level of expectations, if it can be considered to fulfill the promise that it makes to the client. The battles between brands is given always in the mind and the soul of the man, and under no circumstance within the advertising spots or in the publications' pages, which are not more than tools and under no circumstances the goals of a real brand.

The brand represents what tourists believe about that place, their perception. According to the marketing optics, the perception is in fact the reality. As a result, of importance are the opinions of the tourists about the region, and not the locals' opinion.

The tourism branding represents the creation and the maintenance process of a brand in the hospitality industry, the totality of the methods by which an organization or a product communicates, symbolizes and differentiate itself to its audiences.

The destination branding assumes the capitalization of the cultural and natural heritage through the creation of a historical preservation plan, the identification of the locations of major interest and the creation of the promotion materials in order to introduce them in the tourism circuit.

The tourism branding consists of the identification and/or the creation and then the exploitation of some sustainable competitive advantages, in our case we talk about the strengths of the product/the tourism region of Bucovina.

We talk about a process of developing a tourism product (from the marketing point of view), its launch on tourism market and especially creating the connection between the consumer and that product based on the product's qualities (or its "uniqueness").

The implementation, development and experimentation of tourism branding strategies can encounter the following problems:

- Insufficient development of general tourism and/or the marketing strategy;
- An underdeveloped organization structure of the tourism destination can impede the professional elaboration of a strategy of marketing positioning;
- The volume of the budget allotted allows undergoing short-term campaigns, but also the implementation of medium and long-term strategies.

PROMOTING THE TOURISM BRAND OF BUCOVINA

The multitude of tourism forms which can be practiced in Bucovina must become well-known, the possible visitors knowing the fact that they can practice also other forms of tourism beside the religious one, and this is why it is necessary to create the tourism brand of Bucovina.

When we are analyzing the issue of conceiving and implementing a process of destination branding for the Bucovina region, it is necessary to answer the following questions:

- Is the Bucovina region known as tourism destination?
- What distinguishes it from the other tourism areas?
- Which is the first thing the visitors are thinking about regarding Bucovina?

Only after we get the answers to these questions we can initiate an action plan in order to create an image/an identity of that region which should draw the tourists at the national and international level and to ensure a distinct position on the tourism market of Romania.

The promotion of the tourism brand of Bucovina became a strategic priority for the officials in the county of Suceava, especially after 2007, at the same time with the Romania's adhesion to European Union. One of the ex-administrative leaders of the county of Suceava has proposed that the region he administrated to be named "the county of Bucovina," because this brand is known abroad and, as a consequence, it is easier to promote in view of drawing here tourists and investors.

In order to gain notoriety, an international brand as Bucovina assumes rethinking the distribution politics and, namely, a more efficient collaboration with the biggest European tour-operators.

The recreation and the promotion of a tourism brand of Bucovina can bring numerous economic and social advantages to the area. Amongst the most important advantages, we mention:

- The differentiation of the tourism product of Bucovina form the other similar products, granting it an extra value;
- Growing the perception of the global product, triggering and favoring the selling price of the private tourism products related to Bucovina;
- The possibility of launching new products much faster and more efficiently;
- The creation of the conditions of collaboration with the greatest international tour-operators.

Unfortunately, the local tour-operators rarely carry out incoming activities, preferring to center mainly on the outgoing activity, which is more profitable and easier in relation to the sale of local tourism packages.

In view of promoting all the tourism attractions from Bucovina under a unique brand (which will include also the destination of Dorna) we must begin with the performance of a SWOT analysis of the tourism product of Bucovina.

Amongst the strengths of the tourism product of Bucovina we can mention: The alternative tourism potential, the traditional houses, handicraft, sports tourism possibilities (summer-winter), an increased natural potential (for instance, the existence of the natural springs), special relief forms, the well preserved natural environment, special diversity, attractive natural landscapes (with forests, rivers, lakes, mountains), local gastronomic specialties, tradition cuisine, New Eve's customs, masks, traditional music/dances, winter sports, agritourism, eco-tourism (green tourism); The tourism resorts: Vatra Dornei (balneary and climatic), Cimpulung; the mineral springs, the folklore and the festivals (The Folklore festival of Radauti, the international festival from Cimpulung Moldovenesc), the historical and ethnographic museums from Suceava, Radauti, Gura Humorului, Cimpulung Moldovenesc, etc., the fresh air, the memorial houses, the natural environment fit for relaxation, the agritourism hospitality, the medieval fortresses, ceramics and traditional painting exhibition, the unique monuments at the international level, the numerous natural reservations, the possibility to organize a tourism circuit (monasteries' tour being the most appreciated), handicraft, archeological sites, black ceramics (Marginea); The multitude of types of tourism practiced in Bucovina: itinerant tourism with cultural valences, the balneary tourism, rural tourism, ecotourism, transit tourism, hunting and fishing tourism, riding tourism, winter sports tourism, congresses and reunions tourism, leisure and recreational tourism. The cultural tourism has great possibilities to attract foreign tourists through the integration of the national cultural heritage in the European and worldwide heritage (the monasteries ranked by UNESCO and having international significances – granting the prize "Pomme d'or" by the Tourism Journalists and Writers International Federation). Of great importance, in what the cultural potential of Bucovina is concerned, is the fact that the German media uses the slogan "Bucovina - the country of the 100 churches," drawing the attention on the special development of the ecumenical and pilgrimage tourism.

The weaknesses of the tourism product of Bucovina (with the mention that they are mostly found also at the level of the entire Romania): the lack of communication and cohesion between the human communities for the accomplishment of the objectives of mutual interest; the mentality of certain people to make money rapidly more than to provide quality services, people's impassivity regarding the environment; the large number of beggars; the insufficient training of some workers in the hospitality industry, the lack of motivation of the personnel, the relatively weak quality of the tourism services offered in the region, the reduced index of occupation of the accommodation capacity, the disruption of transportation cause by the state of the access roads (week infrastructure, the absence of street directories, pits); tourism infrastructure deficiencies: the absence of specialty shops (sports items, souvenirs, maps, guides, flyers, etc.), the preservation and cleanliness condition of some monuments, the absence of tourism markings, the existence in some cases of poor accommodation conditions, the lack of cleanliness; the insufficient leisure offer, the territory very little recreational and sports equipment for the tourists, the insufficient development of the existing tourism potential; the insufficient promotion of some tourism objectives (the absence of traffic signs and efficient signaling devices for tourism information), the reduced number of tourists information centers; the absence of promotional materials like the brochures freely offered in the accommodation establishments; the absence of cultural guide-books from which the tourist can be informed on the cultural activities and events which take place during his stay; the absence of organization regarding the events which emphasize local traditions and customs; the seeming poverty seen from the outside and the impression of neglect regarding many monuments situated even in historical areas.

The promotion program of the brand of Bucovina must take into account two main objectives: presentation in a more attractive way of the advantages of visiting the Bucovina region and the creation of a good reputation regarding the tourism services provided here.

The objectives and the strategies regarding the promotion on the market of Bucovina as a tourism brand should be implemented through a National Marketing and Promotion Program of the brand of Bucovina, which should involve actions addressed to the tourism' professionals and/or the possible tourists. The program will be revised and periodically adapted (and preferable on a yearly basis) and will enclose:

- The assessment of tourism activities;
- The assessment of the undertaken promotional activity;
- The evaluation of the tendencies of tourism demands;
- The assessment of the services and products offered;
- The identification of new products and services which can be successfully brought to the market;
- The settlement of the expenditures necessary for the program implementation;
- The establishment of the organizational frame for the realization;
- The evaluation of the impact the program application will have on the internal tourism market (the number of tourists, incomes from tourism).

The promotion program of the brand of Bucovina must consider two main objectives: the presentation in a more attractive way of the advantages the tourists will have by visiting the region and the creation of a very good reputation of the tourism services provided in this area.

An important condition for the elaboration and the implementation of the National Marketing and Promotion Program of Bucovina is represented by the creation of the adequate organizational frame – partnership type – between the public organisms of the central and local administration, economic agents, professional associations and organizations, having their own organization and operating statute.

The brand of Bucovina offers support in the fulfillment of the social, cultural and economic objectives advanced by the above-mentioned factors. The zonal branding reconciles in a mutual venture the initiatives of the local authorities, of the entrepreneurs and inhabitants of Bucovina. The creation of the trademark of Bucovina will refresh the image of the region, emphasizing the cultural and natural attractions in view of increasing the number of visitors and, namely, of the income generated from tourism.

For most of the destinations, to create a slogan represents a necessity of the destination brand strategy. Of importance, regarding the cultural potential of the region is the fact that the German press uses the slogan "Bucovina- the country of the 1000 churches," drawing the attention on the potential of developing the ecumenical and pilgrimage tourism.

The invitation forwarded by the slogan "Come as tourists, leave as friends of Bucovina!" will have a greater success if it is supported by the existence of a strong brand, a positive image and, especially, a reality which should carry the message transmitted to the possible tourists of this region.

The promotion program of the brand of Bucovina must include also:

- The increase of the quality of the services provided to tourists by the operators (the organization of training and further training courses in: marketing, gastronomy, behavior, specialized guides, legislation, the imposition of superior standards of quality of the tourism offer and services, through the assistance and stimulation of the tenders of tourism services);
- The increase in the number of tourists in Bucovina;
- The increase of the incomes obtained from tourism;
- The creation and permanent updating of a database comprising the objectives and the tourism companies in Bucovina; the identification of the main attractions (both cultural and natural) which can be arranged and promoted in order to enter the tourism circuits of the great tour-operators from Romania which provide tourism packages; the identification of the secondary attractions (farms, craft workshops, etc.) which can be arranged in order to receive tourists and thus to encourage the development of the agritourism;
- The performance of an inventory of all information centers for tourists on the county's territory;
- The establishment of tourist's information points/centers in the communes which represent the limits of the county, the border localities and in the localities having a great tourism potential;
- The elaboration and the promotion of the yearly calendar of events: festivals, fairs, annual fetes;
- The elaboration of marketing and business plans for the local entrepreneurs;
- The creation of a tourist trademark of Bucovina: the registration of the tourism trademark of Bucovina at the OSIM (logo, brand), the creation of a site for the tourism products from Bucovina; the identification of a small number of rural, original and new tourism products for the external market; the elaboration of some unitary customized offers of Bucovina, which should allow to keep tourists for 6 nights in the area; the identification/arrangement/rearrangement of some country structures for tourists; the construction of tourists structures with traditional architecture, both at the inside and at the outside, which should create a specific atmosphere; enclosing, in the tourists schedules, beside the visitation of some cultural attractions (monaster-

ies, museums, churches, fortresses), of some optional programs like: rides on the inflatable boat on Bistrita, horse-riding in Lucina and Radauti, horse carriages rides in Suceava and Vatra Dornei; conceiving and promoting a voucher which should allow to visit the monasteries or more museums, at a promotional price; the promotion of some small prices for minimum services packages offered by tourism structures in Bucovina;

- Organization of round-tables, seminars, conferences, etc.;
- Elaboration of studies and analysis on subjects of tourism interest;
- The increase in the quality and the number of web pages which should promote the area;
- The promotion of Bucovina by an activity of motivation and support brought to the tour-operator agencies in order to conceive tourism programs for this regions;
- Editing of quality promotional materials;
- The aggressive promotion of Bucovina on tourism fairies, both on national and international level;
- The promotion of the tourism projects with foreign financing (the support of the projects which make the most of the Romanian cultural, spiritual and traditional objectives and events; the accomplishment of some projects which should emphasize the cultural-historical and rural architecture elements of the national heritage; the promotion of the tourism programs in the country-side tourism – the traditional cuisine with ecological agri-food products, the local communities which are maintaining and practicing old ethno-folkloric traditions, naturist medicine, etc.);
- Sending information to the communities inhabitants regarding the local development, agritourism and eco-tourism;
- The promotion of the partnership and the voluntary programs (identification of mountain roads for cyclists, for hiking and recreation; the development of partnerships between mayoralties and transportation operators in order to ensure the necessary means of transportation for tourist routes, by establishing attractive routes and schedules; the participation of volunteers, NGO members to the preservation of the scenery quality and accuracy; the conclusion of partnerships for carrying out the project "At home at the popular craftsmen"); creation of local action groups which should contribute to the development of a business in the domain of tourism or the exploitation of the local crafts, the promotion of the cooperation with the central and local administration; the promotion of the cooperation and of the efficient communication between the Government institutions and those non-governmental and the organization of round-tables for this purpose);

- The professional promotion of the County of Suceava as tourism destination (the performance/updating of the tourist offer for the county of Suceava, the participation of the companies and the professionals and the employers' association to specialized promotional manifestations; the elaboration of complex tourism products, with the promotion of combined offers form the other areas; the organization of "hospitality trips," with the participation of the mass-media representatives from the country and abroad; the participation to international tourism exhibitions, with the organization of the Bucovina's nights, the elaboration of the advertising flyers, maps, CDs, promotional materials for Bucovina, comprising of the tourism offer of Bucovina in the catalogues of the great tour-operator companies; the promotion and the introduction in the eco-tourism circuits of the natural parks and reservations; the elaboration of a tourists information street point based on a software application for tourism promotion);
- The promotion of the cooperation with the central and local administration; for this purpose, it should be mentioned the initiative of the three mountain resorts from Suceava county (Vatra Dornei, Campulung Moldovenesc and Gura Humorului) which will not organize any tourism manifestation of importance in the same period of the year, in order to prevent overlapping events);
- The promotion of an efficient cooperation and communication between the government and non-government institutions and the organization of round-tables for this purpose;
- Drawing programs which should increase the accessibility of the tourism in Bucovina;
- ensuring the sustainable use of natural resources and the exploitation of the ethno –cultural traditions by drawing the tourism agencies in the environment preservation and maintenance, as fundamental element of the tourism offer;
- The creation of the selling exhibitions of the craftsmanship of Bucovina;
- The protection, preservation and the enrichment of the heritage;
- Establishing the extended list of tourism objectives which will receive funds for repairs, renovations, restoration, equipment, modernization, with the identification of the financing sources.

The representatives of the central and local public administration must keep in mind that they must take actions for ensuring the easy access of the tourists to the attraction points, by plane, cars, buses, or by train. It should be distributed brochures, CDs with movies to the voyage agencies and possible visitors. All the hotels and guesthouses should provide video materials for private viewing, which should help the visitors planning their itineraries, make reservations to events or visiting different tourism objectives. Transport companies from Suceava should prepare circuits both for the city and the surroundings which can last half a day or even one day which should include the main points of attraction of the city of Suceava or of the Bucovina in general.

The characteristics of the promotion of the tourism destination brand of Bucovina must be centered on the cultural and spiritual values. Of notice is the organization of the Stefan cel Mare Medieval Arts festival. According to the statements made by the local public administration representatives, the brand "Bucovina – the land of monasteries" will be maintained, but it will also include the eco-tourism and the adventure tourism.

For the mountain area of Suceava County to have manifestations during the entire year in order to attract tourists, it is indicated that the main resorts to organize festivals on each season. Thus, for the winter period, in the municipality of Vatra Dornei it will be organized "The winter feasts," manifestation which is carried out for a period of eight weeks which includes different concerts and winter sports contests.

In the municipality of Campulung Moldovenesc it will take place, each year, at the beginning of March, the Spring Festival, and at the end of the month of August the beginning of September, the Autumn festival, a farmers and berries festival, while in the month of June, the Gura Humorului resort will organize the same festival. The city festival with national and international actions like 'Humor in Gura Humorului'.

This way, all the manifestations will be able to draw tourists to the three mountain resorts of national interest from the county of Suceava during the entire year. Until now, they were involved in a false competition, each wanting to attract tourists during the season periods, but it was established that there are no extra-season in Bucovina and, under these circumstances each resort should be complementary to the other one during the entire year.

The mountain resorts of Suceava should create brands related to these festivals which, together, should constitute a part of the brand of Bucovina.

Bucovina represents not only monasteries, but also mountain tourism, recreational and wellness tourism. On a bottom-up process is also the business tourism, many large companies or professional associations organizing here meetings, conferences and congresses.

To create the tourism brand of Bucovina one should consider that it is necessary for this product to be a complete one, and should include: visiting cultural attractions (monasteries, museum, churches, fortresses, etc.), balneary treatment, sports tourism (hunting and fishing, paragliding, mountain-biking, trekking, river-rafting), leisure and recreational tourism, the rural tourism included in more optional programs. In order to keep tourists in the area more than 2 days, one must conceive supplemental attractions aside the monasteries as, for instance, creating ski runs in Gura Humorului (Arinis), Campulung, Vama, Botus; one must promote the adventure tourism (for instance inflatable boat rides on Bistrita, mountaineering, paragliding, mountain-biking), equestrian tourism (Lucina, Radauti), circuits with the trains of the age (Suceava-Vama-Moldovita), horse carriages rides in Suceava and Vatra Dornei (similar with the ones in Vienna).

Regarding the creation of accommodation structures (an activity which increased much lately), we consider that it is necessary to create a traditional architecture, both at the interior and at the exterior, which should create the proper atmosphere. It is obvious that foreign tourists are not drawn by the standard accommodation establishments which do not comply with their need to see something special, different, that should enchant and determine them to return here, to tell about their experiences they have had in Bucovina to their acquaintances. For this purpose, it is necessary to build and to rearrange some rustic establishments, which should largely use wood, as building material. Moreover, within the tourism products, one should exploit the specific and traditional cuisine and to include the cultural manifestations, the values of the popular culture (for instance, the organization of the folkloric programs on the occasion of dinners).

CONCLUSION

As in many areas of the Romanian economy, foreign investment is critical if a revival of the country's tourism is to take place. This should lead to a radical improvement in quality, as infrastructure is upgraded to Western standards, staff are trained in basic service skills and prices are set to match comparable facilities in other countries.

All types of tourism brands offered by Romania (including Bucovina brand) encounter fierce competition on Western European markets, while the competing destinations offer a wide range of facilities for all the tourists.

Bucovina area is among the most popular cultural destinations in Romania, together with Transylvania and Maramures. What Bucovina stands out for centuries is its Orthodox-Christian religion. Also, 'hosting' the UNESCO (United Nations Educational, Scientific, and Cultural Organisation) World Heritage Sites on its territory makes it a unique place in the world. Bucovina attracts wide range of tourists, from backpackers to businessmen, who come to 'gaze' upon the frescos and experience a mixture of heritage, cultural and religious tourism.

When we talk about cultural tourism in Romania, we immediately think about the medieval monasteries of Bucovina with their wonderful exterior frescoes, which are considered universal cultural heritage and are under the UNESCO protection, such as Voronet, Moldovita, Sucevița, Humor, Arbore, Dragomirna, to mention just a few.

A promotional campaign which aims the tourism brand of Bucovina must consider the following aspects:

- If the advertising which is made in favor of Bucovina isn't' appropriate, also the possible clients' feelings will be inappropriate;
- A tourist won't go thousands of kilometers in order to see something that he can also find in his country; as a consequence, the advertising should present something unique;
- The advertising should arise, in the spirit of the person who sees it or reads it, an unforgettable image of the tourism destination of Bucovina;
- The advertising messages must be expressed in a vivid, interesting language, waiving the conventional clichés.

The most efficient means of promoting tourism, in Romania in general and in Bucovina in particular, is represented by the "mouth to mouth" advertising, performed by the tourists who have visited us and who were satisfied with both the tourism objectives, and the quality of services they received. Ideally, the satisfied tourists would recommend to their acquaintances to visit the region, namely to use the same tourism agency or accommodation establishment which has risen to their expectations.

In Bucovina the tourist can discover the tradition of monastic life in historic monasteries, the beauty of the Orthodox services, cultural treasures of Romania and the peace of the countryside. A great wise man said that God has left blissful places to the humans, in order to remind them that the Heaven really exists. Come to Bucovina and you will live saying: "It really exists!"

REFERENCES

Aaker, D. (2006). *Brand portfolio strategy*. Bucharest, Romania: Brandbuiders Group.

Aaker, D. (2006). *Capital managenment brand*. Bucharest, Romania: Brandbuilders Group.

Aaker, D. A., & Joachimsthaler, E. (2000). *Brand leadership*. New York: Free Press.

Anholt, S. (2003). *Brand new justice: How branding places and products can help the developing world*. Oxford, UK: Butterworth-Heinemann.

Aronczyk, M. (2008). "Living the brand": Nationality, globality and the identity strategies of nation branding consultants. *International Journal of Communication*, *2*, 41–65.

Danta, H. (1999). Destination branding, niche marketing and national image projection in Central and Eastern Europe. *Journal of Vacation Marketing*, *3*(5).

Daye, D. (2006). History of branding. *Branding Strategy Insider*. Retrieved 18th May 2014 from http://www.brandingstrategyinsider.com/2006/08/history_of_bran. html#.URziYaWDhSQ2013-04-05

De Chernatony, L. (2001). A model for strategically building brands. *Brand Management, 1*(9), 32–44. doi:10.1057/palgrave.bm.2540050

Douglas, S. P., Craig, C. S., & Nijssen, E. J. (2001). Integrating branding strategy across markets: Building international brand architecture. *Journal of International Marketing, 2*(9), 97–114. doi:10.1509/jimk.9.2.97.19882

Duncan, T., & Moriarty, S. E. (1998). A communication-based marketing model for managing relationships. *Journal of Marketing, 2*(62), 1–13. doi:10.2307/1252157

Fan, Y. (2006). Branding the nation: What is being branded? *Journal of Vacation Marketing, 1*(12), 5–14. doi:10.1177/1356766706056633

Fetscherin, M. (2010). The determinants and measurement of a country brand: The country brand strength index. *International Marketing Review, 4*(27), 466–479.

Ghodeswar, B. M. (2008). Building brand identity in competitive markets: A conceptual model. *Journal of Product and Brand Management, 1*(17), 4–12. doi:10.1108/10610420810856468

Gilmore, F. (2002). A country – Can it be positioned? Spain – The success story of country branding. *Journal of Brand Management, 4*(9), 281–293. doi:10.1057/palgrave.bm.2540078

Hanna, S., & Rowley, J. (2010). Towards a strategic place brand management model. *Journal of Marketing Management, 27*, 5–6.

Harris, F., & de Chernatony, L. (2001). Corporate branding and corporate brand performance. *European Journal of Marketing, 35*(3/4), 441–456. doi:10.1108/03090560110382101

Hatch, M. J., & Schultz, M. (2008). *Taking brand initiative*. San Francisco: Jossey-Bass Inc.

Hoeffler, S., & Keller, K. L. (2003). The marketing advantages of strong brands. *Journal of Brand Management, 6*(10), 421–445. doi:10.1057/palgrave.bm.2540139

Kapferer, J. N. (2008). *New strategic brand management* (4th ed.). London: Les Editions d'Organisation.

Kavaratzis, M. (2005). Place branding: A review of trends and conceptual models. *The Marketing Review, 5*(4), 329–342. doi:10.1362/146934705775186854

Keller, K. L. (2001). Mastering the marketing communications mix: Micro and macro perspectives on integrated marketing communication programs. *Journal of Marketing Management*, *17*(7-8), 819–847. doi:10.1362/026725701323366836

Keller, K. L. (2009). Building strong brands in a modern marketing communications environment. *Journal of Marketing Communications*, *15*(2–3), 139–155. doi:10.1080/13527260902757530

Kotler, P., & Gertner, D. (2002). Country as brand, product, and beyond: A place marketing and brand management perspective. *Journal of Brand Management*, *9*(4/5), 249–261. doi:10.1057/palgrave.bm.2540076

Kotler, P., Haider, D. H., & Rein, I. (1993). *Marketing places*. New York: The Free Press.

Lagergren, H. (1998). *Varumärkets inre värden*. Göteborg: ICT Education.

Moilanen, T., & Rainisto, S. (2009). *How to brand nations, cities and destinations: A planning book for place branding*. New York: Palgrave Macmillan.

Nandan, S. (2004). An exploration of the brand identity-brand image linkage: Communications perspective. *Brand Management*, *12*(4), 264–278. doi:10.1057/palgrave.bm.2540222

Nedelea, A. M. (2003). *Tourism marketing policy*. Bucharest, Romania: Economica.

Nedelea, A. M. (2009). *Marketing in exercises*. Bucharest, Romania: Economica.

Papadopoulos, N., & Heslop, L. (2002). Country equity and country branding: Problems and prospects. *Brand Management*, *9*(4-5), 294–314. doi:10.1057/palgrave.bm.2540079

Pike, S. (2005). Tourism destination branding complexity. *Journal of Product and Brand Management*, *14*(4), 258–259. doi:10.1108/10610420510609267

Risitano, M. (2006). The role of destination branding in the tourism stakeholders system: *The Campi Flegrei case*. Paper presented at The XV Simposio Internacional de Turismo Y Ocio Esade – Fira, Barcelona, Spain.

Ritchie, R. J. B. (2000). The branding of tourism destinations. In *Tourism: Principles, practices and philosophies*. New York: John Wiley.

Sanchez, R. (2004). Conceptual analysis of brand architecture and relationship within product categories. *Journal of Brand Management*, *3*(11), 233–247.

Sinclair, M. T. (1998). Tourism and economic development: A survey. *The Journal of Development Studies*, 5(34), 1–51. doi:10.1080/00220389808422535

Steinecke, A. (2001). *Keynote presentation*. Paper presented at the Conference on Cultural Tourism at the ITB, Berlin, Germany.

Suceava County Council. (n.d.). *Strategy development and promotion of tourism in Suceava*. Retrieved from www.tourisminbucovina.ro

WTO. (n.d.). Retrieved from http://www.wto.org/english/tratop_e/devel_e/d1who_e.htm

WTTC. (n.d.). Retrieved from http://www.wttc.org/research/economic-impact-research

KEY TERMS AND DEFINITIONS

Brand: The essence of one's own unique story. It is a container for a customer's complete experience with the product or company, a singular idea or concept that you own inside the mind of a prospect. A brand is the meaningful perception of a product, a service or even yourself – either good, bad or indifferent – that marketers want people to believe based on what they think they hear, see, smell, taste and generally sense from others around them.

Branding: An ongoing process of looking at your company's past and present… and then creating a cohesive personality for the company and its products going forward. Branding is the sub-total of all the "experiences" your customers have with your business. Branding is the encapsulation of a company's mission statement, objectives, and corporate soul as expressed through the corporate voice and aesthetic. Branding is the art of aligning what you want people to think about your company with what people actually do think about your company.

Destination Branding: In tourism, branding is most often associated with destinations. There may be many warm weather winter destinations, but each of these destinations differentiates itself from the other via branding. Cities, states, regions and countries increasingly create specific brands for their destination to differentiate them from one another. Destination branding relies on quality, specific attributes and reputation, but it adds another important component - emotion. Marketers want consumers to "feel" the destination, and many brand their product as "experiences" through words, visuals and sounds. Destination branding is largely confined to the use of logos and slogans. It can be defined as the development and active management of destination brands.

Destination Marketing: Tourism destination marketing is now widely recognized as an essential component in the management of destinations, an integral part of developing and retaining a particular location's popularity. Destination marketing is designed to motivate particular groups of visitors and influence their behaviors including: the type of product and activities they choose, the times of the year they visit, the type of accommodation they stay in, and their expenditure patterns.

Place Branding: Believed to be a way of making places famous. The purpose is to enhance the brand image of the place. It is related with nation branding, region branding and city branding. Place branding is the process of image communication to a target market. It is invariably related to the notion that places compete with other places for people, resources, and business.

Tourism Brand: A tourism brand embodies the imagination and emotion a country inspires in visitors. It has a major influence on where people choose to travel. It therefore needs to reach out and strike an emotional chord with travelers. Tourism brands, whether related to a single business or entire destinations, communicate an important message to potential visitors. A brand enables tourism producers to charge more money for their products and services, while it also gives them the responsibility of maintaining and enhancing the brand reputation.

Tourism Marketing: The application of marketing concepts in the travel and tourism industry. Tourism marketing could be complex due to the product being an amalgam of many different industries such as accommodation and transportation. The markets also vary widely, and determining the consumers´ preferences could be difficult. Tourism marketing refers to the organized, combined efforts of the national tourist bodies and/or the businesses in the tourism sector of an international, national or local area to achieve growth in tourism by maximizing the satisfaction of tourists. In doing so, the tourist bodies and businesses expect to receive profits. Branding, positioning and knowledge of consumer psychology have become essential elements in the marketing of tourism and travel, along with the use of strategic partnerships and targeted communications.

Chapter 3
Branding and Brand Management:
Case of Amul

Anupam Sharma
Thapar University Patiala, India

ABSTRACT

In the appearance of globalization and liberalization, both brand and branding have become essential parts of every competitive business firm. To become part of the competitive and ever-changing business world and to maintain the existing business image, business organizations have been continuously focusing upon introducing innovative branding practices and strategies. This chapter focuses on brand and branding strategies of Indian brand name dairy cooperative, AMUL, in western India (Gujarat Cooperative Milk Marketing Federation [GCMMF]), which has developed a successful model for doing business in the large, emerging Indian economy. Amul has been primarily accountable, through its inventive practices, and adaptive to market changes, for India's becoming the world's largest producer of milk. This chapter draws various lessons from the experiences of AMUL that would be useful to business organizations globally.

ORGANIZATION BACKGROUND

Amul (Anand Milk-producers Union Limited), formed on December 14, 1946, is a dairy cooperative organization of India. The brand name Amul, has been originated from the Sanskrit word *Amoolya*, it means *priceless*. It is a brand name managed

DOI: 10.4018/978-1-4666-7393-9.ch003

by cooperative organisation, Gujarat Co-operative Milk Marketing Federation Ltd. (GCMMF), which today is jointly owned by some 2.41 million milk producers in Gujarat, India. It is situated in Anand town of Gujarat and has been a true example of a co-operative business organization's success. The Amul Pattern has established itself as a completely suitable model for rural expansion and growth. Amul has promoted the White Revolution of India, which has contributed in making India the largest producer of milk and milk products in the world. Gujarat Cooperative Milk Marketing Federation (GCMMF) is India's leading food goods marketing organisation. In state of Gujarat Amul is a state level head body of milk cooperatives which aim to endow with remunerative returns to the farmers and also gratify the interests of customers by continuously providing quality products according to varying needs of customers also by providing good value for money. Amul's product range consist of milk, milk powders, ghee, butter, cheese, curd, chocolate, ice cream, cream, shrikhand, paneer, gulab jamuns, basundi, Nutramul brand, and others.

The Kaira District Cooperative Milk Producers' Union Limited was established as a response to utilization of marginal milk producers in the city of Anand (in Kaira district of the western state of Gujarat in India) by traders or manager of existing dairies. Producers of milk had to travel long distances for delivery of milk to the only dairy, named as the Polson Dairy in Anand – frequently milk went sour, particularly in the summer time, as producers had to physically carry milk in containers individually. In winter, the producer was either left with excess of unsold milk or had to sell it at very low prices. Moreover, the government at that time had given particular monopoly rights to Polson Dairy (during that time Polson was the well known butter brand in the country) to collect milk from Anand and was supplied to Bombay city in turn (about 400 kilometers away). India ranked nowhere

Figure 1. Amul starting point

amongst milk producing countries in the world by the end of year 1946 (Akoorie & J.Scott (1999)).

The manufacturer of Kaira district took guidance of the nationalist leaders, Sardar Vallabhbhai Patel (first Home Minister of free India) and Morarji Desai (Prime Minister of India). They guided the farmers to form a cooperative firm and supply milk directly to the Bombay Milk Scheme instead of selling it to Polson (who did the same but offer low prices to the milk producers). As a result of this the Kaira District Cooperative was established to collect and to process the milk in the district of Kaira. The new milk plant had the potential to pasteurize 300,000 pounds of milk per day, and manufacture 10,000 pounds of butter per day, also 12,500 pounds of milk powder per day and 1,200 pounds of casein per day. With the help of R&D and technology development at the Cooperatives had led to the success of production of skimmed milk powder from buffalo milk. This gave birth to a modern dairy industry in India.

In 1946, initiative of milk production was taken by Sardar Vallabhai Patel. Patel has developed innovative ideas and thoughts adjacent to the privately owned Polson dairy and established as the first cooperative society known as Kaira District Cooperative Milk Producers' Union Limited (KDCMPUL). The motto behind establishment of cooperative society was "No Cooperation, No Progress!" spreader very fast and milk was used as a sign to object against British hegemony, throughout a 15-day farmers' strike. Amul is the leading dairy brand name in India and has seized its position against rivalry from international established brands such as Nestle.

Involvement

It was Patel's vision to organize the farmers and to make them enable to manage over procurement, processing and advertising while removing the middlemen from the existing system. Initially Amul started with 2 village societies and collected 247 liters of milk per day. The society grew and, in 1973, the Gujarat Cooperative Milk Marketing Federation (GCMMF) was established in the state of Gujarat for marketing the milk and milk products of cooperative unions. In the year 1980s the word Amul was transformed into a brand. At present, in the state of Gujarat, Amul manufactures 10.16 million liters of milk daily, that is collected from 2.7 million farmers, further processed by30 dairy plants, and circulated through 500,000 retail outlets. The annual sales return has reached USD 1,504 million (2008-2009).

The Amul replica turn out to be so successful that it was replicated in the '70s, after the government standardized the importance of milk cooperatives as a revenue of promoting socio-economic progress in rural areas while at the same time growing milk production in India.

The National Dairy Development Board (NDDB) initiated the Operation Flood programme (OF) to generate a nationwide milk grid. During the 26 year of Amul from 1970 to 1996, this established association between rural milk producers and urban consumers by organizing farmer dairy cooperative societies. Total investment of USD 439 million has engendered an incremental return of USD 8.778 billion. Amul emerged as a world's largest rural developments programme that: "supported dairy farmers in their own development growth and improvement, by placing control of the resources they generate in their own hands. A National Milk Grid links milk manufacturer throughout India with clients in over 700 towns and cities, reducing recurring and regional price disparity while ensuring that the producer gets fair bazaar prices in a transparent way. Dairy engineer Dr. Varghese Kurien, who was chairman of NDDB at that time, was the architect of the programme and is considered as the father of India's "White Revolution."

Now we move to year 2000. The image of Indian dairy industry and particularly in the State of Gujarat it's been redefined or overtaken by the brand name Amul. Mean time India has emerged as the largest milk producing country in the world (Table 1). Gujarat emerged as the most successful State in terms of milk production and milk product production with its cooperative dairy movement. The Kaira District Cooperative Milk Producers' Union Limited, Anand turn out to be the focal point of dairy growth in the entire region and AMUL emerged as a one of the most renowned brands in India, also ahead of many international brands.

Marketing

Starting with a single common plant at Anand and two village cooperative societies for milk procurement, the dairy cooperative movement of State of Gujarat had developed into a network of 2.12 million milk producers (i.e., farmers) who are organized

Table 1. International milk production

Country	Milk Production (Million Tonnes)		
	1961	**1999**	**2000**
Japan	2.10	8.46	8.50
Canada	8.32	8.20	8.10
Europe	132.40	216.30	214.3
USA	57.02	73.8	76.1
Australia	6.28	10.49	11.17
New Zealand	5.22	10.88	12.23
India	20.38	78. 90	81.8

in 10,411 milk collection cooperatives (called Village Societies). These Village Societies (VS) further supply milk to thirteen independent dairy cooperatives (called Unions). AMUL is a one such Union. Milk and other related milk products from these Unions are marketed by a general marketing organization (called Federation). Figure 3 gives the hierarchical structure of this extensive network of cooperatives.

Amul Butter: Pricing Strategy

Today GCMMF is India's largest exporter of Dairy Products. It has been known as a "Trading House" status. GCMMF has received the APEDA Award from Government of India for Excellence in Dairy Product Exports continuously for the last 9 years.

When Amul was formed, consumers were having very limited purchasing power, and reserved consumption levels of milk and other dairy products too. Thus Amul followed a low-cost price strategy to make its products affordable to the masses and attractive to consumers by assuring them value for money.

Figure 3. Dairy cooperative structure and details for state of Gujrat

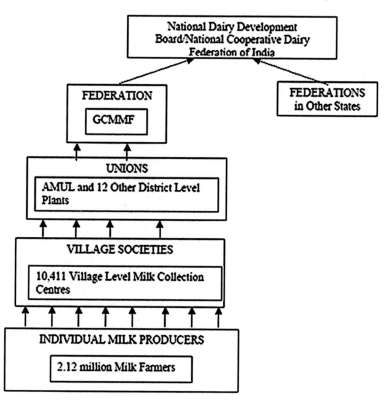

Despite of high competition in the dairy product segment from firms such as Hindustan Lever, Nestle and Britannia, GCMMF guarantees that the product mix and the series in which Amul launch its products is reliable with the core values of delivering butter at a basic, reasonable price to plea the common masses (Table 2 and Figure 2). This price strategy initially helped AMUL BUTTER to create its brand image in the domestic sector of the society.

Table 2. Product range manufactured under brand name Amul

Product Name	Tag Line	Composition	Range
Amul Butter	'UTTERLY BUTTERLY DELICIOUS'	Milk Fat 80% Moisture 16% Salt 2.5% Curd 0.8%	Amul Butter Amul Lite Low Fat Bread spread Amul Cooking Butter
Amul Cheese			Amul Pasteurized Processed Cheddar Cheese Amul Processed Cheese Spread Amul Pizza (Mozarella) Cheese Amul Shredded Pizza Cheese Amul Emmental Cheese Amul Gouda Cheese Amul Malai Paneer (cottage cheese) Utterly Delicious Pizza
Amul Ethnic Sweets			Amul Shrikhand (Mango, Saffron, Almond Pistachio, Cardamom) Amul Amrakhand Amul Mithaee Gulabjamuns Amul Mithaee Gulabjamun Mix Amul Mithaee Kulfi Mix Avsar Ladoos
Pure Ghee			Amul Pure Ghee Sagar Pure Ghee Amul Cow Ghee
Milk powder			Amul Full Cream Milk Powder Amulya Dairy Whitener Sagar Skimmed Milk Powder Sagar Tea and Coffee Whitener
Fresh Milk		3% fat 6% fat 4.5% fat 1.5% fat 0% fat	Amul Taaza Toned Milk Amul Gold Full Cream Milk Amul Shakti Standardized Milk Amul Slim & Trim Double Toned Milk Amul Saathi Skimmed Milk Amul Cow Milk
Amul Curd			Yogi Sweetened Flavored Dahi (Dessert) · Amul Masti Dahi (fresh curd) · Amul Masti Spiced Butter Milk · Amul Lassee

continued on following page

Table 2. Continued

Product Name	Tag Line	Composition	Range
Amul Ice cream			**Royal Treat Range** (Butterscotch, Rajbhog, Malai Kulfi) **Nut-o-Mania Range** (Kaju Draksh, Kesar Pista Royale, Fruit Bonanza, Roasted Almond) **Nature's Treat** (Alphanso Mango, Fresh Litchi, Shahi Anjir, Fresh Strawberry, Black Currant, Santra Mantra, Fresh Pineapple) **Sundae Range** (Mango, Black Currant, Sundae Magic, Double Sundae) **Assorted Treat** (Chocobar, Dollies, Frostik, Ice Candies, Tricone, Chococrunch, Megabite, Cassatta) **Utterly Delicious** (Vanila, Strawberry, Chocolate, Chocochips, Cake Magic)
Milk drink			Amul Kool Flavored Milk (Mango, Strawberry, Saffron, Cardamom, Rose, Chocolate) Amul Kool Cafe Amul Kool Koko Amul Kool Milk Shake (Mango, Strawberry, Badam, Banana)
chocolate		Kcal 541 Energy from Fat, Kcal 261 Total Fat, g 29 Saturated Fat, g 17 Added Sugar, g 45 Total Carbohydrates, g 62	Amul Milk Chocolate Amul Fruit & Nut Chocolate

Effective implementation of pricing strategy of Amul resulted that, at present Amul has 2.41 million milk producer members with average milk collection of 5.08 million litres/day. Moreover India, Amul has penetrated overseas markets such as Mauritius, UAE, USA, Bangladesh, China, Singapore, Australia, Hong Kong and a few South African countries. Its proposal to enter Japanese market in 1994 had not accomplished, but now again Amul is planning to enter Japanese markets. Other potential markets under consideration include Sri Lanka.

Brand Promotional Strategy of Amul

In 1966, Sylvester daCunha, joined ad agency of Amul. At that time, situation of India was like one couldn't afford to have food and food products. Sylvester daCunha decided it was time to change the image. Scott Bradbury, the marketing genius behind success of Nike and Starbucks, once said "A giant brand is a legend

Figure 2. Sardar Patel encouraging farmers

Figure 4. Range of products offered by brand Amul

that is never completely told. A brand is a symbolic story that's developing all the time. Stories create the exciting context that people need to locate themselves in the larger practices."

Since the Sixties to the Nineties, the Amul ads have come a long way. whereas most citizens agree that the Amul ads were at their peak in the Eighties they still continue that the Amul ads continue to rag a laughter out of them The Amul ads are one of the greatest running ads based on a theme, now vying for the Guinness proceedings for being the fastest running ad movement ever. While most of the public agreed that the Amul ads were at their highest point in the Eighties they still maintain that the Amul ads continue to tease a laughter out of them The Amul ads are one of the longest running ads based on a theme, now vying for the Guinness records for being the longest running ad campaign ever.

Many researchers believe that the charm of Amul publicity and popularity lies in the catchy lines followed by them in the advertisements (Figure 3). Because the humor created by adds was enjoyed by all. They don't mention on anyone's nationality or hurt people's sentiments. These ads are pure and simple, everyday fun.

Figure 5. Promotional strategy of Amul

Introducing Higher Value Products

Starting with liquid milk offered by Amul, GCMMF enhanced the product mix through the progressive addition of superior value foodstuffs while maintaining the preferred growth in existing products.Brand extension is an extensively established brand strategy to attach an existing renowned brand name for a new product introduction in a different product category (Swaminathan & Reddy, 2001). And these strategies were generally used because of the thought that built influential brand positioning, to boost awareness among customer and quality alliance and reduces the new product risk for consumers (Taylor & Bearden, 2002).

Despite of high competition in the high value dairy product segment from established firms such as Hindustan Lever, Nestle and Britannia, GCMMF guarantees that the product mix and the range in which Amul introduces its products is steady with the core philosophy of providing milk at a basic, and affordable price. In early 1950's studies have shown that usage of mobile veterinary dispensaries, wireless sets to connect mobile units to service centers, developing a programme of cross breeding of cows in early 1970s etc. that have led to a exceptional rise in efficiency of milk (Patel, 1988). With the changing customer demands Amul is launching new products and introducing innovation in existing range of products. Customers are also enjoying the changing new added flavors and taste. For any competitive firm's growth understanding customer needs by taking care of special reference to product need, product flavor, product availability, and product pricing is very important. We are in the era where only those firms can have survival who understands customer's latent requirements (refer Figure 6). We are in the economic age where there is no room for errors, defects and delayed deliveries and this is created in Japan. Amul is among one of the India's leading firms who are not only understanding customers present needs but also taking care about future emerging needs of the customer by investing on research and development. As Amul has opened Amul Scooping Parlors/Cafes/GRD Parlors Consumer offers from 20th Jan to 31st March, 2014 across India:

- **Delhi Zone:** Includes Punjab, Haryana, J&K, UP, Uttarakhand, and Himachal Pradesh markets.
- **Chennai Zone:** Includes Kerala, Tamilnadu, Karnataka, Andhra Pradesh, and Calicut markets.
- **Kolkata Zone:** Includes West Bengal, Orissa, Jharkhand, and Bihar markets.
- **Guwahati Zone:** Includes Assam, Meghalaya, Nagalend, Arunachal Pradesh, Mizoram, Tripura, and Manipur; "http://www.amul.com/m/amul-parlour-consumer-zone."
- **Mumbai Zone:** Includes Maharashtra and Goa markets.

Figure 6. New range of Amul products

- **Ahmedabad Zone:** Includes Gujarat, Rajasthan, Madhya Pradesh, and Chhattisgarh markets; "http://www.amul.com/m/ amul-parlour-consumer-zone."

With increasing income and with the changing lifestyles people of India also love to spend quality time with the family members outside the home where they can have variety of choices and options for themselves and children too. By keeping this idea in mind across the country Amul has started Ice Cream Scooping Parlors. Here one can have options to choose from world class ice creams, Sundaes, variety of shakes and other ice cream concoctions in a warm and pleasant ambience of these parlors. It's like a more of fun time for the whole family.

At present Amul has opened Scooping Parlors across the country including cities like Mumbai, Chennai, Delhi, Bangaluru, Thane, Pune, Kolkata, Nagpur, Ahmedabad and Coimbatore. Apart from these cities, Amul is planning to open up Amul Scooping Parlors in different parts of the country too.

These Parlors have been well welcomed by customers and are doing cheerful business. Some of the recipes offered at these Parlors include:

- Simply Delicious Ice Cream Scoops,
- Double and Triple Sundaes,

Table 3. List of Amul Parlor in India

Delhi Zone		
Product	**Pack**	**Scheme**
Ice-cream	1 Ltr Tub	Rs.10 off
Kool Range (till 28.02.14 only)	Kool Cans	Rs.2 off
Kool Range (till 28.02.14 only)	1 Ltr Tetra	Rs.10 off
Mitahi mate	400g Tin	Rs.5 off
Amul Lite	100/200/500g	Rs.3/5/15 off
Gulabjamun	500g/1kg	Rs.5/10
Chennai Zone		
Product	**Pack**	**Scheme**
Ice-cream	1 Ltr Tub	Rs.10 off
Kool Range (till 28.02.14 only)	Kool Cans	Rs.2 off
Kool Range (till 28.02.14 only)	1 Ltr Tetra	Rs.10 off
Mitahi mate	400g Tin	Rs.5 off
Amul Lite	100/200/500g	Rs.3/5/15 off
Gulabjamun	500g/1kg	Rs.5/10
Kolkata Zone		
Product	**Pack**	**Scheme**
Ice-cream	1 Ltr Tub	Rs.10 off
Kool Range (till 28.02.14 only)	Kool Cans	Rs.2 off
Kool Range (till 28.02.14 only)	1 Ltr Tetra	Rs.10 off
Mitahi mate	400g Tin	Rs.5 off
Amul Lite	100/200/500g	Rs.3/5/15 off
Gulabjamun	500g/1kg	Rs.5/10
Guwahati Zone		
Product	**Pack**	**Scheme**
Ice-cream	1 Ltr Tub	Rs.10 off
Kool Range (till 28.02.14 only)	Kool Cans	Rs.2 off
Kool Range (till 28.02.14 only)	1 Ltr Tetra	Rs.10 off
Mitahi mate	400g Tin	Rs.5 off
Amul Lite	100/200/500g	Rs.3/5/15 off
Gulabjamun	500g/1kg	Rs.5/10
Mumbai Zone		
Product	**Pack**	**Scheme**
Ice-cream	1 Ltr Tub	Rs.10 off
Kool Range (till 28.02.14 only)	Kool Cans	Rs.2 off

continued on following page

Table 3. Continued

Kool Range (till 28.02.14 only)	1 Ltr Tetra	Rs.10 off
Mitahi mate	400g Tin	Rs.5 off
Amul Lite	100/200/500g	Rs.3/5/15 off
Gulabjamun	500g/1kg	Rs.5/10
Ahmadabad Zone		
Product	**Pack**	**Scheme**
Ice-cream	1 Ltr Tub	Rs.10 off
Kool Range (till 28.02.14 only)	Kool Cans	Rs.2 off
Kool Range (till 28.02.14 only)	1 Ltr Tetra	Rs.10 off
Mitahi mate	400g Tin	Rs.5 off
Amul Lite	100/200/500g	Rs.3/5/15 off
Gulabjamun	500g/1kg	Rs.5/10
Shrikhand (from 1st Feb to 31stMarch 2014) only for Gujarat	1 Kg	Rs.10 off

- Double Swirl/Magic Swirl,
- Thick Shakes, and
- Amul Kool Drinks.

Amul also offers a brilliant business prospect to entrepreneurs who want to open up franchisees of the Amul Scooping Parlors and can become part of the rising ice cream industry with India's most admired brand.

Amul Café

Amul has launched "The CDR (Casual Dining Restaurant)" a brand from Amul. The idea behind launch of Amul Cafe is a Casual Dining Restaurant with a pleasant ambience that offers customers scrumptious delicacies options of

- Pizzas,
- Amul Butter Pavbhaji,
- Amul Cheese Sandwiches,
- Butter, Cheese, and Panner Dosa,
- Chhola Bhatura,
- Amul Cheese Burgers,
- Ice-creams and Sundaes,
- Milk Shakes and Much More.

Figure 7. Amul café outlook

Fundamentals for Cafe Amul

GCMMF today reaches customers in all parts of the India, with a singular main center on marketing and distribution of right products to the right customer.

A state level governing body of milk co-operatives started from Gujarat has been a venture of GCMMF that provides remunerative profits to the farmers by serving the interest of different consumers by providing different range of quality products by taking care for good value for money.

Amul Made India a Flourishing Ice Cream Market

Today ice creams are not only popular among youth but equally trendy among children and grown-ups. Consumption of ice creams has turn out to be an occasion for celebration. In India alone, the structured ice cream manufacturing has a total turnover of around Rs. 1000 Cr. and the market is spectatoring a blooming growth rate of from 12-15% per annual.

In India per capita consumption of ice creams is around 250 ml in comparison to 23 liters in the US, 18 liters in Australia, 14 liters in Sweden and only 800 ml in neighboring country Pakistan. This data figures show that, a huge opportunity is there for investment in the organized players in the ice cream industry.

For opening up Amul café in any state basic requirements are given as follows also refer Table 4 for the same.

- 1000 to 1500 sq.ft space.
- Brand Deposit: Rs.3 lacs.
- Equipment required:
  - Middleby Marshall Pizza Oven,
  - Dosa Maker,
  - Hot & Cold Bain Maries,
  - Sandwich Grillers,
  - Visicooler,
  - Scooping Cabinet,
  - Deep Freezers,
  - Chest Coolers, etc.

Table 4. Total investment required for opening up Amul Café

Particulars	Investment in Rs.
Interiors & Renovation (1000 sq.ft)@ Rs.1600 per sq.ft	16 lakhs
Brand Deposit	3 lakhs
Equipment (Kitchen, Parlour & storage)	11 lakhs
Total	30 lakhs
Note: *Actual investment may vary with time*	

Table 5. Revenue generated by Amul

Indicative ROI (Return on Investment)		
Particulars	Amount Per Month in Rs.	
Total Sales per Month	900,000	-
Gross monthly margins @25%Approx.	225,000	-
Monthly Operating Expenses	152,000	-
Shop Rental @50 per sq ft per month	-	60,000
Manpower(10 persons @ Rs.6000)	-	60,000
Electricity Charges	-	25,000
Consumables/Disposables/Carrybags	-	5,000
Misc (incl. Telephone etc)	-	2,000
Net Contribution per month	73,000	-
Note: *ROI Statement is indicative only*		

MEDIA STRATEGY

Advertising is any paid form of non-personal communication to create awareness, develop perceptions and persuade the audiences to make a specific purchase. Media strategy means the organized selection of the medium of media to be used so that the preferred message must reach the target audiences. Thus, depending upon the product or service and also depending upon target customer's need media of advertisement and the target market, a promoter makes choices among the types of media that will provide maximum efficiency and benefit the product and service too. Brand reputation has been stated in term of consumers perception about quality associated with a brand Aaker & Keller (1990); Barone & Romeo (2000). Amul butter is mostly advertised using inventive and innovative hoardings, slogans, usually mocking or depicting the recent issues. Media strategies helped Amul a lot to build its strong brand reputation over the customers. As a brand Amul is very well advertised by using intermediates like TV commercials, print advertisements, and by outdoor advertising. But the company has not paid a lot of attention for the advertisement of Amul Chocolates which is apparent from the lack of awareness and disinterest from the public.

Types of Media Used

Print Medium

Amul Chocolates started publicity with print advertisement in the 1970s.

But the occurrence and reach of these advertisements was restricted and unsuccessful to create the desirable buzz in the market.

Amul Chocolates also advertised in Indrajal Comics, a series of comics launched by The Times of India, in 1964 which was relatively popular in 1970s and 1980s.

TV Commercials

Series of these advertisements were launched on TV with filling the blanks by the right words of this punchline. In one of the adds, a young teenage girl sings 'I am 2 old for dolls, 2 young for the disco', her elder sister (I think!!), sings back, "But I think you are just right for Amul chocolates" in the year 2000, There were two famous TV advertisements that were aired in year 2005.

Figure 8. Media strategies followed By Amul

Father/Son Advertisement

Father role played by actor Ram kapoor is flying back home from trip and has bought Amul chocolates for his kid. He habitually keeps the chocolate in the right side of his coat but this time to puzzle his kid he keeps the chocolate on left side. On coming home the kid checks the left side only and is very happy to find the chocolates. And in the background of add the wife is shown smiling. The ad focuses on strength of a father son relation is, similarly a consumer will have an enduring connection with Amul Chocolates.

Rose Day

This advertisement have the tagline that for somebody you love, is acceptable by showing a boyfriend gifting his girlfriend Amul chocolate which give to happiness the girl.

Inspite of these advertisements being aired for six years old; they were also aired during the cooking reality show, Master Chef India (Amul sponsors) in 2011. This evidently shows that the advertisement was not altered with the new changing times.

Distribution Network

In over 500,000 retail outlets Amul products are available across India throughout and network of over 3,500 distributors. There are 47 warehouses with dry and cold storehouse to buffer stock of the complete range of products.

GCMMF manage on a progress demand draft center from its wholesale seller instead of the cheque method implemented by other major FMCG corporations. This practice is reliable with GCMMF's attitude of upholding cash dealings during the supply chain and it also diminishes dumping.

Wholesale dealers carry record that is just sufficient to take care of the transfer time from the branch storehouse to their building. This is just-in-time (JIT) inventory strategy that improves wholesalers return on investment (ROI). All GCMMF branches employ in route setting up and have devoted vehicle operations.

Umbrella Brand

The network of Amul Company follows an umbrella branding strategy. Amul is the general brand having majority of product categories produced by different unions: liquid milk, milk powders, butter, ghee, cheese, cocoa products, sweets, ice-cream and condensed milk.

Amul's sub-brands consist of variants such as Amulspray, Amulspree, Amulya and Nutramul. The edible oil goods are grouped around Dhara and Lokdhara, mineral water is sold under the Jal Dhara brand while fruit drinks bear the Safal name.

By maintaining on an umbrella brand, GCMMF not only competently avoided inter-union disagreement but also shaped an opportunity for the union members to collaborate in developing products.

Managing the Supply Chain

However the cooperative system was created to carry together farmers, it was recognized that professional managers and technocrats would be requisite to administer the network successfully and make it commercially feasible.

Coordination

From the large number of associations and entities in the supply chain and having decentralized responsibility for various actions, effective coordination is critical factor to be controlled for efficiency and cost control. GCMMF and the unions played a major role in this progression and helped in jointly achieving the preferred degree of control within the organization.

Buy-in from the unions is assured as the plans are approved by GCMMF's board. The board is drawn from the heads of all the unions, and the boards of the unions comprise of farmers elected through village societies, thereby creating a situation of interlocking control.

The federation handles the distribution of end products and coordination with retailers and the dealers. The unions coordinate the supply side activities.

This include monitoring milk collection supplier, the supply of animal feed and other supplies, provision of veterinary services, and educational activities.

Organization of Third Party Service Providers

From the establishment of business organizations, it was recognized that the unions' core activity set in milk processing and the manufacturing of dairy products. Accordingly, marketing efforts (i.e., brand development) were implicit by GCMMF. All supplementary actions were entrusted to third parties. These include logistics of milk gathering, delivery of dairy products, sale of products through dealers and retail stores, prerequisite of animal feed, and veterinary services.

It is significantly noting that a number of these third parties are not in the structured sector, and many are not efficiently managed with slight regard for quality and product service.

This is a mostly significant issue in the logistics and transport of a consumable commodity where there are already weaknesses in the essential infrastructure.

Introducing Best Practices

A key foundation of competitive advantage has been the project ability to constantly implement best practices across all elements of the system: the federation, the unions, the village societies and the supply channel.

In developing these practices, the organization and the unions have adopted successful models from around the world. Implementation of various TQM practices and strategies like quality circles, housekeeping, kaizen and good accounting practices at the village society level contributed in success of Amul. Major focus of TQM strategies has been on regular continuous improvement for accomplishing long term targets rather than just achieving short term profits.

This improvement program across the Amul involved large number of members and employees for the implementation of various strategies and this made success rate consistently high.

For example, every Friday, without stopping, from 10.00 a.m. and 11.00 a.m., all employees of GCMMF gather at the closest office, it can be a department or a branch or a depot for the discussion of their various quality issues/problems.

In advance each meeting has its pre-set plan in terms of Purpose, Agenda and Limit (PAL) with a process check at the closing stages to record how that meeting was carried out. Similar methods are been implemented in village societies, at the unions and even at the wholesaler as well.

Benefits accomplished by implementing TQM strategies consist of reduction in transportation time from the depots to the wholesale trader, improvement in ROI (rate on investment) of wholesale dealers, achievement of Zero Stock Out through enhanced accessibility of products at depots and also the implementation of JIT (Just-in-Time) in finance to reduce the float.

Kaizen (gradual improvement) at the unions have facilitated to improve the quality of milk in terms of acidity and sour milk. (Kaizen is another TQM strategy to improve the quality; this is extremely focused on projects to increase the quality) For example, Sabar Union's records show a decline from 2.0% to 0.5% in the quantity of sour milk/curd received at the union.

The most inspiring feature of this large-scale roll out is that development processes are spinning the village societies into individual improvement centers.

Technology and E-Initiatives

In the ever changing globalized world modern technology and various e-initiatives taken up by Amul also contributed in the success of the brand. GCMMF's technology strategy is composed of four distinctive components i.e., new products, process technology, and complementary assets to enhance milk production and e-commerce.

Few dairies of the world have the extensive assortment of foodstuffs as produced by the GCMMF network. Village societies are expectant during subsidies to establish alarming units. Automation in processing and packaging areas is regular, as is

Figure 9. Brand promotional strategy of Amul

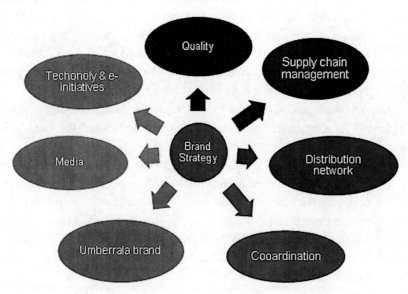

HACCP certification. Amul aggressively follow progress in embryo transfer and cattle breeding to regulate and to improve cattle quality and to increases in milk yields.

GCMMF was among one of the first FMCG (fast-moving consumer goods) firm in India to utilize Internet expertise to execute B2C commerce.

Today customers can select a diversity of products through the Internet and be secure of timely delivery with cash on payment option.

Another e-initiative undertaken by the Amul is to provide farmers access to information relating to markets, technology and best practices in the dairy industry during net enabled kiosks in the villages.

GCMMF has also implemented a Geographical Information System (GIS) at both ends of the supply chain, i.e. milk gathering as well as the promotion process.

Farmers now have improved access to information on the output as well as sustained services while providing a superior planning tool to marketing personnel.

Corporate Social Responsibility (CSR)

Emergence of globalization and liberalization has given confinement to numerous key proposals into Indian economy. Forces and factors enforced by globalization into Indian economy are quality conscious movement, conscious consumer and corporate social responsibility.

Corporate social responsibility (CSR) has been defined as a "assurance of business and firms to contribute for sustainable economic growth by working with employees, workers their families, serving the local community, and society at large to improve the quality of life, in a way that both society and business get the development."

To convene the CSR practices it is anticipated that a business in its whole procurement-production-processing-marketing chain should center on human development by connecting the supplier, the manufacturer, the worker, the consumer, the civil society, and the environment too.

Most businesses would certainly struggle in not being capable to accomplish at least one or many of those expectations of society. But AMUL has revealed the way of success is possible by following win-win strategy. That is to improve the work culture Amul is providing various facilities to the families of workers, So that they can associate with the firm as a family.

CSR-Sensitive Organizational Structure

AMUL is a three tier co-operative organisation. The first tier of the co-operative society is the village, whose milk producers are voluntary members, administrating the co-operative throughout by democratically electing 9-member for managing committee, and doing business by procuring milk from members and selling it to the district level co-operative. In the village more than 11,000 co-operatives of Gujarat are working for this.

The second tier of the state level co-operative is that processes milk into various milk products, markets locally and sells excess to the state co-operative for national and international selling. There are 12 regional co-operatives each being directed by a 15-member board selected by the college comprise the nominated legislature or chairmen of the village co-operatives.

Third tier of the district co-operative of the Gujarat Co-operative Milk Marketing Federation (GCMMF) accountable for national and international marketing of milk and milk products produced and sold to it. The GCMMF is managed by the board democratically elected by and from amongst the chairmen of the district co-operatives.

The entire three-tier structure with the GCMMF at its peak is a unique foundation because it encompasses the complete chain from manufacturing of raw material to delivering the consumer with the end good quality product. Every function engages human intrusion: 23.60 lakh primary milk manufacturer; 35,000 rural workmen from more than 11,400 village societies; 12,000 workers in 15 dairy plants; 750 promotional professionals; 10,500 salesmen in distribution network and 600,000 salesmen in trade network. The GCMMF is quite perceptive towards CSR initiatives. It trusts that technology, infrastructure and capital are replicable inputs but not the human capital/workforce. Since humans are the basis for accomplishing the CSR, the GCMMF puts prominence on their expansion into proficient, chivalrous, credible, reliable, communicators and performers.

CSR Practices for Staff

The GCMMF appoint and educate employees so that they can have advantage over its competitors. Amul has established its in-house modules for training and capability building to develop and promote their information system, knowledge base; communication skills to understand the customer behavior, to be reactive to customer necessities, future demands and needs of customers. To improve the trustworthiness and constancy of the customers it is very important that firstly managers and employees have to be happy and satisfied with the working culture so that they will be able to perform consistently and correctly every time and at all times. The primary and foremost the staff must get contentment from the job they are doing. Amul recognize individual employee's efforts and awards them for their contributions.

Figure 10. Emergence of corporate social responsibility

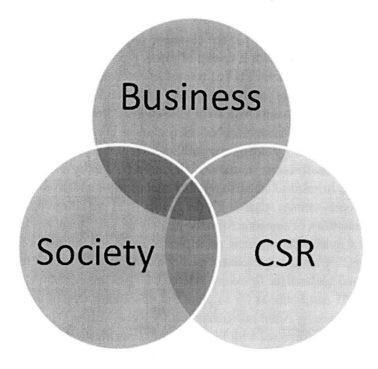

Figure 11. Impact of CSR

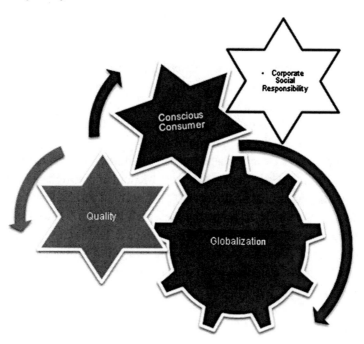

Quality

Quality definition changes as per the customer requirements but one thing that has been always attached with it inspite of place, product, price is satisfaction of customer needs and requirements i.e., termed as conformance to customer needs. For more than twenty long years India enjoyed a free market because of monopoly, no competition and customers with no or little choices. But with the opening up of markets after 1991, now customers had many choices in context to product, price, popularity of brand etc. By having competition from global players Indian markets, producers and manufacturers started realizing need for quality and quality product manufacturing. Amul absolute all the quality management initiatives to its business and production associates whether it's the farmer from the village or a distributor form the metro town or someone from the production unit. Amul has learned a lot form the total quality management principles of Japan and inspired a lot from the concept of quality hence implemented quality management system of international standard. Amul has been the first dairy in India who gets accredited with ISO 90001 and 2200: 2005 certifications for its plant and operations. One of the remarkable achievements made by Amul into Indian history is that village Dairy Co-operative Societies of Amul accredited with ISO 9001:2000 certification.

For export of dairy products to international markets Amul plants and production houses are certified by Agricultural and Processed Food Exports Development Authority (APEDA). Gujarat co-operative milk marketing federation (GCMMF) which markets and exports dairy products of Amul brand won excellent performance award from APEDA for 13th time, IMC Ramkrishna Bajaj National Quality Award – 2003, "Best Best of All" Rajiv Gandhi National Quality Award - 1999, The International Dairy Federation Marketing Award (2007) for Amul pro-biotic ice-cream launch. For the continuous maintenance of quality management systems and hygiene factors are sporadically audited by agencies like Export Inspection Agency (EIA), Armed Forces, by various Indian Statutory Bodies, International statutory Bodies and Quality Management Agencies.

Amul Research and Development centre is working very effectively and have been associated with a centre of excellence in the field of research and development of cattle breeding and animal health care. This Centre of research and development is renowned as a Scientific & Industrial Research institute by the Department of Scientific & Industrial Research, Ministry of Science & Technology, and Government of India. This centre provides knowledge and education to workers about quality semen for artificial insemination plan; impart training to inseminators, prevention and control of diseases.

Amul has not only focused upon improvement and maintenance of quality of milk and dairy products alone but also improved quality of life of farmers associated with Amul. Farmers were continually working with Amul for providing milk for the production of dairy products on daily basis. In a way it helped and brought better social infrastructure of the village by making improvements in roads, communication system, health care centers for man and animal, and opening up of schools, providing water facilities and opening up new banks etc.

Conscious Consumer

Globalization and changing market structures have given birth to new term that is consumer consciousness. Now consumers have too many options to choose from and availability of too many options made the customer conscious for their every purchase decision. Amul is always aware about customer needs and promise to give superior quality products on reasonable price.

CSR Program

The GCMMF has recognized the distributors and retailers as its significant relation with its dealer and supply chain. During analysis the GCMMF found that 90% of the distributors do not have any chance to experience the modern management practices. The GCMMF realized that corporate social responsibility initiatives are very important to support the core business process starting from collection of raw material from vendor to its distributors so as to keep them in mainstream business. The GCMMF has developed and educated all its distributors about Value-Mission-Strategy through Workshops, Amul Quality Circle summit, computerization, and electronic commerce activities.

Relief Trust of Amul

A shocking earthquake (7.9-Richter scale 9) strike Gujarat on 26th January 2001. The epicenter of the shake was positioned in Kutch district. It caused death of thousands of citizens, tens of thousands were offended, hundreds of thousands were turn into homeless and harm of billions of Rupees was made.

Amul put step forward to help the needy ones and in 2001 GCMMF created a particular association named "Amul Relief Trust" (ART) under the supervision of Dr. V. Kurien. Association made a donation of Rs. 50 Millions for reconstruction of the school buildings damaged by the earthquake in year 2001 in the Kutch area. The Trust restructured 6 schools broken by the earthquake with a total cost of Rs. 41.1 millions in Kutch district of Gujrat.

Figure 12. A school reconstructed by Amul Relief Trust

Gujarat Green Tree Plantation Movement by Milk Manufacturers of Dairy Cooperatives: Amul Workers Planted More than 311.98 Lakh Trees

Gujarat Dairy Cooperatives- also known as AMUL celebrated the nation's Independence Day by involving all milk producing members for the novel cause by planting lakhs of saplings across the Gujarat and have taken up an determined plan to save the natural environment by planting more and more trees, and taken a pledge to make India green and hence by minimizing the effects of global warming. There onwards the milk producers of Gujarat Dairy Cooperatives society are carrying out mass tree plantation campaign every year on Independence Day. In the years from 2007 to 2011 the milk producers of Gujarat have planted around 311.98 lakhs trees. The most remarkable attribute of these complete programmes was that it has been commenced by milk manufacturer members of the dairy cooperatives society. The distinctive fact about this initiative was that the milk manufacturer members have taken up the oath to protect tree saplings till it endure and grows into big trees.

As fact natural resources are depicting at a faster pace, and Gujarat is not an exception, over the time, demanding agriculture and dairying a variety of natural resources are getting consumed on daily basis at a faster pace in Gujarat state of

India too. On this serious note the state level apex body of dairy farmers of Gujarat has taken a serious consideration in this direction and discovered a novel scheme of giving back to the nature, so that momentum should be maintained. The idea was formulated in such a way that "one member one tree" plantation idea was introduced on our 60th Independence day on 15th August 2007.To set this idea as a regular practice a management proposed a team constituting of legislative body of member unions were created these teams will look after for regular execution of the idea. The team accepted the idea open heartily and right away decided to extend it along with farmer members of village Gujarat dairy cooperative societies. Then the details of the scheme were communicated to the farmer members and they all also welcomed it and excitedly agreed to put into operation the idea.

The complete plantation movement was synchronized with all the three tiers of Anand pattern system at village, district and state level dairy cooperative societies. This was just the foundation of social responsibility initiative at Amul. From now onwards, the Gujarat Village Dairy Cooperative Societies institutionalized tree plantation program as a mark of respect for our nation determined to carry out such event on regular basis on every Independence Day and acknowledged 15th

Figure 13. Green Revolution Day by a forestation to protect mother Earth from pollution, depletion of natural resources, climate change and global warming

Table 6. Total no. of trees planted

Sr. No.	Year of Tree Plantation	No. of Trees Planted (In Lakhs)	No. of Trees Survived (In Lakhs)	Survival Percentage
1	2007	18.90	11	58
2	2008	52.74	26	49
3	2009	84.24	38	45
4	2010	83.5	39	47
5	2011*	72.6	34	47
Total		311.98	148.122	47

*Estimated (as survey for survival percentage of the saplings planted in year 2010 is ongoing).

August (Independence Day) as a "Green Revolution Day by A forestation to Protect Mother Earth from Pollution, depletion of natural resources, Climate change and Global Warming."

Hence by following their promise Gujarat Dairy Cooperative Societies, milk producers of GCMME planted around 311.98 lakhs of tree saplings in approximately twenty one districts of Gujarat. This has shown that the farmers/milk producers have strong determination, commitment, concern and awareness for the betterment of the society, mankind. And their persistent effort made the idea of 'green revolution day' a successful idea.

AMUL ACHIEVEMENTS

The determined effort of Amul, Gujarat milk production cooperative society provided green wrap to the earth was also recognized and brought fruitful results when the state level apex body of Gujarat Dairy Cooperatives GCMMF received prestigious award "SRISHTI's G-Cube Award" for four successive years i.e., from year 2007, 2008, 2009 to year 2010 for having Good Green Governance in "Service Category."

In addition to this "Amul Green" movement has also been awarded during the 4th Global Dairy Conference held at Salzburg Congress Center, Austria on 28th April, 2010 by International Dairy Federation for best initiatives for environment persurvance in the "sustainability category."

It has been anticipated that when one tree is sliced, in monetary terms there is total loss of Rs. 33 lakhs (Oxygen value of Rs. 5.3 lakhs, Land Fertility of Rs. 6.4 lakhs, Rs. 10.5 lakh for decline of pollution of atmosphere and Rs. 5.3 lakh decline in Flowers/Fruits and habitation to birds and animals). As nature is priceless so benefits accrued by mankind when a tree is planted cannot be measured in monetary terms

Figure 14. Amul achievements

The members of GCMMF have actually put an example for all the other coopera-tive societies and other institutions to turn India green in the age of Global warming and environmental crisis.

In a period of global warming when world is is suffering from the serious problem of environment pollution, Amul has contributed a lot of its share in making Gujarat flourishing green state. In this way, the milk manufacturers of Gujarat are escorting in a silent revolution of greening Gujarat.

CONCLUSION

Business organizations that are intelligent enough to extend control processes throughout with better usage of equipped to perform and supply chain synchroniza-tion are the ones that are capable to provide large volumes and take pleasure in top line growth in revenues.

Growth of dealer necessitates promotion with a long-term perspective. It is exciting to note that this success was attained by AMUL through a procedure of education and social progress activities - activities that are not generally measured to be standard business practices. This type of 'out of the box' visualization is necessary for emerging innovative mechanism in new, different atmosphere where construction of relationship with consumers goes much ahead of advertising and marketing messages and useful product offerings.

Environments with immature or underdeveloped markets and suppliers (as in the case of AMUL) add one more aspect of difficulty concerning to the relative speed of growth of these two areas. Through its pricing approach, AMUL has been able to make proficient balance in the growth of markets and suppliers and has attained some degree of synchronization. Brand management and brand value should be the top precedence of the company Amul is among those companies who have realized the need for the same. And have measured it as a strategic matter that should be dealt on regular basis, because in the past companies were differentiating on the basis of products they manufacture. But now companies who are able to meet and discover customer's latent requirements for the long run only these types of brands stay in business. Need of the hour is to discover next generation needs before they demand for it and making the customer aware about extended brand products availability udder same brand name.

REFERENCES

Aaker, D. A., & Keller, K. L. (1990). Consumer evaluation of brand extensions. *Journal of Marketing, 54*(1), 27–41. doi:10.2307/1252171

Akoorie, M., & Scott-Kennel, J. (1999). The new zeal and dairy board: A case of group-internalization or a monopolistic anomaly in a deregulated free market economy? *Asia Pacific Journal of Management, 16*(1), 127–156. doi:10.1023/A:1015466304266

Amul. (n. d.). *Cafe Amul: The CDR (casual dining restaurant) brand from Amul.* Retrieved from http://www.amul.com/m/cafe-amul

Amul. (n. d.). *Website.* Retrieved from http://www.amul.com/chairmanspeech_annual07.html

Barone, M., & Romeo, J. B. (2000). The influence of positive mood on brand extension evaluations. *The Journal of Consumer Research, 26*(4), 386–400. doi:10.1086/209570

Heredia, R. (1997). *The Amul India Story.* New Delhi, India: Tata McGraw Hill.

Patel, A. S. (1988). Co-operative dairying and rural development: A case study of AMUL. In *Who shares? Cooperatives and rural development* (pp. 362–377). Oxford University Press.

Sexana, R. (2010). *Marketing management.* McGraw-Hill.

Swaminathan, F., Fox, R. J., & Reddy, S. K. (2001). The impact of brand extension introduction on choice. *Journal of Marketing, 65*(4), 1–15. doi:10.1509/jmkg.65.4.1.18388

Taylor, V. A., & Bearden, W. O. (2002). The effect of price on brand extension evaluations: The moderating role of extension similarity. *Journal of the Academy of Marketing Science, 30*(2), 131–140. doi:10.1177/03079459994380

KEY TERMS AND DEFINITIONS

Advertising: Advertising is any paid form of non-personal communication to create awareness, develop perceptions and persuade the audiences to make a specific purchase. Media strategy means the organized selection of the medium of media to be used so that the preferred message must reach the target audiences. Thus, depending upon the product or service and also depending upon target customer's need media of advertisement and the target market, a promoter makes choices among the types of media that will provide maximum efficiency and benefit the product and service too.

Brand: Mark, name or symbol that is been used for the trading purpose by the business firms so that customers and marketers can distinguish between their companies product from competitors product. Brand act as a mark that gives representation to the company's products. By using brand name (related to business or products or commodities produced/manufactured by the firm) business firms launch the product in the market. Brand or brand name also helps the customers in making the purchase decision.

Branding: Branding is done by the business firm's for promotion of products manufactured and launched by the firm under some brand name. It covers advertisement or use of banners, posters, slogans used by companies to make people aware about their company's range of products and services. Now a day's branding is done by endorsing a popular celebrity in the advertisement of the brand, so that customers can relate themselves with their favorite celebrity and can be attracted towards buying companies product. Aim of branding is to increase sales of the product hence increased sales will result into high profits and more popularity of the brand.

Conscious Consumer: Globalization and changing market structures have given birth to new term that is consumer consciousness. Nowadays, customer is treated as a king and focus of the firms is on customer's latent requirements. Now consumers have too many options to choose from and availability of too many options made the customer conscious for their every purchase decision. Amul is always aware about customer needs and promise to give superior quality products on reasonable price. With the awareness among the consumers about the product, brand, branding, pricing, motivated the firms to produce quality products only and business firms are focusing upon delivering quality services to the customers.

CSR (Corporate Social Responsibility): The term CSR is defined as a responsibility of corporate house or business firm towards society. Or it is a payback method so that momentum or balance can be maintained between inputs taken from the society; this will help in perseverance of natural resources too. Emergence of globalization and liberalization has given confinement to numerous key proposals into Indian economy. Forces and factors enforced by globalization into Indian economy are quality conscious movement, conscious consumer and corporate social responsibility. Corporate social responsibility (CSR) has been defined as an "assurance of business and firms to contribute for sustainable economic growth by working with employees, workers their families, serving the local community, and society at large to improve the quality of life, in a way that both society and business get the development."

Globalization: Globalization means across the globe. It is used to denote whole globe as one entity. Despite of cultural differences, regional differences, language differences, geographical location barriers all the business units can operate under one umbrella by following common set of rules and norms. All this is been made possible by introduction of term globalization. Now firms and business units can freely do business across the nations. This helped the business in making their brand more popular across the nations and resulted into more demand of branded products. Also helped the companies to design their products and branding advertisements as per varying customers' needs across the nations.

Quality: Definition of quality changes from person to person and from customer to customer this variation is as per the customer requirements but one thing that is been common among all in spite of place, product, price, promotion, popularity of brand is satisfaction of customer needs and requirements i.e., named as conformance to customer needs/customer requirements. For a very long time i.e., more than twenty years India and Indian firm's enjoyed a free market that is monopoly in market, no competition and customers with no or little choices. But with the opening up of markets after 1991, now customers had many choices in context to product, price, popularity of brand etc. By having competition from global players Indian markets, producers and manufacturers started realizing need for quality and quality product manufacturing. By having competition from global firms local firms have also given due importance to the term Quality, quality of products and services offered by the firm.

Chapter 4
Service Branding through Quality Practices in Public and Private Telecommunication Organization

Archana Krishnan
University of Delhi, India

ABSTRACT

This chapter focuses on comparative analysis of service branding of two telecommunication organisations–one in the public and one in the private sector–through the implementation of quality initiatives. This case was designed after extensive interviews with senior managers to understand the practical issues and challenges involved in improvement of service branding of an organisation through the implementation of quality initiatives, such as benchmarking, leadership, service orientation, continuous improvement, and knowledge management, and their subsequent impact on organisation culture and organisation effectiveness. Even though the public sector organisation has taken several measures to improve service branding through quality in its services, it is engulfed in its own internal issues as compared to the private sector organisation. The real life scenarios of both the organisations presented in the case could facilitate young managers to address the challenges involved in improving the service branding of the organisation through the implementation of quality practices in the future.

DOI: 10.4018/978-1-4666-7393-9.ch004

INTRODUCTION

Quality practices are increasingly being used by organisations around the world as a brand management tool. This comes as a result of growing competition among the business organisations to position them globally. According to Kumar et al (2009) quality management leads to less work defect, shorter work process and use of fewer resources which facilitates in achieving lower cost of operations. Quality practices facilitate the organisations to improve their products and services which earn them loyalty of the customers and subsequent increase in the market presence.

The growth of quality consciousness spread in the 1880's and 1890's with F.W. Taylor's principles of scientific management which emphasised on standardisation, improving efficiency, effectiveness, reducing waste and rework by employing empirical methods to the processes through rationality and work ethics (Taylor, 1910). The wave of quality consciousness which started from the manufacturing industry has now spread to the service industry with significant success being achieved in the implementation of quality practices, around the world and in India in particular (Hasan & Kerr, 2003). The main feature of the service industry is its intangibility and it comprises of different segments such as advertising, promotion, public relations, communication and information, editing and printing, banks, finance and insurance, data processing and software, health care, consulting, auditing and counselling, education and formation, legal and management, research and engineering, real estate, fashion, design and art, leisure and entertainment, hotels, travel and restaurant, distribution, retail sales, wholesale, transportation, repairs, maintenance and recovery, public service (power, gas, etc.) and other government services (Delazaro Filho,1998). The organisations are increasingly experiencing an improvement in the value of their organisation as service brand as a result of implementation of quality practices.

There is a greater realisation of the fact that customer is the essence and customer satisfaction the ultimate goal (Krishnan, 2013). Hence, all organisational measures are now directed towards strengthening the relationship with the end customer by providing service par excellence with quality practices. Several of these service organisations have been recognised with some distinguished awards such as Japanese Deming Prize, USA's Malcolm Baldrige National Quality Award (MBNQA), European Quality Award (EQA) and the UK Quality Award. In India in particular, quality awards such as Rajiv Gandhi National Quality Award, The Golden Peacock National Quality Award, CII-EXIM Bank Award for Business Excellence and IMC Ramkrishna Bajaj National Quality Award have been constituted by different authorities to encourage quality consciousness among the Indian business organisations (Mohammad & Mann, 2010).

Quality has been defined as meeting or exceeding the expectations of the customers (Feigenbaum, 1961), conformance to requirements (Crosby, 1979). ISO 8402 defines Total Quality Management (TQM) as an organisation's management approach, which is quality centred, involving the participation of all its members, aiming at customer satisfaction and providing benefit to all the members of the organisation and society at large (Ljungstrom & Klefsjo, 2002). Olabode (2003) defines TQM as a technique to improve efficiency, effectiveness, flexibility and competitiveness as a whole which involves every individual at every level across the various departments. Siddiqui and Rahman (2007) describe TQM as an initiative, which is delivered through statistical control, procedural design and deployment of policies using the techniques of human resource management centred on the customer. Though, distinctions can be made between the quality management and total quality management, most researchers use the two terms interchangeably. The same practice will be followed throughout the paper for simplicity.

Brand has been described as a combination of images, feelings, beliefs and experiences that the stakeholders both internal and external have about an organisation (The Centre, n.d.). The stakeholders must associate and identify themselves with the organisation which should reflect their hopes and needs. According to Kotler (2000), brand is the name, associated with one or more items in the product line, which is used to identify the source of character of the item(s). The term branding originated from England in the medieval times where livestock cattle were branded with a hot iron as a means for establishing proof of ownership. The American Management Association (AMA) defines branding as 'a name, term, design, symbol, or any other feature that identifies one seller's good or service as distinct from those of other sellers'. Kotler and Armstrong (2006) define branding as a name, term, sign, symbol or design or a combination of these, intended to identify the goods or services of one seller or group of sellers and to differentiate them from the competitors. Stine (n.d.) opines that branding enables the organisations to create an individual niche in the consumer's psyche. It creates a perception in the minds of the customers that their product, service, organization or community is unique. The distinction could be a result of function, form, ease of use, price or prestige.

Brand building and management are essential marketing skills in the process of marketing of any product, service, organization, person, place or cause as it is the driving force that shapes the marketing mix and provides a platform for an organization's strategies and tactics (Kotler & Armstrong, 2006). In this era of high completion even the best of the best product and services get outdated in no time unless the organisation concerned takes some strong measures to establish itself as a differentiated brand. Kotler (1999) throws light on five dimensions of product, services, personnel, channel and image through which a company can differenti-

Figure 1. Differentiation variables

Product	Services	Personnel	Channel	Image
Form	Ordering	Ease	Competence	Coverage Symbols
Features	Delivery	Courtesy	Expertise	Media
Performance	Installation	Credibility	Performance	Atmosphere
Conformance	Customer training	Reliability		Events
Durability	Customer consulting	Responsiveness		
Reliability	Maintenance and Repair	Communication		
Reparability	Miscellaneous			
Style				
Design				

ate its market offering. Figure 1 describes the various differentiation variables for organisational competitiveness.

The present case study focuses on comparative analysis of service branding of two tele-communication organisations–one each in the public and private sector through the implementation of quality initiatives. Extensive interviews with senior managers were conducted to understand the practical issues and challenges involved in improvement of service branding of the organisations through the implementation of quality initiatives such as benchmarking, leadership, service orientation, continuous improvement and knowledge management and their subsequent impact on organisation culture and organisation effectiveness.

The study on service branding is still in the nascent stages and is important as increasingly service organisations are now focusing on branding of their services rather than the products offered by them. This is because customers often evaluate the kind of hassle free service offered to them first rather than the features of the products. De Chernatony & McDonald (1998) emphasise that the branding of services is even more important than branding of products since the customer has no tangible attributes when assessing the brand. Product branding discusses the relationship between the customer and the actual product while in service branding, the organisation itself is the primary brand. In addition to this Richard (2011) mentions how Marc Pritchard, the global marketing and brand building officer at Procter & Gamble, emphasised that organisations must change their mindsets from marketing to consumers to serving consumers. In other words, organisations must shift their focus from brand building from selling products to that of serving consumers to create and improve brand image.

The case focuses on tele-communication organisations in India as tele-communication organisations (irrespective of whether public or private) are the lifeline of common man which facilitates them to connect with each other across India's vast demographic and geographic divide, significantly bridging the gap between the rich and the poor. It is therefore essential for tele-communication organisations in both public and private sectors to improve service branding in their organisations through institutionalisation of quality practices in their work processes to evolve as better service brand.

According to Delazaro Filho (1998), the service sector displays some special characteristics such as attitude, promptness in delivery, equipment and facilities, product and consumer satisfaction as a result of application of quality tools. Personnel rendering service need to possess attitude such as kindness and courtesy, promptness in delivery as any delay in delivery of service is unacceptable, equipment and facilities interms of cleanliness, adequacy and appearance of uniforms, tools, state of art offices and buildings, product(and services) must be free of defects, achieve consumer satisfaction in spite of the fact that services are complex delivery systems, time-sensitive, consumer involvement is unpredictable, consumer standards are difficult to identify, frequently involving preferences or even mood. In addition to this, the author also mentions relevant quality drivers as presented in Figure 2 where the relative importance in a scale is depicted from 1 (very low) to 5 (very high). The most important drivers of quality (in decreasing order) were greater quality requirements of product, opportunities offered by computing/communications, need to reduce operating costs, growing international competition, better usage of resources and better education of their personnel.

The present study highlights two tele-communication organisations one each in the public and private sector named XXX and YYY in the study. The original names of the organisations have been withheld as a respect to their privacy and confidentiality.

Figure 2. Quality drivers

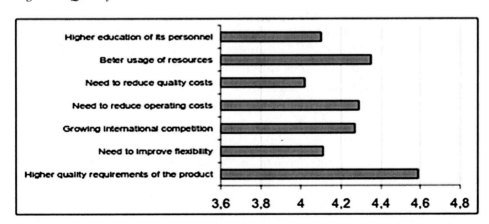

ORGANISATION BACKGROUND

The public sector organisation XXX has been presently labelled as a 'Navratna' by the Indian Government and was established nearly three decades ago for bringing improvement in the quality of tele-communication services, expanding the tele-communication network, adding new services to the domain and raising the revenue to the tele-communication department for further development. 'Navratna' was initially a status given to a set of nine Public Sector Enterprises (PSEs) having competitive advantage and were identified by the Government of India for giving them greater autonomy to compete in the global market and become global giants. The organisation mainly provides fixed line telecommunication services and mobile services in one of the major metropolitan cities of the country. The organisation aims to remain a leader for providing world class tele-communication and IT services while keeping the end customer delighted at all times.

In the recent past, the organisation has witnessed an all-round development, growth and improved operational efficiency. Currently, the organisation provides telecom services such as fixed telephone service, GSM (including 3G services) and CDMA based Mobile service, Internet, Broadband, ISDN and Leased Line services based on state of the art technology at most affordable rates. The organisation was the first to launch some of the latest telecom technologies in the country like ADSL2+ & VDSL2 in broadband, IPTV on MPEG4 technology, VOIP and 3G Mobile service.

The organisation has about 39,264 working employees as compared to 62000 in the year 1997-98. The reduction in staff strength has been attributed to VRS and natural attrition. However, XXX is still grappling with acute overstaffing which leaves a financial burden on the organisation. The organisation has not been able to take any substantial measures to address this problem.

The organisation is administering multi-layered checks and balances to ensure transparency, integrity and accountability in its practices consciously in accordance with the guidelines laid down by Department of Public Enterprises (DPE) on Corporate Governance. The Corporate Governance at XXX lays down procedures for constitution of the board of directors which includes details of their responsibilities, duties, required level of expertise and commitment to discharge their functions effectively. It emphasises on policy on risk assessment and minimization, prevention of insider trading and code of conduct for senior management personnel. The organisation enforces fair and equitable treatment of all its stakeholders including employees, customers, shareholders and investors.

Constant efforts are being taken by the organisation XXX to improve industrial relations. The organisation XXX ensures industrial peace and harmony through healthy employee relations. Grievances are brought to the management's notice by employee unions/associations and redressed through regular meetings and interactions between management and employee unions/associations. Further, joint management workers participation is encouraged in critical issues relating to business and employees through various meetings.

The organisation lays immense stress on the human resource development by focussing on the quality of the intellectual capital. It believes that knowledge and skill of its employees are a determining factor in the realising its corporate objectives. Recently, more thrust on human resource activities such as training and development through the various training centres have raised the capability of the employees to successfully face the threats in the competitive environment and service the end customers in a better manner. The training thus imparted focuses on not only reorienting the employees towards greater organisation purpose but also bridging any existing skill gap in relation to the current technology. Training is offered to employees across the organisation hierarchy in the areas Telecom, IT, computer system and management. The training centre is well equipped with necessary infrastructure, technical and academic competence and excellence for providing training in specialized courses in the field of GSM, broadband technology, switching, transmission, external plant, IT, computer system and management.

The organisation takes special care to improve the working conditions of women employees. The management is continuously focussing on gender sensitization amongst the employees. Management is sensitive to the women working in the night shifts. Special cells have been constituted within the organisation for addressing complaints on sexual harassment in the workplace. Special grants have been allocated for women welfare committees for looking after the needs of the women employees.

The primary need and objective of the organisation is to develop leaders at every level. This is because the organisation is becoming flatter by the day which requires dynamic leaders to spearhead the organisation's objectives. Competitive market environment requires the leaders to formulate strategies for speed, flexibility and the ability to lead in uncertain situations. In this regard, the organisation is implementing an effective and unique leadership program. The management has started with certain measures such as engaging top executives in aligning leadership strategies and development with evolving business goals. XXX also focuses on developing leaders across the hierarchy who could spearhead organisation goals with support from lower rung of employees. Local leaders are nurtured to become global leaders so they are able to address the local issues and challenges with a global perspective. The organisation is also developing succession leaders who could manage the business in the absence of the top leaders in position. Such enriched leaders create an image of progress in the eyes of the customers, thereby improving their service branding.

The private sector tele-communication organisation YYY is one of the fastest growing telecom service providers which has managed to grow its customer base with its best-in-class solutions, partnerships and domain expertise to address the requirements of service providers, enterprises and consumers. YYY is proud to have a pan India presence with the launch of GSM mobile services and mobile internet through its apps which has facilitated it to quickly establish itself as a market leader. The organisation has won the bid for 3G and BWA spectrum which enabled it to provide high speed data and multimedia services in its circles and became the largest operator in India with spectrum secured for next generation wireless technologies. It has also been rewarded for highest customer satisfaction by some distinguished associations due to its voice and data services.

YYY is a leader in data connectivity solutions and was the first operator in India to launch Wi-MAX technology. The range of services includes networking, data centres, managed services, collaboration services, SaaS (Software-as-a-Service) and mobility solutions. World-class internet services are supported by highly redundant, carrier grade mesh network. Internet Leased Line services are offered over various last mile options viz. Wi-MAX, Fiber and P2P radio to ensure cost effective solutions of high uptimes and redundancies in network connectivity with minimum latencies.

The organisation culture at YYY focuses on collaboration where employees across the hierarchy work together. The employees work with a sense of engagement, passion and constantly work towards a 'higher purpose'. It is an endeavour to find simpler and innovative methods of performing work continuously. All organisation members are guided by core values such as – simple, creative and trustworthy which is reflected in all work aspects.

YYY follows the philosophy of growing leaders within the organization and giving them opportunities to explore new avenues. The environment encourages internal growth and learning from taking risks. The organisation supports the development of leaders within the organisation and much support is provided to the budding leaders for exploring new areas of interest.

The organisation works towards the integration of personal and organisational growth. It also rewards the employees for their merit, initiative at work and support for a collaborative culture throughout the organization. This recognition and reward for performance motivates the employees for higher achievements and fosters a culture of appreciation. This in turn reflects in increased customer satisfaction.

The organisation has found a novel way of encouraging appreciation among the employees as a part of the corporate culture wherein a physical 'smile box' is placed on each employee's workstation. The employees need to drop appreciation cards in the box as a gesture of gratitude for the help or assistance they receive from their colleagues.

Enough importance is given to the learning and development at YYY. The organisation stresses on the motto of 'Grow Outward, Grow Inward'. The focus on self-realization and external growth also manifests itself in the official logo– 'the Wishing Tree'. The objective is to allow the employees to scale new heights and at the same time be deep rooted in knowledge and skills. Employees have to go through five Colleges of learning and development which includes areas such as leadership, service management and retail, sales, marketing and distribution, technology and professional support services in the learning academy. Apart from this, Learn, Know, Grow (LKG) process helps them to learn throughout the year through various techniques such as on-the-job, self-paced, web-based, instructor-led and mobile learning.

SETTING THE STAGE

The case study is based on scenarios in a two organisation's in the tele-communication industry each in the public and private sector. Views of senior managers from both the public sector tele-communication organisation named XXX and private sector tele-communication organisation named YYY on the service branding efforts through implementation of quality initiatives- benchmarking, leadership, service orientation, continuous improvement and knowledge management and its impact on organisation culture and organisation effectiveness, were taken through a structured interview. The senior managers have also thrown light on challenges that are being faced during the implementation of these 'quality initiatives' to brand their services in a more effective manner. Since implementation of quality initiatives are an ongoing change initiative, the case study only focuses on the current challenges and issues involved in the implementation of these initiatives. Figure 3 depicts the model showing the relationship between quality initiatives, organisation culture, organisation effectiveness and service branding for the purpose of this case study.

CASE DESCRIPTION

The case describes the various quality initiatives being implemented in the study in both the public and private sector tele-communication organisations in order to improve the organisational service branding position in the perception of the various stakeholders.

Benchmarking

Benchmarking has been defined as the 'search for industry best practices that will lead to superior performance' (Camp, 1989). Benchmarking has also been defined as 'continuous, systematic process of measuring products, services and practices

Figure 3. Relationship between quality initiatives, organisation culture, organisation effectiveness, and service branding

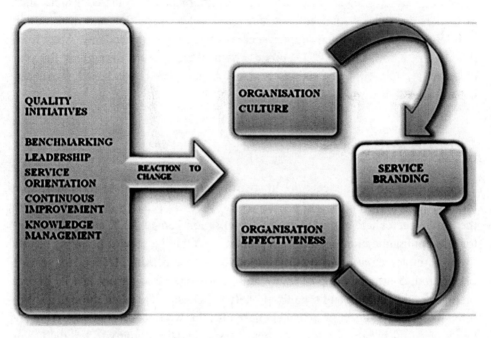

against the companies considered to be superior with the idea of bridging any performance 'gaps' (Kouzmin et al,1999).

In the public sector tele-communication organisation XXX, high competition has been a determining factor in the institutionalisation of benchmarking and improvement of organisation's internal work processes. The senior management opines that better products, service and customer care in comparison to their competitors could give them an edge over others. Hence, increasingly, every employee is encouraged to know about the organisation's products and tariffs to improve, modify and induce services to meet the need and satisfaction of customers. This may develop a perception in the minds of the customers that they are being cared for. There is a common perception that the organisations as a whole must imbibe certain best practices, learn from the best in business and implement the same strategies in XXX by establishing certain short and long term goals which are essential for the organisation's survival.

The level of benchmarking practice in this organisation is not satisfactory, as opined by majority of the employees. This could be attributed to the fact that it is a governmental organisation and the bureaucratic process delays the adoption of new products and alteration of existing practices. In certain cases, innovative projects fail to see any light. Also, the delay in the decision making by the authorities adversely affects the process of benchmarking and its implementation. Currently, the organisation does not have any standard process or policy for benchmarking.

However, the existing benchmarking practices have started modifying the organisational culture. As a result of learning from the best in class, leaders have started recognising employees by means of promotion, motivation and incentives. With the introduction of Management Information Systems (MIS) efforts are being made to have seamless managerial communication. Constant innovation is encouraged towards the introduction of new services and tariffs for attracting customer base. Greater stress is being laid to employee empowerment as empowered employees play a vital role in developing organisation's competency, thereby developing a collaborative culture. Benchmarking has also been influential in increasing the organisational effectiveness as it has streamlined the processes, reduced time to achieve the targets and brought more clarity while realising the organisation goals. On the flip side, institutionalisation of benchmarking has not been a easy task for the senior managers as many a times, as it is observed that subordinates say, 'It is not my work'; 'I am already overloaded' and 'give it to others'. Such reactions affect the overall culture and effectiveness of the organisation.

On the other side, in the private sector tele-communication organisation YYY, majority of the employees believe that the present level of benchmarking practice in their organisation is satisfactory. Although, the benchmarking policy in place, but it is not yielding much benefits as there is absence of implementation. It is rather disheartening that even though the senior managers are aware of the benchmarking standards, they are often seen bypassing the process of benchmarking to achieve organisation goals. Hence benchmarking itself is not useful. All processes in the organisation have well laid out rules. To some extent, checks and controls are carried out in the system itself. Although, benchmarking objectives are set by gathering information from employees past experiences with other organisations in similar work areas, hardly an effort goes into 'how' these objectives will be achieved.

As benchmarking standards are set after a careful consultation from all employees, the process as such facilitates the employees and the management to work together and co-create a culture of cooperation. Employees are recognised through rewards and recognition, individually and in teams. However, the rewards are disseminated at the discretion of the HR manager after recognising an employee's work which may raise questions on the decision making approach. Although, strategies have been laid down by the management for sufficiently empowering the employees, it is up to the employees to utilise those measures that may empower them in the process. Employees are also encouraged to learn and adapt to change through regular training. However, the lack of good communication mechanism acts as a roadblock in disseminating policies for change management among the employees.

Great strides can be achieved in organisation effectiveness if benchmarking is implemented by making the processes coherent through planning, implementation and involvement of all concerned. This organisation still needs to work towards the implementation. On a positive note, the process of benchmarking and its implementation does not have an effect on the work time schedules as process as such cannot dictate schedules. Much depends on internal and external criteria.

The management action of not recognising the employee's work accomplished within a given period of time and more so when the employees finally leave the organisation, certainly affects the overall organisation culture and organisation effectiveness. A certificate of accomplishment during the employees' tenure could bring the employees and the management much closer to each other. This may motivate the two to share a strong and positive relationship even after they leave the organisation. This can also motivate the employees to join back the same organisation later in the future, with much better expertise and skills.

The implementation of benchmarking practices for achievement of higher service related goals projects a customer centric attitude of the organisation. Improved organisation work culture and organisation effectiveness in the work practices creates a good impression about the organisation in the minds of the customers, which reflects in the long term association of customers with the service brand.

Leadership

Leadership has been defined as 'a continuous process of influencing behaviour' (Terry, 1968). Leadership also refers 'to vision, cheerleading, enthusiasm, love, trust, verve, passion, consistency, the use of symbols, creating heroes at all levels, coaching and effectively wandering around' (Peters & Austin, 1985). In the public sector organisation XXX, the degree of leadership commitment in this organisation is not perceived to be satisfactory. The top management has been inefficient in providing enough thrust on HR policies, practices, skilled, professionals and work profile distribution. The decision making authority is limited to a few managers only. Employees usually face the consequences as a result of management callousness. The departments for technical and HR work are not separate; as a result employees are usually over- burdened with work, which brings down their efficiency. The grievance redressal mechanism is also not satisfactory which disrupts a normal flow of work. This has adversely affected the overall performance of the company. The organisation desperately needs an overhaul in the way the top leadership wholeheartedly participates in the issues surrounding the employees and their work. The leaders must move out of their cocoons of bureaucracy and understand the employees with empathy.

Nevertheless, the existing level of leadership has influenced the organisational culture positively. In the past, good leaders have created motivated workforce with a strong sense for achievement. Such leaders have also been helpful in making the organisation effective as their vision adds clarity to the goals and employees understand the ways to achieve them. Common goals were created which helped in building a cohesive workforce. It is essential that leaders align with the mindset of the employees, as a negative employee reaction to leader's ideas can dilute the organisations culture and its effectiveness. A positive reaction can create more loyalists towards the leaders and the organisation, thus making it effective.

In the private sector tele-communication industry YYY as well, the degree of leadership commitment is not very high. This is evident as leaders are not very easily approachable and available to the lower level employees. It is rather, disheartening to note that for most of the leaders, it does not matter much. Some of the leaders do seem to be open to feedback and comments but the implementation of the feedback received is poor. The management focuses on training and development to improve leadership practices in this organisation. Still, leader's will to be 'employee centred' is the biggest challenge in developing leadership. However, employees listen to the senior managers, whether willingly or unwillingly and hence, instances of employee resistance in the organisation are hardly reported. Even if such a situation had risen, no concrete measures were taken to avoid it in the future. Therefore, leaders have not performed their role of being the organisation's backbone in a real sense. Good leadership with regular communication is very much essential for completing the routine tasks else they may lose control over their subordinates.

Improvements in developing leadership as a quality improvement initiative may influence organisational culture. Non-achievement of assigned goals affects the organisation goals. Ultimately it is the leader who motivates his team to accomplish the work goals and take the challenges head on, thereby creating the ability in employees to take calculated risks. Further, a good leadership can guide and motivate the employees well, thereby garnering more commitment and involvement in the tasks whereby employees view the organisation goals as their personal goals making the organisation more effective in the long run. Also, as a good leadership can make the employee happy and contended, a poor leadership can create severe issues in the long run where the employees may strongly resent the same. Hence, employee's reactions to leadership may positively or negatively affect culture and organisation effectiveness.

In both organisations, a stable and a progressive leadership highlights the willingness of the organisation to make significant progress towards taking decisive measures to improve service to its stakeholders. A customer who experiences service in such an environment takes home a positive impression about the organisation's speed and quality of service, thus improving the organisation's service branding.

Service Orientation

Hennig-Thurau (2004) defined service orientation as 'an employee's behaviour during in-person interactions with customers that meets their needs'. This has also been defined as an 'organization-wide embracement of a basic set of relatively enduring organizational policies, practices and procedures intended to support and reward service-giving behaviours that create and deliver service excellence' (Lytle et al, 1998). The present level of service orientation in the organisation XXX is not satisfactory. There are several factors contributing to lack of this initiative. Service orientation mandates the need for flow of information from top to bottom and vice-versa. However, the management is not able to effectively communicate the goals, policies and new services to its employees across the hierarchy. Further, it is essential for the management to obtain feedback from employees about the challenges (hurdles and difficulties) faced during the implementation of these goals. This, the employees opine could be strengthened with regular interactive sessions between the top management and the employees. The employees also expect the management to regularly visit the work place units which can bring the management close to all levels of employees. In this manner service orientation towards both the internal and external customer could well be a backbone for the successful execution of organisation's internal processes.

Institutionalisation of service orientation involves the organisation providing service to the stakeholders by various mechanisms thereby winning over their trust and loyalty. This further spreads a positive word of mouth about the organisation in its immediate environment. The use of MIS for flow of information from top to bottom does have the capacity to strengthen the organisation culture. However, the communication mechanisms needs still to be strengthened. Further, organisational service orientation towards the employees develops more confidence in the management and a sense of hope prevails that all their issues will be taken care of. This sense of hope and reassurance makes the employees work with greater involvement and togetherness. Although, there are instances of employees resisting the initiative, but they can be convinced, motivated and mentored to adapt them to change.

In the private sector, tele-communication organisation YYY, service orientation has proved to be important measure in improving an organisation's internal processes. Though, much depends on the involvement of the seniors towards these initiatives, equally important are the procedures involved in the implementation of the policies thus developed for the customers and employees as such. Overall, employees perceive the level of organisational service orientation towards both external and internal customers to be satisfactory to some extent, although much can be improved with better feedback and communication with the employees. Further, lack of a positive relationship between managers and employees hampers the level of service orientation towards the employees which in turn affects the end customers.

The level of implementation of service orientation is perceived to be inadequate which definitely impacts the organisation culture negatively. This may be attributed to the fact that the management recognises employee's efforts for the objectives achieved by them, though the immediate senior manager may not necessarily recognise the same. Lack of employee recognition by immediate managers creates resentment among the subordinates. Such soured relationships lead to low distribution of available benefits to the employees resulting in reduced morale and effectiveness at work. Nevertheless, the senior mangers feel that measures must be taken to work with greater togetherness with the subordinates and work towards higher customer centric goals leading to a goal oriented culture. A better employee – manager relationship can lead to greater effectiveness. This in turn could lead to better morale, satisfaction and more orientation towards work.

In both the sectors, service orientation towards internal and external customers creates a strong bond between the management and stakeholders which facilitates the customers to place greater trust on the organisation work practices and its service delivery. This in turn creates a positive image in the minds of the customers who spread the organisation's progress through word of mouth which improves the organisation service branding position.

Continuous Improvement

Continuous improvement has been defined as a 'planned, organised, systematic, incremental and companywide change of existing practices aimed at improving company performance' (Boer, 2000). It also focuses on 'setting objectives, measuring outcomes and using the data from the assessment to improve the processes responsible for these outcomes regularly' (Harper, 2008). In the public sector telecommunication organisation XXX, the present level of continuous improvement practices in the organisation is not perceived to be that satisfactory. This may be attributed due to lack of good HR practices, Human Resource Information System (HRIS), Management Information System (MIS), IP-based Multimedia Services (IMS), training and feedback. Employees are recognised by the direct boss, mostly verbally. Also, there is a lack of employee recognition from the side of the management. Employees who are given due recognition by the management have higher satisfaction quotient and are naturally motivated towards their work. Non implementation of such measures creates bottlenecks in the growth of the organisation. As a result of the unsatisfactory implementation of continuous improvement practice, resistance was observed among employees. The management is slowly introducing training for new equipments, methods of work, services and tariffs to align the employees with the organisational objectives.

Nevertheless, continuous improvement practices have brought changes in the overall culture of the workplace by making the organisation proactive. Motivated employees deliver service with greater dedication to the customers. Improved service quality, better customer care, reduced fault duration and fault level and better organised practises through organisational restructuring have increased organisation effectiveness.

In the private sector tele-communication organisation YYY, employees perceive Kaizen as an initiative which brings regular improvements. Bringing drastic changes can bring some serious employee resistance. However, the level of continuous improvement practices in this organisation is not satisfactory. Management is making constant efforts to put forward ideas for improvement by regularly interacting with the subordinates. This process of assisting the employees in successfully completing the routine tasks and engaging them in the work related decisions has led to a culture of continuous achievement and competitiveness. The management regularly conducts HR survey called CSAT (Customer Satisfaction) where a group of customers meet the management and discusses their problems. This facilitates the management to understand the customers view point, develop well organised processes, bring and clarity at work and reduce the instances of waste and rework. Also, with better training and employee development employees are better prepared and accept change positively.

In both the organisations, continuous improvements facilitate in improving the work process through small and incremental improvements. This is mainly implemented with regular feedback and communication from the various stakeholders. This measure of involvement of stakeholders makes them feel an essential part of the organisation and wins their loyalty and commitment. Hence, the initiative positively impacts the service branding of the organisation.

Knowledge Management

Knowledge management refers to 'new knowledge construction, knowledge embodiment, knowledge dissemination and knowledge use' (Demerest, 1997). It has also been expressed as the 'ability of an organisation to use its collective knowledge through a process of knowledge generation, sharing and use of technology to achieve organisational objectives' (Cong & Pandya, 2003). In the public sector tele-communication organisation XXX, level of implementation of knowledge management practices is not satisfactory as employees are not being motivated to share their knowledge through available mechanisms. If implemented well, the initiative can facilitate sharing and transferring knowledge among the organisational members. Knowledge management does lead to an environment of better knowledge sharing and guidance where members (whether experienced or new) learn from each other by overcoming the issues of hierarchy and superiority. This will reflect in the process output. Lack of implementation may bring flaws and lead to weak culture and an ineffective organisation.

Lack of implementation of the initiative may affect the quality of work of the employees as knowledge is the basis of any organisation. In this case, the resistance can be from the organisation as well as the management. Employee's resistance to knowledge management activities may make some individuals power centres of knowledge thereby allowing them to take others for a ride. Lack of knowledge sharing will deprive others of the useful information. At an organisation level, lack of intention to motivate the employees to share their knowledge can affect the work process. The employees feel that management must ensure that they are heard, recognised and appreciated to some extent if not in a big way which could help in bringing positive changes to the organisation culture and organisation effectiveness.

In the private sector tele-communication organisation YYY, knowledge management has not been given enough stress in the development of the organisation. Not enough opportunity is being given to the employees to learn variety of work through on the job techniques such as job rotation, training and development. Also, employees are asked to perform tasks in the same domain which can even the lead to wastage of other skills possessed by the employees. Hence, employees opine that the level of implementation of knowledge management practices in this organisation is not satisfactory. The management is not too keen on implementing the knowledge management, though the scope for institutionalising the same is immense. The management itself has no measures for implementing knowledge management, which is in itself a challenge.

If implemented well, knowledge management can lead to a process oriented culture. This could facilitate in developing an effective work environment, but much depends on both internal and external customers. Further, a positive employee reaction to knowledge management practices may affect the evolution of organisation culture and development of organisation effectiveness while a poor implementation and lack of thrust from the top level management may see more disintegration among organisation members and chaotic work processes.

In both the sectors, knowledge management plays an important role in the increasing the organisation service branding. Better knowledge management practices facilitate the employees to work effectively with upto date customer information. The speed and accuracy of the service reinforces the customers trust and loyalty while improving organisation's reputation in the minds of the customers.

CURRENT CHALLENGES FACING THE ORGANIZATION

Successful implementation of quality initiatives requires the management to overcome the challenges posed by its internal environment. In the case of benchmarking in the public sector, most of the times, the management compromises on quality in order to award tenders to the lowest bidder. This compromise of quality affects work process. Social obligations prevent the organisation from taking unbiased view of the problems. Delay in taking managerial decisions, lengthy paper work and a long bureaucratic channel for planning and implementing new strategies, are some serious road blocks in achieving the established benchmarks. Lack of training, incentives and other forms of motivation have created much resistance among the employees. In such a scenario, the organisation is able to satisfy neither the customer nor the employees thereby affecting the organisation reputation in the minds of the stakeholders. In the private sector, communication is one of the main challenges for benchmarking system. Often the managerial decisions are not effectively communicated across the hierarchy. However, some key policies and objectives are established after careful deliberation among the employees and management which leaves no scope for employees to go against the change initiative. Although, employees are instrumental in designing the process framework, the challenge is to ensure that they implement the same. The organisation has to bridge this gap between theory and practice to deliver the end customer its service promises.

In the public sector, management faces the challenge in terms of the intension of the leaders to understand and act on the comments and feedback from employees about work processes. Comments and suggestions are simply heard but are seldom implemented. In-fact, no measures have been taken to improve the leadership practices in this organisation which has resulted in loss of man days. In case, employee's HR issues are not sorted out by the leader, employee may go to the union and protest by way of demonstration. While some problems may get resolved, some may be forwarded to the upper management level. In such a scenario, employees work for fulfilling their personal objectives first rather than the organisational objectives. The relationship of the leaders with the employees and customers gets affected which in turn affects the service brand. Employees just do their job, what they are paid for. Employees usually say, 'let me do my work first, rest of the work will be done later'. Good leaders have the capability to integrate the individual objectives with the organisational objectives. Further, leaders who are trustworthy and empathetic to the needs of the various stakeholders contribute towards better service brand building. In the private sector, the leader's orientation and empathy towards the subordinates is the biggest challenge in developing leadership. However, the management has not faced any major instances of employee resistance in the organisation. Employees have no option but to listen to the senior managers. In case of any negative feedback in the past as well, no concrete measures were taken to avoid it in the future. Leaders do not provide enough support to the employees in achieving the organisational goals. In such case, dissatisfied customers often provide low quality service to the end customers adversely affecting their position as a service brand.

In the public sector, the non- implementation of service orientation in true spirit is itself a serious challenge to the organisation. It appears that the organisation is embroiled in the web of workers unions, employees, government rules and regulations which prevents it to take progressive decisions. Increasingly, the board finds it very difficult to satisfy the interests of the various stakeholders. Employees experience work related grievances, hurdles and problems related to the new targets, services and goals. As a result employee dissatisfaction is witnessed from the employees during the ongoing work process. In such a case, the immediate managers forward the grievances to the upper management for redressal. Such a measure improves the organisational climate and depicts the responsive behaviour of the management to the outside world. Similarly, hierarchy and feedback (communication) are two important challenges in the private sector. Even though resistance was faced by employees as a result of poor organisational service orientation, the management could bring about only makeshift and not permanent solution to the problem. However, the management consciously seeks a collective view of employees on different issues. Regular communication and involvement of the stakeholders can bring immense benefits in the form of stakeholdership commitment and brand loyalty.

The implementation of continuous improvement also does not come without hurdles. The managers in the public sector opine that lack of implementation of good HR practices, Human Resource Information System (HRIS), Management Information System (MIS), IP-based Multimedia Services (IMS), training and feedback itself is a serious challenge to the organisation. Non implementation of such information systems can collapse the entire service delivery mechanism and immensely affect the manner in which the stakeholders perceive about the organisation. On the other hand, in the private sector, recognition of employee issues by the management is a serious roadblock. Changes cannot be brought in without the management's acceptance and recognition of issues concerning employees. In this case, the management intention to change itself is a challenge. The change in the thought process must be initiated from the top level and flow down to the lower level employees. Lack of such initiatives from management has been causing distress among the employees in the system for some time. Resistance from the employees may be brought down with more communication, feedback and proper training for employees to perform the work function. Organisation must enforce employee recognition programs to appreciate the distinguished service provided by every employee and increase the employee value as well as organisation's brand value.

With regard to the knowledge management practices in the public sector organisation, the biggest challenge is that employees do not want to share their knowledge with their co-workers and the management does not see it as a quality tool. Knowledge management is hardly being enforced by the management as a result of management's lack of attention on the initiative. In the private sector, management intent is itself a challenge as it has no plans or measures for implementing knowledge management. The organisation does not have any standard policy for knowledge management. Managers prefer doing it 'their way'. In both the organisations lack of knowledge sharing in particular among the organisation members about the work process or customer information can leave the organisation in a mess, which would be evident on the service brand value.

CONCLUSION

The scenarios in both the public and the private sector tele-communication organisations towards the implementation of quality initiatives such as benchmarking, leadership, continuous improvement, service orientation and knowledge management depict some important points. While the extent of benchmarking practice seems to be unsatisfactory in the public sector, due to lack of policies, standard procedures and bureaucratic hassles, the private sector seems to be lacking in the implementation of the strategies developed for benchmarking. In the public sector, the level of commitment in the area of leadership has been perceived to be low resulting from lack of proper HR policies and thrust on building leadership capability. A similar scenario is experienced in the private sector tele-communication organisation where a poor relationship between the leaders and the employees has been witnessed. The implementation of service orientation seems to be little better in the private sector, which can further be improved with better channels of communication. Lack of technology and poor implementation of information systems has hit continuous improvement practices in the public sector. In the private sector, continuous improvement also seems to have taken a back seat due to poor employee- management relationship. Again, in both the public and the private sectors, knowledge management and in particular, knowledge sharing has not been given enough thrust. In fact, knowledge management as a quality initiative has not been recognised.

SOLUTIONS AND RECOMMENDATIONS

The case indicates that both public sector and private sector organisations considered in the study have not implemented quality practices in true spirit. Both the organisations are engulfed in their own internal issues. However, the senior managers in both the organisations must be conscious of the fact that employees are the life line of any organisation and they have to be kept highly satisfied at all times. Employees' acceptance to a change process is essential for the change to happen at all. This will facilitate in developing both organisation culture and organisation effectiveness in the long run. Both organisations must focus more on leadership development, better internal communication, support to employees and most importantly a wholehearted will to improve the product and services which could benefit all the stakeholders. All organisational strategies must focus on satisfying the end customers, on which depends the very existence of the organisation. As the legend Walter Landor says 'products are made in the factory; brands are created in the mind', the sole objective of the organisations must be to create a favourable perception in the minds of the customers to distinguish themselves as a service brand.

MANAGERIAL IMPLICATIONS

The case would provide rich learning experience to young managers who are trying to improve their service branding through implementation of quality practices in an unfavourable environment in their organisations. The case highlights the real life scenarios of two major public and private sector tele-communication organisations where quality practices are being implemented in spite of various roadblocks. It would also be interesting for the young managers to learn how the implementation of various quality practices could lead to the development of organisation culture and organisation effectiveness and subsequently contribute towards organisation service branding. It also gives deep insights about the essence of the 'employee reaction' to the change initiatives which if harnessed properly, could be a major determinant in the development of organisation culture and organisation effectiveness.

REFERENCES

Boer, H. (2000). *Changes from suggestion box to organisational learning: Continuous improvement in Europe and Australia.* Aldershot, UK: Ashgate.

Camp, R. (1989). *Benchmarking: The search for industry best practices that led to superior performance.* New York, NY: ASQC Quality Press.

Cong, X. M., & Pandya, K. V. (2003). Issues of knowledge management in the public sector. *Electronic Journal of Knowledge Management, 1*(2), 25–33.

Crosby, P. (1979). *Quality is free*. New York: McGraw-Hill.

De Chernatony, L., & McDonald, M. (1998). *Creating powerful brands in consumer, service and industrial markets*. Oxford, UK: Butterworth-Heinemann.

Delazaro Filho, J. (1998). *Gestão da qualidade no Brasil: Setor de services*. São Paulo: Núcleo de Pesquisas e Publicações, Fundação Getúlio Vargas.

Demarest, M. (1997). Understanding knowledge management. *Long Range Planning, 30*(3), 374–384. doi:10.1016/S0024-6301(97)90250-8

Feigenbaum, A. V. (1961). *Total quality control*. New York: Mc Graw Hill.

Harper, B. J. (2008). *Continuous improvement attitudes and behaviors- Assessing faculty practices in academic programs*. Paper presented at the Annual Meeting of the American Educational Research Association, New York, NY.

Hasan, M., & Kerr, R. M. (2003). The relationship between total quality management practices and organisational performance in service organisations. *The TQM Magazine, 15*(4), 286–291. doi:10.1108/09544780310486191

Hennig-Thurau, T., & Thurau, C. (2003). Customer orientation of service employees–Toward a conceptual framework of a key relationship marketing construct. *Journal of Relationship Marketing, 2*(1-2), 23–41. doi:10.1300/J366v02n01_03

Kotler, P. (1999). *Marketing management: Millennium edition* (10th ed.). Prentice-Hall.

Kotler, P. (2000). *Marketing management: The millennium edition*. Upper Saddle River, NJ: Pearson.

Kotler, P., & Armstrong, G. (2006). *The principles of marketing* (11th ed.). Pearson.

Kouzmin, A., Loffler, E., Klages, H., & Kakabadse, N. K. (1999). Benchmarking and performance measurement in public sectors: Towards learning for agency effectiveness. *International Journal of Public Sector Management, 12*(2), 121–144. doi:10.1108/09513559910263462

Krishnan, A. (2013). Effectiveness as an outcome of quality initiatives. In *Proceedings of International Conference on Technology and Business Management* (pp. 701-706). Dubai, UAE: Academic Press.

Kumar, V., Choisne, F., Grosbois, D., & Kumar, U. (2009). Impact of TQM on company's performance. *International Journal of Quality & Reliability Management, 26*(1), 23–37. doi:10.1108/02656710910924152

Ljungstrom, M., & Klefsjo, B. (2002). Implementation obstacles for a work development-oriented TQM strategy. *Total Quality Management, 13*(5), 621–634.

Lytle, R. S., Hom, P. W., & Mokwa, M. P. (1998). SERV*OR: A managerial measure of organizational service-orientation. *Journal of Retailing, 74*(4), 455–489. doi:10.1016/S0022-4359(99)80104-3

Mohammad, M., & Mann, R. (2010, January 9-13). *National quality/business excellence awards in different countries.* Retrieved February 6, 2014, from NIST: http://www.nist.gov/baldrige/community/upload/National_Quality_Business_Excellence_Awards_in_Different_Countries.xls

Olabode, A. J. (2003). The impact of total quality management on banks performance in Nigeria. *Advances in Management, 3*(1), 79–85.

Peters, T., & Austin, N. (1985). *A passion for excellence: The leadership difference.* New York: Random House.

Richard, B. (2011). The new leadership paradigm. Raleigh, NC: lulu.com.

Siddiqui, J., & Rahman, Z. (2007). TQM principles' application on information systems for empirical goals: A study of Indian organizations. *The TQM Magazine, 19*(1), 76–87. doi:10.1108/09544780710720853

Stine, G. (n.d.). *Supplemental information for the branding essentials workshop.* Retrieved from www.polaris-inc.com/assets/pdfs/9_Principles_of_branding.pdf

Taylor, F. W. (1910). *The principles of scientific management.* Retrieved February 6, 2014, from http://nationalhumanitiescenter.org/pds/gilded/progress/text3/taylor.pdf

Terry, G. R. (1968). *Principles of management.* Ricard D. Irwin.

The Centre. (n.d.). Getting your organisation's branding right. *The Centre for all Your Training Needs.* Retrieved April 17, 2014, from www.the-centre.co.uk/documents/A_short_guide_to_branding.pdf

KEY TERMS AND DEFINITIONS

Benchmarking: Involves measuring the success of organisation's internal work process as against the competitors by setting targets, learning new ideas, methods, processes, sharing information among members and aligning short term goals with the long term goals for improving quality at work.

Continuous Improvement: A set of measures for constantly developing and nurturing the work processes through regular employee trainings, innovative work methods, quick detection and correction of errors using teamwork.

Knowledge Management: The process by which employees are motivated to share knowledge among them and contribute to company's knowledge database which could result in significant reduction in training time.

Leadership: The process by which leaders set strategic targets and motivate employees to participate through open channels of communication for clarifying work related issues with an intention to improve the level of work quality.

Organisational Culture: An internal environment created as a result of quality practices where the employees work with high motivation, team spirit, creativity, learn from past experiences through empowerment, recognition, control and coordination, training, growth opportunities, open communication channels provided by the management.

Organisational Effectiveness: The extent to which an organisation realises its outcomes through fair time schedule, proactive planning, realistic objectives, well intentioned communication, legal provisions, leader's guidance, togetherness and unconditional working spirit.

Public and Private Sector: Public sector organisations are run and financed by the government while private sector organisations are run and financed by private players.

Quality Initiative: An organisational effort to deliver service to the customer as expected.

Service Branding: The process of creation of a positive image in the minds of the customers as a service brand by establishment of a competitive position through various strategies of differentiation.

Service Orientation: The set of organisational measures for satisfying the employees by providing relevant work information, encouraging suggestions, ensuring high employee spirits and the customers by improving service delivery though updated database, regular feedback and prompt grievance redressal.

Tele-Communication Industry: Involves the facilitation of sending or receiving information between the source and the destination electronically.

Chapter 5

The Importance of Supply Chain Management in Positioning and Creating Brands of Agro–Based Products

Aroop Mukherjee
Universiti Putra Malaysia, Malaysia

Nitty Hirawaty Kamarulzaman
Universiti Putra Malaysia, Malaysia

ABSTRACT

This case aims to provide information on the importance of supply chain management in creating and positioning of brands of products by companies. Supply chain management entails configuration, collaboration, and coordination. The company that uses only costing for creating brands without resource availability exposes its supply chain to an insufferable risk. Consequently, the company hoping to create its brand in the world market needs to be more resilient in the supply chain process and resources. A strategic and holistic approach to supply chain in collaboration with different companies will help to identify the different strategies, which can be more resilient and efficient supply chain. Supply chain management acts as branding tool and is vital for conveying branded goods to the market in optimal time and cost. The creation of a brand name is linked to management strategies, but persistence and character are possible solely by using supply chain efficiently.

DOI: 10.4018/978-1-4666-7393-9.ch005

ORGANISATION BACKGROUND

The best supply chains aren't just fast and cost-effective. They are also agile and adaptable, and they ensure that all their companies' interests stay aligned. - Lee (2004)

Palm oil is the second most consumed oil in the world after soybean oil. Malaysia is the biggest exporter of palm oil in the world, which currently produces 39% of the world palm oil, and exports 44% of its total production. As Malaysia is also the largest producers of palm oil and palm oil products, it plays a major part in meeting the growing demands of sustainable products from Unilever, which is the largest user of palm oil. Unilever buys 1.3 million tons of palm oil in a year to make products such as Dove soap, TRESEMME shampoo, and Flora Margarine (Evans, 2014) (Figure 1).However, by the end of 2014 Unilever has decided to stop buying unsustainable palm oil that cannot be traced(Evans, 2014) in the supply chain due to 'green movement'. The Malaysian palm oil industry could achieve another milestone as in the 80s, which bolstered the Oleochemicals industry to grow due to an ample supply of palm and palm kernel oil.

Malaysia is now the second largest manufacturer of palm oil products after Indonesia, which took over the number one position in 2007.The oil palm, *Elaeisguineensis*, originates in a region from Angola to Senegal from West Africa and

Figure 1. Use of palm oil in various final product
Source: Patel, 2013.

| BEVERAGES | FOOD | COOKIES,CANDY & ICE CREAM | PERSONAL CARE PRODUCTS | CLEANING PRODUCTS | COSMETICS |

was first introduced to Malaysia as an ornamental plant in 1870 by the British under the colonial rule (Figure 2). The leading producer of palm and palm oil until 1960 was Nigeria, however, now Nigeria is an importer of crude palm oil (CPO). Malaysia started producing refined palm oil after gaining independence in 1950s. Since 1960, the planted area had increased at a rapid pace and the innovations in technology helped the government of Malaysia to overcome Nigeria's dominance. In 1985, 1.5 million hectares were set with palm tree, which increased to 4.917 million hectares by 2011 and palm oil has become the most important commodity crop in Malaysia (Palmoilworld, 2014). The Malaysian government made attempt to displace upward the value chain by running across the refining and marketing abroad. Malaysia has led the other Asian states to diversify its export by developing the palm oil cluster.

The palm oil plant grows within 10 degrees in latitude from the equator, whereas the ideal growing condition is within 5 degrees, but due to global warming the area has been increased to 15 degrees in latitude from the equator. Hence, Malaysia is naturally gifted to produce palm, as long as the land resources exist. The oil palm plantations (Figure 3) have evolved in ensuring that the palm oil produced is according to set standards. The oil palm systems inherent advantages are to have high productivity and efficient carbon assimilation. The oil palm is credited to have a higher yield per unit area as compared to other crops like soybeans, sunflower, and rapeseed (Figure 4). The palm oil planted current yields about 4.0tons of palm oil per hectare along with 0.5 tons of palm kernel oil and 0.6 tons palm kernel cake

Figure 2. Palm fruits at glance
Source: MPOB, 2014.

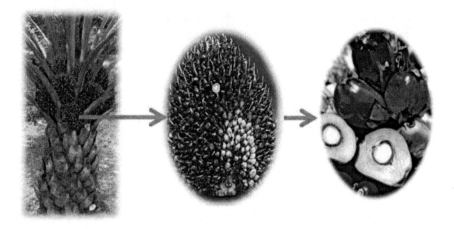

Figure 3. Oil palm plantation
Source: MPOB, 2014.

Figure 4. Production of oil palm with soybean, sunflower, and rapeseed
Source: MPOB, 2014.

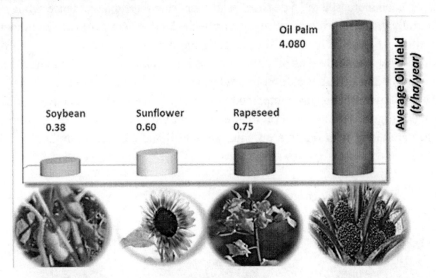

(Palmoilworld, 2014). The oil palm has an economic life of around 25 years, and usually the harvesting of the palm could begin 30 months after field planting (Palmoilworld, 2014) (Figure 5).

Broadly, the palm fruit is roughly the size of a small plum and is based in large bunches that weigh 10-15 kilograms. The fresh fruit bunch (Figure 6) can have up to 2,000 of palm fruits, and each consists of a hard kernel (seed) within a shell (endocarp) which in turn is coated by a fleshy mesocarp that is constituted of approximately 49% oil and around 50% kernel (Figure 7).The two oils (palm oils and kernel oils) have very different compositions, the palm oil from the mesocarp contains mainly palmitic acid and oleic acid, which is the most commonly fatty acids

Figure 5. Age of oil palm tree
Source: MPOB, 2014.

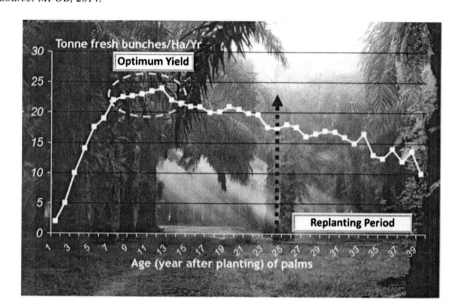

in natural oils and fats and is close to 50% saturated whereas from palm kernel oil it holds more than 80% saturated and contains mainly lauric acid.

Palm oil production has increased over the years from 4.1 million metric tons in 1985 to 18.9 million metric tons in 2011 (Figure 8).The projected production of palm oil is to reach19.4 million metric tons in 2014. The palm oil industry in Malaysia easily meets the local oils and fats demand, and the surplus can be exported to other countries (Palmoilworld, 2014). The palm kernel oil production in 1999 was 1.3 million metric tons and had reached 4.7 million metric tons in 2011. Mostly, the palm kernel oil was exported back in 1970 and since 1979 it has started producing locally the crude oil, palm kernel oil and palm kernel cake. In Malaysia, the palm oil is the highest yielding oil crop among the other crops per hectare per year.

BUSINESS SERVICE

The Malaysian Palm Oil Industry (MPOI), which is the major source of the gross domestic product (GDP) of the country which aspires to advance the country's earning to RM21.9 billion during the 10thMalaysian Plan Period (2011-2015). The Malaysian palm oil industry is clustered into two major groups namely public sector and private sector. The public sector includes the Malaysian Palm Oil Board

Figure 6. Fresh fruit bunch - oil palm
Source: MPOB, 2014.

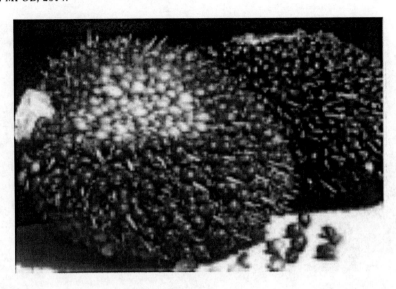

Figure 7.Cross section of fresh fruit oil palm
Source: Capitine, 2010.

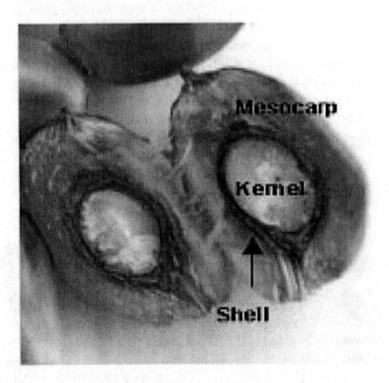

Figure 8. Production of crude palm oil in Malaysia
Source: MPOB, 2014.

(MPOB), which is contained by an Act of Parliament by merging the functions of the Palm Oil Research Institute of Malaysia (PORIM) and the Palm Oil Registration and Licensing Authority (PORLA) (Palmoilworld, 2014). The sector, which was run for more than 20 years to concentrate more on effective services and to provide greater accessibility of internal and international industry(MPOB, 2014). Further, the public sector includes Oil Palm Growers Association (OPGA), Palm Oil Refiners Association of Malaysia (PORAM), Federal Land Development Agency (FELDA), Malaysian Palm Oil Promotion Council (MPOPC), Kuala Lumpur Commodity Exchange (KLCE) and collaborating among the various growers and supply chain linkages for CPO (MPOPA), the refining process (PORAM) and for risk management (KLCE) (MPOB, 2014). According to the Malaysian Palm Oil Board (MPOB, 2014) to accomplish the object layer, the MPOI will be furthered as a planetary hub for the palm oil and make Malaysia as the preferred location for the foreign investments.

Altogether, the major players have a well-established supply chain. Malaysian government has decided to develop the Malaysian palm oil industry as a strategy for the country's economic development. Mainly, all the companies are having a similar supply chain management, which is linked to players and other entities, which is important for the development, and form the clusters that include upstream activities, downstream activities, exporters and importers, customers, government agencies, and industry organization. A single supply chain, which is a set of entities, includes the collection of all the clusters, which is primarily involved in streamlining the supply chain. The entire supply chain management can be reckoned as the group of activities that can coordinate from the beginning to the end and in the end create customer value and client commitment. According to Mentzer *et al.* (2001), the activities like integration of behavior, sharing information, sharing risk, cooperation, focus on serving customers, the integration of process and creating and maintaining long term relationship will lower down on implementing supply chain management at lower costs and improved customers value, make customer satisfy and have a competitive advantage.

ORGANISATION STRUCTURE

The panel members are nominated by the Minister of Plantation Industries and Commodities. The chairperson is the representative from three ministries namely Finance (MOF), Plantation Industries and Commodities (MPIC), and International Trade and Industry (MITI). The representative from Federal Land Development Authority (FELDA), National Association of Smallholders (NASH), Malaysian Estate Owners Association (MEOA), Malaysian Palm Oil Association (MPOA), Malaysian Edible Oil Manufacturers Association (MEOMA), Palm Oil Millers Association of Malaysia (POMA), Palm Oil Refiners Association of Malaysia (PORAM), Malaysian Oleochemical Manufacturers Group (MOMG), Sarawak State Government, Sabah State Government, East Malaysia Planters Association and the Director-General of Malaysian Palm Oil Board (MPOB). Various committees from the areas of Research, Finance and Development, Tenders, Establishment, Registration and Licensing Audit also assist the board. The director-general and deputy director-general from research and development and the deputy director-general from services administer manage the Malaysian Palm Oil Board (MPOB). The board is divided into eight divisions that is headed by directors. The eight divisions are Biological Research, Engineering & Processing Research, Advanced Oleochemical Technology, Product Development Research & Advisory Services, Economics & Industry Development, Finance, Management & Development, Information Technology & Corporate Services, and Licensing & Enforcement (Figure 9).

MARKET ASSESSMENT

The Malaysian agriculture sector is governed by oil palm, which accounted for 71% of its national agricultural land bank (Performance Management and Delivery Unit, 2010). The industry is more than 100 years old, which have recorded remarkable success. The industry will remain a major contributor to the Malaysian economy over the next 10 years (Performance Management and Delivery Unit, 2010). The two major core advantages over other substitute are:

Figure 9. Organization structure
Source: MPOB, 2014.

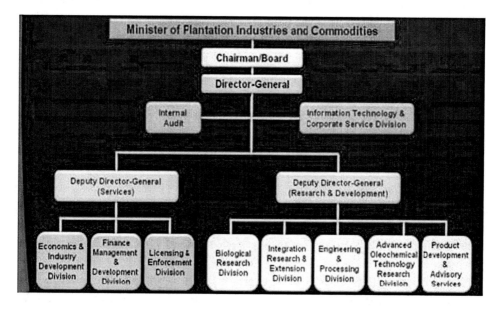

1. **Rising Relative Demand vs. Substitutes:** The demand for oils and fats have increased sharply at an average growth rate of 7% over the past 10 years, which was driven by increasing global population, changing dietary habits and rising per capital income. Comparatively, at the same time the demand for palm oil is increased at the rate of 10 percent; and

2. **High Oil Yield per Hectare vs. Substitutes:** Oil palm produces 4 to 5 tons of oil per hectare, which is 8 to 10 times higher than any other oilseeds such as soybean, sunflower, and rapeseed.

FINANCIAL STATUS

The Malaysian oil palm industry (MPOI) saw a mixed performance during the last year 2013. As the crude palm oil production and export demand increased, the imports were low throughout the year. The costs for crude palm oil (CPO) have shown uptrend from a low of RM2, 221 (USD 689) in January 2013 to close to RM2,574 (USD 799) in December 2013 even though the median monetary value was low as compared to the previous year. In 2013, the total oil palm planted reached5.23 million hectares, which was an increase of 3% as against of 5.08 million hectares recorded 2012 because mainly an increase in the newly planted areas in Sarawak have recorded an increase of 7.9% or 84,660 hectares. The biggest oil palm planted state is still being headed to be Sabah with 1.48 million hectares or 28% of the total planted area, followed by Sarawak with 1.16 million hectares or 22%, and 2.59 million hectares or 50% is accounted for Peninsular Malaysia.

Crude palm oil (CPO) production recorded an increase of 2.3% from 18.79 million metric tons to 19.22 million metric tons in the year 2013 from 2012. This was due to an increase of fresh fruit bunch (FFB) yield by 0.7% with additional new matured areas for producing the palm fruits especially in Sarawak area. In the Peninsular Malaysia where there was an addition of 0.1% to 10.33 million metric tons, Sabah increased by 4.2% to 5.78 million metric tons. The fruit for the fresh fruit bunch (FFB) for 2013 was higher by 0.7% to arrive at 19.02 tons per hectare from 18.89 metric tons per hectare. Sabah registered an increase of 2.4% to 20.88 tons per hectare, as 65% of the planted field is in the peak production years (10 to 24 years). Further, the Peninsular Malaysia recorded an addition of 1.1% to 19.26 metric tons per hectare, Sarawak registered a decrease of 1.7% at 16.23 metric tons per hectare.

Oil Extraction Rate (OER) has registered a fall of 0.5% to 20.25%, which was primarily due to excessive rainfalls, hot and dry weather in June 2013 and July 2013 and because of the low quality of crops from the new matured areas coming into production from Sarawak. The oil palm products consist of palm oil, palm kernel oil, palm kernel cake, Oleochemicals, biodiesel, and finished products have increased by 4.5% to 25.70 million metric tons in 2013 from 24.59 million tons of total exports. The total export revenue was declined by 14.1% to RM61.36 (USD [1]19.05)billion as compared to RM71.45 (USD22.18)billion in 2012 due to the export price of all palm products was low. A reduction of 14.6% to RM45.27 (USD14.05) billion as compared to previous year price for palm oil was recorded as RM52.99 (USD 16.45) billion tons.

The higher demand for palm oil from China P.R, India, Bangladesh, the European Union, Iran, and Pakistan has suggested an increase of exports of palm oil by 3.3% to 18.15 million metric tons, which have an impact on the CPO export duty structure in Figure 10. The CPO export duty structure was increased in export of processed palm oil by 9.5% from 12.95 million metric tons in 2012 to 14.16 million metric tons in 2013.

Since 2002, China, P.R has maintained the position of largest palm oil importer with total consumption of 3.70 million tons or 20.4% of the total palm oil exports, which is followed by the European Union (EU) to 2.34 million tons (12.9%), India 2.33 million tons (12.8%), Pakistan 1.43 million tons (7.9%), USA 1.01 million tons (5.7%), Iran 0.64 million tons (3.5%) and Japan 0.50 million tons (2.8%) or from the total the Malaysian palm oil export in 2013, 65.9% or 11.69 million tons were exported to these seven countries.

Figure 10.Top 10 importers 2008 – 2014
Source: Patel, 2013.

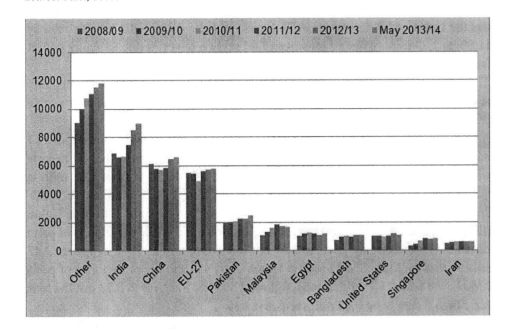

The substantial growth of palm oil export to China, P.R., was at 5.6% to 3.70 million metric tons in 2013 from 3.50 million metric tons in 2012.This increase was due to lower imports of soy oil which amount to 0.89 million metric tons. There was a higher increase of export of palm oil was recorded from 0.19 million tons to 0.47 million tons i.e. 68.7% in Benin, and this is mainly due to re-exports to its neighboring countries such as Nigeria and Togo. Export to Bangladesh has shown an increase of 61.6% from 0.27 million metric tons to 0.44 million tons is due to competitiveness, price as against the other vegetable oils. The monetary value of palm oil was competing at a deduction of USD 200 per ton against soybean oil and against rapeseed oil, it was discounted of USD 225 per ton.

European Union (EU) has increased the import of palm oil by 5.2% to 2.34 million tons from 2.22 million tons in 2012 due to competitive price of other vegetable oils as well as increased consumption for biodiesel in generating electricity and heat. The increase in export of palm oil to Pakistan by 6.8% to 1.44 million tons is mainly due to lower import of rapeseed and sunflower seed for domestic crushing activity. Export to Iran has discovered an increase by 15.8% to 0.64 million metric tons from 0.55 million metric tons during the same point from last year 2011. Ithas contributed to arise from the financial sanctions imposed on the country due to the reduced imports of oilseeds and oilseed products, which have shown a favorable shift in demand of palm oil imports from Malaysia to Indonesia.

While the majority has registered an increase of palm oil exports, but some markets have registered a decline in exports of palm oil namely India, Philippines, and the United Arab Emirate (UAE). Export of palm oil to India has declined by 11.9% to 2.33 million metric tons from 2.64 million tons was due to higher import from Indonesia at competitive costs. The export of palm oil was also declined by 27.5% to 0.21 million metric tons from 0.29 million metric tons due to availability of coconut oil in surplus for domestic use of goods and services at an unattractive price for export.

The export to the UAE was down by 25.6% to 0.13 million metric tons from 0.17 million metric tons due to re-export activity in Iran. The palm kernel oil exports were increased to 7.9% from 1.17million metric tons in 2013 from 1.08 million metric tons. The market for palm kernel oil with China, P.R., was around 0.27 million tons, which is followed by the USA at 0.22 million tons, the European Union (EU) at 0.21 million tons and Japan at 0.08 million tons. While the exports of palm kernel cake increased by 7.9%, to 2.67 million metric tons in 2013 as against 2.47 million tons in 2012. The European Union (EU) was the major importer of palm kernel cake with 0.83 million tons, followed by New Zealand to 0.78 million tons and South Korea to be 0.48 million metric tons.

Exports of oleochemical products rose by 4.8% to 2.73 million tons in 2013 from 2.60 million tons in 2012. The export of oleochemical product was increased due to higher demand from the European Union, China, P.R., the USA, and Japan. The market for oleochemicals where the European Union with 0.63 million metric tons (23%), China, P.R with 0.47 million metric tons (15%), the USA with 0.26 million metric tons (9.7%), Japan with 0.21 million metric tons (7.7%) and India with 0.15 million metric tons (5.3%).

The decline in imports of palm oil by 60.1% to 0.56 million tons from 1.39 million tons recorded in 2012was due to higher domestic palm oil production, which lead to higher supply availability. The major origin of palm oil, which was imported, was from Indonesia, accounted for 89% of palm oil imports in Malaysia.

In 2013, the stock of palm oil was down by 24.4% to close at 1.99 million metric tons as compared to 2.63 million tons recorded in 2012. This was because mainly due to higher exports by 3.1% to 18.12 million tons and was declined the imports by 60.1% to 0.56 million metric tons.

The overall CPO price has shown uptrend in price performance, because of restructuring the CPO export duty. The cost increase was marginal by RM170 from the level of RM2,221 in January2013 to reach RM2,391 in February 2013. The price reflected a downward trend until May 2013 with the second lowest level at RM2,270 which resulted in market fears over the build-up in domestic palm oil inventory levels. However, the price of CPO rebounded to its highest level of

RM2,574 in December 2013 mainly supported by higher export performance during the 3rdquarter of the year.

In 2013, the average annual price of CPO was lower, reaching RM2,371 per ton as against of RM2,764 per ton in 2012 with main market pressure by market sentiments of higher palm oil inventory level of 2.56 million tons and 2.43 million tons in January and February 2013 respectively. In response to the overall decrease of local CPO price, coupled with weaker Brent crude oil price in 2013,the concerns over the uncertainty in global economic outlook in the first half of the year affected the demand for vegetable oils in the world and put pressure to average the price of the processed palm oil products. Brent crude oil price is the benchmark price for purchases of oil worldwide. Brent crude is extracted from the North Sea, and comprises of Brent Blend, Forties Blend and Oserberg and Ekofisk crudes and is also known as BFOE Quotation.

The monetary value of the palm kernel declined in 2013 by RM151 or 9.9% to RM1,371.50 as compared to RM1,522.50 during the same period in 2012. This was mainly due to lower domestic of crude palm kernel oil (CPKO) price during the first half of the year. The price showed down trend of approximately RM590 (18.2%) to RM2, 659.50 from RM3,249.50 which was registered during the same point last year 2012. Fresh Fruit Bunch (FFB) price was lower at 1% Oil Extraction Rate (OER) by 19.2% to RM24.39, which was down from RM30.18 from the last year 2012. The average price of FFB in 2013 was equivalent to RM485 per ton as against of RM615 per ton from the last year 2012 based on the National Oil Extraction Rate. Table 1 shows the performance of Malaysia palm oil industry 2012-2013.

Table 1. Performance of Malaysia palm oil industry 2012-2013

	2012	2013	Differences	
			Volume/Value	%
Planted Area (Hectares)				
Malaysia	**5,076,929**	**5,229,739**	**152,810**	**3.0**
Peninsular Malaysia	2,558,103	2,593,733	35,630	1.4
Sabah	1,442,588	1,475,108	32,520	2.3
Sarawak	1,076,238	1,160,898	84,660	7.9
CPO Production (Tons)				
Malaysia	**18,785,030**	**19,216,459**	**431,429**	**2.3**
Peninsular Malaysia	10,319,774	10,328,025	8,251	0.1
Sabah	5,542,649	5,776,459	233,810	4.2
Sarawak	2,922,607	3,111,975	189,368	6.5

continued on following page

Table 1. Continued

	2012	2013	Differences	
			Volume/Value	%
Closing Stocks (Tons)				
Crude Palm Oil	1,575,103	1,118,531	(456,572)	(29.0)
Processed Palm Oil	1,052,316	868,580	(183,736)	(17.5)
Total Palm Oil	**2,627,419**	**1,987,111**	**(640,308)**	**(24.4)**
Export (Tons)				
Palm Oil	**17,575,486**	**18,146,823**	**571,337**	**3.3**
Palm Kernel Oil	1,084,618	1,170,800	86,181	7.9
Palm Kernel Cake	2,473,732	2,668,393	194,661	7.9
Oleochemicals	2,601,377	2,726,930	125,553	4.8
Biodiesel	28,983	175,032	146,049	6 Folds
Finished Products	361,143	367,161	6,019	1.7
Other Palm Products	465,686	447,568	(18,118)	(3.9)
Total Exports (Tons)	**24,591,025**	**25,702,707**	**1,111,682**	**4.5**
Export Revenue (RM Million)				
Palm Oil	**52,994.56**	**45,269.23**	**(7,725.33)**	**(14.6)**
Palm Kernel Oil	4,097.34	3,406.38	(690.96)	(16.9)
Palm Kernel Cake	1,027.81	1,278.66	250.85	24.4
Oleochemicals	11,458.38	9,297.66	(2,160.72)	(18.9)
Biodiesel	98.44	502.61	404.17	5.1 Folds
Finished Products	1,494.71	1,356.29	(138.42)	(9.3)
Other Palm Products	276.92	252.52	(42.40)	(8.8)
Total Revenue (RM Million)	**71,448.16**	**61,363.35**	**(10,084.81)**	**(14.1)**
Import (Tons)				
Palm Oil	**1,391,483**	**555,776**	**(835,707)**	**(60.1)**
Palm Kernel Oil	366,684	140,435	(226,249)	(61.7)
Price (RM/Tons)				
FFB (Mill Gate)	615.00	485.00	(130.00)	(21.1)
CPO (Local Delivered)	**2,764.00**	**2,371.00**	**(393.00)**	**(14.2)**
Palm Kernel (Ex-Mill)	1,522.50	1,371.50	(151.00)	(9.9)
CPKO (Local Delivered)	3,249.50	2,659.50	(590.00)	(18.2)
RBD Palm Oil (FOB)	2,970.50	2,478.50	(492.00)	(16.6)
RBD Palm Olein (FOB)	2,963.00	2,525.50	(437.50)	(14.8)
RBD Palm Stearin (FOB)	2,786.00	2,257.00	(529.00)	(19.0)
PFAD (FOB)	2,522.50	1,883.50	(639.00)	(25.3)

continued on following page

Table 1. Continued

	2012	2013	Differences	
			Volume/Value	%
OER (%)				
Malaysia	**20.35**	**20.25**	**(0.10)**	**(0.5)**
Peninsular Malaysia	19.98	19.86	(0.12)	(0.6)
Sabah	21.02	21.05	0.03	0.1
Sarawak	20.43	20.12	(0.31)	(1.5)
FFB Yield (Tons/Hectare)				
Malaysia	**18.89**	**19.02**	**0.13**	**0.7**
Peninsular Malaysia	19.05	19.26	0.21	1.1
Sabah	20.40	20.88	0.48	2.4
Sarawak	16.51	16.23	(0.28)	(1.7)

Source: MPOB, 2014.

STRATEGIC PLANNING

Malaysia generates around 11% of Gross National Income (GNI) from the agriculture sector. Palm oil industry is the largest contributor of the total GNI of the country, accounted for 8% or almost RM50 billion(Singh, 2011).Biomass Strategy 2020 which mainly focuses on oil palm as a starting point to have biomass, which can be returned to the field to release its nutrients and replenish the soil. This will lead to ensure the sustainability of fresh fruit bunch (FFB) yields. The variety of uses has very different risk-return policy that gives different technological maturities, global demand potential and competitive dynamics. By 2020, Malaysia's palm oil industry will be generating about 100 million dry tons of solid biomass from empty fruit bunches (EFB), mesocarp fibers (MF), palm kernel shells (PKS), and from oil palm fronds and trunks. The decision for all the palm oil mills will make long term commercial and sustainability merits to reduce the carbon dioxide (CO_2) emission by 12%. For the success of the Biomass Strategy 2020,it is proposed to rely upon strong collaboration among many government agencies, private sector, and research institutions.

The Malaysian government in its 11[th]Malaysia Plan (11MP) will focus more on developing the local palm oil industry, which has supported the gross domestic product (GDP) of the country. The 11[th]Malaysia Plan (11MP) will begin from 2016 and will focus on enhancing the palm oil sectors productivity and sustainability while expanding the markets. The efforts will be taken to enhance and to strengthen the research and development (R&D) and technologies with value added services to downstream activities. Innovative products and the new range of financial contract mechanisms will be inculcated for the prosperity of the Malaysian palm oil industry. This will lead to generate better business strategy and will have better means of risk pricing. Hence, it is a matter of strategic importance to examine the relative strength and to synergies because of rising competitors. The Malaysian palm oil industry (MPOI) is looking at diversifying into niche downstream activities that can fetch higher market value.

To achieve full potential, the Malaysian palm oil industry (MPOI) requires significant coordination and cooperation structures among the plantation owners, which is critical to mobilize the Entry Point Project (EPP) and to accelerate the opportunity. For the success of Malaysia, it is important to make the palm oil industry of very high value industries, so that it can build blocks for future prospects. The Malaysian palm oil industry (MPOI) has committed itself towards transforming Malaysia into a high-income nation by 2020.

TECHNOLOGY TRANSFER

The entrepreneurs are welcome to setup the technologies for commercialization under the mutually agreed terms and conditions. This would help the newcomers and existing players to get the benefit and with this condition, the Malaysian palm oil ultimately transfer the technologies across the industry for better productivity of crude palm oil (CPO). The technology transfer is done through licensing the technologies to the interested parties who would perform the production of the CPO and marketing of the products by itself (Adnan, 2010). The different features of technology transfer are listed in Table 2.

Vision

Sustainable palm oil production occurs in Malaysia by 2020 wherein to have high conservation value area that no longer converted to plantations and measures are in place to reduce biodiversity losses arising from plantation activities.

Goal

Sustainable palm oil production occurs in Malaysia by 2016 where high conservation value forests (HCVF) are no longer converted for plantations and measures are in place to reduce biodiversity losses arising from plantation activities. All palm oil producers commit to and follow the principle of zero conservation of high conservation value areas.

Table 2. Technology transfer features

Serial No.		Technology Transfer Features
1	Licensing	The interested entrepreneurs wish to use the licensed technologies, which are licensed by the Malaysian Palm Oil Board (MPOB), the parents and knowhow of the technologies for commercialization under mutually agreed terms and conditions of the terms of payments of royalties. The licensee will carry out the production and marketing activities by itself and the royalties will be imposed as a percentage of sales or as a lump sum, or both. Licenses can be exclusive or non-exclusive.
2	Plan Development	The Malaysian palm oil board (MPOB) can conduct development work of new products or by using new technologies that can be scaled up as a pilot level. The incurring cost will be negotiated and for some time the governments have provided grants to perform and implement new technologies.
3	Incubator Facilities	The facilities can be used for trial manufacturing and marketing of their products on the payments of fees. Therefore, the entrepreneur can test the product and market on a small scale before making decisions on investing on to start in full swing in producing the products.
4	Consultancy	Technical support will be provide by MPOB the researchers and if required even after commercial production. The consultancy will help in finding the oil palm industry by its research findings for the industrial operations.
5 .	Research & Development Collaborative	Collaboration with outside parties to develop certain technologies on mutually agreed terms and condition. The new technologies will then be transferred to the Malaysian palm oil.

Source: MPOB, 2014.

NATIONAL PROGRAMME STRATEGIES (SUSTAINABLE PALM OIL)

According to World Wide Fund (WWF)-Malaysia Strategies (2012-2020) report, supports and promotes sustainable palm oil production in Malaysia through its conservative strategy. It also addresses the Malaysian palm oil footprint through collaboration with WWF locally and internationally on campaigns and advocacy in the European Union and US markets and in the near future with China, P.R and India(WWF-Malaysia, 2012).The national sustainable palm oil strategies are:

Strategy 1: Advocate spatial planning with consideration of HCV and degraded land.
Strategy 2: Sustainable production and sourcing of palm oil.
Strategy 3: Facilitating partnerships between smallholders and big companies for Best Management Practices (BMP).

The corporations have operations or activities with a significant impact on priority conservation areas. It has recently expanded its efforts in palm oil work by examining the certified sustainable palm oil (CSPO) supply chain, engaging investor markets to promote responsible financing and advocating for smallholder schemes to be Roundtable Sustainable Palm Oil (RSPO) Certified.

In 2013, the demand for palm oil had overtaken the supply of 57.6 million tons. The palm oil production in 2008 was at 43.5 million tons against the demand of 42.6 million tons. According to the Ministry of Plantation Industries and Commodities (MPIC), the industry will be starting the certification scheme based on Malaysian palm oil standards. This scheme will help to raise the image of Malaysian palm oil products in the international markets

CASE DESCRIPTION

Management and Organizational Concerns

The palm oil produced in Malaysia is exported to China, P.R., India, the European Union, United States and other countries constitute around 44% of the total production across the world. It is the world's highest yielding oil crop with an output of 5-10 times greater per hectare than other leading vegetable oils. The oil price in the global market is comparatively low with relative shelf stability and reported nutritional benefits that have natural advantages for a long-term staple of the global diet (Levin, 2012). With an increasing global population and changing consumption habit have increased the demand from crude palm oil (CPO). According to Mielke (2011), the demand for palm oil will increase in the near future to about 65% by 2020.The yields range from less than one to more than 7metric tons of crude palm oil per hectare demonstrates the flow of palm oil from the primary production regions of palm oil i.e., Malaysia to the respective flows into the world's primary palm oil in the consumer markets (India, China, P.R., European Union, and U.S.).

The palm oil production is grown by a proper processing system in a company where the supply chains are easier to manage for quality and consistency. The production using better supply chain, which is complex in nature, requires multiple modifications in corporate ownership with every bit of palm oil passes from growers to mills, refiners, traders, chemical processors, manufacturers to finally create brand name of the products on the shop shelves. The supply chain is an important tool for the creation and position of the brand. It helps by benefiting the wide-range of rural and urban in the developing and developed countries. Considering the supply chain, it can improve competitiveness, reduce overall costs, increase efficiency, and add value to the products. The operation of the supply chain will enhance the efficiency, economic benefits, and proper distribution to ensure the quality and safety of the products. Hence, the supply chain management strategies have great significance to implement brand value without delay.

The supply chain management strategies that perform the brand valuation are not only significant for economic benefits, but also maximize the utilization of resources and reduce resource consumption. It will help to perform the environmental assessment, reduce environmental pollution, and reduce unnecessary negative impacts. Hence, the supply chain which is dynamic and having an integrated system to obtain the optimization of the whole chain (Aimin, 2011). The counterfeit to be a low probability event in the supply chain would carry high risk due to the potential threat to consumer safety and brand equity. As the supply chain becomes increasingly global and complex and its counterfeit has become more proficient the counterfeit goods and components will become more difficult to detect, prevent and remove from the right supply chain (Dollase *et al.*, 2014). As the front of the product is being placed through the fabrication and distribution process many channels have taken in representing an opportunity to counterfeit the product and to enter the supply chain that find its way from consumers to consumers who assume the degree of quality and safety when they buy brands on being trusted. A given product contains palm oil from a single plantation is impossible to be confirmed unless the palm oil is certified across each step of the supply chain. The palm oil supply chain involves many steps from plantations to mill to refinery for further processing and manufacturing of the final products to be used.

The brand Nutella uses palm oil. The company Ferrero that makes Nutella had announced in April 2013 that it will switch to 100% certified Segregated Palm Oil. The Certified Sustainable Palm Oil (CSPO) now represents over 10% of the global palm oil markets (Levin, 2012). The major brands such as Unilever, Walmart, Marks & Spencer, Nestle and many more have made a decision to source only 100% certified sustainable palm oil (CSPO) by 2015. There are currently three main supply chain systems for CSPO; Segregated & Identity Preserved, Mass Balance, and Book and Claim. The segregated palm oil can be traced throughout the supply chain and allows mixing from the multiple certified plantations. The CSPO is collected from the certified plantations in dedicated tanks and is kept separately from non-certified palm oil to the end users. Hence, the end users receive 100% certified palm oil, which is fully traceable. The segregated CSPO systems are managed by UTZ-CERTIFIED (Levin, 2012). The Mass Balance systems are where the certified palm oil is mixed with non-certified and record is kept of the total amount of non-certified palm oil is mixed with the certified palm oil. At the time of selling of palm oil to the end users, palm oilis sold as per the volume of certified and non-certified palm oil and hence mixing of the palm oil takes place in the supply chain without affecting the total volume of the palm oil. It is also managed by UTZ-CERTIFIED (Levin, 2012). The Book and Claim system, the sale of CSPO is separate from the sale of the physical palm oil. In this case, it is being sold as normal, uncertified palm oil, which record the total volumes that can sell Book and Claim certificates to other downstream entities in the supply chain who wish to "offset" the non-sustainable palm oil. It is very easy to monitor, as it is purely a paper-based process. The Book and Claim certificates trading platform is managed by Green Palm (Levin, 2012). However, RSPO provides a time-bound plan that is accountable, which result in timely execution of the best practices on all levels. The firms also report that the RSPO formal systems for managing interactions with local communities that help to make the existing social engagement costs to be more effective. Table 3 shows relative costs and benefits of supply chain mechanism for CSPO.

All the three systems required the plantations to be successfully audited against the CSPO principles and criteria. By adopting the segregation model, the commodity roundtables have copied the supply chain solutions to develop the certification schemes. With a comprehensive production standard and certificate systems, the Roundtable on Sustainable Palm Oil (RSPO) includes better management and agricultural practices, environmental and social risk and management tools and systems to verify and credibly about the information passed to the end users. The RSPO vision is to transform the market into a sustainable palm oil. The RSPO normally looks for developing, implementing, verifying, monitoring, and reviewing credible global standards for the entire supply chain for sustainable palm oil and to involve all the supply chain stakeholders along with civil society and government in the process (Levin, 2012). According to Teoh Cheng Hai, a former Secretary-General of RSPO in Levin (2012) that the success story of certification of the commodity is determined by large extent from the positive business case from the major players along the supply chain. In the case of palm oil, the business case is easy dominated by the financial benefits of undergoing certification and the major key interest is

Table 3. Relative costs and benefits of supply chain mechanism for CSPO

Supply Chain Mechanisms	Overview	Implementation Costs	Level of Traceability
Segregated	CSPO that has been separated and directly tracked throughout the supply chain. Involves coordination of all actors.	High	High
Mass Balance	Delivered palm oil not directly linked with the CSPO at source, but the % CSPO purchased is guaranteed, involves coordination of entire supply chain.	Medium	Medium
Book and Claim	Final product is not CSPO, instead end-user offsets noncertified palm oil purchases with certificates, which are generated by CSPO producers who are not able to sell their product as such. Does not involve coordination of the supply chain.	Low	Low

Source: Levin, 2012.

because of getting the premium price in an effort to meet the stringent requirements of the RSPO. The disagreement between the growers prefer a two-tier market whereby certified palm oil will be supplied to get the premium price to those who need it in the developed countries, while the bulk market perform the Business-As-Usual (BAU) for the uncertified palm oil. The European consumers mainly the multinational companies see sustainability performance as a market requirement, rather than looking as significant aspect for two-level marketplace. The survey, conducted in May 2011, among the nine plantation companies revealed that around 45% of the total production of CSPO globally have showed the implementation of RSPO principles that have resulted in considerable improvements in their triple-bottom line performance. In the plantation level, the effective implementation of best management practices would require RSPO standard that has resulted in the improvements in the operational efficiencies and reductions of the costs. This can be achieved by implementation of the RSPO's eight principles (Table 4)of continuous improvement as a key driver for long term economic viability and also creating its brand image in the dynamic market(Colchester & Jiwan, 2009).The RSPO has1,470 members of which 25% are consumer good manufactures, 22% are palm oil processors and traders, around 8% are growers, and remaining are environmental and conservation NGO's, retailers, and banks and investors (RSPO, 2014) and around 1.97 million hectares of plantation are being certified by RSPO (RSPO, 2014).

Recently, the major companies like Kellogg's, Mars, L'Oreal, Procter & Gamble, and Willmar have pledged to develop full traceable, deforestation-free supply chain (Reusner, 2014). As these companies have made policy for ensuring all palm oil players must be fully traceable back to the growers. While some of the companies

Table 4. RSPO - 8 principles

Serial No.	Principles
1	Commitment to transparency
2	Compliance with applicable laws and regulations
3	Commitment to long-term economic and financial viability
4	Use of appropriate best practices by growers and millers
5	Environmental responsibilities and conservation of natural resources and biodiversity
6	Responsible consideration of employees and of individuals and communities affected by growers and mills
7	Responsible development of new plantings
8	Commitment to continuous improvement in key areas of activity

Source: RSPO, 2014.

have a vision 2020 for achieving this compliance and others like Kellogg's, Willmar along with Unilever, Nestle have recognized the urgency about the need for certified sustainable palm oil in their supply chain by 2015. Due to the companies concerned about the risks associated with deforestation and climate change, which have influenced the Malaysian Palm Oil Industry (MPOI) to adopt and to make commitments and drive change through the supply chain.

To have secure deforestation free supply chain of palm oil, the industry is working to achieve natural segregation of the supply chain where the entire refineries only can process palm oil that is fully traceable to growers. Once the company is committed to make sure to have 100% of certified sustainable supply chain palm oil, the process will lower the cost of logistics and will have overall complexities to secure separate supply chain of palm oil.

Supply chain management has emerged as a vivacious domain for which the companies can be a substance to have the opportunity to overcome the competitions and create a position in the competitive market. Supply chain management strategies are the driving force to reduce price of the product, reduce logistics cost, accelerating the introductions of product and to be a competitive organisation to maintain product availability on the shelf (Kenney, 1998). The supply chain for palm oil is an extremely complex process. According to Shewchuk (1998) there is a requirement of most fitted supply chain management approach depends on the type of business and on the context where the organisation is working. The major contributor in terms of strategy is basically related to lean versus agile. Generally, the main focus is on eliminating waste, reducing costs, and increasing efficiency in lean systems, whereas for agility it mainly focuses on speed, flexibility and responsiveness, which is suitable for highly volatile and unpredictable environments. The potential mixing of supplies from different sources at multiple stages in the supply chain often becomes impossible to trace the sustainability of palm oil. The Malaysian palm oil industry (MPOI) is changing in an effort to underway to develop systems to track and trace certified sustainable palm oil in each of the stage across the supply chain. Moreover, the society also wants to build customer brand loyalty, the optimization of supply chain becomes important aspects of the company as well as the supply chain manager.

Once harvested, the palm fruit must be taken to the mill within 48 hours before it gets rots. Currently, Malaysia is expected to produce 19 million tons whereas the neighbor country, Indonesia is on the track to produce 31 million tons. As per the Ministry of Plantation Industries and Commodities, Datuk Amar Douglas Uggah Embas said that the government is in the consultation with the industry to get the sustainability certification and to experience a sustainable supply chain that will improve transparency within its supply chain.

Current Challenges

In the 21st century, the companies are facing many challenges ranging from globalization, economic uncertainties, increase in demands of the customer and reduce cost by implementing effective and efficient supply chain. According to Mentzer *et al.* (2001), the supply chain is referred to as a set of three or more companies that are directly linked by one or more of the upstream and downstream flows of the products, services, finance, and information from a source of customer. The supply chain has become more and more complex with many challenges that often stand in the way for stakeholder's value and profitability. Due to globalization effect, there will be an increase in pressure to make right decisions for better supply chain to have better performance. Supply chain management has materialized as a critical arena where organizations can significantly have cost reduction and give them cost advantage over competitors and create value in the market. According to Flint (2004), enhanced supply chain can facilitate marketing strategy (e.g. branding, positioning and segmentation), which lead to the creation of superior customer value, satisfaction and loyalty which in turn lead to improved product profit margins on overall firm profitability, corporate growth, and create and sustain brand image.

In the near future, the market environment will be highly challenging and competitive for effective and smarter supply chain to create the product position in the market. In the dynamic environment, a better supply chain management and its strategy could be able to manage efficient chain that will enforce a better brand value of the product. According to Flint (2004), the successful market opportunity analysis in brand positioning and repositioning for new or existing product development will depend on being able to understand how changes occur for customers throughout the supply chains across the globe. Therefore, the supply chain relationships will enable the governing body to define the market coordination in rapid responses to produce changes in the customer value and its competitor move for more dependable performance. With an efficient and effective supply chain management involvement, companies will get the right product, to the right place at the right time, in the right condition, with right price. Due to more turbulent environment and having higher uncertain on decision-making, it will require companies to have strong supply chain management to facilitate marketing strategy implementation. Hence, to respond to economic pressure, the supplier base is in the favor of building better supply chain that will share and reduce the costs (Davis, 2003). Thus, focus mainly on managing the brand in the consumer markets will ignore the need for critical downstream customers and fails to capitalize the potential for using brand that influence to create added value with upstream suppliers (Davis, 2003).

The need for edible oils has increased from the last decade, and there is an increase in the areas of oil crop cultivation particularly for soybean and oil palm. The world output of soybean has increased to 47% to meet the market demand and the major countries that contribute to the world requirement comprising Brazil, Argentina, Bolivia, and Paraguay (Palmoilworld, 2014).The soybean has recorded 92% in output and 66% growth in plant area in the last 5 years. Whereas, the world production of palm oil has grown drastically with a significant jump in production and embedded fields. The rapid growth in the yield of palm oil has touched the rain forest in the South-East Asia area with growing worry about the expansion would result in deforestation that would indirectly affect the rains and the major concern about the very rare species, which are dying to be out. The palm oil is widely used vegetable soil in the world, and over half of that is used for package products on supermarket shelves from bakery snacks to cosmetics and lipstick. Mostly, the brand executives and marketing personnel spend very less time in thinking about the company's supply chain process which they think as a nuisance or as irrelevant (Benson & Kinsella, 2004). Lack of coordination between the supply chain and marketing is a brand nightmare and supply chain capabilities can make or break the ability to give impact on brand equity positively or negatively. Customers want to associate with the brands that keep the promises. This majorly requires knowledge of supply chain to meet the brand needs and thus the supply chain should support and build the brand. However, it is an era of customer demands and supply chain is often represented as a critical opportunity for the organisation to build or to destroy brand equity (Benson & Kinsella, 2004). Hence, it is important for the marketing executives to pay more attention to their supply chain management.

If the world output of palm oil is expected to grow at the current pace, then palm oil growing is to receive a more honest apprehension of several subjects related to forestry, sustainability of the palm oil organisation, possessing a sustainable supply chain, and creating and preserving brand loyalty for the Malaysian palm oil industry (MPOI).The major players in the Malaysian palm oil industry (MPOI) are being grouped into clusters covering upstream production, downstream producers, exporters and importers, customers, government authorities and other actors such as NGOs.

Major palm oil consuming companies such as Unilever, Nestle and Starbucks, which have taken steps to address the impact of their supply chain by promising to purchase only certified sustainable palm oil are developing the pressure including consumers and investors. Rather than buying from any sources that do not follow any standards of supply chain, the companies are purchasing large quantities of palm oil for their branded products and leveraging their purchasing power to influence the palm oil supply chain. If the palm oil production continuities with the clearing of forests, destruction of biodiversity and carbon emission then the industry is likely to seal its own fate. Adopting sustainability practices with a more sustainable supply chain measure, might have short term implementation costs, but will lead to significant price premiums (Grayson & Stampe, 2012) that will have an effect in placing the products. By adopting the sustainable palm oil practices, palm oil companies can increase access to global markets, provide commercial opportunities, and enhance brand reputation. The companies that join the RSPO can enhance the palm growers to access large US and European Union markets who are moving towards sustainable proprietary supply chain to have control over the source of materials. This will help to gain trust within the government and among the local and international growers to have expanded opportunities from the preferred supplier.

SOLUTIONS AND RECOMMENDATIONS

The one promise that is expected of every brand is by delivering the right product, to the right place, at the right time. The supply chain capabilities can make or ruin companies' ability to live up to that hope. Consequently, the supply chain can powerfully affect brand equity, positively or negatively. Brands with substantial equity favorably influence the purchasing behavior and command a price premium, and have the referral to generate customers (Benson & Kinsella, 2004). The efficient and effective supply chain would also help to create a better marketing strategy that will lead to place the product in the market and will create satisfied customers and create brand loyalty towards the product (Flint, 2004). Thus, integrating supply chain is the key aspects of creating success factors for brand management and its activity that will have great impact on creating and protecting the brand in the market (Newman, 2013). Hence, the lack of coordination with supply chain and marketing will generate a brand nightmare for the product. So poor supply chain integration will drive the customers away.

Positive buying experiences will set the stage for positive using experiences. Customers want to associate themselves with brands that maintain their promises. The companies think that the brand understands their needs, and they feel honest about practicing it. These customers can be the most forgiving when a product requires repair or replenishment and tend to be among the most loyal customers when repurchase decisions come around.

The new level of supply chain completions would present tremendous challenges to brand managers (Davis, 2003). While the companies that have not invested in supply chain among the partners in the brand management may be advised to do so to secure their positions among the trade partners in their supply chain and also to be an agile firm. Agile firms will be able to leverage upon the high levels of brand awareness and its positive brand image that will increase marketing communication effectiveness. This calls for both knowledge of supply chain and the leadership to regulate it to satisfy trade name needs. Besides, this will be a starting point for the company to start out using supply chain to sustain and build brand (Benson & Kinsella, 2004).

CONCLUSION

This case exhibits the importance of supply chain management and its strategies in creating and positioning of the brand of the product in the dynamic market. It will play a fundamental role in understanding the concept and importance of supply chain transparency in the companies. This case study suggests the pathway of understanding the importance of right decision at the right time that will create and understanding of the supply chain to retain customers, to provide excellent services, and to have clear communications. The importance of supply chain management became the vital importance of placing the product in the market. The strategies have been designed to drive costs and discover a clearer sense of the relationship between supply chain management and brand equity. It is important for a supply chain manager to understand that there is an immense amount of responsibility that creates the brand of the product on every action. So everyone right down to the person from harvesting of the fresh fruit bunch (FFB) to delivering of the FFB to the mills and to refineries and to all the activities of the downstream to perform their job will enhance or destroy the brand across the complete supply chain of Malaysian Palm Oil Industry. Hence, every bit of supply chain is important to create and position the product as a brand and to enhance customer loyalty.

REFERENCES

Adnan, H. (2010). Dealers unsung heroes in palm oil supply chain. *The Star Online*. Retrieved May 27, 2014, from http://www.thestar.com.my/Story/?file=/2010/12/21/business/7656951&

Aimin, H. (2011). A research on the supply chain management of brand agricultural products. In *Proceedings of Internet Technology and Applications (iTAP)*. Academic Press. doi:10.1109/ITAP.2011.6006258

Benson, J. P., & Kinsella, B. (2004). How your supply chain can build or destroy your brand. *SSRN Electronic Journal*. doi:10.2139/ssrn.611543

Colchester, M., & Jiwan, N. (2009). *RSPO principles and criteria for sustainable palm oil production*. RSPO. Retrieved March 15, 2014, from http://rspo.org

Davis, D. F. (2003). The effect of brand equity in supply chain relationships. Knoxville, TN: University of Tennessee. Retrieved from http://trace.tennessee.edu/utk_graddiss/1996

Dollase, S., Joyner-Payne, S., Small, R., Milligan, R., Schneitler, G., Weavil, M., … Asher, R. (2014). *Brand protection and supply chain integrity: Methods for counterfeit detection, prevention and deterrence a best practices guide*. Grocery Manufacturers Association. Retrieved from www.gmaonline.org

Evans, P. (2014). Unilever commits to sustainable palm oil by end of 2014. *European Business News*. Retrieved April 5, 2014, from http://online.wsj.com/news/articles/SB10001424052702304644104579I

Flint, D. J. (2004). Strategic marketing in global supply chains : Four challenges. *Industrial Marketing Management*, *33*(1), 45–50. doi:10.1016/j.indmarman.2003.08.009

Grayson, J., & Stampe, J. (2012). *Palm oil investor review: Investor guidance on palm oil the role of investors in supporting the development of a sustainable palm oil industry*. RSPO. Retrieved from http://panda.org

Kenney, J. (1998). Meeting the challenge of supply chain management. In *Competing through supply chain management* (pp. 1–6). Academic Press.

Lee, H. L. (2004). The triple-A supply chain. *Harvard Business Review*, 102–112. PMID:15559579

Levin, J. (2012). *Profitability and sustainability in palm oil production - Analysis of incremental financial costs and benefits of RSPO compliance*. WWF, FMO, and CDC. Retrieved from http://panda.org/finance

Mielke, T. (2011). Global supply and demand outlook of palm and lauric oils - Trends and future prospects. *MPOC*. Retrieved April 28, 2014, from http://www.pointers.org.my/report_details

MPOB. (2014). *The official portal of Malaysian palm oil board*. MPOB. Retrieved February 15, 2014, from http://www.mpob.gov.my

Newman, W. (2013). Focused brand management via supply chain visibility. *Supply Chain Management (SAP SCM)*. Retrieved January 20, 2014, from http://scn.sap.com/community/scm/blog/2013/05/15/focused-brand-management-via-supply-chain-visibility

Palmoilworld. (2014). *Palmoil world*. Retrieved March 28, 2014, from http://www.palmoilworld.org

Patel, S. (2013, July 18). Outline of production: Palm fruit to product. *Bloomberg Business Week*. Retrieved from http://www.schusterinstituteinvestigations.org/#!palm-oil-supply-chain/c1q1d

Performance Management and Delivery Unit. (2010). Deepening Malaysia's palm oil advantage. In *Economic transformation programme: A roadmap for Malaysia* (pp. 281–314). Academic Press; doi:10.1002/047167849X.bio071

RSPO. (2014). *Roundtable sustainable palm oil*. Retrieved March 28, 2014, from http://rspo.org

Shewchuk, J. P. (1998). Agile manufacturing : One size does not fit all. In U. S. Bititci & A. S. Carrie (Eds.), Strategic management of the manufacture value chain (vol. 2, pp. 143–150). Springer US. doi:10.1007/978-0-387-35321-0_16

Singh, K. J. D. (2011). *National biomass strategy 2020: New wealth creation for Malaysia's palm oil industry*. Academic Press.

von Reusner, L. (2014). How investors are changing the palm oil supply chain. *greencentury.com*. Retrieved April 28, 2014, from http://greencentury.com/how-investors-are-changing-the-palm-oil-supply

WWF-Malaysia. (2012). *WWF-Malaysia strategy 2012-2020*. WWF-Malaysia. Retrieved May 8, 2014, from www.panda.org

KEY TERMS AND DEFINITIONS

Brand Equity: A group of brand assets and liabilities of different attributes of the brand to increase value to the firm's balance sheet to endow a product as perceived by an individual consumer.

Malaysian Palm Oil Industry (MPOI): The multi-stakeholders eventually have useful information resources to get people together and prosper them. The leaders in the Malaysian palm oil industry are very moderate and willing to put their time and resources to get the most of it and at the same time maintaining an eye on sustainability topics.

Palm Oil: It is extracted from the mesocarp of the fruit of an oil palm species called *Elaeis guineensis*.

Roundtable on Sustainable Palm Oil (RSPO): A non-profit association with multi-stakeholder initiative and dedication to promote sustainable production of palm oil worldwide through cooperation and open dialogue for the ultimate goal of transforming markets to make sustainable palm oil norms. Palm growers, oil processors, dealers, consumer goods manufacturers, retailers, investors and social and environmental NGO's as the member of RSPO.

Supply Chain Management: An integrative philosophy to manage the sourcing, total flow of distribution channel from supplier to end user, and control of materials utilizing total systems perspective across the multiple functions.

Supply Chain Strategies: The way the business operates and have an impact on efficiency and productivity on other business in the supply chain. Supply chain strategies are divided into various categories namely lean, agile, postponement, and speculation.

Sustainability: An endurance of systems and processes for everything that need for the survival and well-being for present and hereafter. It compromises of three pillars as social, economic and environment.

ENDNOTES

[1]   1USD=RM3.22 as on 28 May, 2014.

Chapter 6
Building and Development of Dairy "Dana" Brand

Boris Milović
Sava Kovacevic Vrbas, Serbia

ABSTRACT

For success it is not enough to have the best and highest quality product, best price, the best distribution network, and excellent promotion; the most important thing is how the consumer values it. The market for dairy products in Serbia is dominated by products that were perceived as average and ordinary, consumed simply to meet basic nutritional needs. Agricultural company Sava Kovacevic had great products, but not brands. Development of brand "Dana" is focused on that specific benefits found to provide consumers a brand as well as a range of values that a new brand represents. The very brand strategy is developed after a detailed analysis of the product, consumers for which it is intended (their lifestyles, habits, attitudes, etc.), competition and market conditions, market position of competing brands, and their communication with customers and the general public. Therefore, brand image of the product is built along with its unique position in the market.

COMPANY OVERVIEW

Agricultural joint-stock company "Sava Kovacevic" was founded in 1946 and since 2003 after privatization exists as a joint-stock company representing an influential agro complex in Backa which includes significant agricultural production.

DOI: 10.4018/978-1-4666-7393-9.ch006

- Husbandry and olericulture on 4000 ha (wheat, barley, corn, sunflower, soybean, sugar beet...).
- Animal husbandry (dairy cows, beef cattle, calves, 2500 head of cattle).
- Meat production.
- Production and processing of milk.
- Seed processing.

Dairy farm does business within the company since 1948 and it was first conceived only for milk pasteurization. However with the growth of the company the dairy farm was developed also and other dairy products were introduced. "Mlekara Sava Kovacevic" was fitted for production work for the first time in 1961 at the location at which it resides to this day. Capacity for milk processing was on average around 2000 litres per day. Milk was delivered from a nearby farm, and also bought from private farms.

After that in 1971 reconstruction of the dairy farm was carried out and the capacity was increased to 8000 litres of milk per day. Today installed capacity of the dairy farm is 35000 litres of raw milk. Its production mix includes 12 different dairy products.

"Mlekara Sava Kovacevic" joint-stock company has in 2007 introduced a new product brand of yogurt with 3.2% milk fat content which can today be found in the market under the name "Dana." During 2007 all of the product line of the dairy farm are placed on the market with this name. It employs 34 employees that process about 2'300'000 litres of milk annually, with a tendency of increasing the amount of processed milk, introduction of new products etc. Website of the dairy farm is http://www.mlekaradana.rs/.

"Mlekara Sava Kovacevic" represents one of the medium sized dairy farms in Serbian market and the development of this brand is crucial for its existence and growth. Brand strategy is made after detailed analysis of the product itself, analysis of consumers for whom it was intended (their lifestyle, habits, views...), analysis of competition and state of the market, analysis of market positions of competing brands and their communication with consumers and general public. These efforts are directed toward finding specific benefits consumer gains from the brand as well as values which the new brand represents. Based on this the brand image of the product is built and its unique position on the market as well as in the consumer's mind is determined.

CHARACTERISTICS OF THE DAIRY PRODUCTS MARKET AND MARKET ENVIRONMENT

Intense competition in the market and variable conditions of business are steering companies to constantly seek new sources of competitive advantages. Market globalization has unified consumers in the demands they ask of companies and benefited the development of new marketing strategies which enable the growth of satisfaction and loyalty of consumers toward the brand, directly implying the improvement of financial performance in business. Brand management allows companies to reach global market relevance for a longer period of time. In accordance with dynamic changes in the environment and with anticipating competing trends, company management formulates long-term marketing and brand strategy. Creating and maintaining strong brands allows companies higher market dispersion, because of which brand management activities have become marketing priority. Brand management has become a critical factor for company competitiveness as a response to the dominant effect of globalization on business, market liberalization, removal of trade barriers and more intense competition in the business environment. Complex functions of brand management and the strategic significance of creating a brand of high value demands a systematic approach to business. Everyday expansion of new brands and their global availability points to a large profit potential of this field. Application of brand management concept isn't limited to specific types of activity, which further contributes to the concept value. Accelerated trend of globalization and company efforts to keep existing and gain new consumers in conditions of rapid technological changes and innovative accomplishments, and under pressure from strong competition, implies business analysis in conditions of globalization.

Brand serves to identify products and services, as well as the manufacturer (salesman). However at the same time it often serves to identify consumers themselves. Main task of marketers is monitoring and research of existing and newly developed possibilities in the dairy company environment. Ability and speed of adjusting to changes in the environment are critical variables in the success of the company in modern economy. Degree of adjustability is higher if the company is forward thinking and capable to learn from its and other's experience. Environment constantly creates new possibilities. Significance given inside the company to the strategic analysis of economic environment depends, firstly, on the degree of influence of the environment on the dairy company business, and secondly from its character (first of all level of turbulence). Environment is a starting point from which "Mlekara Sava Kovacevic" starts researching possibilities and detecting threats. Environment is comprised of all forces and agents which influence the ability of the dairy company to successfully do business on the target market. Analysis of the dairy companies' environment represents determination of possibilities and dangers for each company individually. The study of marketing practice cases of different cultures is useful for a company wishing to expand its business horizons and become part of the competitive environment. Collecting marketing data is conditional for development of marketing plans. On the market, on one side, demands and needs converge, and on another side, differences in demands and needs as a consequence of cultural differences are observed. Marketing is regaining the strategic role in modern business. By developing a single approach for several markets, company can achieve benefits on the basis of economy of scale, through time saving and cost effective development of special strategy for individual culture. (Solomon, Bamossy, Askegaard, & Hogg, 2006.)

In Serbia there are 230 dairy farms which annually buy and process 900 million litres of milk. The country produces 1.8 billion litres of milk annually, and around 50% is spent. In times when cattle numbers in Serbia drop by a factor of 1.5-2%, milk production has stabilized to the level of minimal consumption of 100 litres per capita annually. Currently in Serbia there are around a million head of cattle, including 700'000 cows and in-calf heifers. This is the same number of cattle as in 1910. At the same time, with reducing the livestock numbers, the number of mini dairy farms has increased, especially in the last three years, when there was the most intense process of privatization. In short, decrease of milk production and the available market attracted foreign investors, which bought large dairy farms. This sets the task for the "Mlekara Sava Kovacevic" to create a recognizable product and with that a new policy was adopted to distribute the dairy farm products under the brand Dairy Farm "Dana."

Stating the factors which influence the complex creation of brand values requires five gradual steps (Lindemann & Valuation, 2004):

1.   Market segmentation,
2.   Financial analysis,
3.   Demand analysis,
4.   Competitiveness benchmark, and
5.   Calculating brand value.

While researching the brand of dairy products it is necessary to pay attention to individual characteristics of the market:

- Existence of a large number of need holders. In principle there is an entire series of need holders that are dislocated across the entire Serbian market, although density varies in regards to soil configuration, road development, population intensity of individual regions in the country etc.

- With consumers of dairy products mostly emotional motives prevail while shopping. Large role in the forming of habits have experiences of others, subjective views of consumers, salesman recommendation, promotion influence etc.
- Dairy products market is characterized by a certain dynamics of sales. There is a pronounced growth of sales in different times of year, for example higher sales of milk during winter and yogurt during summer.
- Products compete with each other with different brands.
- Competitiveness on this market is extremely strong due to a large number of manufacturers of the same or similar products.
- Channels of distribution with these products are more complex. Manufacturers are unable to completely control distribution channels. The majority of them ship their products to the wholesaler, while the vast majority of consumers supplies themselves in retail shops. The only complete control manufacturers can achieve is through owning a retail network.
- Products of dairy industry are subject to the influence of trendiness, style, habits, taste. So for most of these products constant perfecting and adjusting of the design, packaging, product mix and innovations is necessary.
- Packaging, packing and labeling of products have different functions for these products: product protection, ability to easily manipulate and promotional function.
- It is necessary for the dairy companies to be connected with trade companies in order to be able to notice and react to consumer demands in time.

DAIRY PRODUCTS MARKET SEGMENTATION

Segmentation of the dairy products market can be defined as company efforts to group consumers in such manner so that their reaction to the marketing mix instruments (dairy product, its price, marketing channels and forms of promotion) is similar, in other words that reactions vary more between different segments compared to within the segment.

Dairy products market segmentation essentially means division of the entire market into smaller segments in order to conduct special company strategy on these smaller parts of the market. Important condition of segmentation is that the segments be as homogenous as possible. Determining of the target segment or "focus group" on the market serves the process of production optimization.

Market segmentation starts from heterogeneity of the market and the fact that it comprises of a larger number of smaller homogenous submarkets. By dividing the market we observe different degrees of satisfied needs of individual consumer segments. Market segments whose needs aren't satisfied present potential possibilities for the company. Segmentation leads to a clearer overview and a more complete satisfaction of consumer needs, medium and long term and not just short term satisfaction of consumer needs.

Every focus group requires its own research approach, its own model with which we achieve depth, and overview of the market.

Market segment, as a relatively homogenous whole enables the dairy company the following:

- Establishing contact with need holders, meaning to perceive their desires, needs and possibilities,
- More efficient positioning relative to the competition (to achieve competitive advantage of one relative to other dairy companies),
- Overview of tendencies to change in different market segments,
- Getting ideas to expand the mix of dairy products.

Dairy products market segmentation also enables lowering of competitive pressure in the dairy products market; by choosing the focus segment, or differentiating products or the whole line of products relative to the competition. Brands identify the source or the creator of a product, and enable consumers – either individuals or organizations – to impose liability on a certain manufacturer or distributor. Consumers can assess the same product differently relative to their previous experience with that product and its marketing agenda. Consumers also recognize which brands satisfy, and which do not satisfy their needs. Since consumers' lives are becoming more and more complex and fast, as well as the fact that they have less and less time, ability of the brand to simplify decision making and reduce risk is truly priceless. Brands can represent a certain synonym for a certain level of quality, so that the satisfied consumers can easily choose again. Loyalty to the brand enables the company predictability and certainty of demand, and also forms barriers that complicate entering of other companies on the market. Competing companies can easily copy manufacturing processes and product design, but they cannot easily rival long lasting impressions in minds of individuals and organizations, that result from years of marketing activities and product experience. From this angle, branding is a powerful tool for securing competitive advantage. Dairy farm "Dana" as a small dairy farm neglects differences in market segments and approaches the entire market with a single offer.

Criteria for Dairy Products Market Segmentation

Brands influence the choice of consumers, but the influence varies depending on the market in which the brand exists. It is necessary to divide the market into homogenous consumer groups that do not overlap according to the criteria such as: product or service, distribution channels, consummation habits, level of purchase subtlety, geographically, existing and new customers etc. Brand is valued in each segment and by summing up values of all individual segments the total brand value is obtained.

Determining the basis for market segmentation is a critical factor in defining the target market. Authors state different bases for market segmentation. According to one of them criteria for segmentation can be divided into:

- **Demographic:** Age, sex, occupation, education, size of family, etc.
- **Geographic:** Country, region, city, village, climate, population density, etc.
- **Psychological:** Sociability, traits, ambitions,etc.
- **Customer Behavior:** Sensitivity to quality, prices, consumer habits, loyalty to the dairy product brand or manufacturer, purchase motives, etc.

Most often as the basis for segmentation geographic, demographic and economic traits of consumers are used.

Geographic segmentation is characterized by flexibility and simplicity which contributes to its widespread use in practice. Geographic segments are often available through local media (newspapers, TV, radio and local magazines). As it is based on static approach instead of causality, it is only a useful starting point for segmentation. Geographic segmentation, as one of the oldest bases for market segmentation, is based on the assumption that people living in the same region have similar needs and desires, tastes and preferences and that they are different from the needs and desires of people in other regions. Despite the fact that people are more uniform today, regional differences still exist.

In Serbia village settlements make for 78%, mixed make for 17% and 5% city settlements. In cities with over 100'000 inhabitants resides 16.5% of citizens. Share of city population since 1948 to 2002 has increased from 17% to 47% of population. Dairy companies decide to appear in one or more geographic areas and modify their marketing mix according to different regional tastes and preferences.

Family, its size and phase in the life cycle is also an important variable for segmentation. The fact is that the needs, desires and preferences differ in individual phases of life cycle of a family because of differences in the financial situation and priorities of needs and confectionery companies adjust their product line to accommodate them.

Next important and probably the most used method of segmentation is division of the market based on demographic variables. Reason for this is based on the fact that desires and preferences of consumers and the degree of use are often tightly connected to demographic variables and the fact that they are easier to identify and be measured compared to most other types of variables.

Age is a useful and often used variable because desires and capacities of consumers are changed during their life. The entire population of Serbia are consumers of dairy products, and according to age groups they prefer different products.

Estimates of population structure indicate an aging population. At the same time generation between 20 and 34 years of age are diminishing. For milk and dairy products manufacturers and also for Dairy farm "Dana" this means orientation toward seniors and their needs. At the same time packaging of products will be directed primarily on this segment of consumers.

Consumers within the same geographic or demographic group can exhibit highly distinctive psychological profiles. That is why those characteristics should be taken into account and divide consumers based on their affiliation to a certain social stratum or class, way of life or personal characteristics.

In order to maximize the use of market segments they have to fulfil the following conditions:

- They have to be able to be identified in regards to different needs or benefits they require, geographic, demographic or psychological traits,
- Members of a market segment have to express reactions to instruments of marketing to justify their special treatment,
- Segments have to be large enough, in order to be profitable, and stable in size and structure, or more preferably to grow,
- They have to be available, to be able to communicate with them.

Dairy companies should discern consumers of individual types of dairy products. For example, companies offering different kinds of yogurt are making a choice of an individual market segment. Thus, for example "Suboticka Mlekara" for special consumer segments of diabetics and "healthy food consumers" offers yogurt Ella, AB yogurt (probiotic), Yogurt 5 (with vitamins).

The goal of market segmentation for Dairy Farm "Dana," at the same time its significance, is identifying and choosing target markets considering that the potential of a dairy company is limited and has to be rationally focused on individual segments. Market segmentation reveals possibilities of a certain market segment that Dairy Farm "Dana" is facing. Market segmentation directs positioning of a product toward consumers of dairy products and competition. Market segmentation assists dairy companies to accommodate certain needs of consumers. By dividing the market company observes a different degree of satisfaction of individual groups of consumers. Parts of the market whose needs aren't satisfied represent potential for the company. Segmentation leads to a clearer overview of needs of individual groups of consumers (Milisavljevic, 2004).

Adapting the instruments of the marketing mix of Dairy Farm "Dana" to the special needs and demands of individual consumer segments, based on market segmentation, more complete consumer satisfaction is achieved, while simultaneously realizing profit and good customer relations.

Dairy products market segmentation directs manufacturers to address certain consumer segment with their marketing mix in order to increase product consumption. It is estimated that, due to decreased natality, by 2011 20% of population of Europe will be people over 60 years of age, and at the same time population between 20 and 34 years of age will have a tendency to diminish so dairy companies will adapt their product line for this consumer segment.

Dairy products are intended for human nutrition and as such fall into a fundamental group of human food. Basic characteristic of human food is inevitability of everyday consumption. Need for every human to access a certain amount of food with nutrients every day imposes conscious organizing of its production and consumption. Basic characteristic of dairy products is high content of proteins necessary for normal growth and development of organism and performing vital functions.

The most numerous consumers of these products are the population, which in their nutrition use dairy products. Number of citizens directly determines the scale of total consumption of dairy products. Supplying the population for the most part is done through retail.

Serbia isn't really a large consumer of milk. While in Romania annual consumption of milk is around 1.5 billion litres, in surrounding countries: Bulgaria 676 million, Hungary 644 million, in Serbia it is around 382 million litres. What can be viewed as positive while talking about Serbian market is an increase in consumption of milk and dairy products during the last five years.

Table 1. Consumption of milk and dairy products per member of the household in Serbia

	All Households		Non-Agricultural Households	
	1991	**2002**	**1991**	**2002**
Milk, litres	98.1	93.9	105.0	95.3
Dairy products	14.7	9.5	15.9	9.0

Source: Poll about household consumption 2003, Republic Statistics Bureau Belgrade, 2003.

Structure of dairy capacities built by the end of 1970s in Serbia was determined by non-market factors. Problem of working capital was solved by crediting which involved monetary expansion and price ratios were incompatible with price ratios in the global market. Long-term development strategy was based on large investments resting on large loans and high degree of market closure toward foreign competitors.

COMPETITIVENESS OF DAIRY PRODUCTS

Control of competitive ability is a very important point for all companies in the dairy industry. Activities and acting of competing dairy companies, concepts and strategies of appearances on individual markets largely influence the behavior of Dairy Farm "Dana." Analysis of competition enables scanning of the environment and provides data for timely response and formulation of a competitive brand strategy. Companies should monitor their competitors, in order to devise and implement adequate brand positioning strategy. Identifying competitors is only seemingly simple task. "Competitive Myopia" – focusing on actual competitors instead of latent – helped displace some businesses (Kotler & Keller, 2006). Managers often view competition too narrowly, assuming it only happens between current competitors.

There are three main types of competition:

- **Generic Competition:** This competition implies competition between dairy companies and all other participants in the distribution of national income.
- **Competition between Products:** Implies, for example, contest between two different dairy products.
- **Competition between Companies Manufacturing the Same or Similar Products**: Implies competition between dairy industry companies.

Industrial dairy farms are the biggest manufacturers of pasteurized milk. Small dairy farms don't participate in the production of pasteurized milk, seeing as they don't have any interest in producing base product whose added value is lowest. The most developed dairy in Serbia is "Imlek" covering 40% of total milk production in the country (TGI-Serbia, 2014).

Understanding the concept of competitiveness and knowing the competition are necessary in the process of creating a business strategy of a company. Based on an estimate of internal capacities and research of the competition, company differentiates its assortment. Strategy of branding can be the source of competitive advantage. Managing competitiveness enables gaining sustainable competitive advantage in the long-term. In that context we start at analysis of competitiveness concept on a macro and micro level, and the important elements in the process of creating a competitive strategy. Building a strong brand in the market is the goal of many organizations because it provides a host of benefits to a firm, including less vulnerability to competitive marketing actions, larger margins, greater intermediary co-operation and support and brand extension opportunities. (Delgado-Ballester & Munuera-Alema, 2005).

New competition manifests itself in different ways: competitors wish to increase sales in new markets, they are searching for more cost effective ways of expanding distribution, designing private brands in order to offer cheaper alternative to the consumers or use the power of their megabrands and by their extension enter into new categories of products.

Competitors to Dairy Farm "Dana" besides large are also small dairy farms and imported products – above all else companies "Danone" and "Lura," which is the leader in the region when it comes to dairy industry. "Danone" started an aggressive campaign with their fruit yogurts, and "Lura" Zagreb has managed to become the owner of "Somboled."

Managing the data, Dairy Farm "Dana" starts to develop its own strategy, which means to create product policy, prices, promotions, distribution, which should secure the following:

- Better product or of the same quality as the competitor's.
- Affordable price.
- Availability for the consumer.
- Availability of information about the dairy product to the consumer and potential consumer.

For successful marketing appearance and competitiveness in the market of dairy products it is necessary to execute organizational changes in the company, as a prerequisite to accepting the marketing concept in business.

Dairy Farm "Dana" is oriented toward satisfying the needs and desires of consumers. By satisfying consumers an image of dairy products and/or manufacturer is created and loyalty of the consumers is established, which implies increase in revenue and profit.

SWOT ANALYSIS

The fundamental problem of managing marketing activities of a dairy company as it was mentioned consists of harmonizing controlled variables (products, prices, marketing channels and promotion, to put it simply: marketing mix), on which confectionery companies can directly influence with their decisions and actions, with uncontrolled variables (competition, suppliers, public, intermediaries and also demographic economic environment, technological, sociocultural and political and legal environment in which the dairy company does business), to which the company has to adjust.

Uncontrolled variables are external, given conditions in which the organization has to exist, while controlled variables are the instruments of the marketing mix under its direct control with whose help it adjusts to the conditions of the environment, in order to successfully achieve set marketing goals through planning, organizing, execution, control.

As the basis of decisions about allocating resources on instruments of the marketing mix and in order to define possible models, combination of mentioned methods was used, information and results discovered by researching instruments were included in the SWOT matrix in order to predict the future. SWOT matrix is a concept which should enable the dairy industry systematic analysis of threats and possibilities of the environment as well as their harmonization with its own strong and weak points. SWOT analysis points only to the key factors, such as: fundamental differences between dairy companies of Serbia and Dairy Farm "Dana," quality of the dairy product, prices, channels of distribution, market share etc. This model is given in Table 2.

By observing the aforementioned Dairy Farm "Dana" can conclude the following:

- Consumers have a wide assortment of dairy products offered by the competition.

Table 2. SWOT matrix for dairy farm "Dana"

Strengths:	Weaknesses:
• Consumer loyalty for traditionally known products of the Dairy Farm "Dana." • Market knowledge. • Possibility of innovating existing products. • Existence of owned distribution network.	• Underdeveloped brands. • Obsolete technologies. • Underdeveloped market image. • Vulnerability from foreign competition. • Lack of funds for investments in new technologies and developing new brands. • Inadequate product packaging.
Opportunities:	Threats:
• Increase in purchasing power and living standards of consumers. • Development of new, unique technologies. • "Health food" trend.	• Inability to adopt new technological solutions. • Developed and numerous competition. • Change in needs, desires and demands of customers and the inability to adjust. • Sudden change in general level of prices in retail.

- Products of the dairy industry can quantitatively satisfy the local demand and the market is dominated by large manufacturers. So for example direct competitors in markets in which Dairy Farm "Dana" does business are Dairy Farm Novi Sad, Dairy Farm Subotica, Imlek and Somboled.
- Products of Dairy Farm "Dana" aren't equipped with an adequate packaging.
- Products of Dairy Farm "Dana" are technologically behind foreign products.
- The most prospective market for long-term placement is health-safe food as a trend present amongst consumers. Dairy Farm "Dana" uses only milk from its own farm.
- Higher quality of dairy product allows for a higher price.
- Higher price of the dairy product leads a consumer to think the product is of higher quality.
- Prices of dairy products follow the increase of retail prices.
- Dairy Farm "Dana" has long-term relationships with distributors.
- In places of supply consumers have a possibility of multiple choices.
- Higher expenditures for economic advertising reduce the sensitivity of consumers in regards to the price, meaning that it is possible to obtain consumer preference towards a certain dairy product.
- Expenditures for economic propaganda have greater impact on product sales with lower prices rather than with higher.
- Bigger expenditures for economic propaganda reduce the total cost of sales.
- Economic propaganda represents the most important instrument of the promotion mix in the phase of introducing potential customers with the dairy product because it is directed to the widest possible auditorium.
- Price of products of Dairy Farm "Dana" is acceptable compared to its competitors.

Fundamental strength of Dairy Farm "Dana" is the ability to completely satisfy the level of consumption in the market in which it does business and the product assortment that enables the sales of all processed amounts. However Dairy Farm "Dana" should still realize rational allocation of its resources on individual instruments of the marketing mix because it has limited funds. The choice of strategies for the appearance of the dairy company in the market should provide satisfaction of consumers' needs and realization of profit. Turbulent factors of the environment in which Dairy Farm "Dana" does business demands an active relationship of the company and those factors so management needs a marketing plan.

Goals of Development of the Brand Dairy Farm "Dana"

Role of the brand in gaining consumers and the influence on the satisfaction as a result of created and delivered value is significant. Branded world becomes a reality, and business people see this as a chance and/or threat for business and results. Most of consumers live with brands and some even develop a higher level of affection (loyalty) and personalization. By developing Dairy Farm "Dana" brand the following will be enabled:

- Faster development of marketing functions of the company,
- Satisfaction of desires and needs of consumers in a faster and more efficient way,
- Brand enables business prosperity for Dairy Farm "Dana."

Brand is an important tool in marketing, because it enables bringing products and services closer to the customers. New findings discovered while working with brands of products and services can be used in marketing practice.

Oscillations in quality of procured raw materials can very badly influence the quality of the product which in conditions of the same competition in the market can lead to loss of the market, inability to place products on the market and increase in production costs.

Dairy Farm "Dana" will because of changed market conditions, customer demands, fierce competition be forced to direct its activity on new development programs. Within its promotional activities it is important that Dairy Farm "Dana" created its web site on the internet to establish business connections with distant partners for more successful realization of its products as well as to obtain the best quality raw materials and also to enable contact with customers of Dairy Farm "Dana" products, still these efforts are not sufficient.

DAIRY PRODUCT

Dairy Product, represents the basic instrument of the marketing mix on which depend and by which are other instruments directed. By one definition product is a package of physical, service and symbolic advantages expected to satisfy or be useful for the customer. Product is, in essence, carrier of growth and development of every dairy company. By constant discovering, launching of new and changing existing products, dairy companies achieve their growth. In essence, marketing orientation of dairy companies means planning inside the dairy company and development of products (manifests itself in adequate modifying and differentiating of products), adapting in order to satisfy demands, needs and desires of consumers and potential consumers.

- Milk contains all nutrients in ratios which suits the needs of the human body. Average content of water in milk is 87.5%, in which the other ingredients are – emulsified, dispersed or diluted.
- Yogurt and sour milk are two related products which are produced by lactic acid fermentation of milk. During fermentation lactose is transformed into lactic acid, with partial coagulation of proteins. Sour milk is produced only in packaging of 0.2 litres because the process of production demands a special way of production for this product which consists of starter cultures, process of homogenization and storing the product in cups in thermal chambers where sour milk changes its consistency and gains firmness.
- Cream is a product obtained by separating fats from the milk. It is sold as: cream, pasteurized cream, sterilized cream, sour pasteurized cream and whipping pasteurized cream with or without sugar.
- Butter is made by processing non fermented (sweet) and fermented (sour) cream. By technological processing of cream (churning) fat droplets are merged and buttermilk is extracted. Raw butter is then rinsed, mashed, shaped and packaged.
- Cheeses are the most numerous category of dairy products. Their production is based on extracting proteins, fats and part of the mineral content from milk by coagulating with rennet – enzyme complex of microbial or animal origin. Technological process of producing white cheeses in Serbia isn't standardized, and it varies by region, and depends on climate conditions and tradition.

Overview of production scale for the period of 10 years has changed in the following manner and the scale of processed milk in litres:

2000: 1,888,465
2001: 1,768,264
2002: 1,669,806
2003: 1,621,150
2004: 1,346,266
2005: 1,952,752
2006: 2,277,358
2007: 3,120,624
2008: 2,991,260
2009: 2,627,443.

By analyzing indicators it is clear that the processed amount of milk since 2000 until 2005 has been decreasing partly because of reduced quantity of milk, and partly because outdated equipment, which has encouraged the management to invest in equipment. Also it is evident there is increase in cumulative products which achieve greater profit, and the production of pasteurized milk has decreased having small profit for unit of product. Dynamic market, technological and social factors lead to the open problem of grading and establishing balance between social needs and available resources.

According to Nelson, one of the most important forms of non-material investment is technological know-how. Technology enables innovation, which secures differentiating assortment and establishes a certain degree of competitive advantage (Teece, 2011). Application of modern technology has become imperative in business in conditions of today's economic and political globalization and directly influences the process of making marketing decisions. Only companies that have technological capacities are able to design a product which will achieve desired results in the market with competitive prices (Altshuler & V.V, 2010).

Brand Creation

Modern literature and economic practice show that the brand is created by long-term, persistent, patient and dedicated work on product assortment. Every company or entrepreneur can, while founding, create its own brand, which is logical and required for business. Dairy Farm "Sava Kovacevic" since 2007 creates the brand Dairy Farm "Dana." It cannot be expected for the brand to be established in the moment of its creation, that is to say by announcing it.

All brands do not become "brands," just like all competitors are not equal. Brand has its higher or lower values. Careful planning and large long-term investment are fundamentals for creation of a "strong" brand. Brand management becomes key component of marketing management.

Expressing factors which influence the complex creation of brand values requires five gradual steps:

1. Market segmentation,
2. Financial analysis,
3. Demand analysis,
4. Competitiveness benchmark, and
5. Calculation of brand value.

Development of the plan and strategy of production mix should be based on data of consumer's product evaluation, its weaknesses and advantages compared to competitor's products (positioning dairy products based on data of market segments) and evaluation based on objective data of real factors and optimal marketing strategy for dairy product doesn't determine only instruments of the marketing mix but also level of investment as well as disposition for individual instruments. As the needs and demands of consumers constantly change it is necessary to adjust dairy products and complete production program with constant research and modification of dairy products. Coordinating the potential of dairy company with needs and demands of consumers, as a basic demand of marketing is most directly manifested in the structure and quality of its production assortment.

Brand serves to identify products and services, as well as the manufacturer (salesman). However at the same time it often serves to identify consumers themselves. Therefore, the notion of brand should be expanded, it represents the way the consumer sees, observes and understands a certain brand in every dimension. Purchase of known and preferred brands carries with it reduced risk of wrong purchase, but also establishing specific emotional bonds with the brand, "connection" with other people who use the same brand etc. From this we can conclude that the "plus value" which consumer gets by purchasing a certain brand, is a consequence of a series of benefits, namely functions that the brand provides for the consumer, and which are still subject of analyses.

Changes in the purchasing power of the consumer, changes of their needs and demands, appearance of new products in the competition system, force dairy companies the need to accept change. Innovation and expansion of product mix is a necessity and prerequisite for the existence of the company. There is a market pressure namely consumers and channels of distribution on the manufacturers to expand production program and narrowing production.

Marketing research deals with the question should the market (and which segments) be offered one or more levels of quality of the same dairy product? With different levels of quality different instruments of the marketing mix are provided which can enable offerors of dairy products bigger gain.

By observing the share of individual products in the structure of total production even in this short period some important differences can be noticed. Local companies offer to consumers of dairy products larger amounts of products based on their earlier expressed preferences.

By applying the BCG matrix on data from Table 3, the results shown in Table 4 are obtained.

High growth rate and large market share are related to the group of dairy products (yogurts and sour milk products) which will greatly advance in the future. However, yogurt and similar products demand added investments (development of new kinds of yogurt, enrichment of the existing with new ingredients, strong promotion etc.), and with the goal of keeping the position of the leading product. Low

Table 3. Production mix of dairy farm "Dana" 2005-2009

Product	2005	2009	Product	2005	2009
PASTEURIZED MILK	1178	1200	FRESH CHEESE	49	36
Share in %	69	60,5	Share in %	2,8	2
YOGURT 1/1	246	251	CHEESE IN SLICES	8	8
Share in %	14	13	Share in %	0,4	0.5
YOGURT ½	64	161	BUTTER	8	-
Share in %	14	8,5	Share in %	0,11	-
YOGURT 0,2	53	107	CREAM	100	93
Share in %	3	5	Share in %	3	4.5
SOUR MILK	30	52	KASHKAVAL	-	-
Share in %	17	2,5	Share in %	-	-

Source: Internal data Dairy Farm "Dana" Vrbas – department for planning and analyses.

Table 4. BCG matrix of dairy products of Dairy Farm "Dana" vrbas

		Market Share	
		High	Low
Market Growth	H I G H	Products-Market leaders Yogurt "Dana" and Sour milk products	Inferior products Fresh cheese
	L O W	Products-Generators of current revenue Pasteurized milk	Products – Candidates for elimination Butter

growth rate, and large market share is observed with pasteurized milk, these products have gone through the growth phase and right now they are in the phase of maturity. They represent the source of income for confectionery companies and should maintain this phase as long as possible. While butter production doesn't generate enough profit.

In the business environment characterized by dynamism, companies in order to remain competitive, strive to continually introduce innovation. Innovation is a critical factor for survival and development of the company, and can be defined as "creation, acceptance and implementation of new ideas, processes, products or services." (Huang & Huddleston, 2009)

Innovative planning system for development of dairy products is based on marketing research which, based on evaluating a series of interdependencies, reveals possibilities to enhance realization and acceptance of the new dairy product, and undertaking necessary changes in the product characteristics, which will ensure market success up until the halt of further investments in the product, at which point it doesn't have any perspective in the market.

Especially significant are three aspects of innovation influence on business: (Bowonder, Dambal, Kumar & Shirodkar, 2010)

- Creating new assortment or experiences which excite consumers;
- Market competitiveness;
- Entry on the new markets or new business ventures.

Modified product implies a product which has some of the physical properties changed, enhanced or has modified packaging. Such is the case with yogurt "Dana" of the Dairy Farm "Dana."

Dairy Farm "Dana" seeks to introduce new products in its production program based on consumer needs and demands, it is less common to first develop new dairy product and then create a market for it. Prerequisite for success is a planned approach, namely creating a program of introducing the new dairy product which is based on the needs and demands of consumers. Dairy products have their nutritional characteristics which are significant in human nutrition.

Packaging is more and more pronounced as an active element of dairy product strategy. Packaging of dairy products has two basic functions to protect the product during storage, transport and manipulation, the packaging in question is the transport packaging, and to attract attention of consumers, to inform and influence the decision to purchase: commercial packaging.

Packaging is an integral part of dairy products and it is necessary to be adjusted for the needs and demands of consumers. Stronger dairy companies have access to more adequate product packaging. Dairy Farm "Dana" places its product in packaging which isn't modern because of the lack of funds for modern Tetra Pak packaging or PET, which presents a problem of entering large supermarket chains and partially in the sense of conserving the quality of the product. Still old packaging has been replaced by new and modern:

Strategic Role of a Brand and Brand Strategy

In the process of developing a new product, when creating a name, logo and other specific markings, potentially a new successful brand is created. Branding is a priority for the top management in the last decade, and the strategic role of brands comes from the fact that brands often represent the most valuable non-material property of the company.

Figure 1. Old packaging has been replaced by new and modern

Brand is probably the most powerful instrument of communication, and yet only a small number of organizations purposely create and use brand identity for sales of its products or services.

Brand strategy is built on the positioning of the brand, brand mission, brand assortment value (and personality), promise of the brand and brand architecture. First step in effective branding of the assortment is to understand precisely what your customers want from you and to provide it for them. There are different definitions of a brand. One of the widespread in the literature is the one that the American Marketing Association (AMA) gave: "Brand is a name, term, sign, symbol, or design, or a combination of them, intended to identify the goods and services of one seller or group of sellers and to differentiate them from those of competitors." (Keller, 2003).

Designing branding strategy involves precise interpretation of the results of previous analysis of the brand. In addition, when determining the direction of the brand strategy, it is necessary to estimate what is justified and what can be done immediately. Top management has to support leadership and management of the brand – otherwise it is not possible to conduct brand strategy. Branding is a process of building awareness in consumers about the existence of the brand and creating their loyalty to the brand. To brand means to create a strong emotional connection between the brand and the consumer, which signifies a high degree of identification of the consumer with the brand and the values it symbolizes. Brands have always been commercial agents and brand managers take pride in their ability to meet the needs of their target. (Veljković & Đorđević, 2010) However, these two desires are in conflict with the recent trend towards positioning brands as "authentic," emphasizing the timeless values desired by consumers while downplaying apparent commercial motives. The dual problem for the firm is in creating images of authenticity while dealing with the challenge that authenticity presents for brand management. (Beverla, 2005)

Brand has a role of a communication bridge between the company and the consumer, because of numerous functions and benefits it realizes. It is considered that the brand represents (Milisavljevic, 2004):

1. Ownership sign,
2. Means for differentiation,
3. Functional means,
4. Symbolic means,
5. Means for risk reduction,
6. Memory (experience) which translates meaning to the product,
7. Legal means, and
8. Element of company assets.

Focusing attention on the accompanying characteristics of dairy products is a result of knowledge that consumers buy image, brand, packaging and not just the physical product. Design of dairy products should be visual, attractive for potential consumers, to add value in the consumer's eyes. Brand "Dana" of the Dairy Farm "Dana" products increases the value of the dairy products in the eyes of consumers and also it is an important instrument for the dairy products strategy. It is especially important in communicating dairy products, as a way to identify manufacturer, retail salesman and others and as a legal protection of the dairy products. Brand isn't only a label by which to differentiate dairy products. When the brand is successful it becomes a symbol which has multiple attributes for the consumer awakening in him certain associations. It enables the creation of a notion in public. Dairy product brand is used while segmenting target customers, determining level of quality and other characteristics of the product, adds to the image of the product and the dairy company.

Successful brand of a dairy product is the one the customers want, seek, insist upon and purchase with trust. It accomplishes great effects through the size of the scale of turnover of the dairy company. Brand "Dana" which Dairy Farm "Dana" uses for all its products is a multipurpose brand. This brand strategy can be labelled as: one brand – multiple products compared to the strategy of each product one brand.

Advantages of this type of usage of the brand are:

- Using the right of brand for all products instead of registering each individually.
- Consumers that have positive experience with one of the products will buy other products thanks to the same brand.
- Possibility of including new products under the same brand.
- Lower costs of advertising and promotion.

Branded innovation improves business and can (Aaker, 2007):

- Create company assortment, differentiate it and make it more attractive. Innovation can be presented by the brand or sub-brand, branded characteristic, ingredient or service.
- Create new sub-category of a product and act in the direction of consumer habits change. Challenge of branding is managing the perception of the consumer and influencing the choice of relevant brands.
- Influence greater respect of the consumer towards the company or corporate brand, because of innovativeness which makes the new product offer more credible.

Well positioned brand enables companies' placement with higher prices than the competitors. In the product strategy creating the brand is one of the main moments, because that way, primarily increases the product value. Also, in the struggle for differentiating products brand is the weapon of choice. Customers trust products with brands more than products without one. Besides attracting the customer and connecting him to the product, or brand, helps segment the market and create the image of the dairy company, brand also legally protects the product. Dairy Farm "Dana" has introduced by the end of 2007 a new brand for yogurt, under the name of Dana.

Creating a good brand implies large expenses – to create and promote, label, packaging, legal protection etc. – global companies consider it an inevitable investment in the future.

Significance of the brand management strategy concept is viewed in the fact that orientation towards the brand determines the performance of the brand in the market (Wong & Merrilees, 2007). Strategic brand management begins its activity with the development of the brand vision and on it "relies" the concept of orientation towards the brand. Brand vision is defined as the ability of the company to recognize current value of the brand, brand potential and the possible future value of the brand.

There is a high degree of interdependence between different activities of the strategic brand management, which can be systematized in the following manner (Cravens & Piercy, 2006):

- **Construction of the Brand Identity:** The goal of the brand identity is to define a unique set of associations towards the brand, which the company wishes to create or maintain. Elements of the identity should be complementary with the holder of the brand.
- **Brand Implementation:** Initiative determines which elements of the identity should be communicating with the target group and how to establish com-

munication. Elements of the identity are used for positioning the brand in the consumers' minds.

- **Brand Management Over Time:** Implies managing during the life cycle of the brand. Branding strategy can be adjusted over time, but it is always in the function of achieving the primary goal. Goal of the branding strategy is the construction of strong brands and all activities which could harm the brand are avoided.

- **Managing the Brand Portfolio:** Activity includes coordinating brands comprising the company's portfolio with the purpose of reaching the optimal performance in the system. Management researches the profitability of brands in the portfolio and their connections.

- **Brand Leverage:** Leverage includes the transfer of the essential identity on the new additions to the production line or a new category of a product. Expansion and extension of the brand give the possibility to cover new market segments.

- **Brand Value:** Every activity within strategic brand management can have a positive and negative influence on the brand value. It is necessary to identify key determinants of brand value with the goal of creating the highest possible value of the brand over time.

- **Strategic Brand Analysis:** Procedure provides basic data for decision making for every activity of the brand management. Involves market analysis, customers, competitors and brand information.

Brand strategy is always based on the essence of the brand, its values, and associations. Products and services are an integral part of the brand. Content and meaning of these dimensions change over time and they are managed by the management through decisions they make. Definition of the current status and future perspective are great challenges in building brand strategy. Consistency between different aspect of the brand and the authenticity of the company and the pressure from the market environment are a never-ending challenge for the management. Need for economic sustainability and investing in the brand value have to be taken into consideration in every marketing decision making.

Price

Price is one of the instruments of the brand which by itself or in combination with other instruments enables realizing the business goals. In the conditions which exist in Serbia the situation is that the price is still the primary factor during purchase. Market is a significant source of data necessary to determine the degree of reaction of the consumer to the level and change of prices. Degree of sensitivity of the consumer to the prices and their change is governed by the structure of needs, purchasing power, product characteristics, habits, traditions, climate, the existence of substitutes etc. therefore, by the demand for dairy products. Understandably, the level of demand is influenced by the price of the product, substitute products, complementary and competitive products. Price is one of the factors of competitiveness, which significantly determines the financial result of Dairy Farm "Dana." Price should be adjusted to cover the expenses of business and achieve certain profit, and at the same time to correspond to the perceived value by the consumer. With the price dairy companies realize their participation in the primary distribution, which significantly determines its economic standing. Dairy Farm "Dana" is highly sensitive to change in prices of its products because they directly reflect on production ability and profit. Critical element for developing pricing strategy is the consideration of competition and probable reactions of competition to the pricing. Analysis of the probable reaction of competitors is an important determinant while choosing the price. Company should determine the relationship of its prices with the prices of competitors, whether it will be the same, lower or higher. The price of dairy products should be taken into account as well as other expenses of consumers because they are often ready to pay more to save time and effort.

With the number of dairy product kinds even the small change in prices provoke the change in preference in customers. That is why dairy companies more and more while introducing new products in the production program start at one orientation price and it falls on the research and development department to create a product that will be successfully realized at that orientation price.

In the conditions of inadequate competition, prices of sour milk products are freely formed. That is why the average prices of these products are high, and there is also a large difference in prices between manufacturers and places of purchase.

Demand for dairy products is the next factor in line. Decisions about pricing must have information about demands in individual market segments.

On the price of the dairy product the following have influence: manufacturer policy in the area of prices (set goals, tasks, strategy), characteristics of product differentiation, elements of an "image" of the product and production or trade organization, institutional measures of society, market constellation etc.

Consumers form the standards of pricing, what they consider a fair price and it serves to estimate prices of dairy products. There is a certain tier, framework around the price standard within which the amount of purchased goods will probably not change or the brand of dairy products because greater change of prices is needed to produce noticeable difference.

Marketing Channels

Marketing channels are instruments of marketing mix used by dairy companies to reach customers. Marketing channels involve all activities undertaken with the goal of forwarding individual dairy products from the manufacturer to the consumer. While making decisions involving sales channels existing product policies are taken into account, price and promotions but also every decision about marketing channels influences later decisions involving the product, price and promotion. In essence they represent the bridge between dairy companies and consumers of dairy products.

Dairy products are subject to spoilage, which also influences the choice of placement of the product in the market. On shaping the channel strategy the state and the expected changes in economic, sociological, political and legal environment also have an effect. Situational analysis of macro-environment is important because it points to potential problems and possibilities, which is especially important with environment channels because they change very slowly. Characteristics of the competition (size, financial and marketing strength, market share etc.) and the way they distribute dairy products Dairy Farm "Dana" takes into account while creating its channels of distribution. Control over distribution channels enables the company to monitor how much the needs and demands of consumers are respected and to take corrective actions.

Dairy Farm "Dana" has to choose the number of levels of its marketing channels, or how much levels of intermediaries it wants to have in the distribution of its products to customers. With regards to that is the question of selectiveness (wholesale, retail...).

Creating loyalty for the shop is one of the main goals of retail. Model for the shop choice shows that loyalty can be created if the image of the shop confirms consumer priorities. For example, consumers that value commodities, namely ease of purchase will be loyal to the closest supermarket, and consumers that prefer personalized relationships will be loyal to the classic shops in which they form close contacts with sales staff and feel right at home.

All parameters indicate that in the majority of European countries exists accelerated growth of large retail facilities which are also a kind of wholesale. With the growth of hypermarkets and supermarkets the number of small retail shops and kiosks has dramatically decreased, and with that the need for wholesale.

Promotional Activities

Promotional activities of Dairy Farm "Dana" as one of the elements of brand construction represent a continuous communication process of exchange of information, messages and introducing the company with closer and further environment. This process of communication is permanent.

In the world there is a prevailing tendency of manufacturers to have control over their own brands. Control is reflected in clearly defined contents which make the brand, and in accordance to that brands communicate with consumers. The paradox in this situation is that actually none of the brands is under complete control of the manufacturer. The reason is the existence of perceptive filters in humans. So the communication directed towards consumers never reaches them in the way initially formulated rather it is perceived from the position of the individual. Conveying brand contents to the consumers aren't simple and clear messages which cannot be hindered or even understood differently. These are complex messages containing character, feelings, features, explanations and because of that they experience serious deviations in the context of perception. Obstructions of meaningful, creative character originate on the sender side as well as on the receiver end (Vracar, 2010).

Each instrument of the promotional mix has its specificity contributing to the image creation of Dairy Farm "Dana." Instruments of promotion in combination and with adequate dosing make the promotional mix.

To adjust to the new trends Dairy farm "Dana" has to change standing rules and find new ways to communicate and better understand its customers. Managing promotion is connected to decision making involving application of individual forms of promotion and their combination, namely the promotional mix which gives to the target market information about dairy products, raising awareness about the products etc. Goals of managing promotion are profit gain and formation of the planned image of the Dairy Farm "Dana." Each instrument of the promotional mix has its specificity and corresponding contribution to creating consistent image and presenting the company on the market. In the integrated marketing communication company has a policy with which it ensures synergy of all forms of promotional mix.

Economic propaganda is a paid mass communication with the end purpose of conveying information, developing preferences and encouraging actions for the benefit of the propagandist. Dairy Farm "Dana" pays for the exposure through media, with the purpose of influencing public opinion or action. Economic propaganda is any form of public advertising or information with the intent to directly or indirectly help with the sales of products. Economic propaganda is therefore, a form of promotion which represents creative, communicative process, coordinated with the interest and the needs of consumers and manufacturers. Dairy Farm "Dana" has since 2006 in cooperation with marketing agency Kitchen and Good Wolf Novi Sad made promotional material emphasizing the origin of milk. Farm milk is a term used while advertising on the local radio and TV station. Corporate propaganda actions are frequent with large and known companies, because creating the image is very hard and lengthy process especially if it involves new market or the market with very strong competition. Economic propaganda informs about new dairy products, suggests new uses of products, informs about price change and explains ways to use dairy products.

Personal sales, is a creative direct communication with one or large number of consumers of dairy products in order to create favorable pre purchase mood, realizing sales and maintaining post purchase satisfaction and general atmosphere harmonized with the interests of the manufacturer, consumer and society in general. Personal sales, is therefore part of the communication mix, in which there is a direct communication between the company, salesman and consumer. With dairy products personal sales do not involve end consumers but only intermediaries in the turnover. Dairy companies through their sales representatives communicate with wholesalers. Goal of sales improvement is to establish conditions for the customer to sample the certain dairy product in the hopes that he will develop loyalty for that product.

Sales improvement is connected to direct sales of the products. Sales improvement of Dairy Farm "Dana" directed towards consumers can be achieved with the following groups of actions:

- Dairy Farm action which enabled the consumers of cream for the price of one to get another at a lower price or for free.
- Dairy Farm action in which a new product would be promotionally given.
- Promotional action in facilities where customers could sample new cheeses.

Sales improvement oriented towards public takes place at fairs and exhibitions. The fair represents a manifestation where at one place there is a gathering of manufacturers, customers, consumers and general public. Manufacturer, or salesman can at the same place present its results and achievements, and the customer can observe the entire overview of manufacturers and competition. Chamber exhibitions serve to promote products and companies. Exhibitions serve to introduce and inform potential customers and audience to the company's products.

Promotion of the brand at the place of sales takes place through placement of different promotional materials in order to attract attention of the consumers to the product in the moment of purchase decision and in order to remind the consumer of the messages he received through other channels. In parallel in large number of retail facilities activities are organized to encourage consumers to sample products in order to resolve any dilemma concerning the taste or quality of the product.

Publicity is a form of public advertisement. Economic publicity of Dairy Farm "Dana" represents publication of positive information about the dairy company and its products in the media. Primarily it is information about product quality prizes and awards, awarded certificates and acknowledgements but also information about new products, achieved profit etc. With economic publicity accent is on the information about the company or its products and not on persuasion to buy company's products. Economic publicity of Dairy Farm "Dana" is used to increase affection towards dairy company and its products. Prospects are introduced to the existence and activity of the company. To be successful economic publicity should be interesting for a wider audience. But still, dairy farm cannot influence the content of the news published like with propaganda messages.

To build brand awareness, communicate basic brand idea and stimulate the desire to experience the brand the most effective is TV communication. Keeping that in mind Dairy Farm "Dana" sells the slogan "milk from our farm" accentuating the known origin of the raw materials for products and control of the milk.

Marketing public relations activity creates in a certain manner positive climate in which it is easier to launch and sell products. This activity of Dairy Farm "Dana" must be permanent. If Dairy Farm "Dana" with its marketing activities succeeds in making the customer feel good after purchase, and if it reassures him that he made the right decision, road to long-term cooperation has been paved. Marketing of good relations is an attempt to influence the consumer behavior, and the end goal is to fortify the connection between customer on one side, and dairy companies and their products on another.

Dairy Farm "Dana" doesn't have the funds to be able to execute a more aggressive approach. Still in modern conditions it cannot neglect this field of its actions. Modern conditions of business and promotional campaigns of financially stronger competitors condition the need for professional management's promotional policy of Dairy Farm "Dana," hence it hired a marketing agency to assist it.

SOLUTIONS AND RECOMMENDATION

Dynamic business ambient presents a challenge for marketing experts to find a solution which will offer cost-effective and efficient response to constant changes in the demands of consumers. Management accepts the facts that each market and region has its own characteristics and each consumer has specific interests, and as a response it implements new solutions.

First step of the company in further development of the brand "Dana" for building relationships with consumers was starting a call centre (consumer helpline) which is available to consumers at all times. Dairy Farm "Dana" would in this manner create everyday direct contact with consumers, to hear their comments, and to meet their demands and needs. Also consumers can get information about the company, production program of Dairy Farm "Dana," new products, price reduction etc. Information technology and e-business become unavoidable in modelling organization, managing and increasing competitiveness, with which the company's business becomes part of the global business trends. It is considered that the creation of the global consumer market in most part is a consequence of technological achievements (Milisavljevic, 2004).

It is very important to create a personalized relationship with consumers. Personalization through internet technology involves delivery of adapted content to customers through internet presentations or e-mail (Chaffey, Mayer, Johnston, & Ellis-Chadwick, 2000). Personalization represents special commodity which enables the delivery of personalized service or product to individual customer and often it is possible to realize with minor expenses over the internet of cellular telephony.

Benefits of the brand in marketing are realized by manufacturers and consumers. Effects of built brand come from valuable, but intangible property which marketing managers manage more and more carefully.

Modern practice of marketing clearly shows there are significant differences in realizing market results of products and built brand, which further implies the existence of real market value of a brand.

Dairy Farm "Dana" will monitor the performance of its processes during exercising activities planned by an annual plan. After conducted promotional actions dairy farm will conduct research with the goal of determining the number of consumers familiar with the marketing campaign, in order to examine whether marketing campaign influenced the increase in demand for Dairy Farm products.

So many things should be considered during creation of the global market strategy that the list of factors that need to be taken into account may appear very large. Positive and negative sides must be measured in creating one global design. However, despite these complications, large number of brands penetrate basic human needs and desires. There is no stronger platform of a brand than the one speaking directly to consumers and enhancing their lives – no matter how big the enhancement.

Consumers are prepared to pay more for products designed according to their standards, taste, style, and companies, with the advancement of technology, fast exchange of information and higher production flexibility, are capable to satisfy specific demands of consumers, with similar efficiency of mass production (Chang & Chen, 2009). Positioning of the brand "Dana" is a key process of successful brand management. Brand must be directed towards right consumers in the right way. Therefore positioning is considered as a process of creating company assortment and corresponding image, which will take special and preferred place in the thoughts of consumers in the target segment.

Since different segments value brands in different ways, it is important to know them and choose target segments, which will receive primary attention and company assortment will be adjusted for them. For a successful brand management, it is necessary to have the ability to monitor continuous changes in the market environment and minds of consumers. Mission and vision of a company must be clear, and while managing the brand it is important to maintain constant balance. Foundations of the mission and vision are created by experienced managers, while in brand development it is important to give opportunities to younger staff, which are capable, hardworking and imaginative. Equally important is to have their ideas and views of the brand checked, while giving them space to advance in the ever-changing cultural environment of the company. Brand is a living organism which develops and grows. Therefore Dairy Farm "Dana" should develop a special brand for each consumer segment. Managers must be aware that the opinions of consumers change after every purchase. Company must manage certain number of brands or strong and carefully nurtured corporate brand representing the entire company. The choice of a brand is a very difficult process. It is possible that the company is forced to sacrifice short-term scale of sales and results in order to invest in a brand which will hold a solid and long-term strategic position. Consequence of such investments are unique advantage and long-term profit. Companies must know their brand and manage it, and be aware that their existence in the market depends on it.

Long-term goal of Dairy Farm "Dana" is building a distinctive image, which will benefit its competitiveness and successful business on local and global market.

Distinctiveness of the brand image presents a barrier for the competition. Noticeable and original image cannot be copied by the competitors. Existence of a powerful positive image is a good foundation for further diversification of business, reallocation of resources and transfer from one industry to another.

REFERENCES

Aaker, D. (2007). Innovation: Brand it or lose it. *California Management Review*, *50*(1), 12. doi:10.2307/41166414

Altshuler, L., & Tarnovskaya, V. V. (2010). Branding capability of technology born globals. *Brand Management*, *18*(3), 212–227. doi:10.1057/bm.2010.47

Beverla, M. (2005). Brand management and the challenge of authenticity. *Journal of Product and Brand Management*, *14*(7), 460–465. doi:10.1108/10610420510633413

Bowonder, B., Dambal, A., Kumar, S., & Shirodkar, A. (2010, May-June). Innovation strategies for creating competitive advantage. *Research Technology Management*, 19-32.

Chaffey, D., Mayer, R., Johnston, K., & Ellis-Chadwick, F. (2000). *Internet marketing*. Harlow, MA: Pearson.

Chang, C. C., & Chen, H. Y. (2009). I want products my own way, but which way? The effects of different product categories and cues on customer responses to web-based customizations. *Cyberpsychology & Behavior*, *12*(1), 7–14. doi:10.1089/cpb.2008.0111 PMID:19113951

Cravens, D. W., & Piercy, N. F. (2006). *Strategic marketing*. New York: The Mc-Graw Hill.

Delgado-Ballester, E., & Munuera-Alema, J. L. (2005). Does brand trust matter to brand equity? *Journal of Product and Brand Management*, *14*(3), 187–196. doi:10.1108/10610420510601058

Huang, Y., & Huddleston, P. (2009). Retailer premium own-brands: Creating customer loyalty through own-brand products advantage. *International Journal of Retail & Distribution Management*, *37*(11), 981.

Keller, L. K. (2003). *Strategic brand management, building, measuring, and managing brand equity* (2nd ed.). London: Prentice Hall International Inc.

Kotler, P., & Keller, K. L. (2006). *Marketing menadžment*. Pearson Education.

Lindemann, J., & Valuation, B. (2004). Brand valuation, a chapter from brands and branding. In *An economist book*. New York: Interbrand.

Milisavljevic, M. (2004). *Strategijski marketing*. Beograd: Centar za izdavačku delatnost Ekonomskog fakulteta u Beogradu.

Paula, E., Chaves, S., & Moura Engracia Giraldi, J. (2014). Financial and economical value od country brand: Concept, conceptual definition and operational definition. *Asian Journal of Business and Management Sciences*, *3*(05), 42–55.

Solomon, M., Bamossy, G., Askegaard, S., & Hogg, M. K. (2006). *Consumer behaviour*. Harlow, MA: Pearson.

Teece, D. J. (2011, March/April). Dynamic capabilities: A guide for managers. *Ivey Business Journal*, 1.

TGI-Serbia. (2014, january 5). *Superbrands*. Retrieved August 4, 2014, from http://www.superbrands.rs/images/bible/60-61imlek.pdf

Veljković, S., & Đorđević, A. (2010). Vrednost brenda za potrošače i preduzeća. *Marketing*, *41*(1), 3–16.

Vračar, D. (2010). *Strategije tržišnog komuniciranja*. Beograd: Ekonomski fakultet Univerziteta u Beogradu.

Wong, H. Y., & Merrilees, B. (2007). Closing the marketing strategy to performance gap: The role of brand orientation. *Journal of Strategic Marketing*, *15*(5), 390. doi:10.1080/09652540701726942

KEY TERMS AND DEFINITIONS

Brand Management: It is a strategic question. It represents a set of activities tied to the launch of the brand in the market and managing the brand throughout its life cycle. The goal is to create and increase the value of the brand for consumer as well as for the company. If the consumer recognizes added benefits (values) of a brand, it results with a higher level of total satisfaction which the consumer has after the purchase (and/or use).

Brand Strategy: It is built upon positioning of the brand, brand mission, value of the brand (and personality), promise of the brand and brand architecture. Content and meaning of these dimensions are changed over time and they are managed by management through decisions they make.

Brand Strength: It primarily depends on the position the brand has in the minds of consumers with regards to other brands. The branding tale couldn't be started without previous understanding of the idea of positioning which led to today's revolution in marketing thinking.

Brand: It is the most significant property of the company and their highest value. It represents everything that reminds us of a product or service. The entire success in the market lies in the reputation of a brand and collective knowledge about the company. Brand adds characteristics which in a way are different from a product or satisfying same needs. The best brands represent quality guarantee.

Customer Satisfaction: It represents long-term foundation for profitability of individual products and services as well as the complete company assortment. It depends on comparison of observed performances of products and their expectations. Successful companies give promise only for the values they can deliver, and then deliver more than they promised consumers. Companies can only increase satisfaction by ways of lower prices, or providing added services, which only in exceptionally rare cases, results in lower profit. Brand often implies a certain level of quality and consumer satisfaction.

Market Segmentation: It implies division of the market into parts based on previously defined criteria. It is necessary to divide the market into homogenous groups of consumers which do not overlap with each other by criteria such as: product or service, distribution channels, consummation habits, purchase subtlety level, geographic, existing or new customers etc. Brand is valued in each segment and by summing the values of each individual segmented values we obtain the total value of a brand.

Marketing Strategy: It enables the company to concentrate their limited resources on the best opportunities in the environment with the goal of expanding sales and reaching sustainable competitive advantage. By analyzing the competition, with detailed research of consumers and their decisions the company makes a long-term strategy for conquest of new and keeping existing consumers.

Packaging and Labeling: Have a role of a channel for broadcasting identity. Design of packaging and the way of labeling of the brand partake in the construction of the brand's identity with the goal of original packaging attracting attention of the customers, and increasing the chance of purchase and stimulate impulsive purchase.

Slogan: It represents a short associative sentence or a phrase which represents the essence and mission of a brand. Slogan is important during brand positioning, should be well accepted in the market and in general public, and is placed parallel to the brand name. Slogan serves as a communication device between the company and the consumer. Its success is measured by the ability to attract consumer attention by promoting views and values the campaign stands for.

Chapter 7
Simply Food:
The Crossroads in Front of a New–Born Food Brand

Hakim A. Meshreki
American University in Cairo (AUC), Egypt

Maha Mourad
American University in Cairo (AUC), Egypt

ABSTRACT

Simply food is the first food brand that was launched in September 2013 by "Orange International" company. Simply food's aim is to provide a high quality food round the corner for young students and business professionals who are seeking a high quality meal during their lunch break or their evening outing. Simply Food team has many prospects to work upon in terms of the management of the stores in addition to expansion and creation of other simply brands. Issues facing management are which simply sub-brands to launch that would be integrated into the simply brand and how to expand simply stores in Egypt and the region. Furthermore, what is the proper marketing strategy given the limited budget available that would help strengthening the simply brand? What is the proper regional expansion strategy that would enable the simply brand to the fast food destination for customers in the region?

DOI: 10.4018/978-1-4666-7393-9.ch007

ORGANIZATION BACKGROUND

History of the Company

Based in Cairo Egypt, Orange International is a company that was founded in 2011 by a group of Enthusiastic, professional, young entrepreneurs and top executives that have experiences spanning many business sectors starting from food and beverage, marketing, telecommunication, energy management, higher education and other fields. This blend of various experiences enables the team to successfully realize the mission and vision of the company which is mainly specialized in the food and beverage business. Its aim is to create and manage high-quality, food brands for consumers all over the world starting from Egypt and growing through the MENA region.

Fast Food Market in Egypt

The fast food business in Egypt has been growing in the past years with an accelerating trend with Egyptians lifestyle changes. Most of the world renowned fast food chains opened in Egypt fostered by the opening of many mega shopping malls and business/leisure hubs. According to the American Chamber of Commerce in Egypt, The Egyptian Fast-food market is dominated by US-based franchisors including Bakin Robbins, Burger King, Chili's, Cinnabon, Cold Stone Creamary, Dairy Queen, TGI Fridays, Hardee's, Mc-Donald's, Hard Rock Café, Outback Steakhouse, Pizza Hut, Starbucks and Ruby Tuesday. In addition to this many well established local fast-food chains are present in Egypt (for Example: Mo'men, Cook D'or, Smileys' Grill, which constitute old and strong fast food players within the Egyptian Market. According to Euromonitor (EUROMONITOR, 2013), the fast food industry in Egypt recovered from 2011 drop caused by the revolution, thanks to a recovery in tourist volume, a relative return to stability and competitive prices implemented by the country's operators. However, the weakened economy, general uncertainty and decrease in purchasing power hindered this recovery. As a result, transaction volume growth only reached 1% in 2012, compared to a review period CAGR of 2%, while current value sales rose by 8.4% in comparison to a review period CAGR of 10%.

The Egyptian Fast food business however is still viewed as possessing a strong growth potential. It is expected that chains continue leading the fast food category. However, outlets and transactions volume are expected to witness a CAGR of 1.2% and 6% respectively, compared to a reviewed period of 9% and 11%. Leading chains from Americana and Mo'men group are likely to wait a complete return to stability before directing strong investments in outlet expansion.

Simply Food

As a start, Orange launched their first brand called "SIMPLY FOOD." Simply Food is a concept chain built around today's fast-paced lifestyle. It offers a specialized line of food that is tasty, fresh and fast. The overall experience of each specialized outlet will enable customers to enjoy fine dining cuisine quality in a trendy, selective and clean environment with hundreds of varieties to choose from. One is able to create his own base and toppings the way he wants allowing him to indulge in dishes that serve his taste buds justice. The main thing is that simply represents "fine dining on the go ."The founders of Simply have allocated a gap in the fast food Egyptian Market which is split between fast food chains (always categorized as Junk food) and fine dining restaurants which could be sometimes very expensive to a big sector of the Egyptian consumers. The concept of "fine dining on the go" is expected to fill this gap by providing the quality of food usually found in a fine dining restaurant but at a service speed of a fast food chain.

Simply stores are designed to reflect the simply brand identity which is simple, neat, clean and relaxing on the go environment. This is reflected through the white walls and store façade (See Figure 1).

Simply Management

The management of Simply Food is headed by the company CEO "Mr. Hani Ossama" who is overlooking the whole operations. Simply food has five board members including Mr. Hani Ossama who set the business strategy for the company and guide the company growth. The management team of simply food is also comprised of an

Figure 1. Simply Pasta store

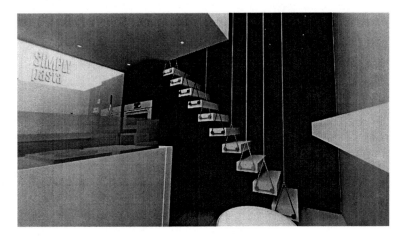

operational director" Mr. Kamal" who takes care of all the operations in the central kitchen and within the store with the assistance of a cost controller and an accountant. The cost controller is responsible for calculating the food cost, conducting reconciliation on monthly basis and negotiating deals with suppliers of food components, packaging material and other supplies needed by both stores. An Executive Chef directly reporting to the CEO is managing the hiring of cooks and chefs, cooking and food preparation procedures taking place within the central kitchen and in the stores. Furthermore he is responsible of assuring food standardization procedures creation and implementation within the central kitchen as well as in the stores.

Financial Outlook of Simply

By taking a financial outlook of simply, the fixed and variable costs are summarized in Table 1.

Since the opening in September 2013 the Monthly sales for simply food are shown in Table 2. As noted the highest sales were realized at the month of December where simply food had the opportunity to be present in GUC for a trial for the first fourteen days of the month. GUC daily sales sored very high and had a great impact on the overall simply revenue.

Branches and Operations

Simply currently has two branches located in Zamalek. The owners decided to start by Simply Pasta which offers a variety of creative pasta dishes by mixing and matching pasta types, toppings and sauces. Upon entering the store customers find a menu board describing the three steps for ordering starting by choosing the types of pasta that is offered whether it is fettuccine, penne, bowtie, spaghetti or fusilli.

Table 1. Fixed and variable costs of Simply Pasta and Simply Potatoes

Fixed Cost Items	
Fixed Cost Item	Value (EGP) [1]
Salaries/Month	40,000 EGP
Rent/Month	44,000 EGP
Utilities/Month	3,000 EGP
Total Fixed Cost/month	87,000 EGP
Variable Cost	
Food component	32% of Sales Price
Packaging	15% of Sales Price

Simply Food

Table 2. Simply Food monthly sales since the start

Month	Year	Monthly Revenue (EGP)	Comments
September	2013	44,246	Only 10 days of operations (Opening was September 21st)
October	2013	103,931	
November	2013	112,604	
December	2013	210,658	Opening of a new branch in German University in Cairo
January	2014	141,359	
February	2014	89,854	
March	2014	124,585	

For all these types of pasta customers can choose between whole wheat pasta or regular pasta depending on their request. The second step is to choose the type of sauce that will be added to the pasta ranging from red sauces, white creamy sauces, brown and "rose" sauces. The final step is to add toppings on the pasta to jazz it up. These steps are explained by the line cooks and the cashier. Customers are able to customize more than 150 combinations of pasta based on their selection of pastas, sauces and toppings. In addition, simply Pasta offers soft drinks and mineral water.

The other branch is Simply Potatoes which embraces the same Simply concept and identity offering hence a variety of potato types starting with baked potato, chips, fries and ending with sweet potato. Similarly customers can mix and match potato types, toppings and dippings to enjoy more than 200 combinations of potato dishes.

Each store accommodates 4 seated customers on high chairs. Customers can watch the last stages of their pasta and potatoes being made in front of them which enriches their experience and at the same time builds rapport between the customer and the store team all along with creating trust in the food quality the customer is eating. Simply crew was selected with care. They have to reflect cleanness, friendliness and they received fine training in the food category they are serving in order to help customers create their own optimum value in a cheerful yet professional ambience. Each store contains a line cook and a cashier that are present on daily basis from 12 pm till 11 pm. To assure the cleanness of each store, 3 Stuarts are cleaning the stores on hourly basis to maintain the hygiene level within the stores.

Initial preparation for food ingredients is done in a central kitchen rented by the company. Within this central kitchen all inbound food components and final packages are received, checked for quality approval by the executive chef and then stored. Afterwards, main bulk sauces for the pasta shop is prepared and stocked on daily basis based on the sales feedback received from the system. Similarly potatoes with their respective ingredients are received in the central kitchen for preparation which includes cutting, pre-frying and baking in order to realize the "7 minutes order "model that was initially set by top management in the stores. Basically, a customer should enter any simply store and receive his order within a maximum of 7 minutes from the ordering time. This has in turn some requirements on the amount of cooking that takes place in the stores versus the amount of cooking that takes place in the central kitchen.

In early December 2013, Simply food was approached by the German University in Cairo to cater food during an employment fair in exchange for an allowance to serve food at the University for 14 days without any charge. At the end of this period, both Simply food management and the German University in Cairo would evaluate the experience and decide whether to expand to a full permanent contract or not. The experience was excellent for both sides and Simply food signed a contract with GUC to have a permanent booth serving Simply Pasta and Simply Potatoes Menu at GUC (see Figure 2).

Simply Food launched its delivery services one month after the start of the stores. Founders were initially aiming to make Simply Food the ordering hub for fast food. A mobile number with an easy to memorize combination was assigned as a first step until a good and easy to memorize short number could be purchased. A spe-

Figure 2. Simply Food booth at GUC, Cairo, Egypt

cific person was assigned to answer the phone calls and to store customers' data in addition to their respective orders in the system.

Upon placing the order customers were promised 45 minutes to receive their orders. Delivery bags were carefully branded with the Simply Food logo and delivery guys were dressed in nice and trendy uniforms.

SETTING THE STAGE

Values and Philosophy

Orange International is built on a set of internal principles that they call "Our Way." They believe in doing business in concert with "Our Way," which constitute the values platform that helps guide their everyday efforts and helps keep integrity at the core of the operations.

The values as stated by the management are:

- **Innovation:** We always see this value as our first priority since by this value we could meet each and every customer wants and needs.
- **Employees:** We respect every employee; take care of him and his family. We recognize our mutual need to be safe, healthy, and successful. We value each other for our diverse ideas, experiences, and backgrounds.
- **Encouraging:** We encourage our people to be innovative, to take action, to make independent decisions, and to be accountable for their actions.
- **Leadership:** Each and every one of us is a leader in his own field but all of us work in cross-functional teams to serve each other in order to come out with the best.
- **Continuous Improvement:** We insistently pursue doing the right things better and accept each new idea that would push us a step forward in our improvement efforts.
- **Technology:** We are committed to providing the resources to develop technology that will build and sustain our business.
- **Ethics:** We are fair, honest, and consistent in our business and personal practices.

The above standards were in turn transferred to SIMPLY FOOD and were explained carefully by the top management to line cooks, chefs, Stuarts and administrative employees.

Marketing and Branding

Simply founders had in mind that they are not just launching a fast food chain but rather their focus was on building the Simply brand. The simply brand promise was "Expanding your food senses by taking your food experience to different level through tastes from around the world ." In order to achieve this brand promise, the role of simply stores was to deliver high-end quality food round the corner. Simply brand personality was designed to convey a professional, passionate, personal, and young and playful brand. Each of these constituents of Simply brand personality were then translated into a set of important rules that should be considered while designing the stores, menus, uniforms and packaging which were all carried out by a specialized branding consulting agency that was chosen by the founders. The professional look of the brand was supported by a staff look inside the stores, their attitude, and the simple yet professional ordering process and flow. The personal dimension of the brand was built using a database system where customer's data and order history were stored. In addition the high level of food customization in the simply menu enabled each customer to have his own recipe and dish made with his name. Simply did not yet activate any loyalty program within the stores to further emphasize personal contact with customers. The passionate dimension of simply brand personality was conveyed through an enthusiastic and welcoming staff within the stores and the dynamic colors chosen for the brand in addition to the focus during communication on the food passion that is built around trying simply food. Finally the young and playful dimension was stressed in the design of the packaging material suited for customers on the move accompanied by a use of a dynamic color pallet that is full of energetic colors. This young and playful look was further confirmed by the communication tools used to transmit the brand identity.

Having watched the fast-food competitive landscape, simply founders have set three key differentiators upon which they will build their competitive advantage within the fast food market in Egypt. Firstly, value for money was an important key differentiation factor within a highly price sensitive market like Egypt. In order to achieve this, simply food menu was done to simplify the calculation process for customers. All pasta types had the same pricing and each sauce had a price and each topping had a price. These prices were calculated after a thorough market research of similar pasta stores. Hence, prices were set slightly above the junk-food prices and below fine dining restaurants by 15%. Secondly, customers ought to have an unmatched experience within the stores. This was reached by a white look of the stores to reflect a clean environment, speed of service whereby customers receive their orders within seven minutes from order time. In addition, and as previously highlighted packaging was designed with care to match hygiene and food contact regulations all along allowing for eating on the go without any hassle. Thirdly, an important key differentiator was the high quality ingredients used to assure the fine dining promised taste.

In designing their communication strategy, simply food founders were relying heavily on social media given its high prominence within the Egyptian market and its effectiveness in reaching specific target segments of consumers. Initially the social classes targeted by simply were class A of students in private universities and fast paced business professional who are seeking high quality meals on the go. The main social media tools that were adopted were Facebook®(https://www.facebook.com/SimplyFoodEg), Twitter®(https://twitter.com/SimplyFoodEg), and Instagram®. A nice Facebook page featuring Simply Food logo and Simply food slogan "Cooking Good Food" were present on the page and managed by a professional Facebook page management company whereby regular posts of food shots and in store pictures were done. Customers' feedbacks and comments were received via the Facebook page. This page has currently 2757 likes which is considered still a small number but the management team is less concerned about the number of likes versus the quality of interaction that takes place on the page and the amount of brand buzz that occurs due to the word of "MOUSE." Similarly Simply food has also a Twitter account and customers were allowed to send tweets to this account in order to further collect feedback from them. The number of followers on Twitter is yet still very small and reached 322 followers so far. Finally, Instagram was also used to post all pictures posted on Facebook in addition to allow consumers to send their pics within the stores or while eating to allow for a more personal feel of the brand. The interaction on Instagram was seen as much better than twitter with 416 followers and more people posting their experiences in Simply to their friends and peers. On each store's glass door, one would find stickers pointing to simply social media accounts.

CASE DESCRIPTION

Upon the start of the operations, many issues became evident to the management team. Food consistency was the first issue that had to be dealt with. Pasta sauces were made of raw ingredients with high variability from one batch to the other. This variability would not allow food consistency and hence would not help in the initial brand image that was made by the company offering consistently high quality food. In order to overcome this problem, the operation manager in association with the executive chef conducted a complex suppliers' evaluation and inconsistent food suppliers were removed from the approved supplier list within the first month of operation. Furthermore, they have set some standard operating procedures aimed to standardize the preparation process. For example in what relates to making baked potatoes, a special potato type, size and diameter were set to accept inbound potatoes from suppliers. Moreover, cooking time and order were standardized and put in front of central kitchen cooks and line cooks in stores.

The board members aimed to build personal rapport with customers by being regularly present within the stores to collect fresh insights from customers' comments, gestures and expressions. Any customer concern was as much as possible solved.

In the first couple of months of operations sales were rising from month to month and Simply founders received many franchising offers from people who wished to take Simply Pasta or Simply potatoes franchises. Additionally, Simply Food catered in two events using a mobile booth whereby a very positive customer's feedback was received regarding the quality of food, speed of service and friendliness of the staff.

However, things were not always as rosy as they appear. In January, the main executive chef left Simply accompanied by a set of assistant chefs who were attached to this executive chef. As the handover between old and new chefs was not enough, the food quality got affected and complaints started to rise in front of Simply management. This has resulted in turn in a decrease in the sales figures for both stores and for the delivery which represented a big problem to management. Only 85% of the total cost was covered by revenue. As much as this represents a financial problem for Simply owners their fear on tarnishing the brand image (Keller, 1993; Aaker, 1991) and positioning that they had wished was greater. With all the controversies that were initially present in their expansion plan, the business growth was questioned given the current status of operations and their financial position. Simply founders have made an effort to restore the food quality to normal in order to retrieve the original food taste. However, still many challenges are still facing them which they have to tackle with prompt decisions.

CURRENT CHALLENGES FACING THE ORGANIZATION

Simply team is faced with many challenges some of them relate to how to restore and maintain a certain level of the business that would assure the pre-planned brand positioning by the founders. This is expected to be fostered by proper operations, consistent quality and good communication with current and potential customers. In this regard, many questions arise: Are the current social media tools like Facebook, Twitter and Instagram sufficient to properly position the company brand in consumers' mind as planned by the management team or is there a need to use further communication tools that would help emphasizing this position? Furthermore what is the proper promotional mix (Kotler, 2000) given the limited budget available that would help strengthening the simply brand?

Simply team has also many prospects to work upon in terms of the management of the operations in addition to expansion plans. Given the current success that was realized at the German University in Cairo, is it suitable to hunt for launching other booths in other similar universities like the American University in Cairo which is considered one of the best private universities in the region? Moreover, given a recent offer from some renowned clubs and cafes, would it represent a good opportunity for Simply Food to be present in these well-known clubs or cafes with small booths? Would this cause any harm for the "Simply" brand image previously planned by the founders.

Given that simply food is built upon launching more simply sub-brands which are not limited to Simply Pasta and Simply Potatoes to better become the fast-food ordering destination, what is the long-term expansion plan? Would a horizontal expansion strategy whereby more Simply Pasta and Simply Potatoes stores are launched to cover other locations than Zamalek be better or would a more vertical strategy where more priority is given to launch other Simply sub-brands be better in terms of strengthening the brand image? If a horizontal expansion strategy is chosen, where are the hot spots that could be allocated for the stores? Is it better to find new business/leisure hubs that are trending within the Egyptian market or would it be better to limit the location of the stores to big shopping malls and pedestrian areas within Cairo? If a vertical strategy is chosen, what are the best sub-brands that would match the Simply brand Identity and would assure further emphasis on Simply brand Image?

SOLUTIONS AND RECOMMENDATIONS

Simply founders in addition to the management team have many cross-roads and it would be sensible to think on some plan of actions. Firstly, given the limited budget that Simply possesses as a startup business, relying on social media tools could represent a very good opportunity for the company to further create a brand buzz. However, currently, social media hasn't proven its effectiveness from the management perspective. Simply management was advised to launch some ads on Facebook and some contests on best food combination including pasta and potatoes dishes contests to help further increase customers' interaction on the page and foster more brand awareness. The presence in other cafes and clubs represents a very good opportunity to management since it can create good brand awareness and at the same time could be a good revenue streams for the company to help overcome budget limitations. Nevertheless, management should approach these offers with great care. From one side, being present in several places could represent a very good opportunity but the place choice here represents a great challenge since this place's image could spill-over the Simply brand image. The management has to ensure that the club or the café from which they received the offer has a good image and is frequented by the correct target customers that are sought by the simply brand offering. Also, from an operational point of view, food quality, staff experience and friendliness and booths look have to be consistent with the stores look and feel in order to maintain a consistent brand image of Simply Food in consumers mind. In conclusion, it would appear that the management has a golden opportunity to expand in clubs and café from which it received the offer, however care should be taken in execution and operations.

Secondly, deciding on launching more stores having simply brand name is another important challenge facing management. From one side, it represents a big investment required which creates a financial burden on the investors, and from the other side it is crucial for brand equity building whereby more brand awareness is required and further emphasis on building the right image in consumers 'mind. Initially, the founders had an intention while they were launching the simply brand to create many sub-brands that would help simply food further grow. Hence, launching another Simply sub-brand besides the currently present sub-brands; namely Simply Pasta and Simply Potatoes would help execute this plan. To launch another sub-brand, involves a lot of investment; however Simply investors are willing to follow this trend if they feel that it would really strengthen their company both from an image and a financial perspective. An attractive idea was tingling in the founder's mind to open a new Simply Sub-brand in another location and combine both the horizontal as well as the vertical expansion strategies facing them. This represents a double-edged sword solution. From one side, it constitutes less investment and a good combination and from the other side, one store in another location could not create enough brand buzz and a failure to promote it well would lead to a deteriorating brand image. One of the founders suggested in a board meeting "why don't we opt for franchising our current sub-brands to others and we focus our efforts on launching other sub-brands. This would create a great buzz and would help us overcome the lack of cash that we might face?"

Given the multitude of decisions facing the management which reflects the crossroad that they are in the right way to follow is still not clear. Each set of decisions have their future implications on Simply Food brand.

ACKNOWLEDGMENT

We would like to acknowledge all the help and support done by El-Khazindar Business Research and Case Center (KCC), Egypt, during the preparation and submission of this case.

REFERENCES

Aaker, D. A. (1991). *Managing brand equity: Capitalizing on the value of a brand name*. New York: The Free Press.

EUROMONITOR. (2013, November). *EUROMONITOR international*. Retrieved from http://www.euromonitor.com/fast-food-in-egypt/report

Keller, K. L. (1993). Conceptualizing, measuring,and managing customer-based brand equity. *Journal of Marketing, 57*(1), 1–22. doi:10.2307/1252054

Kotler, P. (2000). *Marketing management*. Upper Saddle River, NJ: Prentice Hall.

Webster, F. E., & Keller, K. L. (2004). *A roadmap for branding in industrial markets*. Academic Press.

KEY TERMS AND DEFINITIONS

Brand Buzz: Refer to a very specific type of word-of-mouth communication about a brand or product that leads to explosive self-generating demand–or ruin.

Brand Equity: The deferential effect that brand Knowledge has on consumer response to marketing of a brand (Keller, 1993; Kotler, 2000).

Brand Identity: How a business wants a brand's name, communication style, logo and other visual elements to be perceived by consumers.

Brand Personality: Human traits or characteristics associated with a specific brand name.

Ordering Hub: An effective central destination for food ordering.

Social Media: Social media is the interaction among people in which they create, share or exchange information and ideas in virtual communities and networks.

Spill-Over: The phenomena whereby an entity (brand, place) would influence another brand.

ENDNOTES

[1]   1 US$ = 7.03 EGP.

Chapter 8
Branding and New Product Development:
A Case of Glemma

Dennis Damen
Glemma, The Netherlands & Fontys University of Applied Sciences, The Netherlands

Miao Wang
Fontys University of Applied Sciences, The Netherlands

Tim Wijnhoven
Glemma, The Netherlands & Fontys University of Applied Sciences, The Netherlands

ABSTRACT

The Glemma case explains brand management of a young startup company located in Eindhoven, The Netherlands. The case describes background, the current status, and present challenge of Glemma. Since the company is still in a very early stage, the management system is not mature yet. Hence, the Glemma case falls into the new product development category in the book. In addition, Glemma was a Web design company in the beginning; they released a universal reservation system on June 2013. Therefore, branding here is not only for Glemma itself but also for the new product they developed. The Glemma team has tried many times with various different approaches. In the early stage, the team really focused on brand image. They took on enormous projects just to deliver a professional image to customers. However, they did not reach their goal. A nice website didn't bring them any customers. Along with their experience, they figured out that brand experience is more important than brand image.

DOI: 10.4018/978-1-4666-7393-9.ch008

ORGANIZATION BACKGROUND

Glemma is registered as a VOF (vennootschap onder firma or general partnership) and started out as a web development company. It was founded in March of 2010, Eindhoven, the Netherlands. The company is run by three students from Fontys University of Applied Science. They specialize themselves in creating a fitting online experience for customers. They design and build websites and web shops for a wide variety of companies with different strategies. Promoting and maintaining these sites is also a part of their service. This includes setting up successful search engine optimization strategies. The development of the company is in its early stages. Its online marketing is still in a weak position and the customer can only find them on the Internet. This has been a predetermined decision. It was never the idea to keep working on websites but to evolve into something more permanent and maintainable.

Starting from June 2013, Glemma decided to finally pivot away from making websites and started developing a universal reservation system (A computerized system for customers to make reservations online). It is a universal system that targets both the customers as well as the users. Their first target audiences were barbershops and beauty salons. For this new approach they still needed to learn a lot and the current way of working in the company wasn't sufficient anymore. They needed to be more agile in their approach and make prioritized decision for the product to reach success.

The management structure of Glemma is simple. Three employees work as a team, they help each other's work in order to make achievements. They have cooperated with outsourced co-workers before, but the result was not effective. So they decide to keep three employees at this moment. In addition, they decide to work together as a remote partnership in long distance. The reason is that one of them has a one-year job contract in New York, the United States. The rest continue work in the Netherlands. Thus, they work through Google Hangout and make sure everything is according to the plan. The advantage of this method is that they can save money for circulating capital of the company, and they can work without location restriction.

The main income for the company is still from web design since reservation system is not fully out yet.

SETTING THE STAGE

Before Glemma pivoted their way towards the development of a product they branded themselves a company that loved design and technology. They spend countless number of hours in developing the right way of presenting themselves designing multiple logos and keep changing their website. The idea was that the way "you presented yourself towards your audience seemed most important." The image of the company needed to be right. They used a similar approach for customers.

As a web development company they only had little structure in the approach they maintained. It was a little uncoordinated. The most common approach for most of the projects was to set up a concept. This concept meant a couple of design where the customer could choose from which then got completely developed. Most of the time, this resulted in a lot of changes that had to be made afterwards because the customer was not closely involved in the project.

Technology Utilization

There were several aspects in the development of Glemma that needed attention. Coding was one of them. The code that was used to develop websites was not a standardised way of coding. This let to incompatible code with future implementations. Though they did make use of frameworks they still had a particular way of coding to and tried to create authenticity. The downside was that a lot of code was not reusable and took more time to develop.

Every product that they develop needs to be accessible for multiple people. Unfortunately this was not always the case. Some products were made locally and could only be accessed after sharing.

Another aspect that they worked on was platform independence. A aspect that they already applied because most of the projects were web applications and therefore supported a wide range of devices.

Organizational Concerns

The biggest problem the company faced was their inability to properly finish a project. It was never good enough. Whenever a project seemed to be finished a new idea came around the corner. This is no specifically aimed at the projects for customers but mostly projects that were initiated for the company itself. Logo's, websites and projects that innovated the company itself. By constantly improving their skills, every time a project seemed to be finished, it wasn't good enough anymore. Implementing newly developed aspects and automations was not structured.

To give the development inside the company structure Glemma had regular meetings. A lot of these meetings were long. Too long, and during most of the meeting they strayed from the actual subjects of the meeting. Though these long meetings did delivered them new insights they were not specific enough and derailed the active project they were working on.

It's clear that the company envisioned high quality for their products, both for customers as for the company itself. But instead of focusing on the experience this brought, they focused on the way the product showed their image.

CASE DESCRIPTION

Introduction to the Case Description: Opposite of What's Stated Down Here

Glemma learned that the way they looked didn't make much of a difference, at least not in the early stages of the company. The experience that people got from the service or products showed more potential. They got the idea that if you could convince the users of the functionalities and the possibilities the service or product had to offer, users could be convinced to return. This meant that the company culture had to change and rigorous actions needed to be applied.

Technology Concerns

Glemma uses the latest technologies to develop their product. They actively study for more efficient ways of developing. They find it very important to work efficient and therefore invest time and money in ways of making development meet their standards. A few requirements are:

In this ever evolving market it is important to keep up with new technologies and innovations. That is why they actively study for more efficient ways of developing and organizing work. To keep up with the high pace the market is evolving they needed a more structured approach. An approach that focused on validated learning and innovate in iterations rather than developing fully functional product based on a idea. To accomplish this they needed to meet a few requirements:

- **Standardized Coding:** Every (future) developer needs work according to the company standards. This way they can ensure that code maintains it readability and compatibility. Mistakes can be resolved faster and with less effort. Because technology is unparalleled in its speed of innovation, these standards will be most important to stay agile.
- **Using Frameworks and Platforms:** While the company finds authenticity important they also don't want to reinvent the wheel. By using different frameworks and platforms they ensure that as little time as possible is wasted on creating different components of the product. This enables them to get the most validated learning out of newly developed components and iterate

through development cycles faster and more efficient. Because most of these frameworks and platforms are open, they can still apply their own vision whilst making sure compatibility does not suffer.

- **Centralization:** An important aspect of the development is centralized management. This enables the company to hire external developers to contribute on the project. No time will be wasted in setting up a work environment for a new developer. There are several aspects that they have centralized to ensure their iterative process continues as fast as possible. One of the most important aspects was communication. Not only internal communication but also towards customers. They use a open platform where communication inside the company and towards the customers is combined in one place. This makes sure that everybody is on the same page during the development. Changes that may occur can be dealt with head on without delay.

The same approach applies to planning, although there are two aspects here. They make use of a milestone planning that is transparent for the customers while internally they heavily rely on the individual. Everybody needs to be up-2-date about upcoming changes and overall progress. This makes sure they can easily adapt to changes in the market without wasting a lot of resources like time and money. This automatically means there are more resources available for creating the best experience they can offer.

- **Platform Independent:** One of the last aspects is its platform independence. No matter what device the user uses, if it supports internet and a browser it should work. This does not mean that the product won't be developed in the form of an application. If by analyzing the feedback and use of the customers shows that people want to use the service in the form of an app, this could alter the course of the concept. Simply put: be where the user is.

Organizational Concerns

After careful consideration, a lot of research and three years of hard work and practice, Glemma found a suitable way to run the company. The Glemma team found a balanced combination of three popular working methods; "Agile," "Scrum" and "the lean startup model." They believe, as do many other companies, that the agile approach of working is essential in this time. Markets change at fast pace and its hard work to keep track of all these changes. The old model where a team works for a predetermined time to finish the product the way the company had envisioned has been outdated. It is essential that the company can react on changes in the market as fast as possible to keep ahead of the competition.

To be able to keep track of all the work that needs to be done they have adapted some of the practises from scrum. The most important adaptation is the product backlog. Glemma has evolved this list into a priority update list that consists of three parts: Long term, short term and important now.

- **Long Term:** The long term list contains every idea, or backburner, that has a possibility of being implemented in the feature. It's a list that makes sure not a single idea gets lost and will be reconsidered when the time is right.
- **Short Term:** The short term list is what Glemma considers important on a short term. 1 week till a month although it does not have a predetermined date.
- **Important Now:** The important now list is the list that the team is working on now. This can be compared to the sprint backlog from scrum. It has a maximum amount of items it can hold to make sure things won't get overlooked.

Glemma combines this priority update list with specific agreements and a tight schedule. It starts with something very simple; do your research. Everyone in the company has the obligation to know what's on the market, see the new trends and be able to predict what the "next hot thing" will be. Each member of the team keeps a list of the ideas that flow out of this. This is essential.

Every month there will be a long meeting. This meeting will "sync" all the individual ideas into the long-term list. Each new idea will be presented and its possible impact will be discussed. The priority of the discussed items will also be determined. Is it something that we need to act on right now, or would an implementation is too early?

Every week there will be a hourly meeting. In this hour all the items in the short-term list will be evaluated together with the items in the important now list. Do items need to shift based on the wishes of the market? Have items been outdated? Do new items find their ways to the important now list? This hourly meeting gives Glemma an overview of what is important and needs attention.

To keep everything on track a 10-minute daily hangout has been introduced to keep the workers up to date with what has been working on now. This is a fixed time and everybody needs to attend. Are there finished items? Are there complications or is everything going according to plan? The essential part here is that the hangout cannot take longer than 10 minutes. If specific question take longer they will be planned in the weekly hour meeting where there is more time to discuss this subject.

The Lean Startup Method

As described earlier, Glemma works based on the lean startup methodology. Glemma doesn't decide what the market needs, the market decides what they want and Glemma makes it in the best way possible.

The lean startup approach states that everything emerges from validated learning. Using the Lean Startup approach, Glemma creates order by providing tools to test a vision continuously. It is about putting a defined process and methodology around the development of a product (Fried et al., 2013).

A core component of Lean Startup methodology is the build-measure-learn feedback loop. The first step is figuring out the problem that needs to be solved and then developing a minimum viable product (MVP) to begin the process of learning as quickly as possible. They started out with a list of assumptions and prioritize the most essential ones. The ones that need to be proven first will be the feature that needs to be built and tested first. In the case of the reservations system one stood out above the others: "Do people want to make online reservations instead of making a reservation via phone?" Once the MVP is established, the process of learning can

Figure 1. Build, measure, learn cycle
Ries (2011).

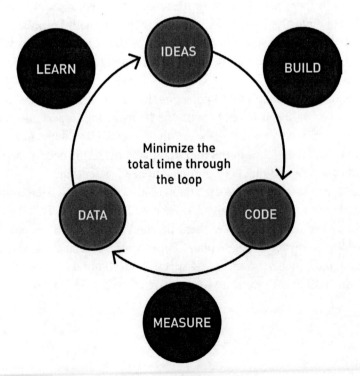

be started. This will involve measurement and learning and must include actionable metrics that can demonstrate cause and effect question.

They use different tools to gather the information necessary to learn is the following.

- **Ab-Testing:** By dividing users in groups and show them different concepts can be deducted which concept has the best outcome, A or B. These can include subtle changes like colors to totally different layout and content. Based on the analytics they receive they can evaluate which approach works best. Of course there no single concept that works for everybody so by using behavioral targeting they can show relevant content to specific groups while keep improving the experience.

- **Social Media Analyses:** Different social media platforms will be monitored for specific expressions. These expressions give insight in the way the customers experience the product. There are several tools that the company uses to keep track of social media expressions. They use these tools to track certain groups of people based on what they are posting. The main reason for this is to be able to give a personalised response to messages that describe a bad experience. Doing so they hope they can convince the customer to use their product because it can help them solve their own described problems. An added value to this approach is the personal interaction we get with customers. Not only is this good for the customer, but it also gives the company more data which they can base the overall experience of the product on (Kniberg, 2007).

- **Interviews with Users and Customers:** To get a more detailed insight on the way customers experience the product Glemma conducts interviews with the customers. By asking the right questions they can learn a lot about the wishes and uses from the customers. This information is invaluable for the company to steer their development.

- **Enquetes:** Together with the interviews they conduct several enquetes to the user of the product.

- **Analytics:** The data that comes from analytics outputs actionable metrics. Most of these metrics are based on analytics from Google and Mouse flow. Both give insight in the use of the product and the ease of use for customers. Based on this information it is possible to improve the overall experience of the product. Aspects like content placement, user interaction and specific functionalities could be altered based on the collected information.

Customer Empathy Maps

Making different empathy maps helps Glemma to consider how people are thinking, feeling, doing, seeing, and hearing. Not only while using the product but also in general. It helps them to consider the emotional value of customers. Based on this information they can find the right approach for this customer segment to amplify the ease of use and popularity of the product. It can even help priorities the priority list.

Business Model Generation

Glemma does not have a fixed business model. Instead they see it as a growing and evolving part of the business. By developing the MVP's and constantly test in in the market different revenue streams may evolve and costs can be shifted. They use this tool to actively brainstorm for new ideas and possible business models. It's a part of the monthly meeting and essential to get a good feeling for the targeted groups or to find new ones.

The first markets they are targeting are barbershops and beauty shops–a market that has yet been digitalized. Most of these shops still rely on customers making a phone call for a reservation, while the current trends tell us that people are more likely to make a reservation online. It saves time and with the use of modern smart phones nowadays you can have a much broader overview and ease of selection.

Figure 2. Customer empathy maps
(Willsgire, 2014).

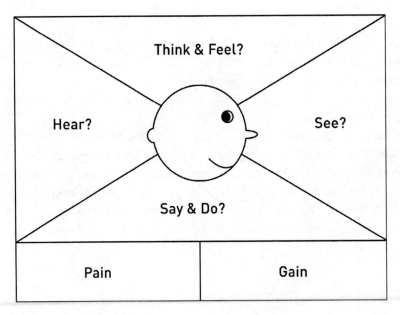

Figure 3. The business model canvas
(Osterwalder et al., 2010).

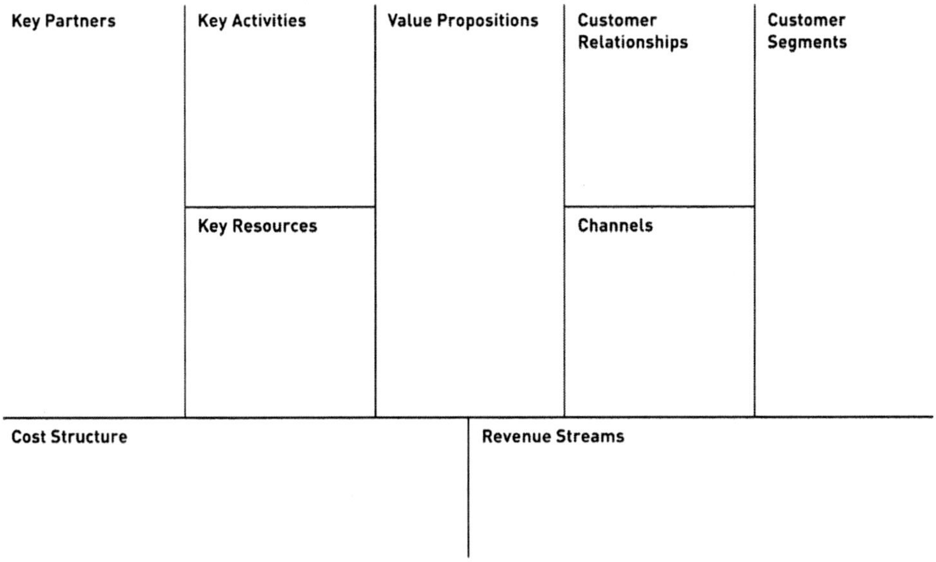

Key Partners	Key Activities	Value Propositions	Customer Relationships	Customer Segments
	Key Resources		Channels	

Cost Structure	Revenue Streams

Lean Canvas

While the Business Model Generation applied the methodologies used by Skype and Apple to attain product success in the market, the Lean Canvas concentrates on the way timeline affects the revenue stream of the company. It is therefore more target-specific and incorporates both small and large businesses effectively.

"The Lean Canvas is more actionable and entrepreneur-focused. It deeply focuses on startup factors such as uncertainty and risk. Four elements were added by replacing key activities and resources, customer relationships and key partners with the following:

- **Problem:** A problem box was included because several businesses do fail applying a lot of effort, financial resources and time to build the wrong product. It is therefore vital to understand the problem first.
- **Solution:** Once a problem has been recognized the next thing is to find an amicable solution to it. As such, a solution box with the Minimum Viable Product "MVP" concept was included.
- **Key Metrics:** A startup business can better focus on one metric and build on it. The metrics include the range of products or services you want to provide. It is therefore crucial that the right metric is identified because the wrong one could be catastrophic to the startup.

- **Unfair Advantage:** This is basically the competitive advantage. A startup should recognize whether or not it has an unfair advantage over others."

Brand experience is more important than brand image.

- **Used Software:** Adobe Suite; Illustrator, Photoshop, Dreamweaver.
- Webhosting.
- Domain registration(s).
- **Test Devices:** Computer (OS X and Windows), Android phone(s), iPhone(s), Android and Apple tablets.
- **Languages:** HTML, CSS, JavaScript, PHP.
- **Frameworks:** Sass, bootstrap, jquery, angularJS, doctrine, laravel, Zend Framework 1 and 2.
- **Platforms:** Magento, Wordpress.

Management and Organizational Concerns

The company contains three members Tim, Paul and Dennis. They all serve different roles in the company, which are based on the Belbin team roles. These roles make sure that the company (or eventually different teams in the company) can work together like a well oiled machine. They consist of the following roles:

Figure 4. The lean canvas
(Osterwalder et al., 2010).

Problem	Solution	Value Proposition	Unfair Advantage	Customer Segments
List the top 1-3 problems	Outline a possible solution for each problem	Single, clear, compelling message that turns an unaware visitor into an interested prospect	Something that can't be easily copied or bought	List your target customers and users
Existing alternatives List how these problems are solved today	**Key Metrics** List the key numbers that tell you how your business is doing		**Channels** List your path to customers	**Early Adopters** List the characteristics of your ideal customers

Cost structure	Revenue Streams
List your fixed and variable costs	List your sources of revenue

Implementer

The implementer is the one who organizes the team. He is disciplined, orderly and task-oriented. The implementer converts plans and ideas into executable tasks.

Resource Investigator

The resource investigator is an extroverted person. They have a lot of contact inside as well as outside of the company and are one of the roles that still need to grow to its full potential.

Plant

The plant is the creative thinker at the company. It is a person who comes up with surprising solutions to complex problems. They normally don't bother with the details but has an extraordinary gift in seeing the bigger picture.

Monitor

The monitor is the analyst in the company. This person is always analyzing different situations to get to the bottom of them. He has a clear-minded and broad view on problems and he moves slowly but analytical to find the best suitable solution to problems.

Shaper

The shaper in the company is very passionate about what he does. He is driven and has a strong urge to perform at his best. He looks for challenges and makes sure that project get going.

Coordinator

As the name implies this person coordinates the company. He looks after procedures and helps clarify intentions. He is also very competent in recognizing abilities in others. He is not afraid to delegate tasks when has found the right person for them.

Completer/Finisher

The completer is all about the details. He tests components rigorously and makes sure no mistakes slip through the cracks. He has a talent to always feel what could go wrong and works as a perfectionist.

Team Worker

The team worker is the sensitive kind in the company. He is helpful and helps create and maintain a pleasant atmosphere. This role is essential for a company to work together as a real team.

Specialist

The specialist focuses on his work and knowledge in his specific field. He as a immeasurable understanding of the work that he is doing.

Although the company only consists of three people at the moment, they do find these roles very important. They make sure that the described roles are implemented. That of course means each person fulfills multiple roles at this time. Which is fine for now but these roles need to be reconsidered after hiring more employees to ensure good teamwork.

CURRENT CHALLENGES FACING THE ORGANIZATION

The biggest challenges of the organization by far is how to successfully entre Dutch market, and let customers aware of the brand Glemma. In order to solve the problem there are three sub questions should be asked:

1. How to build a brand strategy for Glemma?
2. How to actually implement all the assumptions in reality? (How to prioritize the assumptions need to be tested in reality?)
3. How to successfully remote control staff in long distance?

All things are difficult before they are easy. That is why the biggest challenge of Glemma is to enter the market; to find the very first customer; to engage with the customer. This is the most difficult part of the business plan, especially for a startup company like Glemma.

As it mentioned above, the Glemma team suggests many assumptions so as to runs the company productively. However, how to find and and prioritize the assumptions and how to actually implement all the ideas is still a big problem.

The communication problem was occurred during last projects in Glemma. The employees can't reach each other sometimes due to the time difference and totally different working environment. Consequently, a plan of approach for remote control is necessary.

SOLUTIONS AND RECOMMENDATIONS

According to IDS technology marketing, there are three steps to build a brand strategy for a small business:

1. Define your brand.
2. Communicate your brand.
3. Engage with your target market.

In Glemma case, they have defined their brand very well by their own business model caves. Therefore the problem is how to communicate the brand and engage with the target market.

To communicate the brand, social media is high recommended. Particularly, more and more people like to use Facebook or Instagram after their new haircut. This is a very good channel to let people engaged with a barbershop as well as Glemma reservation system. In cause of answer the question better, a book named Start-up Owners' Manual in 2012 also has contributed to this case study. It is suggested that get out of the buildings, get real contact with customers (Blank etal., 2012). All the startups should ask them several questions:

- Who influences a sale? Who recommends a sale?
- Who is the decision-maker? Who is the economic buyer? The saboteur?
- Where is the budget for purchasing the type of product you're selling?
- How many sales calls are needed to make one sale?

The Glemma team should actually get in to a real barbershop and make sure they get all answers above.

How to actually implement all the assumptions in reality? They can start with the biggest assumption. How to define the biggest assumption? It can be decide by answering the following questions:

- Which assumption has the biggest impact?
- What could disprove the current idea?
- What data tells you?

In addition, they should start small so that they can change it fast. Do not do many assumptions at a time.

To answer the third question, which is, How to successfully remote control staff in long distance? According to the book of Remote: Office Not Required in 2013, there are some very excellent points to solve the problem. Here is the selection and conclusion of the book.

- First they need to set a stander working time, make sure everybody informed about time schedule.
- Centralized communication tools so everybody is up-to-date.
- Make shared resources like Google drive make files accessible to Centralize file management.

REFERENCES

Blank, S., & Dorf, B. (2012). *Start-up owners' manual*. K&S Ranch Inc.

Fried, J., & Hansson, H. (2013). *Remote: Office not required*. New York: Crown Publishing Group.

Kniberg, H. (2007). Scrum and xp from the trenches. InfoQ.com.

Osterwalder, A., Pigneur, Y., & Clark, T. (2010). *Business model generation: A handbook for visionaries, game changers, and challengers*. Hoboken, NJ: Wiley.

Ries, E. (2011). *The lean startup: How today's entrepreneurs use continuous innovation to create radically successful businesses*. New York: Crown Business.

Willsgire, J. (2014). *Empathy mapping with Lego figures*. Retrieved June 22, 2014, from http://smithery.co/random-inspiration-2/empathy-mapping-with-lego-figures/

KEY TERMS AND DEFINITIONS

Brand Strategy: A long-term approach for create or develop a brand into a market, and accepted by customers. An excellent brand strategy offers the company a huge competitive power.

New Product Development: A whole procedure which aims bring a new product into a certain market. According to business dictionary that "New product development is essential to any business that must keep up with market trends and changes."

Small Business Management: A strategic action in order to make a small business achieve their special goal. This is combination of marketing strategy and management skills.

Startup Company: In the early stage of company operations. Most of them are still in the development phase. There is limited capital and staff, and company system is often imperfection.

Strategic Business Plan: Different from traditional business plan. Strategic plan always takes planning ahead of company goals. And it also can utilize these goals to get more business advantages.

Technology-Based Company: A special organization with scientific and technological knowledge system. They also produce their products or service with high advanced value.

Chapter 9

Factors Influencing the Buying Behavior of Female Consumers with Reference to Top Three Brands of Make–Up Cosmetics in Pune City

Mukta Srivastava
Allana Institute of Management Sciences, India

ABSTRACT

Customers are the end beneficiary of all the marketing activities. No matter what type of cosmetics a company is making (natural or chemical), what type of company it is (national or international), it has to satisfy the needs of the customers. No marketer can ever be successful until and unless it is able to understand the buying behavior of the end users. Hence, the current study addresses issues, such as, 'what factors are influencing the buying behavior of female consumers with reference to make-up cosmetics?' Has there been a relationship existing between the demographical factors and other influencing factors? How female consumers make decisions for buying a particular brand of make-up cosmetics and what factors affect the decision?

DOI: 10.4018/978-1-4666-7393-9.ch009

INTRODUCTION

The global cosmetic industry has been fascinated by India in a mesmerizing way–the world's second most populous country has seen a massive growth in the cosmetics industry. India's retail beauty and cosmetics industry, currently estimated at $950 million, is likely to almost treble to $2.68 billion by 2020 (TOI, 2013). The industry has been growing at an annual rate of almost 15-20 per cent in the coming years, which is twice as fast as that of the United States or Europe. The Indian cosmetic industry has witnessed robust growth in the past decade and has been ranked 5th largest in Asia (TOI, 2013).

The Associated Chambers of Commerce and Industry of India (ASSOCHAM, 2013) has published a survey which stated that 65% of the teenagers claimed that their expenditure on branded cosmetics had increased 75% in the past 10 years. In India, the target range for cosmetics is from 30 plus age group as against the western countries, where 55 plus age category is the target group.

The increasing disposable income of the urban Indian youth is encouraging them opt for better choices, especially in terms of grooming. Furthermore, people are now spending lavishly owing to the changing mindset. The changing face of the Indian cosmetic industry has certainly worked both for the country and its investors, and it undoubtedly looks ready to amaze.

LITERATURE REVIEW

Marketing Mix Factors

According to Kotler & Armstrong (1989), marketing mix and personal character-istics play important role in influencing the purchase behavior of consumers. Most of the studies have shown that the marketing mix factors have a strong impact on the purchasing behavior of the consumer. The study by Gupta (1988) shows that marketing mix have a strong relationship with consumers buying patterns, brand choices and incidences of purchase. Hence the relationship with brand and the marketing mix factors can be analyzed.

Product

The product characteristics such as package, durability, and quality of a make-up product play a significant role. The attributes are evaluated by the consumer based on his/her own values, beliefs, past experience (Peter & Olson, 1990). The product attribute of make-up product may include attractive packaging, color, ease to handle, variety and many more expected by the consumers.

Price

The price of the product may differ based on the economic conditions and consumer perceptions. It could influence the perceived value of a brand. Many consumers use price as an indication of the quality of the brand which is an important factor in purchasing decision (Nilson, 1998; Kotler & Armstrong, 1989).

Place

Place or the distribution channel is a combination of institutions through, which a seller markets product to user or ultimate consumer (Peter & Donnelly, 1992). Many companies take the advantage of a strong distribution channel to keep the brand in a strong position. They use different places such as super markets, high end groceries and retails to sell the brand. These selling points are also categorized based on the scale of the operation and the ultimate objective of the shareholders.

Promotion

Promotion is communicating information about the product between a seller and a buyer in order to create brand values and brand profile (McCarthy & Pereault, 1984). The four main elements of promotion mix are advertising, sales promotion, public relations and personal selling. The major objective of advertising can be inform, persuade, or remind through the mass media. The advertising includes television, radio, billboards, POSM, etc. In a first purchase situation, consumers will have to rely on advertising in order to decide whether to buy or not (Peter & Olson, 1990; Nilson, 1998). Sales promotions include sampling operations, free banded issues, money-offs and games among consumers, etc. These activities will uplift the sales volumes. Successful sales promotion has to be consistent with the brand values and be consistent with all other aspects of the brand (Peter & Olson, 1990; Nilson, 1998).

Demographical Factors

The impact on demographical factors also plays a significant role in consumers buying behavior. Age group is an attribute which has a direct impact on person's attitude towards a brand. In the make-up product categories age group is used to define the targeted market segment. Based on the maturity the preference for make-up or any other product may vary. The education level of a person also influence in the decision making process. A well educated person may analyze the ingredients in particular cosmetic brand but less educated person may not, due to lack of knowledge.

Income level of a person has a direct impact on the purchasing of a product. When the income levels rises naturally people tend to buy more luxury/premium products. The income affects the type of goods that consumers are likely to buy (McConnell & Brue, 1999). Since the demographical factors help to identify the target groups, the relationship between brand and the demographical factors can be analyzed.

Age

Age is a factor which plays a vital role in purchasing behavior of cosmetic, because it is considered as a criterion in the segmenting process. As an example some cosmetics are targeted to females' age between 16-24 years and some other brands are targeted to age between 16-45 years. Therefore each brand has its own targeted market. The purchasing behavior in age categories may be similar and or vice versa.

Marital Status and Years in Marriage

Consumers buy products over their lifetime. Buying behavior will be shaped by the family life cycle, which defines the marital status and life time as young single, young married, middle-aged single, middle aged divorced, older married, and so on (Onkvisit & Shaw, 1994). For an example unmarried consumer may have been using brand "A," but after that consumer got married she may be using brand "B" because of the enhanced level of income or influence of her husband/daughter etc.

Education

Based on the education level of a person buying behavior could vary. A well educated consumer may read the ingredients of cosmetics before the buying decision is made. At the same time consumer with a lesser education level may decide to buy the product due to the attractiveness of the package. Hence analysis of the relationship of education level and the brand is very important.

Employment Status/Occupation

The occupation of a consumer could vary during the life cycle or else may be occupied in the same occupation until retired, besides field of occupation also may be different during the life cycle. It enables the consumer to build up different types of reference groups around. Moreover it has a relationship with the income level, attitude, interest and life style of the consumer. Hence above factors results in various buying patterns (Guiltinan & Joseph, 1991).

Income Level

Income implies the purchasing power of a consumer. Because purchasing of a lower grade or a highly premium brand is decided based on the income level of the consumer. Even though there is a requirement to purchase a premium brand the income level of a consumer may not support it. Hence income and consumption are positively related. Generally when the income rises, consumers increase their purchases & consumption. But this is not applicable for inferior goods. Further more income also affects the type of goods that consumers are likely to buy (McConell & Brue, 1999; Onkvisit & Shaw, 1994).

Other Factors

Apart from above mentioned factors, there are some other factors that have been found responsible for the purchase of a particular brand of cosmetics over the other. They are discussed below.

Skin Type

Since make-up is applied directly to the skin, brand selection may occur due to the nature of the skin. Because some brands may be harmful to different skin types depending on the ingredients included. Therefore consumer may pay an especial attention to the skin type, when the brand is purchased. Skin types can be categorized as oily, dry, mixed, normal and sensitive.

Social Factors

The social factors refer to the influences made by the consumer's reference groups such as the family and friends. The weight and powerfulness of the influence may vary depending on the significance of the relationship between the consumer and the reference group. Reference groups can influence the beliefs, attitudes and behavior of a consumer in different circumstances. As result of that purchasing behavior and brand preference could get changed of a consumer. Consumers are more likely to be influenced by word-of-mouth information from members of reference groups than advertisements or sales people (Stanton et al, 1991), in terms of benefit, selecting or changing brands.

Friends/Colleagues and Others

The influence of friends/colleagues and other parties such a presenter/sales person also plays a vital role in the purchasing behavior of consumers. These friendship groups are classified as informal groups since they are with lack of authority levels. The options and preferences of friends are an important influence in determining the products or brands selecting, especially to a single person, who live alone (Schiffman & Kanuk, 2000). Hence friends and other interacting parties can be considered as influences to a consumer when a product is purchased.

Brand Preference

A brand can be a label of ownership, name, term, design, or symbol. Further brand can be product, service or concept. Brand preference is measure of brand loyalty in which consumers will choose a particular brand in presence of competing brands (http://www.businessdictionary.com/definition/brand-preference.html). Also it can be defined that the degree to which consumers prefer one brand over another (http://www.answers.com/topic/brand-preference). A greater brand loyalty among consumers leads to greater sales of the brand (Howard & Sheth, 1969). Brand loyalty leads to certain marketing advantages such as reduced marketing costs, more new customers and greater trade leverage (Aaker, 1991).Quality and personal habits thus influence this situation because consumers prefer risk reduction in familiar products not as in a trial (Nilson, 1998). Hence analyzing the brand preference of consumers is an interesting area for the marketers to develop the marketing strategies for their brands.

OBJECTIVES OF THE STUDY

Based on the Literature Review and the gap found, following objectives have been framed:

1. To know factors influencing the buying behavior of female consumers with reference to top three brands of make-up cosmetics.
2. To know the relationship between marketing mix factors and the brand preference of female consumers with reference to top three brands of make-up cosmetics.
3. To know the relationship existing between the demographical factors and the brand preference of female consumers with reference to top three brands of make-up cosmetics.

4. To know the relationship existing between the other factors (e.g. skin type, social factors) and the brand preference of female consumers with reference to top three brands of make-up cosmetics.

RESEARCH METHODOLOGY

- **Sample Design:** The present study is based on the primary data. The primary data were collected from 66 sample respondents. These 66 respondents were selected by using convenience sampling technique.
- **Data Collection:** The present study is purely based on the primary data. Questionnaire method was used to collect data. The questionnaires were mailed through e-mails.
- **Area and Period of the Study:** This study is confined to Pune city (Maharashtra, India). The study was conducted during the months of October-December 2013.
- **Framework and Tools for Analysis:** Data collected through questionnaire were presented in a master table and required sub-tables were prepared. For analyzing the data, Chi-square test and Percentage Analysis were applied. Statistical calculations and computations were done through IBM SPSS statistical package (version 19.0).

DATA ANALYSIS AND INTERPRETATION

- **Null Hypothesis:** There is no relationship between respondent category and the brand preference of female consumers with reference to top three brands of make-up cosmetics.
- **Alternative Hypothesis:** There is significant relationship between respondent category and the brand preference of female consumers with reference to top three brands of make-up cosmetics.
- **Statistical Test:** Chi-square test.
- **Level of Significance** $= 0.05$.

From Table 1:

- Out of 66 respondents, 32 are students, 26 are working women and 8 are housewives.
- Out of 32 students, 16 prefer Lakme, 10 prefer Revlon and 6 prefer L'Oreal.

Table 1. Respondent category * brand preference cross-tabulation

			Brand			Total
			Lakme	Revlon	L'Oreal	
Respondents category	student	Count	16	10	6	32
		Expected Count	15.0	10.2	6.8	32.0
		% within respondents category	50.0%	31.2%	18.8%	100.0%
	working women	Count	10	8	8	26
		Expected Count	12.2	8.3	5.5	26.0
		% within respondents category	38.5%	30.8%	30.8%	100.0%
	housewife	Count	5	3	0	8
		Expected Count	3.8	2.5	1.7	8.0
		% within respondents category	62.5%	37.5%	0.0%	100.0%
Total		Count	31	21	14	66
		Expected Count	31.0	21.0	14.0	66.0
		% within respondents category	47.0%	31.8%	21.2%	100.0%

- Out of 26 working women, 10 prefer Lakme, 8 prefer Revlon and 8 prefer L'Oreal.
- Out of 8 housewives, 5 prefer Lakme, 3 prefer Revlon and none of them prefer L'Oreal.

From Table 2:

- The Pearson Chi-square is 3.875.
- Degree of Freedom = 4.
- P value = 0.423 which is more than level of significance 0.05. Therefore the null is accepted.

Table 2. Chi-square tests

	Value	df	Asymp. Sig. (2-Sided)
Pearson Chi-Square	3.875	4	.423
Likelihood Ratio	5.420	4	.247
Linear-by-Linear Association	.071	1	.789
N of Valid Cases	66		

- **Null Hypothesis:** There is no relationship between age and the brand preference of female consumers with reference to top three brands of make-up cosmetics.
- **Alternative Hypothesis:** There is significant relationship between age and the brand preference of female consumers with reference to top three brands of make-up cosmetics.
- **Statistical Test:** Chi-square test.
- **Level of Significance** = 0.05.

From Table 3:

- Out of 66 respondents, 43 are between the age of 15-25 years, 17 are between 25-35 years, 4 of them are between 35-45 years, and only 2 are between 45-55 years.
- Out of 43 respondents who are between the age of 15-25 years, 19 prefer Lakme, 15 prefer Revlon and 9 prefer L'Oreal.
- Out of 17 respondents who are between the age of 25-35 years, 10 prefer Lakme, 3 prefer Revlon and 4 prefer L'Oreal.
- Out of 4 respondents who are between the age of 35-45 years, none prefer Lakme, 3 prefer Revlon and only 1 respondent prefers L'Oreal.
- Both the respondents who are between the age of 45-55 years prefer Lakme only.

From Table 4:

- The Pearson Chi-square is 8.332.
- Degree of Freedom = 6.
- P value = 0.215 which is more than level of significance 0.05. Therefore the null is accepted.

*Table 3. Age * brand preference cross-tabulation*

		Brand			Total
		Lakme	Revlon	L'Oreal	
Age	15-25	19	15	9	43
	25-35	10	3	4	17
	35-45	0	3	1	4
	45-55	2	0	0	2
Total		31	21	14	66

Table 4. Chi-square tests

	Value	df	Asymp. Sig. (2-Sided)
Pearson Chi-Square	8.332	6	.215
Likelihood Ratio	10.486	6	.106
Linear-by-Linear Association	.178	1	.673
N of Valid Cases	66		

- **Null Hypothesis:** There is no relationship between marital status and the brand preference of female consumers with reference to top three brands of make-up cosmetics.
- **Alternative Hypothesis:** There is significant relationship between marital status and the brand preference of female consumers with reference to top three brands of make-up cosmetics.
- **Statistical Test:** Chi-square test.
- **Level of Significance = 0.05.**

From Table 5:

- Out of 66 respondents, 20 are married, 44 are unmarried and 2 are widows.
- Out of 20 married respondents, 11 prefer Lakme, 7 prefer Revlon, and 2 prefer L'Oreal.
- Out of 44 unmarried respondents, 18 prefer Lakme, 14 prefer Revlon and 12 prefer L'Oreal.
- Both widow respondents prefer Lakme.

*Table 5. Marital status * brand preference cross-tabulation*

		Brand			Total
		Lakme	**Revlon**	**L'Oreal**	
Marital Status	Married	11	7	2	20
	Unmarried	18	14	12	44
	Widow	2	0	0	2
Total		31	21	14	66

From Table 6:

- The Pearson Chi-square is 4.888.
- Degree of Freedom = 4.
- P value = 0.299 which is more than level of significance 0.05. Therefore the null is accepted.
- **Null Hypothesis:** There is no relationship between number of years of marriage and the brand preference of female consumers with reference to top three brands of make-up cosmetics.
- **Alternative Hypothesis:** There is significant relationship between number of years of marriage and the brand preference of female consumers with reference to top three brands of make-up cosmetics.
- **Statistical Test:** Chi-square test.
- **Level of Significance** = 0.05.

From Table 7:

- Out of 20 married respondents, 4 are married since less than one year, 9 are married since 1-5 years, 3 are married since 5-10 years and 4 are married since 10-20 years.
- All the 4 respondents who are married since less than one year prefer Lakme.
- Out of 9 respondents who are married since 1-5 years, 4 prefer Lakme, 4 prefer Revlon and only 1 respondent prefers L'Oreal.
- All the 3 respondents who are married since 5-10 years prefer Lakme.
- Out of 4 respondents who are married since 10-20 years, none prefer Lakme, 3 prefer Revlon and only 1 respondent prefers L'Oreal.

From Table 8:

- The Pearson Chi-square is 11.079.
- Degree of Freedom = 6.

Table 6. Chi-square tests

	Value	df	Asymp. Sig. (2-Sided)
Pearson Chi-Square	4.888	4	.299
Likelihood Ratio	5.879	4	.208
Linear-by-Linear Association	.051	1	.821
N of Valid Cases	66		

*Table 7. Number of years in marriage * brand preference cross-tabulation*

		Brand			Total
		Lakme	Revlon	L'Oreal	
No. of Years in Marriage	<1year	4	0	0	4
	1-5	4	4	1	9
	5-10	3	0	0	3
	10-20	0	3	1	4
Total		11	7	2	20

Table 8. Chi-square tests

	Value	df	Asymp. Sig. (2-sided)
Pearson Chi-Square	11.079	6	.086
Likelihood Ratio	15.192	6	.019
Linear-by-Linear Association	3.907	1	.048
N of Valid Cases	20		

- P value = 0.086 which is slightly more than the level of significance 0.05. Therefore we can say that there is partially significant relationship between number of years of marriage and the brand preference of female consumers with reference to top three brands of make-up cosmetics.
- **Null Hypothesis:** There is no relationship between number of children and the brand preference of female consumers with reference to top three brands of make-up cosmetics.
- **Alternative Hypothesis:** There is significant relationship between number of children and the brand preference of female consumers with reference to top three brands of make-up cosmetics.
- **Statistical Test:** Chi-square test.
- **Level of Significance** = 0.05.

From Table 9:

- Out of 22 respondents (20 married and 2 widows), 4 respondents do not have any child and the remaining 18 respondents have 1-2 kids.
- All the 4 respondents who do not have any child prefer Lakme.
- Out of 18 respondents who have 1-2 kids, 9 prefer Lakme, 7 prefer Revlon and 2 prefer L'Oreal.

*Table 9. Number of kids * brand preference cross-tabulation*

		Brand			Total
		Lakme	Revlon	L'Oreal	
No. of kids	Nil	4	0	0	4
	1-2	9	7	2	18
Total		13	7	2	22

From Table 10:

- The Pearson Chi-square is 3.385.
- Degree of Freedom = 2.
- P value = 0.184 which is more than level of significance 0.05. Therefore the null is accepted.
- **Null Hypothesis:** There is no relationship between employment and the brand preference of female consumers with reference to top three brands of make-up cosmetics.
- **Alternative Hypothesis:** There is significant relationship between employment and the brand preference of female consumers with reference to top three brands of make-up cosmetics.
- **Statistical Test:** Chi-square test.
- **Level of Significance** = 0.05.

From Table 11:

- Out of 66 respondents, 35 are unemployed, 3 are self-employed and 28 are private employee.
- Out of 35 unemployed respondents, 19 prefer Lakme, 12 prefer Revlon and 4 prefer L'Oreal.

Table 10. Chi-square tests

	Value	df	Asymp. Sig. (2-Sided)
Pearson Chi-Square	3.385	2	.184
Likelihood Ratio	4.814	2	.090
Linear-by-Linear Association	2.702	1	.100
N of Valid Cases	22		

*Table 11. Employment * brand preference cross-tabulation*

		Brand			Total
		Lakme	Revlon	L'Oreal	
Employment	Unemployed	19	12	4	35
	Self-employed	0	1	2	3
	Private employee	12	8	8	28
Total		31	21	14	66

- Out of 3 Self-employed respondents, none prefer Lakme, 1 prefers Revlon and 2 prefer L'Oreal.
- Out of 28 private employee respondents, 12 prefer Lakme, 8 prefer Revlon and 8 prefer L'Oreal.

From Table 12:

- The Pearson Chi-square is 7.287.
- Degree of Freedom = 4.
- P value = 0.121 which is more than level of significance 0.05. Therefore the null is accepted.
- **Null Hypothesis:** There is no relationship between annual family income and the brand preference of female consumers with reference to top three brands of make-up cosmetics.
- **Alternative Hypothesis:** There is significant relationship between annual family income and the brand preference of female consumers with reference to top three brands of make-up cosmetics.
- **Statistical Test:** Chi-square test.
- **Level of Significance** = 0.05.

Table 12. Chi-square tests

	Value	df	Asymp. Sig. (2-Sided)
Pearson Chi-Square	7.287	4	.121
Likelihood Ratio	7.863	4	.097
Linear-by-Linear Association	2.174	1	.140
N of Valid Cases	66		

Table 13. Annual family income * brand preference cross-tabulation

		Brand			Total
		Lakme	Revlon	L'Oreal	
Ann. Family Income	< Rs. 1 lac	10	2	0	12
	Rs.1lac-Rs.10 lac	19	15	8	42
	>Rs.10 lac	2	4	6	12
Total		31	21	14	66

From Table 13:

- Out of 66 respondents, 12 have annual family income less than Rs. 1Lac, 42 have income between Rs. 1Lac –Rs. 10Lac and 12 have income more than Rs.10Lac.
- Out of 12 respondents who have annual family income less than Rs. 1Lac, 10 prefer Lakme 2 prefer Revlon and none prefer L'Oreal.
- Out of 42 respondents who have annual family income between Rs. 1Lac – Rs. 10Lac, 19 prefer Lakme 15 prefer Revlon and 8 prefer L'Oreal.
- Out of 12 respondents who have annual family income more than Rs.10Lac, 2 prefer Lakme 4 prefer Revlon and 6 prefer L'Oreal.

From Table 14:

- The Pearson Chi-square is 14.153.
- Degree of Freedom = 4.
- P value = 0.007 which is less than level of significance 0.05. Therefore the null is rejected.
- **Null Hypothesis:** There is no relationship between educational qualification and the brand preference of female consumers with reference to top three brands of make-up cosmetics.

Table 14. Chi-square tests

	Value	df	Asymp. Sig. (2-Sided)
Pearson Chi-Square	14.153	4	.007
Likelihood Ratio	15.714	4	.003
Linear-by-Linear Association	13.068	1	.000
N of Valid Cases	66		

- **Alternative Hypothesis:** There is significant relationship between educational qualification and the brand preference of female consumers with reference to top three brands of make-up cosmetics.
- **Statistical Test:** Chi-square test.
- **Level of Significance** = 0.05.

From Table 15:

- Out of 66 respondents, 25 are Graduate, 38 are Post Graduate and 3 are Doctorate.
- Out of 25 Graduate respondents, 12 prefer Lakme, 10 prefer Revlon and 3 prefer L'Oreal.
- Out of 38 Post Graduate respondents, 16 prefer Lakme, 11 prefer Revlon and 11 prefer L'Oreal.
- All the 3 Doctorate respondents prefer Lakme.

From Table 16:

- The Pearson Chi-square is 6.281.
- Degree of Freedom = 4.
- P value = 0.179 which is more than level of significance 0.05. Therefore the null is accepted.

*Table 15. Educational qualification * brand preference cross-tabulation*

		Brand			Total
		Lakme	Revlon	L'Oreal	
Educational Qualification	Graduate	12	10	3	25
	Post Graduate	16	11	11	38
	Doctorate	3	0	0	3
Total		31	21	14	66

Table 16. Chi-square tests

	Value	df	Asymp. Sig. (2-Sided)
Pearson Chi-Square	6.281	4	.179
Likelihood Ratio	7.475	4	.113
Linear-by-Linear Association	.009	1	.926
N of Valid Cases	66		

- **Null Hypothesis:** There is no relationship between skin type and the brand preference of female consumers with reference to top three brands of make-up cosmetics.
- **Alternative Hypothesis:** There is significant relationship between skin type and the brand preference of female consumers with reference to top three brands of make-up cosmetics.
- **Statistical Test:** Chi-square test.
- **Level of Significance = 0.05.**

From Table 17:

- Out of 66 respondents, 15 have oily skin, 7 have dry skin, 11 have mixed skin, 21 have normal skin and 12 have sensitive skin.
- Out of 15 respondents who have oily skin, 10 prefer Lakme, 2 prefer Revlon and 3 prefer L'Oreal.

*Table 17. Skin type * brand preference cross-tabulation*

			Brand			Total
			Lakme	Revlon	L'Oreal	
skin type	oily	Count	10	2	3	15
		Expected Count	7.0	4.8	3.2	15.0
		% within skin type	66.7%	13.3%	20.0%	100.0%
	dry	Count	3	4	0	7
		Expected Count	3.3	2.2	1.5	7.0
		% within skin type	42.9%	57.1%	0.0%	100.0%
	mixed	Count	2	4	5	11
		Expected Count	5.2	3.5	2.3	11.0
		% within skin type	18.2%	36.4%	45.5%	100.0%
	normal	Count	11	5	5	21
		Expected Count	9.9	6.7	4.5	21.0
		% within skin type	52.4%	23.8%	23.8%	100.0%
	sensitive	Count	5	6	1	12
		Expected Count	5.6	3.8	2.5	12.0
		% within skin type	41.7%	50.0%	8.3%	100.0%
Total		Count	31	21	14	66
		Expected Count	31.0	21.0	14.0	66.0
		% within skin type	47.0%	31.8%	21.2%	100.0%

- Out of 7 respondents who have dry skin, 3 prefer Lakme, 4 prefer Revlon and none prefer L'Oreal.
- Out of 11 respondents who have mixed skin, 2 prefer Lakme, 4 prefer Revlon and 5 prefer L'Oreal.
- Out of 21 respondents who have normal skin, 11 prefer Lakme, 5 prefer Revlon and 5 prefer L'Oreal.
- Out of 12 respondents who have sensitive skin, 5 prefer Lakme, 6 prefer Revlon and 1 prefers L'Oreal.

From Table 18:

- The Pearson Chi-square is 13.719.
- Degree of Freedom = 8.
- P value = 0.089 which is slightly more than level of significance 0.05. Therefore we can say that there is partially significant relationship between skin type and the brand preference of female consumers with reference to top three brands of make-up cosmetics.
- **Null Hypothesis:** There is no relationship between number of years of use of cosmetics and the brand preference of female consumers with reference to top three brands of make-up cosmetics.
- **Alternative Hypothesis:** There is significant relationship between number of years of use of cosmetics and the brand preference of female consumers with reference to top three brands of make-up cosmetics.
- **Statistical Test:** Chi-square test.
- **Level of Significance** = 0.05.

From Table 19:

- Out of 66 respondents, 42 respondents are using cosmetics since less than 5 years, 13 are using since 5-10 years, 6 are using since 10-15 years, 3 are using since 15-20 years, and 2 are using since 25-30 years.
- Out of 42 respondents who are using cosmetics since less than 5 years, 19 prefer Lakme, 12 prefer Revlon and 11 prefer L'Oreal.
- Out of 13 respondents who are using cosmetics since 5-10 years, 5 prefer Lakme, 5 prefer Revlon and 3 prefer L'Oreal.
- Out of 6 respondents who are using cosmetics since 10-15 years, 5 prefer Lakme, 1 prefer Revlon and none prefer L'Oreal.
- All the 3 respondents who are using cosmetics since 15-20 years prefer Revlon.
- Both the respondents who are using cosmetics since 25-30 years prefer Lakme.

Table 18. Chi-square tests

	Value	df	Asymp. Sig. (2-Sided)
Pearson Chi-Square	13.719	8	.089
Likelihood Ratio	15.211	8	.055
Linear-by-Linear Association	.303	1	.582
N of Valid Cases	66		

*Table 19. Years of use of make-up cosmetics * brand preference cross-tabulation*

			Brand			Total
			Lakme	Revlon	L'Oreal	
Years of use of make-up cosmetics	less than 5 yrs	Count	19	12	11	42
		Expected Count	19.7	13.4	8.9	42.0
		% within years of use of make-up cosmetics	45.2%	28.6%	26.2%	100.0%
	5-10 yrs	Count	5	5	3	13
		Expected Count	6.1	4.1	2.8	13.0
		% within years of use of make-up cosmetics	38.5%	38.5%	23.1%	100.0%
	10-15 yrs	Count	5	1	0	6
		Expected Count	2.8	1.9	1.3	6.0
		% within years of use of make-up cosmetics	83.3%	16.7%	0.0%	100.0%
	15-20 yrs	Count	0	3	0	3
		Expected Count	1.4	1.0	.6	3.0
		% within years of use of make-up cosmetics	0.0%	100.0%	0.0%	100.0%
	25-30	Count	2	0	0	2
		Expected Count	.9	.6	.4	2.0
		% within years of use of make-up cosmetics	100.0%	0.0%	0.0%	100.0%
Total		Count	31	21	14	66
		Expected Count	31.0	21.0	14.0	66.0
		% within years of use of make-up cosmetics	47.0%	31.8%	21.2%	100.0%

From Table 20:

- The Pearson Chi-square is 13.140.
- Degree of Freedom = 8.
- P value = 0.107 which is more than level of significance 0.05. Therefore the null is accepted.

Table 20. Chi-square tests

	Value	df	Asymp. Sig. (2-Sided)
Pearson Chi-Square	13.140	8	.107
Likelihood Ratio	15.365	8	.052
Linear-by-Linear Association	2.150	1	.143
N of Valid Cases	66		

- **Null Hypothesis:** There is no relationship between number of cosmetics used per day and the brand preference of female consumers with reference to top three brands of make-up cosmetics.
- **Alternative Hypothesis:** There is significant relationship between number of cosmetics used per day and the brand preference of female consumers with reference to top three brands of make-up cosmetics.
- **Statistical Test:** Chi-square test.
- **Level of Significance = 0.05.**

From Table 21:

- Out of 66 respondents, 48 respondents are using less than 4 cosmetics per day, 15 are using 4-8 cosmetics per day, 2 are using 8-12 cosmetics per day and 1 respondent is using 16-20 cosmetics per day.
- Out of 48 respondents who are using less than 4 cosmetics per day, 24 prefer Lakme, 12 prefer Revlon and 12 prefer L'Oreal.
- Out of 15 respondents who are using are using 4-8 cosmetics per day, 5 prefer Lakme, 8 prefer Revlon and 2 prefer L'Oreal.
- Both the respondents who use 8-12 cosmetics per day prefer Lakme.
- The respondent who uses 16-20 cosmetics per day prefer Revlon.

From Table 22:

- The Pearson Chi-square is 8.736.
- Degree of Freedom = 6.
- P value = 0.189 which is more than level of significance 0.05. Therefore the null is accepted.
- **Null Hypothesis:** There is no relationship between frequency of purchase of cosmetics and the brand preference of female consumers with reference to top three brands of make-up cosmetics.

*Table 21. Number of cosmetics used per day * brand preference cross-tabulation*

			Brand			Total
			Lakme	Revlon	L'Oreal	
no of cosmetics	less than 4	Count	24	12	12	48
		Expected Count	22.5	15.3	10.2	48.0
		% within no of cosmetics	50.0%	25.0%	25.0%	100.0%
	4-8	Count	5	8	2	15
		Expected Count	7.0	4.8	3.2	15.0
		% within no of cosmetics	33.3%	53.3%	13.3%	100.0%
	8-12	Count	2	0	0	2
		Expected Count	.9	.6	.4	2.0
		% within no of cosmetics	100.0%	0.0%	0.0%	100.0%
	16-20	Count	0	1	0	1
		Expected Count	.5	.3	.2	1.0
		% within no of cosmetics	0.0%	100.0%	0.0%	100.0%
Total		Count	31	21	14	66
		Expected Count	31.0	21.0	14.0	66.0
		% within no of cosmetics	47.0%	31.8%	21.2%	100.0%

Table 22. Chi-square tests

	Value	df	Asymp. Sig. (2-Sided)
Pearson Chi-Square	8.736	6	.189
Likelihood Ratio	9.447	6	.150
Linear-by-Linear Association	.060	1	.807
N of Valid Cases	66		

- **Alternative Hypothesis:** There is significant relationship between frequency of purchase of cosmetics and the brand preference of female consumers with reference to top three brands of make-up cosmetics.
- **Statistical Test:** Chi-square test.
- **Level of Significance = 0.05.**

From Table 23:

- Out of 66 respondents, 15 respondents purchase cosmetics more than once a month, 16 respondents purchase cosmetics about once a month, 16 respon-

*Table 23. Frequency of purchase * brand preference cross-tabulation*

			Brand			Total
			Lakme	Revlon	L'Oreal	
frequency of purchase	more than once a month	Count	8	5	2	15
		Expected Count	7.0	4.8	3.2	15.0
		% within frequency of purchase	53.3%	33.3%	13.3%	100.0%
	about once a month	Count	3	8	5	16
		Expected Count	7.5	5.1	3.4	16.0
		% within frequency of purchase	18.8%	50.0%	31.2%	100.0%
	once every 3 months	Count	7	6	3	16
		Expected Count	7.5	5.1	3.4	16.0
		% within frequency of purchase	43.8%	37.5%	18.8%	100.0%
	once every six months	Count	5	0	2	7
		Expected Count	3.3	2.2	1.5	7.0
		% within frequency of purchase	71.4%	0.0%	28.6%	100.0%
	once a year	Count	4	1	1	6
		Expected Count	2.8	1.9	1.3	6.0
		% within frequency of purchase	66.7%	16.7%	16.7%	100.0%
	anytime	Count	4	1	1	6
		Expected Count	2.8	1.9	1.3	6.0
		% within frequency of purchase	66.7%	16.7%	16.7%	100.0%
Total		Count	31	21	14	66
		Expected Count	31.0	21.0	14.0	66.0
		% within frequency of purchase	47.0%	31.8%	21.2%	100.0%

dents purchase cosmetics once every 3 months, 7 respondents purchase cosmetics once every 6 months, 6 respondents purchase cosmetics once in a year and 6 respondents purchase cosmetics anytime.

- Out of 15 respondents who purchase cosmetics more than once a month, 8 prefer Lakme, 5 prefer Revlon and 2 prefer L'Oreal.
- Out of 16 respondents who purchase cosmetics about once a month, 3 prefer Lakme, 8 prefer Revlon and 5 prefer L'Oreal.
- Out of 16 respondents who purchase cosmetics once every 3 months, 7 prefer Lakme, 6 prefer Revlon and 3 prefer L'Oreal.
- Out of 7 respondents who purchase cosmetics once every 6 months, 5 prefer Lakme, none prefer Revlon and 2 prefer L'Oreal.

- Out of 6 respondents who purchase cosmetics once in a year, 4 prefer Lakme, 1 prefers Revlon and 1 prefers L'Oreal.
- Out of 6 respondents who purchase cosmetics anytime, 4 prefer Lakme, 1 prefers Revlon and 1 prefers L'Oreal.

From Table 24:

- The Pearson Chi-square is 11.229.
- Degree of Freedom = 10.
- P value = 0.340 which is more than level of significance 0.05. Therefore the null is accepted.
- **Null Hypothesis:** There is no relationship between monthly expenditure on cosmetics and the brand preference of female consumers with reference to top three brands of make-up cosmetics.
- **Alternative Hypothesis:** There is significant relationship between monthly expenditure on cosmetics and the brand preference of female consumers with reference to top three brands of make-up cosmetics.
- **Statistical Test:** Chi-square test.
- **Level of Significance** = 0.05.

From Table 25:

- Out of 66 respondents, 46 respondents spend less than Rs. 500 a month on cosmetics purchase, 18 respondents spend Rs. 500-Rs. 1000 a month on cosmetics purchase and 2 respondents spend more than Rs. 1000 a month on cosmetics purchase.
- Out of 46 respondents who spend less than Rs. 500 a month on cosmetics purchase, 24 prefer Lakme, 11 prefer Revlon and 11 prefer L'Oreal.
- Out of 18 respondents who spend Rs. 500-Rs. 1000 a month on cosmetics purchase, 6 prefer Lakme, 9 prefer Revlon and 3 prefer L'Oreal.

Table 24. Chi-square tests

	Value	df	Asymp. Sig. (2-Sided)
Pearson Chi-Square	11.229	10	.340
Likelihood Ratio	13.910	10	.177
Linear-by-Linear Association	1.066	1	.302
N of Valid Cases	66		

Table 25. Monthly expenses on cosmetics * brand preference cross-tabulation

			Brand			Total
			Lakme	Revlon	L'Oreal	
monthly expense on cosmetics	less than 500	Count	24	11	11	46
		Expected Count	21.6	14.6	9.8	46.0
		% within monthly expense on cosmetics	52.2%	23.9%	23.9%	100.0%
	500-1000	Count	6	9	3	18
		Expected Count	8.5	5.7	3.8	18.0
		% within monthly expense on cosmetics	33.3%	50.0%	16.7%	100.0%
	more than 1000	Count	1	1	0	2
		Expected Count	.9	.6	.4	2.0
		% within monthly expense on cosmetics	50.0%	50.0%	0.0%	100.0%
Total		Count	31	21	14	66
		Expected Count	31.0	21.0	14.0	66.0
		% within monthly expense on cosmetics	47.0%	31.8%	21.2%	100.0%

- Out of 2 respondents who spend more than Rs. 1000 a month on cosmetics purchase, 1 prefer Lakme, 1 prefer Revlon and none prefer L'Oreal.

From Table 26:

- The Pearson Chi-square is 4.721.
- Degree of Freedom = 4.
- P value = 0.317 which is more than level of significance 0.05. Therefore the null is accepted.

Table 26. Chi-square tests

	Value	df	Asymp. Sig. (2-Sided)
Pearson Chi-Square	4.721	4	.317
Likelihood Ratio	4.999	4	.287
Linear-by-Linear Association	.038	1	.845
N of Valid Cases	66		

- **Null Hypothesis:** There is no relationship between importance of product feel in cosmetics purchase and the brand preference of female consumers with reference to top three brands of make-up cosmetics.
- **Alternative Hypothesis:** There is significant relationship between importance of product feel in cosmetics purchase and the brand preference of female consumers with reference to top three brands of make-up cosmetics.
- **Statistical Test:** Chi-square test.
- **Level of Significance= 0.05.**

From Table 27:

- Out of 66 respondents, for 37 respondents product feel is very important factor in cosmetics purchase, for 23 respondents product feel is fairly important factor in cosmetics purchase and 6 of the respondents are not sure about the same.
- Out of 37 respondents for whom product feel is very important factor in cosmetics purchase, 17 prefer Lakme, 10 prefer Revlon and 10 prefer L'Oreal.
- Out of 23 respondents for whom product feel is fairly important factor in cosmetics purchase, 12 prefer Lakme, 8 prefer Revlon and 3 prefer L'Oreal.
- Out of 6 respondents who are not sure about the importance of product feel in cosmetics purchase, 2 prefer Lakme, 3 prefer Revlon and 1 prefer L'Oreal.

*Table 27. Importance of Product feel * brand preference cross-tabulation*

			Brand			Total
			Lakme	Revlon	L'Oreal	
importance of product feel	very important	Count	17	10	10	37
		Expected Count	17.4	11.8	7.8	37.0
		% within importance of product feel	45.9%	27.0%	27.0%	100.0%
	fairly important	Count	12	8	3	23
		Expected Count	10.8	7.3	4.9	23.0
		% within importance of product feel	52.2%	34.8%	13.0%	100.0%
	I don't know	Count	2	3	1	6
		Expected Count	2.8	1.9	1.3	6.0
		% within importance of product feel	33.3%	50.0%	16.7%	100.0%
Total		Count	31	21	14	66
		Expected Count	31.0	21.0	14.0	66.0
		% within importance of product feel	47.0%	31.8%	21.2%	100.0%

From Table 28:

- The Pearson Chi-square is 2.704.
- Degree of Freedom = 4.
- P value = 0.609 which is more than level of significance 0.05. Therefore the null is accepted.
- **Null Hypothesis:** There is no relationship between purchase of cosmetics based on tester and the brand preference of female consumers with reference to top three brands of make-up cosmetics.
- **Alternative Hypothesis:** There is significant relationship between purchase of cosmetics based on tester and the brand preference of female consumers with reference to top three brands of make-up cosmetics.
- **Statistical Test:** Chi-square test.
- **Level of Significance** = 0.05.

From Table 29:

- Out of 66 respondents, 50 respondents said that they purchase cosmetics based on tester, and 16 respondents said that they do not purchase cosmetics based on tester.
- Out of 50 respondents who purchase cosmetics based on tester, 24 prefer Lakme, 15 prefer Revlon and 11 prefer L'Oreal.
- Out of 16 respondents who do not purchase cosmetics based on tester, 7 prefer Lakme, 6 prefer Revlon and 3 prefer L'Oreal.

From Table 30:

- The Pearson Chi-square is 0.795.
- Degree of Freedom = 2.
- P value = 0.672 which is more than level of significance 0.05. Therefore the null is accepted.
- **Null Hypothesis:** There is no relationship between purchase of other products from the same brand of cosmetics and the brand preference of female consumers with reference to top three brands of make-up cosmetics.
- **Alternative Hypothesis:** There is significant relationship between purchase of other products from the same brand of cosmetics and the brand preference of female consumers with reference to top three brands of make-up cosmetics.
- **Statistical Test:** Chi-square test.
- **Level of Significance** = 0.05.

Table 28. Chi-square tests

	Value	df	Asymp. Sig. (2-Sided)
Pearson Chi-Square	2.704	4	.609
Likelihood Ratio	2.719	4	.606
Linear-by-Linear Association	.222	1	.638
N of Valid Cases	66		

*Table 29. Purchase of cosmetics based on tester * brand preference cross-tabulation*

			Brand			Total
			Lakme	Revlon	L'Oreal	
Have you purchase make-up based on tester?	yes	Count	24	15	11	50
		Expected Count	23.8	16.2	10.0	50.0
		% within have you purchase make-up based on tester	48.0%	30.0%	22.0%	100.0%
	no	Count	7	6	3	16
		Expected Count	7.2	4.8	4.0	16.0
		% within have you purchase make-up based on tester	46.7%	40.0%	13.3%	100.0%
Total		Count	31	21	14	66
		Expected Count	31.0	21.0	14.0	66.0
		% within have you purchase make-up based on tester	47.7%	32.3%	20.0%	100.0%

Table 30. Chi-square tests

	Value	df	Asymp. Sig. (2-Sided)
Pearson Chi-Square	.795	2	.672
Likelihood Ratio	.819	2	.664
Linear-by-Linear Association	.102	1	.750
N of Valid Cases	65		

From Table 31:

- Out of 66 respondents, 61 respondents said that they purchase other products of the same cosmetic brand, and 5 respondents said that they do not purchase other products of the same brand.

*Table 31. Purchase of other products from the same brand * brand preference cross-tabulation*

			Brand			Total
			Lakme	Revlon	L'Oreal	
Purchase of other products from the same brand	yes	Count	26	21	14	61
		Expected Count	28.7	19.4	12.9	61.0
		% within purchase of other products from the same brand	42.6%	34.4%	23.0%	100.0%
	no	Count	5	0	0	5
		Expected Count	2.3	1.6	1.1	5.0
		% within purchase of other products from the same brand	100.0%	0.0%	0.0%	100.0%
Total		Count	31	21	14	66
		Expected Count	31.0	21.0	14.0	66.0
		% within purchase of other products from the same brand	47.0%	31.8%	21.2%	100.0%

- Out of 61 respondents who purchase other products of the same cosmetic brand, 26 prefer Lakme, 21 prefer Revlon and 14 prefer L'Oreal.
- All the 5 respondents who do not purchase other products of the same cosmetic brand prefer Lakme.

From Table 32:

- The Pearson Chi-square is 6.108.
- Degree of Freedom = 2.
- P value = 0.047 which is less than level of significance 0.05. Therefore the null is rejected.

Table 32. Chi-square tests

	Value	df	Asymp. Sig. (2-Sided)
Pearson Chi-Square	6.108	2	.047
Likelihood Ratio	8.022	2	.018
Linear-by-Linear Association	4.771	1	.029
N of Valid Cases	66		

- **Null Hypothesis:** There is no relationship between opinion of friends and the brand preference of female consumers with reference to top three brands of make-up cosmetics.
- **Alternative Hypothesis:** There is significant relationship between opinion of friends and the brand preference of female consumers with reference to top three brands of make-up cosmetics.
- **Statistical Test:** Chi-square test.
- **Level of Significance=** 0.05.

From Table 33:

- Out of 66 respondents, 9 respondents said that they seek the opinion of their friends very often, 16 respondents said that they often seek the opinion of their friends, 31 respondents said that they sometimes seek the opinion of their friends, 5 respondents said that they seek the opinion of their friends very rarely and 5 respondents said that they never seek the opinion of their friends while purchasing cosmetics.
- Out of 9 respondents who seek the opinion of their friends very often, 5 prefer Lakme, 3 prefer Revlon and 1 prefers L'Oreal.
- Out of 16 respondents who often seek the opinion of their friends, 5 prefer Lakme, 5 prefer Revlon and 6 prefer L'Oreal.
- Out of 31 respondents who sometimes seek the opinion of their friends, 18 prefer Lakme, 9 prefer Revlon and 4 prefer L'Oreal.
- Out of 5 respondents who seek the opinion of their friends very rarely, 3 prefer Lakme, 1 prefers Revlon and 1 prefers L'Oreal.
- Out of 5 respondents who never seek the opinion of their friends, none prefer Lakme, 3 prefer Revlon and 2 prefer L'Oreal.

From Table 34:

- The Pearson Chi-square is 10.154.
- Degree of Freedom = 8.
- P value = 0.254 which is more than level of significance 0.05. Therefore the null is accepted.
- **Null Hypothesis:** There is no relationship between recommendation of sales personnel and the brand preference of female consumers with reference to top three brands of make-up cosmetics.
- **Alternative Hypothesis:** There is significant relationship between recommendation of sales personnel and the brand preference of female consumers with reference to top three brands of make-up cosmetics.

Table 33. Opinion of friends * brand preference cross-tabulation

			Brand			Total
			Lakme	Revlon	Loreal	
opinion of friends	very often	Count	5	3	1	9
		Expected Count	4.2	2.9	1.9	9.0
		% within opinion of friends	55.6%	33.3%	11.1%	100.0%
	often	Count	5	5	6	16
		Expected Count	7.5	5.1	3.4	16.0
		% within opinion of friends	31.2%	31.2%	37.5%	100.0%
	sometimes	Count	18	9	4	31
		Expected Count	14.6	9.9	6.6	31.0
		% within opinion of friends	58.1%	29.0%	12.9%	100.0%
	very rarely	Count	3	1	1	5
		Expected Count	2.3	1.6	1.1	5.0
		% within opinion of friends	60.0%	20.0%	20.0%	100.0%
	never	Count	0	3	2	5
		Expected Count	2.3	1.6	1.1	5.0
		% within opinion of friends	0.0%	60.0%	40.0%	100.0%
Total		Count	31	21	14	66
		Expected Count	31.0	21.0	14.0	66.0
		% within opinion of friends	47.0%	31.8%	21.2%	100.0%

Table 34. Chi-square tests

	Value	df	Asymp. Sig. (2-Sided)
Pearson Chi-Square	10.154	8	.254
Likelihood Ratio	12.020	8	.150
Linear-by-Linear Association	.377	1	.539
N of Valid Cases	66		

- **Statistical Test:** Chi-square test.
- **Level of Significance** = 0.05.

From Table 35:

- Out of 66 respondents, 1 respondent said that she purchase cosmetics based on recommendation of sales personnel very often, 10 respondents said that they often purchase cosmetics based on recommendation of sales personnel, 25 respondents said that they sometimes purchase cosmetics based on recommendation of sales personnel, 22 respondents said that they purchase cosmetics based on recommendation of sales personnel very rarely and 8 respon-

*Table 35. Recommendation of sales personnel * brand preference cross-tabulation*

			Brand			Total
			Lakme	Revlon	L'Oreal	
recommendation of sales personnel	very often	Count	1	0	0	1
		Expected Count	.5	.3	.2	1.0
		% within recommendation of sales personnel	100%	0.0%	0.0%	100%
	often	Count	6	4	0	10
		Expected Count	4.7	3.2	2.1	10.0
		% within recommendation of sales personnel	60.0%	40.0%	0.0%	100%
	sometimes	Count	14	5	6	25
		Expected Count	11.7	8.0	5.3	25.0
		% within recommendation of sales personnel	56.0%	20.0%	24.0%	100%
	very rarely	Count	9	9	4	22
		Expected Count	10.3	7.0	4.7	22.0
		% within recommendation of sales personnel	40.9%	40.9%	18.2%	100%
	never	Count	1	3	4	8
		Expected Count	3.8	2.5	1.7	8.0
		% within recommendation of sales personnel	12.5%	37.5%	50.0%	100%
Total		Count	31	21	14	66
		Expected Count	31.0	21.0	14.0	66.0
		% within recommendation of sales personnel	47.0%	31.8%	21.2%	100%

dents said that they never purchase cosmetics based on recommendation of sales personnel.

- The respondent, who purchases cosmetics based on recommendation of sales personnel very often, prefers Lakme.

- Out of 10 respondents who often purchase cosmetics based on recommendation of sales personnel, 6 prefer Lakme, 4 prefer Revlon and none prefer L'Oreal.

- Out of 25 respondents who sometimes purchase cosmetics based on recommendation of sales personnel, 14 prefer Lakme, 5 prefer Revlon and 6 prefer L'Oreal.

- Out of 22 respondents who purchase cosmetics based on recommendation of sales personnel very rarely, 9 prefer Lakme, 9 prefer Revlon and 4 prefer L'Oreal.

- Out of 8 respondents who never purchase cosmetics based on recommendation of sales personnel, 1 prefers Lakme, 3 prefer Revlon and 4 prefer L'Oreal.

From Table 36:

- The Pearson Chi-square is 11.514.
- Degree of Freedom = 8.
- P value = 0.174 which is more than level of significance 0.05. Therefore the null is accepted.
- **Null Hypothesis:** There is no relationship between reading reviews and the brand preference of female consumers with reference to top three brands of make-up cosmetics.
- **Alternative Hypothesis:** There is significant relationship between reading reviews and the brand preference of female consumers with reference to top three brands of make-up cosmetics.
- **Statistical Test:** Chi-square test.
- **Level of Significance = 0.05.**

From Table 37:

- Out of 66 respondents, 13 respondents said that they very often read reviews about the cosmetics before purchasing them, 23 respondents said that they often read reviews about the cosmetics before purchasing them, 12 respondents said that they sometimes read reviews about the cosmetics before purchasing them, 12 respondents said that they very rarely read reviews about the cosmetics before purchasing them and 6 respondents said that they never read reviews about the cosmetics before purchasing them.

Table 36. Chi-square tests

	Value	df	Asymp. Sig. (2-Sided)
Pearson Chi-Square	11.514	8	.174
Likelihood Ratio	14.044	8	.081
Linear-by-Linear Association	6.826	1	.009
N of Valid Cases	66		

*Table 37. Read reviews of cosmetics before purchase * brand preference cross-tabulation*

			Brand			Total
			Lakme	Revlon	L'Oreal	
read reviews of cosmetics before purchase	very often	Count	5	3	5	13
		Expected Count	6.1	4.1	2.8	13.0
		% within read reviews of cosmetics before purchase	38.5%	23.1%	38.5%	100.0%
	often	Count	7	10	6	23
		Expected Count	10.8	7.3	4.9	23.0
		% within read reviews of cosmetics before purchase	30.4%	43.5%	26.1%	100.0%
	sometimes	Count	5	5	2	12
		Expected Count	5.6	3.8	2.5	12.0
		% within read reviews of cosmetics before purchase	41.7%	41.7%	16.7%	100.0%
	very rarely	Count	8	3	1	12
		Expected Count	5.6	3.8	2.5	12.0
		% within read reviews of cosmetics before purchase	66.7%	25.0%	8.3%	100.0%
	never	Count	6	0	0	6
		Expected Count	2.8	1.9	1.3	6.0
		% within read reviews of cosmetics before purchase	100.0%	0.0%	0.0%	100.0%
Total		Count	31	21	14	66
		Expected Count	31.0	21.0	14.0	66.0
		% within read reviews of cosmetics before purchase	47.0%	31.8%	21.2%	100.0%

- Out of 13 respondents who very often read reviews about the cosmetics before purchasing them, 5 prefer Lakme, 3 prefer Revlon and 5 prefer L'Oreal.
- Out of 23 respondents who often read reviews about the cosmetics before purchasing them, 7 prefer Lakme, 10 prefer Revlon and 6 prefer L'Oreal.
- Out of 12 respondents who sometimes read reviews about the cosmetics before purchasing them, 5 prefer Lakme, 5 prefer Revlon and 2 prefer L'Oreal.
- Out of 12 respondents who very rarely read reviews about the cosmetics before purchasing them, 8 prefer Lakme, 3 prefer Revlon and 1 prefers L'Oreal.
- All the 6 respondents who never read reviews about the cosmetics before purchasing them prefer Lakme.

From Table 38:

- The Pearson Chi-square is 14.349.
- Degree of Freedom = 8.
- P value = 0.073 which is slightly more than level of significance 0.05. Therefore we can say that there is partially significant relationship between reading reviews and the brand preference of female consumers with reference to top three brands of make-up cosmetics.
- **Null Hypothesis:** There is no relationship between impulse purchase of cosmetics and the brand preference of female consumers with reference to top three brands of make-up cosmetics.
- **Alternative Hypothesis:** There is significant relationship between impulse purchase of cosmetics and the brand preference of female consumers with reference to top three brands of make-up cosmetics.
- **Statistical Test:** Chi-square test.
- **Level of Significance** = 0.05.

From Table 39:

- Out of 66 respondents, 1 respondent said that she very often purchase cosmetics based on impulse, 3 respondents said that they often purchase cosmetics based on impulse, 24 respondents said that they sometimes purchase cosmetics based on impulse, 33 respondents said that they very rarely purchase cosmetics based on impulse and 5 respondents said that they never purchase cosmetics based on impulse.
- The respondent who very often purchases cosmetics based on impulse prefers Lakme.
- All the 3 respondents who often purchase cosmetics based on impulse prefer Revlon.

Table 38. Chi-square tests

	Value	df	Asymp. Sig. (2-Sided)
Pearson Chi-Square	14.349	8	.073
Likelihood Ratio	16.567	8	.035
Linear-by-Linear Association	9.413	1	.002
N of Valid Cases	66		

Table 39. Purchase based on impulse * brand preference cross-tabulation

			Brand			Total
			Lakme	Revlon	L'Oreal	
purchase based on impulse	very often	Count	1	0	0	1
		Expected Count	.5	.3	.2	1.0
		% within purchase based on impulse	100.0%	0.0%	0.0%	100%
	often	Count	0	3	0	3
		Expected Count	1.4	1.0	.6	3.0
		% within purchase based on impulse	0.0%	100%	0.0%	100%
	sometimes	Count	10	7	7	24
		Expected Count	11.3	7.6	5.1	24.0
		% within purchase based on impulse	41.7%	29.2%	29.2%	100%
	very rarely	Count	19	8	6	33
		Expected Count	15.5	10.5	7.0	33.0
		% within purchase based on impulse	57.6%	24.2%	18.2%	100%
	never	Count	1	3	1	5
		Expected Count	2.3	1.6	1.1	5.0
		% within purchase based on impulse	20.0%	60.0%	20.0%	100%
Total		Count	31	21	14	66
		Expected Count	31.0	21.0	14.0	66.0
		% within purchase based on impulse	47.0%	31.8%	21.2%	100%

- Out of 24 respondents who sometimes purchase cosmetics based on impulse, 10 prefer Lakme, 7 prefer Revlon and 7 prefer L'Oreal.
- Out of 33 respondents who very rarely purchase cosmetics based on impulse, 19 prefer Lakme, 8 prefer Revlon and 6 prefer L'Oreal.
- Out of 5 respondents who never purchase cosmetics based on impulse, 1 prefers Lakme, 3 prefer Revlon and 1 prefers L'Oreal.

From Table 40:

- The Pearson Chi-square is 12.024.
- Degree of Freedom = 8.
- P value = 0.150 which is more than level of significance 0.05. Therefore the null is accepted.
- **Null Hypothesis:** There is no relationship between purchase of cosmetics based on commercial and the brand preference of female consumers with reference to top three brands of make-up cosmetics.
- **Alternative Hypothesis:** There is significant relationship between purchase of cosmetics based on commercial and the brand preference of female consumers with reference to top three brands of make-up cosmetics.
- **Statistical Test:** Chi-square test.
- **Level of Significance** = 0.05.

From Table 41:

- Out of 66 respondents, 42 respondents said that they purchase cosmetics based on commercial while 24 respondents said that they do not purchase cosmetics based on commercial.
- Out of 42 respondents who purchase cosmetics based on commercial, 25 prefer Lakme, 12 prefer Revlon and 5 prefer L'Oreal.
- Out of 24 respondents who do not purchase cosmetics based on commercial, 6 prefer Lakme, 9 prefer Revlon and 9 prefer L'Oreal.

From Table 42:

- The Pearson Chi-square is 8.975.
- Degree of Freedom = 2.
- P value = 0.011 which is less than level of significance 0.05. Therefore the null is rejected.

Time of Purchase

Table 43 shows multiple responses for the variable time of purchase.

Out of total 81 yes responses, 38 were for when cosmetics run out of stock, 12 for whenever I see some ad about some new product, 21 for whenever I go for shopping and 10 were for whenever I see some attractive offer or sale.

Table 40. Chi-square tests

	Value	df	Asymp. Sig. (2-Sided)
Pearson Chi-Square	12.024	8	.150
Likelihood Ratio	12.743	8	.121
Linear-by-Linear Association	.062	1	.804
N of Valid Cases	66		

Table 41. Purchase of cosmetics based on commercial * brand preference cross-tabulation

				Brand			Total
				Lakme	Revlon	L'Oreal	
Do you purchase make-up cosmetics based on commercial?	yes		Count	25	12	5	42
			Expected Count	19.7	13.4	8.9	42.0
			% within purchase of cosmetics based on commercial	59.5%	28.6%	11.9%	100.0%
	no		Count	6	9	9	24
			Expected Count	11.3	7.6	5.1	24.0
			% within purchase of cosmetics based on commercial	25.0%	37.5%	37.5%	100.0%
Total			Count	31	21	14	66
			Expected Count	31.0	21.0	14.0	66.0
			% within purchase of cosmetics based on commercial	47.0%	31.8%	21.2%	100.0%

Table 42. Chi-square tests

	Value	df	Asymp. Sig. (2-Sided)
Pearson Chi-Square	8.975[a]	2	.011
Likelihood Ratio	9.130	2	.010
Linear-by-Linear Association	8.833	1	.003
N of Valid Cases	66		

Table 43. Time of purchase frequencies

		Responses		Percent of Cases
		N	Percent	
Time of purchase	when they run out of stock	38	46.9%	57.6%
	whenever I see some ad about some new product	12	14.8%	18.2%
	whenever I go for shopping	21	25.9%	31.8%
	whenever I see some attractive offer or sale	10	12.3%	15.2%
Total		81	100.0%	122.7%

Influencing Factors (Product) for the Purchase of Cosmetics

From Table 44:

- None of the respondents have ranked attractive packaging, color & ease to handle as their most influencing product feature for the purchase of cosmetics, while 3 respondents have ranked attractive packaging and 2 have ranked ease to handle as second most influencing factor and 10 have ranked attractive packaging and only 2 respondents have ranked ease to handle as the third most influencing product feature for the purchase of cosmetics.
- Quality has been ranked as the most influencing factor by maximum respondents (41). 6 respondents have ranked it as the second most and 2 respondents have ranked it as the third most influencing product feature for the purchase of cosmetics.

Table 44. Influencing factors (product) for the purchase of cosmetics

Promotional Factors	Rank I	Rank II	Rank III
Attractive Packaging	0	3	10
Color	0	0	0
Design & Shape	6	8	2
Quality	41	6	2
Ease to handle	0	2	2
Durability	9	23	13
Variety	5	6	10
Brand Name	4	15	18
Features	1	3	9
Warranties	0	0	0

- 6 respondents have ranked design as most influencing factor, 8 as second most and 2 have ranked it as the third most influencing product feature for the purchase of cosmetics.
- 9 respondents have ranked durability as most influencing factor, 23 as second most and 13 have ranked it as the third most influencing product feature for the purchase of cosmetics.
- 5 respondents have ranked variety as most influencing factor, 6 as second most and 10 have ranked it as the third most influencing product feature for the purchase of cosmetics.
- 4 respondents have ranked brand name as most influencing factor, 15 as second most and 18 have ranked it as the third most influencing product feature for the purchase of cosmetics.
- 1 respondent has ranked features as most influencing factor, 3 as second most and 9 have ranked it as the third most influencing product feature for the purchase of cosmetics.
- **Null Hypothesis:** There is no relationship between price and the brand preference of female consumers with reference to top three brands of make-up cosmetics.
- **Alternative Hypothesis:** There is significant relationship between price and the brand preference of female consumers with reference to top three brands of make-up cosmetics.
- **Statistical Test:** Chi-square test.
- **Level of Significance** = 0.05.

From Table 45:

- Out of 66 respondents, 2 respondents said that the price of their preferred brands is low while 53 respondents said it is medium and 11 respondents said that the price is high.
- Out of 2 respondents who said that the price of their preferred brands is low, 1 prefers Lakme and 1 prefers Revlon.
- Out of 53 respondents who said that the price of their preferred brands is medium, 25 prefer Lakme, 17 prefer Revlon and 11 prefer L'Oreal.
- Out of 11 respondents who said that the price of their preferred brands is high, 5 prefer Lakme, 3 prefer Revlon and 3 prefer L'Oreal.

Table 45. Price* brand preference cross-tabulation

			Price			Total
			Low	Medium	High	
Brand preference	Lakme	Count	1	25	5	31
		Expected Count	.9	24.9	5.2	31.0
		% within brand preference	3.2%	80.6%	16.1%	100.0%
	Revlon	Count	1	17	3	21
		Expected Count	.6	16.9	3.5	21.0
		% within brand preference	4.8%	81.0%	14.3%	100.0%
	L'Oreal	Count	0	11	3	14
		Expected Count	.4	11.2	2.3	14.0
		% within brand preference	0.0%	78.6%	21.4%	100.0%
Total		Count	2	53	11	66
		Expected Count	2.0	53.0	11.0	66.0
		% within brand preference	3.0%	80.3%	16.7%	100.0%

From Table 46:

- The Pearson Chi-square is 0.910.
- Degree of Freedom = 4.
- P value = 0.923 which is more than level of significance 0.05. Therefore the null is rejected.

Place of Purchase

Table 47 shows multiple responses for the variable place of purchase.

Out of total 79 yes responses, 23 were for Super Markets, 13 for Premium Groceries, 30 for Retails (General Stores), 1 for Pharmacy, 6 for both Fancy Shops and Through Personal Selling.

Table 46. Chi-square tests

	Value	Df	Asymp. Sig. (2-Sided)
Pearson Chi-Square	.910	4	.923
Likelihood Ratio	1.291	4	.863
Linear-by-Linear Association	.236	1	.627
N of Valid Cases	66		

Table 47. Place frequencies

		Responses		Percent of Cases
		N	Percent	
Place	Super Markets	23	29.1%	34.8%
	Premium Groceries	13	16.5%	19.7%
	Retails (General Stores)	30	38.0%	45.5%
	Pharmacy	1	1.3%	1.5%
	Fancy Shops	6	7.6%	9.1%
	Through Personal Selling	6	7.6%	9.1%
Total		79	100.0%	119.7%

Influencing Factors (Promotional) for the Purchase of Cosmetics

From Table 48:

- 44 respondents have ranked TV advertisement as the most influencing promotional factor in the purchase of cosmetics, 10 respondents have ranked it as second most influencing promotional factor and 5 respondents have ranked it as third most influencing promotional factor.
- Only 3 respondents have ranked Radio advertisement as the most influencing promotional factor, 18 have ranked it as second most influencing factor and 21 have ranked it as the third most influencing promotional factor.
- None of the respondents have ranked POS & Hoardings as the most influencing promotional factor, 15 respondents have ranked POS and 10 have ranked Hoardings as the second most influencing factor while 18 respondents have

Table 48. Influencing factors (promotional) for the purchase of cosmetics

Promotional Factors	Rank I	Rank II	Rank III
TV Advertisement	44	10	5
Radio Advertisement	3	18	21
POS Promotions	0	15	18
Hoardings	0	10	7
Newspaper/Magazine	15	2	20
Discounts	2	9	2
Free Banded issues	2	0	5

ranked POS and 7 have ranked Hoardings as the third most influencing factor in the purchase of cosmetics.

- 15 respondents have ranked Newspaper/Magazine as the most influencing factor in the purchase of cosmetics, 2 respondents have ranked it as the second and 20 respondents have ranked it as the third most influencing factor in the purchase of cosmetics.
- Discount has been ranked as first most influencing factor by only 2 respondents, while 9 respondents have ranked it as second most influencing factor and 2 as third most influencing factor in the purchase of cosmetics.
- Only 2 respondents have ranked Free Banded Issues as the most influencing factor, none ranked it as second and 5 respondents have ranked it as the third most influencing factor in the purchase of cosmetics.

FINDINGS

Following are the findings of the study:

- There is no relationship between respondent category and the brand preference of female consumers with reference to top three brands of make-up cosmetics.
- There is no relationship between age and the brand preference of female consumers with reference to top three brands of make-up cosmetics.
- There is no relationship between marital status and the brand preference of female consumers with reference to top three brands of make-up cosmetics.
- There is partially significant relationship between number of years of marriage and the brand preference of female consumers with reference to top three brands of make-up cosmetics.
- There is no relationship between number of children and the brand preference of female consumers with reference to top three brands of make-up cosmetics.
- There is no relationship between employment and the brand preference of female consumers with reference to top three brands of make-up cosmetics.
- There is significant relationship between annual family income and the brand preference of female consumers with reference to top three brands of make-up cosmetics.
- There is no relationship between educational qualification and the brand preference of female consumers with reference to top three brands of make-up cosmetics.

- There is partially significant relationship between skin type and the brand preference of female consumers with reference to top three brands of make-up cosmetics.
- There is no relationship between number of years of use of cosmetics and the brand preference of female consumers with reference to top three brands of make-up cosmetics.
- There is no relationship between number of cosmetics used per day and the brand preference of female consumers with reference to top three brands of make-up cosmetics.
- There is no relationship between frequency of purchase of cosmetics and the brand preference of female consumers with reference to top three brands of make-up cosmetics.
- There is no relationship between monthly expenditure on cosmetics and the brand preference of female consumers with reference to top three brands of make-up cosmetics.
- There is no relationship between importance of product feel in cosmetics purchase and the brand preference of female consumers with reference to top three brands of make-up cosmetics.
- There is no relationship between purchase of cosmetics based on tester and the brand preference of female consumers with reference to top three brands of make-up cosmetics.
- There is significant relationship between purchase of other products from the same brand of cosmetics and the brand preference of female consumers with reference to top three brands of make-up cosmetics.
- There is no relationship between opinion of friends and the brand preference of female consumers with reference to top three brands of make-up cosmetics.
- There is no relationship between recommendation of sales personnel and the brand preference of female consumers with reference to top three brands of make-up cosmetics.
- There is partially significant relationship between reading reviews and the brand preference of female consumers with reference to top three brands of make-up cosmetics.
- There is no relationship between impulse purchase of cosmetics and the brand preference of female consumers with reference to top three brands of make-up cosmetics.
- There is significant relationship between purchase of cosmetics based on commercial and the brand preference of female consumers with reference to top three brands of make-up cosmetics.
- Most of the respondents purchase cosmetics when they run out of stock.

- According to maximum number of respondents, quality is the most influencing product feature in the purchase of cosmetics, followed by durability and brand name.
- There is no relationship between price and the brand preference of female consumers with reference to top three brands of make-up cosmetics.
- Most of the respondents purchase cosmetics from Retails (General Stores), followed by Super Markets and Premium Groceries.
- Most of the respondents have ranked TV advertisement as the most influencing promotional factor in the purchase of cosmetics.

CONCLUSION

Nowadays cosmetic has become part and parcel of our daily life. As discussed in the introduction section, the cosmetic industry in our country is growing because of the increasing demand among the users. The Indian cosmetic market has a lot to offer in terms of penetration of new brands. The customers are becoming more aware with the willingness to try new brands and products. This is for a variety of reasons. Firstly, there is greater consciousness among the well-travelled, prosperous middle-class about international brands before they even enter the Indian market. Hence as they enter into the Indian market, they find ready reception. It is also to do with changing retail environment, especially with more number of departmental stores coming up in the last decade. The new international brands see potential in the market and hence lots of brands are coming and launching in departmental stores. Definitely the future seems to be brighter for the industry.

REFERENCES

Aaker, D. A. (1991). *Managing brand equity: Capitalization on the value of a brand name*. New York, NY: Free Press.

ASSOCHAM. (2013). *Youths spend big on cosmetics, apparel & mobile: ASSOCHAM survey: Delhiites ahead of their counterparts on cosmetics, apparel & mobile!*. Retrieved from http://www.assocham.org/prels/shownews-archive.php?id=4128&month=&year=

Guiltian & Joseph. (1991). *Marketing management*. New York, NY: McGraw-Hill.

Gupta, S. (1988). Impact of sales promotion when, what and how much to buy. *JMR, Journal of Marketing Research*, (Nov), 25.

Howard, J., & Sheth, J. (1969). *The theory of buyer behavior*. New York, NY: John Wiley & Sons.

Kotler, P., & Armstrong, G. (1989). *Principles of marketing* (4th ed.). New York, NY: Prince Hall.

McCarthy, E. J., & Perreault, W. D. Jr. (1984). *Basic marketing* (8th ed.). Home-wood, IL: Irwin.

McConnell, C. R., & Brue, S. L. (1999). *Economics* (14th ed.). New York, NY: Irwin-McGraw-Hill.

Nilson, T. H. (1998). Competitive branding. New York, NY: John Wiley & Sons.

Onkvisit, S., & Shaw, J. J. (1994). *Consumer behavior: Strategy and analysis*. New York, NY: Macmillan.

Peter, J., & Donnelly, H. (1992). *Marketing management* (3rd ed.). Chicago: Irwin.

Peter, J. P., & Olson, J. C. (1990). *Consumer behavior and marketing strategy* (2nd ed.). Homewood, IL: Irwin.

Schiffman, L. G., & Kanuk, L. L. (2000). *Comportamento do consumidor*. Rio de Janeiro: LTC.

Times of India. (2013). *India's cosmetics industry may treble by 2020*. Retrieved from http://articles.timesofindia.indiatimes.com/2013-12-24/beauty/45539514_1_cosmetics-indian-spa-creams

KEY TERMS AND DEFINITIONS

Brand Preference: Brand preference is measure of brand loyalty in which consumers will choose a particular brand in presence of competing brands.

Buying Behavior: Buying Behavior is the decision processes and acts of people involved in buying and using products.

Cosmetics: Cosmetics are care substances used to enhance the appearance or odour of human body.

Marketing Mix: The marketing mix is a business tool used in marketing and by marketers. The marketing mix is often crucial when determining a product or brand's offer, and is often associated with the four P's: price, product, promotion, and place.

Chapter 10
A Case Study on Pitfalls in Branding of Boroline

R. Padma
Jain University, India

Pawan Sharma
Jain University, India

ABSTRACT

The Indian FMCG sector is the fourth largest sector in the economy with a total market size in excess of US$ 13.1 billion. The FMCG market is set to treble from US$ 11.6 billion in 2003 to US$ 33.4 billion in 2015. Skin care products are one of the key constituents of the FMCG sector. One of the major products under skin care products are antiseptic creams. In India, the market size of the antiseptic cream markets is approximately US$ 2.94 billion. The major players in the antiseptic cream industry are Betadine Cream, Boroline, Boroplus, Vicco Turmeric Cream, etc. With the growing market and many players, it becomes essential for every organization to retain the brand that it has set in the market. And every organization wants to take advantage the market and one such organization is Boroline.

INTRODUCTION

Boroline is the product of G.D Pharmaceuticals. It was founded by Mr. Gourmohan Dutta, an Indian merchant. It was launched in the year 1929 in Calcutta which is currently known as Kolkota. The name is derived from its ingredients 'Boro' from boric power which has antiseptic properties and 'Oline' derived from Latin word

DOI: 10.4018/978-1-4666-7393-9.ch010

'oleum', meaning oil. The journey of Boroline since 1929 has not been smooth. The brand almost faced extinction in the early 1990's. It almost disappeared from the retail shelves for two years. But however when the brand returned to the market after two years the customers accepted it with open arms. This proved the good will of the brand. And the sales doubled that year. But with more competition in the market both by the domestic and Multinationals the brand might experience again the same scenario. The major competitors for Boroline are Boroplus from house of 'Emami' another major FMCG group of India.

In the present era the companies have a wide market spread across the geography of the world. This has resulted in vast opportunity to the organization as well as a treat because every organization would try to take the opportunity of the wide spread market. And this led to very stiff competition. Today's market is inundated with hundreds and thousands of product providing wide range of choices to the consumer in such a scenario it becomes difficult to retain and attract the consumers unless the company has established a strong brand image in the minds of the consumers.

According to the American Marketing Association (AMA) (2007) defines brand as " name, term, sign, symbol or design, or a combination of them intended to identify the goods and services of one seller or group of sellers and to differentiate them from those of other sellers." According to de Chernatony and McDonald (2003) "a successful brand as an identifiable product, service, person or place, augmented in such a way that a buyer or user perceives relevant and unique added values which match their needs more closely. Furthermore its success results from being able to sustain these added values in the face of competition"

Kotler (1991) defines a brand as "a name, term, sign, symbol or design, or combination of them which is intended to identify the goods and services of one seller and to differentiate them from those of competitors." A brand is intended to persuade the consumer about the quality, reliability, social status, value or safety of a product (Bowbrick, 1992), and it indicates that all products carrying this brand have a common manufacturer, distributor, retailer or country of origin.

From the above definitions it can be understood that brand is any kind of identification which makes the company's product and service different from the other companies. It's how well the customer recognize a particular product or service and differentiate it from that its competitors. This helps the organisation to set apart from its competition. And the process involved in creating a unique identification is known a branding.

Hence is can be concluded brands enable the customers to remember a particular product and service which allows the organization to gain loyal customer base. A brand of a product or service conveys the message to customer and adds values and emotion to the customers.

The case study discusses about the concept of branding. Here, we discuss about the 'Boroline' and the way in which branding has helped 'Boroline' to survive in market.

Brand 'Boroline' has two major problems to take care of one is marketing channel and second retaining the customer loyalty in order to survive in the market. The case study would be dealt in four parts.

1. It would provide a detail background of the company.
2. Throw light on the brand value since 1929 to present days.
3. The challenges faced by the brand at the present stage.
4. Suggestion based on the literature.

About FMCG

Fast Moving Consumer Goods (FMCG) are those products that are sold quickly and at a relatively low cost. They are frequently purchased essential or non essential goods such as food, soft drinks, toiletries etc. FMCG have a short shelf life, because of high demand from the consumers or because the product deteriorates rapidly.

The Indian FMCG sector is the fourth largest sector in the economy with a total market size in excess of US\$ 13.1 billion. The FMCG market is set to treble from US\$ 11.6 billion in 2003 to US\$ 33.4 billion in 2015. It consist of various product categories such as food and beverage, personal care, pharmaceuticals, plastic goods, paper and stationery and household products etc. and one of the booming product category is the personal care and skin care industry.

FMCG sector has grown at an average of 11% a year; in the last five years, annual growth accelerated at compounded rate of 17.3%. The sector is characterized by strong presence of global businesses, intense competition between organized and unorganized players, well established distribution network and low operational cost. Availability of key raw materials, cheaper labor costs and presence across the entire value chain gives India a competitive advantage. Certain facts about FMCG are given in Table 1.

BRAND BUILDING IN FMCG

If the companies have to survive in Fast Moving Consumer Goods (FMCG) sector they have to ensure that they are always ahead of the competition. It is one of the rapidly evolving sectors in the Indian market. In order to stay strong and face the mounting competition the companies have to shell out huge money in advertising and promoting their products and also in launching new products to expand the

Table 1. Fast facts: Indian FMCG industry

Fast Facts
• The Indian FMCG industry represents nearly 2.5% of the country's GDP.
• The industry has tripled in size in past 10 years and has grown at ~17%CAGR in the last 5 years driven by rising income levels, increasing urbanisation, strong rural demand and favourable demographic trends.
• The sector accounted for 1.9% of the nation's total FDI inflows in April 2000- September 2012. Cumulative FDI inflows into India from April 2000 to April 2013 in the food processing sector stood at `9,000.3 crore, accounting for 0.96% of overall FDI inflows while the soaps, cosmetics and toiletries, accounting for 0.32% of overall FDI at 3,115.5 crore.
• Food products and personal care together make up two-third of the sector's revenues.
• Rural India accounts for more than 700 mn consumers or 70% of the Indian population and accounts for 50% of the total FMCG market.
• With changing lifestyle and increasing consumer demand, the Indian FMCG market is expected to cross $80 bn by 2026 in towns with population of up to 10 lakh.
• India's labor cost is amongst the lowest in the world, after China & Indonesia, giving it a competitive advantage over other countries.
• Unilever Plc's $5.4 billion bid for a 23% stake in Hindustan Unilever is the largest Asia Pacific cross border inbound merger and acquisition (M&A) deal so far in FY'14 and is the fifth largest India Inbound M&A transaction on record till date.
• Excise duty on cigarette has been increased in the Union Budget for 2013-14, which would hit major industrial conglomerates like ITC, VST Industries in the short term.

Source: http://reports.dionglobal.in/Actionfinadmin/Reportsretrieved on 06.06.2014.

market share. The leading players in FMCG have a vast portfolio of products and brands to keep growing and meeting the wants of the consumers.

For many companies larger part revenue, approximately up to 60% is received from new product launches. Companies like ITC, Britannia industries; Nestle and Amul are among those, which are currently unveiling dozens of new product. And many leading firms spend approx. 10% of the turnover on advertising and brand promotion. FMCG are not capital intensive but they encourage expenditure on promotional and branding activities. And to ensure continuous growth the companies have to diversify into other sub sectors. The popular promotional strategies are tying up with celebrities as brand ambassadors.

Skin care products are one of the key constituents of the FMCG sector. And one of the major products under Skin care products are antiseptic creams. In India the market size of the antiseptic cream markets is approximately 2.94 billion. The skin care market is at a booming stage in India. With changing life styles, increase in disposable incomes, greater product choice and availability, and influence of satellite television, more people are taking interest in personal grooming. The facial skin care market is booming. Products are competing with one another to take shelf space in the retail stores. Facial skin care products have become an essential part of the beauty market. Like western countries, creams and lotions are applied in India also, in an effort to remove the pimples and the acne, fight stress and worry lines, and to remain young. See Table 2 representing the segmentation of skin care products in Indian Market.

Table 2. Market segmentation of skin care products by volume and value

Category	% Volume	% Value
Antiseptic Creams	14	13
Cold Creams	13	8
Snows	1	Neg
Astringents	1	1
Fairness creams/lotions	48	56
Vanishing Creams	4	5
Calamines/Foundations	2	6
Moisturizing Creams/lotions	17	11
Total	**100**	**100**

Source: Research Report Indian FMCG 2014 retrieved on 6.06.2014.

The market size of the skin-care segment is estimated at Rs 21 billion. Fairness creams, with a market of around Rs 11.75 billion, account for around 56 per cent by value. The contribution of moisturizing lotions and creams was 17 per cent; antiseptic creams 14 per cent and cold creams 13 per cent of the total skin cream market by volume. Vanishing creams, calamines and foundations, snows and astringents remained marginal categories within the skin-care market.

- **Anti-Septic Creams:** The market for anti septic creams, a traditional product on the market for several decades, is estimated to be 3.5 million litres in volume, valued at Rs 2.30 billion in 2006. The market is dominated by three domestic players: Emami's Boro Plus with a 64 per cent share, Boroline with a 21 per cent share and Paras Pharmceuticals' Boro Soft with a 12 per cent market share and 3 percent others. This is a volume-driven segment, and selling purely on functional. The most frequent application for the product is in case of shaving cuts. Table 3 represents Antiseptic Cream market of India.

Table 3. Skin care – antiseptic creams market shares by value

Brand	% Value
Emami	64
G.D. Pharmaceuticals	21
Paras Pharmaceuticals	12
Others	3
Total	**100**

Source: Research Report Indian FMCG 2014 retrieved on 6.06.2014

- **O.T.C Market in India:** An over-the-Counter market, popularly called O. T. C. markets, mainly refers to spot markets as well as those markets of specific commodities, which can be localized. Pharmaceutical companies occupy a significant portion in Indian O.T.C market in India. Over the Counter antiseptic cream market in India as an annual sale of 2.8 million liters valued at Rs 1.8 billion. Table 4 shows categories of OTC products in India.

ORGANIZATION BACKGROUND

Boroline is a one of the major products of GD Pharmaceuticals. GD has two production units. One in Chakbagi, West Bengal, 16 kms from Kolkata and the other unit is in Mohun Nagar Industrial area, Gaziabad, 5 kms from Delhi.

GD has established logistics, distribution and marketing infrastructure with associates who have been working together for more than 30 years. It has existing offices and ware housing facilities in 16 regional headquarters across India. The company is specialised in Over The Counter (OTC) Pharmaceutical products and healthcare cosmetics which caters to vast Indian market through over 750 distribution channels that are situated thought-out the country.

Other products of GD apart from Boroline are, Eleen, Suthol and Glosoft. Eleen is perfumed hair oil enriched with Amla& vitamin E. Suthol is an antiseptic skin shower. It acts as a relief to skin problem such as reashes, itches, prickly heat and other irritations. Suthol was India's first antiseptic skin shower. 'Glosoft' is a face wash which does not act only as a cleanser but also makes the skin glow and soft.

Boroline is the product of GD pharmaceuticals. It is multipurpose cream which provides remedies to problems like minor nicks, chapped lips, cracked feet and a

Table 4.The various categories of O.T.C products

Categories	Products
Analgesic or Cold Table	Crocin, Dcold, Disprin, Stopache. Triaminic, VicksVaporub
Antiseptic Cream or Liquids	Boroline, Boroplus, Borosoft, Dettol
Balm or Rubs	Amrutanjan Joint Ache Cream, Emami Mentho Plus, Himani Fast Relief, Iodex, moov
Cough Lozenges	Halls, Strepsils, Vicks Cough Drops.
Digestives	DaburHingoli, Eno, Hajmola, Pudin Hara
Health Supplements (Tonic and Vitamin)	Boost, Calcium, Sandoz Complan, Dabur Chawanprash, Himalaya, Horlicks, Jeevanprash, Sona Chandi Amritprash.
Skin Treatment (Medicated)	Clearsil, Itch Guard, Krack, Ringguard

Source: Research Report Indian FMCG 2014 retrieved on 6.06.2014.

tonic to dry skin. The name is derived from its ingredients 'Boro' from boric power which as antiseptic properties and 'Oline' derived from Latin word oleum, meaning oil. Boroline is the combination of essential oils, waxes and antiseptic properties which are a result of Boric powder and zinc oxide. Boric acid has the anti bacterial and anti fungal properties. While Zinc oxide is an astringent for the skin and has a soothing and protective action in skin infections. Lanolin is a natural product. It increases the absorption of active ingredients. It acts as an excellent emollient. This is due to the presence of alcohols collectively known as lanolin alcohols. Lanolin alcohols include cholesterol (30%), lanosterol (25%), cholestanol (3%), agnosterol (2%) and various other alcohols (40%).

The affected skin is protected against germs and allows the epidermal cell to rapidly grow due to the combination of these ingredients. And it is this reason that boroline cures cuts and bruises, heals the stitches after operation and protects heels against cracks. It also provides the best healing for sun burnt skin.

BRAND BOROLINE

The brand identity the logo of the product was developed carefully. Elephant was chosen has the Boroline's logo as it had an enormous significance to all Indian's as it symbolises lord Ganesha (elephant god). The logo caught the attention on the customers even those who were not able to read. Boroline was known as the "Hathiwala Cream" (cream with elephant logo).

The brain behind the brand image of Boroline was Mr. Murari Mohan Dutta. He was the son of Mr Gourmohon Dutta the founder of boroline. Mr. Murari Mohan Dutta was a marketing genius and a pioneer to marketing concept. Boroline tried to explore the various avenues of brand building during late 50's even when the concepts like brand image, rural marketing and event sponsorship were unknown to Indian Market. Boroline went on to become a part of people's live. It followed strategies like intensive newspaper, magazine, radio and various other outdoor promotions. It sponsored the players of cricket and football. Since 1982 it had been the sponsor of Jawaharlal Nehru Invitation International Football Gold Cup a popular football match of India.

Boroline kept up its brand image with the pace of the time. it changed its slogan which reflected its promotional platform through the decades. The chronological order for the advertising tag line has been given below:

1950: Tender face cream.
1960: BOROLINE for the skin, skin needs BOROLINE.
1970: BOROLINE has no substitute.

1980: The hard working cream that protects your skin.
1990: The original, BOROLINE skin healthy skin.
2000: WOW FACTOR!!!! BOROLINE works wonders.
2010: Wake up to a happy skin with BOROLINE.

Brand Element of Boroline

- **Name:** Boroline.
- **Logo:** Elephant.
- **Tagline:** Wake up to a happy skin with BOROLINE.
- **Shape:** Tube.
- **Colors:** Green.

Brand Identity of Boroline

Boroline is identified as India's first antiseptic cream. It is identified as the "Khusbuwalacream" which means the cream with fragrance in Hindi.

CHALLENGES FACED BY THE BRAND

Boroline is an 80 year old brand. Till the mid 80's Boroline was an undisputed market leader. It enjoyed 100% market share in antiseptic cream market until 'BoroPlus', from 'Emami' entered the market and changed the pace of the antiseptic cream market. At present the position is taken away by Boroplus which enjoys a market share of 74% in the antiseptic cream market making it the largest selling antiseptic cream in the market in India. In spite of being the best quality product in the antiseptic market Boroline as failed upgrade and attract new customers.

PITFALLS IN BRANDING 'BOROLINE'

Oiliness was the first and foremost factor that worked against 'Boroline'. And second the package of 'Boroline' which is dark green in colour that has not changed over the years. These factors were recognised by Emami group and they entered the market with Boroplus. Boroplus positioned itself with an 'Aurvedic' (indigenous Indian medicine) touch while Boroline had positioned itself as perfumed antiseptic.

'Boroplus' differentiated its product from 'Boroline' by using different packaging. It used white and lavender colour pack. It presented itself in terms of 'being smooth and light'. "Gudiya rani badisayani" the commercial highlighted the word 'plus' implying the value addition it had over its competitor. 'Boroplus' conveyed the message of value addition while 'Boroline' had branded only on the basis of quality. Aspirations over the 'antiseptic' attribute of the brand 'Boroline' got stuck. So much so that 'Boroline' lost out being categorised as a medicinal product and instead got bracketed as a cosmetic one. Concessional levies and taxes built into the pricing of the product too were lost when 'Boroline' started to be treated as any other cosmetic product.

STRENGTH OF THE COMPETITORS

- **Boroplus:** Boroplus is the product of Emami. It is a leader in the antiseptic cream market with a 74% market share; it was launched in the year 1977. It is anall purpose antiseptic moisturising cream with a combination of herb with antiseptic properties and long lasting protection with motorising cream. It is the largest selling cream in India and has a very strong international presence in countries like Russia, Ukraine and Nepal. It has an annual sales volume of US$ 2.5 Million - US$ 5 Million. Amitabh Bacchan, Kareena Kapoor and BipashaBasu (some of the most popular Indian actors)are the brand ambassadors of Boroplus. It launched brand extension with – Body Lotion and Healthy and Fair winter cream. The product has grown at a healthy CAGR of 12% in last three years.
- **Borosoft:** Borosoft antiseptic cream is a product of Paras Pharma. It was launched in the year 1996 at the times where the 'Boroplus' and 'Boroline' were already dominating the antiseptic cream market. Today, BoroSoft is the 3rd largest brand in its category (Boro Antiseptic Creams).
- **Burnol:** Burnol antiseptic cream is a product of Dr. Morepen. It is used for burns as well as cuts like other antiseptic creams. It's one the oldest antiseptic cream brand in India. The first brand owner was Boots and the brand the brand was acquired by Knoll. Later Reckitt and Piramal bought the brand from Knoll. In 2002 the brand was acquired by Dr. Morpean labs and positioned so strongly that the association has become embedded in the mind of the customers.
- **Dettol:** Dettol antiseptic cream was launched in Indian market by Reckitt & Colman of (India) Ltd as a brand extension strategy. It offers Dettol protection in the form of cream for minor cuts, burns, insects bite, wound, boils and rashes.

BRAND VALUE OF BOROLINE.

'Boroline' is the original antiseptic cream of India. 'Boroline' is the eminent front-runner in the O.T.C antiseptic cream market with 21 per cent of market share. The consumers of 'Boroline' are spread across the length and breadth of India. The product reflects the trust of generations of consumers. As it evolved as a trusted product in the minds of the consumer which as lead the company to gain and retain the brand loyalty with its consumers. The integral part of Boroline's brand profile has been the emphasis on the family value and tradition. That is the reason Boroline is regarded as heritage brand in India. The brand enjoys a 34.2 percent dealers penetration and has a 300,000 retail outlets across the country.

MILESTONE OF BRAND BOROLINE

For more than three generation 'Boroline' has maintained its position as one of the most trusted over the counter product in the Indian skin care industry. The brand enjoys a high recall among its consumers. Quality is the main reason for 'Boroline' to retain in the antiseptic cream market as a brand leader and the other reason is due to total quality management (TQM) which provides significant inputs for continuous up gradation of production technologies which results in quality standards. 'Boroline' spends 5per cent of its annual earrings on research and development. And as a result new production technologies have been developed resulting in operational efficiency which enables the firm to set the price of 'Boroline' down. High productivity and an effective distribution channel as made Boroline both accessible and affordable in the price sensitive market.

As an initiative towards environment and conservation of natural resources 'Boroline' has switched to recycling package. A special plantation project contributes as a part of save tree campaign in the factory near Kolkata.

In addition to these, 'Boroline' also maintains a large water reservoir of 6000 sq.mts to provide a balanced ecosystem, biodegrading all pre-treated effluents. From across India, numerous economically under-privileged, terminally ill patients and children requiring heart surgery have applied to 'Boroline' and received financial assistance for treatment.

SUCCESS TO DOWNFALL

'Boroline' entered the Indian market 80 years back, until 1990's 'Boroline' had 90per cent of market share in the antiseptic cream industry. It had positioned itself as all purpose cream. With entry of new products 'Boroline' started to lose its market share launching of 'Boroplus' was the major setback for 'Boroline'. The brand had faced the stage of being extinction in the early 1990's the production was stopped for two years due to stagnant pricing and following the statutory order from the authorities. The production was minimized to a greater extent. The company was incurring greater losses for every 'Boroline' tube it sold. 'Boroline' almost perished from the retail shelves. This condition prevailed for two years.

The product received a overwhelming responses from its consumer when the product re-entered the market the market after two years, this proved the goodwill of 'Boroline'. The product survived remarkable against all the odds in the market where the consumers are provided with wide range of choices.

Factors That Helped 'Boroline' to Survive in the Market

- 'Boroline' had a strong brand recall and had a certain level of brand awareness.
- Distribution factor is one the plus point of 'Boroline' as stated earlier 'Boroline' has a wide range of distribution network the brand enjoys 34.2% dealer penetration and over 300,000 retail outlets.
- 'Boroline' has a strong penetration in East Indian market in places such as West Bengal, Assam and Orissa. 'Boroline' is a market leader in Kolkata market. In this part BoroPlus market share is 55% while 'Boroline' is 60% in the region.
- 'Boroline' brand has a great advantage associated with quality. And the ingredients that worked wonders. The brand established as the cream for skin in 60's. Since then it has continued to be a skin care cream.
- Another important factor is that 'Boroline' is a heritage brand in India. It has come a long ways since 1929. It has established itself has a family brand trusted by generation.
- 'Boroline' has separate marketing division which focuses only on the branding of the product.
- 'Boroline' has a very strong loyal customer base. It has maintained a fantastic relationship with regional distributors.

ACHIEVEMENTS OF BOROLINE

- The company has always tries it best to maintain a good relationship with its customers, business associates, the government authority, various groups and trade association and every individual who the company comes in contact with. And this is the main reason for 'Boroline' to gain a very goodwill in the industry.

- 'Boroline', the flagship brand has been selected as an Indian Superbrand, twice in a row for the year 2004-05 and for the year 2006-07.

RECOMMENDATIONS

'Boroline' could go for brand category extension in order to survive in market. It can venture into products such as face wash, body lotion talcum powder etc especially for summer. It could be successful in the East Indian market as the weather is extreme hoe and cold. Though brand 'Boroline' has 300,000 retail distribution outlets its till very less when compare to its competitors 'Boroplus' with has around 16 lakhs distributors across the country. It can also change the brand image. Boroline has to take initiative to create a new brand image. This could be done by redesigning the logo or by changing the logo, repositioning the brand, re-launching the product or making small changes in the name by adding new word or the design of writing. This would help the brand to attract new generation consumers. Focus on the segments that are neglected segments. 'Boroline' does not have products for different age group, type of skin and for summer.

One approach to attracting a new market segment for a brand while satisfying current segments is to create separate advertising campaign and communication programs for each segment. The management can go for communication program via TV advertisement, radio and print media. The communication program can be done in a phased manner. The management can divide the country in four zones and then launch the campaign as per the zone at different intervals.

The brand has to change its communication style by being present in the popular social networking forum to reach out to the 'netizens' and the youth.

CONCLUSION

The Indian FMCG sector is the fourth largest sector in the economy with a total market size in excess of US\$ 13.1 billion. Skin care products are one the key constituents of the FMCG sector. Antiseptic creams are one of the major products under skin care products. Over a period of time antiseptic cream market has seen a tremendous growth. And every organisation strives to survive the growing competition and to retain its brand in the market. One of the major players in the antiseptic cream market is Boroline.

Boroline is one the oldest brand that exists in the antiseptic cream product. It is product of G.D Pharmaceuticals which was launched in the year 1929. Boroline was one of the house hold brand in the Indian market. But with the entry of the Boroplus a product from Emami, Boroline almost face the extinction and the product disappeared from the shelves for two year. The reason being that Boroplus used a different product positioning and advertising strategies compared to Boroline. Boroline failed to change its product with the changing market. The product re-entered the market and it gained a good response due to its brand value. Boroline had a strong brand recall and the brand awareness was strong. But still it is Boroplus that currently dominates the antiseptic cream market.

Hence it can be concluded that in order to survive in the competitive market it becomes necessary to every organisation to have a loyal customers and create a strong brand image in the minds of the customer and to adapt to the changes of the market.

REFERENCES

Aaker, D. A. (1991). What is brand equity and why is it valuable? *Managing Brand Equity*. Retrieved from http://www.prophet.com/blog/aakeronbrands/156-what-is-brand-equity-and-why-is-it-valuable

Aaker, D. A. (1996). *Building strong brands*. New York: The Free Press.

Aaker, D. A., & Keller, K. L. (1990). Consumer evaluations of brand extensions. *Journal of Marketing*, *54*(January), 27–41. doi:10.2307/1252171

Baker, W., Hutchinson, J. W., Moore, D., & Nedungadi, P. (1986). Brand familiarity and advertising: Effects on the evoked set and brand preferences. *Advances in Consumer Research. Association for Consumer Research (U. S.)*, *13*, 146–147.

Brodie, R. J., Ilic, A., Juric, B., & Hollebeek, L. (2013). Consumer engagement in a virtual brand community: An exploratory analysis. *Journal of Business Research*, *66*, 105–114. doi:10.1016/j.jbusres.2011.07.029

(2006). Bulletin 372 - Origin-based products. Invan de Kop, P., Sautier, D., & Gerz, A. (Eds.), *Lessons for pro-poor market development*. Amsterdam: KIT Publishers.

Davenport, T. H., & Prusak, L. (1998). *Working knowledge: How organizations manage what they know*. Boston: Harvard Business School Press.

De Chernatony, L. (1998). Criteria to assess brand success. *Journal of Marketing Management*, *14*(7), 765–781. doi:10.1362/026725798784867608

De Chernatony, L., & McDonald, M. (2003). *Creating powerful brands in consumer, service and industrial markets* (3rd ed.). Oxford, UK: ELSEVIER Butterworth-Heinemann.

Hislop, M. (2001). *Branding 101: An overview of branding and brand measurement for online marketers*. Dynamic Logic.

Kaplan, A. M., & Haenlein, M. (2012). The Britney Spears universe: Social media and viral marketing at its best. *Business Horizons*, *55*(1), 27–31. doi:10.1016/j.bushor.2011.08.009

Keller, K. L. (1993, January). Conceptualizing, measuring, and managing customer-based brand equity. *Journal of Marketing*, *57*(1), 1–22. doi:10.2307/1252054

Keller, K. L. (2003). *Strategic brand management: Building, measuring, and managing brand equity* (2nd ed.). Upper Saddle River, NJ: Prentice Hall.

Keller, K. L. (2004). *Brands and branding: Research findings and future priorities*. Academic Press.

Kotler, P. H. (1991). *Marketing management: Analysis, planning, and control* (8th ed.). Englewood Cliffs, NJ: Prentice-Hall.

Leif, M. H., De Chernatony, L., & Iversen, N. M. (2001). *Factors influencing successful brand extensions* (Working Paper). Birmingham, UK: Birmingham University Business School.

Leonard-Barton, D. (1995). *Wellsprings of knowledge: Building and sustaining the sources of innovation*. Boston: Havard Business School Press.

Nijssen, E. J. (1999). Success factors of line extensions of fast-moving consumer goods. *European Journal of Marketing*, *33*(5), 450–469. doi:10.1108/03090569910262044

Oliver, R. (1997). *Satisfaction: A behavioral perspective on the consumer*. New York: McGraw-Hill.

Probst, G., Raub, S., & Romhardt, K. (2001). *Managing knowledge: Building blocks for success*. Chichester, UK: John Wiley.

Randall, G. (2000). *Branding: A practical guide to planning your strategy* (2nd ed.). London: Kogan Page Limited.

Reddy, S. K., Holak, S. L., & Bhat, S. (1994). To extend or not to extend: Success determinants of line extensions. *JMR, Journal of Marketing Research*, *31*(May), 243–262. doi:10.2307/3152197

Richards, I., Foster, D., & Morgan, R. (1998). Brand knowledge management: Growing brand equit. *Journal of Knowledge Management*, 2(1), 47–54. doi:10.1108/13673279810800762

Völckner, F., & Sattler, H. (2006). Drivers of brand extension success. *Journal of Marketing*, 70(2), 18–34. doi:10.1509/jmkg.70.2.18

Yoo, B., & Donthu, N. (2001). Developing and validating a multidimensional consumer-based brand equity scale. *Journal of Business Research*, 52(1), 1–14. doi:10.1016/S01482963(99)00098-3

KEY TERMS AND DEFINITIONS

Brand Elements: Brand elements refers to various components such as name, logo, jingles that enable the customers in identifying a particular company's product or service.

Brand Promotion: Brand promotion refers to various elements that are used to influence, remind and persuade the customers to purchase a particular brand.

Brand: Brand refers to the various tangible and intangible elements that allow the customers to identify and differentiate from one manufacturer to another manufacturer.

FMCG: Fast Moving Consumer Goods are those goods that are frequently purchased in the market. They are sold quickly and at a lower cost. Consumers usually purchase FMCG goods frequently, immediately and with very little effort.

Logo: Is a symbol, graphics or design which helps buyers to identify products.

Market Leader: Market Leader refers to the company that holds the majority of the market share in a particular market.

Market: Market refers a place where exchange takes place between buyer and seller.

Chapter 11
Managing Brand Portfolio in a Crisis:
The Case of a Pharmaceutical Company in Egypt

Rafic Nadi
American University in Cairo, Egypt

Ahmed Tolba
American University in Cairo, Egypt

ABSTRACT

Branding in pharmaceutical markets is more challenging than any other market due to the enormous regulations and restrictions from governmental bodies like MOH, Ministry of Health. This case tackles a real challenge that one of the leading pharmaceutical companies in Egypt is facing. Since the company has a well-established brand that has been in the market for more than 30 years, this brand has strong brand equity and is well known by consumers, end users. In the past 5 years with the devaluation of the Egyptian currency, the price of the active ingredients increased. Accordingly, the gross margin of the brand was highly affected, to the extent that it reflects losses in the net operating income. In any other market, it might be an option to increase the price and enhance the gross margin, but in the pharmaceutical industry, companies are price takers and only MOH has the right to set the price.

DOI: 10.4018/978-1-4666-7393-9.ch011

DEFINITION

A serious situation, a mega brand that has been the cash cow for the company is turning into a failure brand in terms of profitability. Yet, still this brand is ranking 3rd in its market, pain market, which is the 2nd biggest market in the country, and has strong brand equity that the company cannot afford to lose. Now the company needs to take crucial decision regarding the brand as it will not be an option to continue with negative net operating income for long time besides it is not an option to lose a mega brand in a large market.

In the Marketing Manager's office, Amr Shawky, the marketing manager is thinking about the business case that he needs to present to the vice president of the company in few days. Suddenly the door knocks and the sales manager of Sonalfen brand, Tamer Hakim, came in holding his laptop and seems worried.

"Hi Tamer, I am thinking about Sonalfen business case. I am extremely worried about Sonalfen's future. This brand is a legacy in the company, and we cannot afford stopping it. As you know, the net operating income is now negative. We have request price increase from Ministry of Health, yet it was refused. We need to think of alternatives to get out of this situation with minimal losses." Said Amr.

"Yes stopping Sonalfen without clear direction will be disaster. It is one of our biggest brands with high sales turnover, in addition it is well known by consumers, and requested by name among 150 other brands in the market. I cannot imagine that we can simply sacrifice this brand equity that took us years to build, I am sure we will find a solution" Says Tamer.

Amr replied "Of course, I have been working in this company for more than 10 years. Sonalfen has been our cash generator till 2004, when we suffered from devaluation of the Egyptian pound. However, the brand remained profitable, but not at the same level. Then in 2011 with the raw material price increase and the devaluation of our currency after the revolution, Sonalfen became a brand that negatively affects our net operating income. We need to study all the pros and cons of possible courses of action to present a solid business case to the VP."

The pharmaceutical industry develops, produces and markets drugs licensed for use as medication. There are different categories of medicine like:

- **OTC Pharmaceuticals and Prescription Drugs:** Over the Counter (OTC) pharmaceuticals can be taken with no need to a prescription in contrast to prescription drugs.
- **Patented and Generic Medicine:** Patented medicine is the original one that is firstly produced and generic medicine is the copy of the original medicine. Patents form the major percentage of the value of drug demand. On the other

hand, generic medicine represented 60.2% of the value of the pharmaceutical sector in 2008.

- **Biologics and Biosimilars:** Biological medicines are produced using biological processes and biosimilar medicines are copies of original biological medicines.

BONDET COMPANY[1]

Bondet Co. is one of the top 5 pharmaceutical companies worldwide. Present in more than 120 countries, has more than 100 industrial sites. Bondet Turnover reached US$40 Billion in 2013 coming from diversified portfolio. Bondet Co. has strong brands in several disease area including chronic, acute and rare diseases, animal health in addition to human vaccines. The company has a strong research and development hub, which keeps its pipeline filled with new innovative drugs. Bondet Co. has strong presence in Egypt. It has a huge factory, and the number of employees exceeds 1500.

GLOBAL PHARMA MARKET

Global pharmaceutical market turnover is around US$ 300 billion. One third of this market is dominated by the top 10 players. Ranking and competition between the top players differs in each country. In local markets there are sometimes serious competitions from strong local players. For example, in Japan, there is a huge local player that is considered a major threat on multinationals. Research and development plays an important role in supporting the pipeline of any company with new drugs. Innovative drugs pass by several phases and approvals before and might take 10-15 years before they enter the market in addition to huge investment as from each 10 new drugs, only 1 drug succeeds to fulfill all the tests and criteria required by regulatory bodies to enter the market. However, an innovative drug usually has a premium pricing and has a quite high profit margin. Regulatory bodies understand the cost that it takes to produce a new drug, and thus a 10-15 years patency is granted to the company producing the new drug. Patency secures that no other company is allowed to produce the same drug for this period of time and thus companies are encouraged to spend on new innovations for their high profitability. When the patency ends, other companies can produce the same drug under different names and they are called generics. The global market can be divided into well developed markets like USA, Europe, Japan and emerging markets. 17 Pharma-emerging markets are being considered as the fastest growing markets and they are divided in 3 tiers. China comes in tier one. Brazil, India and Russia in tier 2 and finally 13 countries; Venezuela, Poland, Argentina, Turkey, Mexico, Vietnam, South Africa, Thailand, Indonesia, Romania, Ukraine, Pakistan and Egypt in tier 3. Since 2010, large companies have started to focus on the emerging markets. Acquiring local brands or even local companies in these emerging markets is a new profitable strategy and it is called branded generics.

PHARMACEUTICAL MARKET IN EGYPT

The pharmaceutical sector in Egypt is one of the oldest strategic sectors in the country, founded in 1939 with the establishment of the Misr Company for Pharmaceutical Industries. The Egyptian pharmaceuticals and cosmetics sector is considered the largest in the region with regards to growth capacity and expansion during the coming five years compared to similar sectors in neighboring countries.

The industry has enjoyed a period of considerable development in recent years. There is a strong domestic production sector and, while the majority is destined for the domestic market and imports play an important role, Egypt has emerged as a leading exporter of pharmaceuticals to Arab, Asian and Eastern European markets. Public production, represented by the state-owned holding company HOLDIPHARMA, accounts for around one-tenth of sales by value and nearly two-tenths by volume.

Large multinationals, including GlaxoSmithKline (GSK), Sanofi-Aventis and Novartis are among the top manufacturers of pharmaceuticals in the domestic market. Other leading multinational companies active here include Pfizer, Bristol-Myers Squibb, Servier, Eli Lilly, AstraZeneca and Otsuka.

Foreign participation in the local production of under-license pharmaceuticals is of major importance to both the Egyptian economy and local consumers, supplying a significant portion of domestic demand at a fraction of the import cost. Locally owned Egyptian companies producing generic products also play a key role in the domestic market with the Egyptian International Pharmaceutical Industries Company (EIPICO) being ranked as the leading manufacturer in the domestic market and the largest Arab pharmaceutical company overall. A top company on the Cairo and Alexandria Stock Exchange (CASE), EIPICO is also one of Egypt's 100 largest exporters.

Pharmaceutical prices in Egypt are based on a cost-plus formula, allowing for a profit margin of 15% on essential drugs, 25% on non-essential drugs and 40% or more on over-the-counter products. The formula, managed by the Ministry of Health and Population, guarantees positive returns for all companies operating in Egypt.

Providing the political situation stabilizes and the economy continues to perform well, the Egyptian pharmaceutical market at retail prices is expected to rise by a double-digit CAGR in US dollar terms between 2011 and 2016.

Espicom1 estimates that the market increased by nearly five times between 1995 and 2010. And went from EGP 18.23 billion in 2011 to EGP 20.33 billion in 2012; a +11.5% in local currency terms. The country's pharmaceuticals market is ranked 13th in BMI's proprietary Risk/Reward Ratings (RRRs) for the region.

Egypt is one of the booming pharmaceutical markets that large multinational companies look at. Total number of companies operating in Egypt is over 700. Top 10 companies contribute to 50% of the total turnover of the market. 5 companies of the top 10 are local companies. The market split is 60% chronic and 40% acute. Chronic diseases are type of diseases that patients have to live with, for the rest of their life, like diabetes and hypertension. More than half of the population suffers from these chronic diseases. While acute market, which is the diseases that occurs for short term period, like headache, heart burn, cough, cold and sore throat The market could be categorized as well by brand nature into OTC, over the counter, which means that any consumer can enter a pharmacy and ask for a medicine without prescription, or RX, prescribed brands, which means that a prescription should be present to be able to get the medicine from the pharmacy. Accordingly, for OTC, consumers have more influence in brand selection rather than RX. Yet due to low level of education, majority of consumers ask pharmacist to recommend a brand for their acute signs and symptoms. Examples of OTC markets are pain killers (analgesics), heart burn, cough & cold, allergy, feminine hygiene, skin and hair care products. While examples of RX diseases are hypertension, diabetes, oncology, psychic products, and usually physicians have the ultimate power in brand selection. Generally, in OTC the role of pharmacist in brand selection surpass the role of physician. Yet from pharmacists' behavior research, it was shown that pharmacists gain confidence in certain brand when they see several prescriptions for this brand. So even in acute market in order to launch a new brand properly, the cycle usually starts by the physician prescribing a certain brand passing the confidence to phar-

Table 1. Projected pharmaceutical market, 2011-2015

	2011	2012	2013	2014	2015
Value USD billion	4.7	5.4	6.2	7	8
% GDP	2	2	1.9	2	2
% Health Expenditure	31	31	30.8	31.6	32.3
Per Capita (USD)	54	61	69	77	86

Source: (ESPICOM, 2011).

macist to recommend and dispense this brand then finally by usage the consumer starts to request the brand by name and this would be the ultimate success point of a certain brand as it gained consumer equity (ESPICOM, 2011).

In Egypt there is no clear definition of the OTC market versus the RX market accordingly all brands can be dispensed without prescription. In Acute market, Pharmaceutical companies compete in different therapeutic classes or disease areas, for example, Allergy market; with a range of therapeutic classes like nasal drops & oral antihistamine, Pain market; oral, topical & parenteral analgesics, steroidal or non-steroidal analgesics, cough and cold market ext... In Egypt pain market is considered the biggest market with 18.5% MS of total Acute market, more than 50 companies are competing in the pain market with more than 150 brands. Pain market is highly fragmented where the top 3 brands has 30% of the market while 70% is distributed among the rest of the brands.

The Top 3 markets are Pain killers (analgesics) and Gastro category (antiulcer ants & antacids) brands, used in treatment of heart burns and peptic ulcers, and Cold preparations market. Accordingly, for any company, in order to have strong presence in the acute market and in order to compete in the overall market, it should have strong existence in at least one or two of these 3 mega markets which contributes to 35% of the total acute market.

In pharmaceutical market, regulatory bodies like MOH, Ministry of Health, plays an important role in regulating the market in terms of setting prices, so companies are price takers. MOH regulates as well all the promotional materials, brands' claims communicated by each company to physicians or pharmacists. It is forbidden to communicate any message including brand names direct to consumers. For consumers, Pharmaceutical companies are only allowed to communicate educational materials about diseases i.e disease awareness yet without any brand names. Accordingly, if a brand reached a phase were it gained equity at consumer level then this brand has made great success.

SWOT ANALYSIS

Strengths

- The new efficient system for new medicine.
- The increasing size of the local market due to increase in the country's population.
- The rising health awareness.
- The improvement in the economic performance and the enhancement in individual's purchasing power.

- The entrance of multinational companies to the local market with their massive financial abilities and their introduction to new technologies.
- The recent Ministry of health's decision of limiting the number of companies that manufacture pharmaceuticals for other companies to32 instead of 120, seeking more adoption of the international quality standards in pharmaceuticals production in Egypt.

Weakness

- Limited research and development expenditure.
- Depending on imported raw materials.
- The absence of strong allies in the local market similar to successful international merges between Glaxo Wellcome and Smithkline or Pfizer and Warner Lambert with more abilities to fund researches and invading new markets.
- Fake or expired medicine sold in pharmacies.
- Very low GDP per capita and also the low per capita consumption.
- Lack of effective patent legislation.
- Difficult access to new markets like administrative and transportation problem in some African countries.

Opportunities

- The government's plan to introduce a basic health insurance that will extend its benefits to more Egyptian's.
- The growing health and pharmaceutical expenditure.
- The ability to open new markets in Africa through bi or multi-lateral agreements like COMESA or Egyptian medicine.

Threats

- The application of the trips would increase the medicine prices because of the need to get the permission from the original inventor to produce the medicine locally.
- Disputes about the pricing policy especially after the administrative court decision to stop the ministry of Health new decision.
- Wrong ideas about the superiority of patented and international medicine over generic and locally produced ones although they undergo the same evaluating processes.
- The difficult access to imported raw materials after the advent of China and India as large for them.

MARKET STRUCTURE

Pharmaceutical companies operating in Egypt fall into three categories: public sector companies (12 companies are affiliates of Holdipharma previously known as Drug Holding Company D.H.C), private sector Egyptian companies and multinational companies.

Before1990s, the sector was dominated by state-owned companies but this has changed with the introduction of privatization program that has made the private sector take the highest share of the production in the domestic market.

The number of pharmaceutical companies that have been established in the period between 1970 and 2009 is 291 companies including 212 Egyptian companies, 61 companies launched by a partnership between Egyptians and foreigners and 18 international companies.

CONSUMPTION

Egypt is the largest consumer of pharmaceuticals in the MENA region with an annual increasing pharmaceutical spending reaching about US $ 2.48bn, by the end of 2009, and experts forecast to continue rising to reach about US $ 4.24 bn. by 2014 at a compound annual growth rate (CAGR) of 11.4%, although Egypt's pharmaceutical expenditure per capita is still one of the lowest in the region.

PRODUCTION

Annual production is recorded to be LE 15 bn. in 2009 with capital expenditure of LE 6 bn. In 2010, the market size has reached US $ 4.1 bn. at retail prices or US $ 48 per capita which represents 1.9% of GDP and 30.6% of health expenditure. Egypt has the largest drug –manufacturing base in the MENA region accounting for around 30% of the regional market. Local production covers around 93% of the market with 7% made up of highly specialized pharmaceuticals not produced locally. Multinational corporations account for about 30% of local sales through domestic manufacturing, and about 35% through licensing agreements, while the remaining ratio represents generic medicines produced by local companies.

This industry has a good potential for the future with investments keep increasing. The number of pharmaceutical factories has increased from 90 factories in 2006 to 120 factories in 2010 with other 70 plants that are under construction (Innovic, 2013).

COMPETITIVE STRENGTHS AND CAPABILITIES

- **Highly Effective Workforce:** Egypt produces more doctors and pharmacists than any other country in the Middle East. Egypt's workforce is the largest in the Arab world and the second largest in the MENA region, after Iran. Egypt's pharmaceutical workforce offers the highest quality of performance standards and simultaneously promotes cost efficiency in the form of low labor costs and a large pool of highly trained professionals. The industry currently employs a total of 39,500 professional staff and production workers.
- **Increase in Investment Appeal:** Egypt is looking to further solidify its stronghold by increasing investment in the sector and expanding production capacity. Pharmaceutical production increased in 2009, reaching EGP3.5 billion. The Ministry of Investment announced plans to build 76 new pharmaceutical plants, bringing the national total to 180, in order to help meet its target of USD1billion in exports by 2015. Investments in Egypt's pharmaceutical industry currently stand at EGP 26 billion.
- **Largest Drug-Manufacturing Base in the MENA:** Egypt has the largest drug-manufacturing base in the Middle East and North Africa (MENA), accounting for 30% of the regional market. With a 75% market share, the private sector dominates pharmaceutical production. The total value of the Egyptian pharmaceutical market is USD 1 billion annually. Local manufacturers of generic drugs supply 52% of the market, while research-based multi-national companies account for the balance, either through "under licensing'" local manufacturing or direct imports.

OPPORTUNITIES

1. The government's plans to introduce a basic health insurance that will extend its benefits to more Egyptians.
2. The growing health and pharmaceutical expenditure.
3. The ability to open new markets in Africa through bi or multi-lateral agreements like the COMESA for Egyptian medicine.

It's expected that the industry will witness an increase in its value through the coming three years to reach USD 8 billion in 2015 with an average CAGR of 14.3%. However, it will keep a consistent percentage of the GDP ranging from 1.9 - 2.0%. This increase is accompanied with the increase in health expenditure to form 32.3% of the market value in 2015. Moreover, per capita share is anticipated to increase to be USD 86 in the same year.

The Pharmaceutical industry in Egypt is rising, stimulated by many factors like the increasing size of the market and the entrance of new investors to the market. The government seeks more liberalization for the industry with less control over prices and more privatization for the sector. This industry faces many challenges like the rising competition with international producers and poor healthcare system in Egypt. However, many specialists have positive expectations that Egypt would become one of the leading countries in that field.

OUTLOOK

Rapid population growth and expansion in healthcare coverage and expenditures are key growth drivers, as are an increasing awareness of health issues and the modernization of the healthcare industry.

Egypt's exports of pharmaceuticals have grown steadily in recent years, topping USD 270 million in FY 2011/2012 compared to USD 238 million in FY 2006/2007.

In April 2008, Novartis became the first multinational drug producer operating in Egypt to add its local facility to its global supply chain. In addition to making 123 products for local consumption, Novartis Egypt will now supply the company's global operations with treatments for ocular and hormonal conditions.

Egypt is the largest consumer of pharmaceuticals in the MENA region with an annual increasing pharmaceutical spending reaching about USD 2.48 billion, by the end of 2009, and experts forecast to continue rising to reach about USD 4.24 billion by 2014 at a compound annual growth rate (CAGR) of 11.4%, although Egypt's pharmaceutical expenditure per capita is still one of the lowest in the region.

Annual production is recorded to be EGP 15 billion in 2009. In 2010, the market size has reached USD 4.1 billion at retail prices or USD 48 per capita which represents 1.9% of GDP and 30.6% of health expenditure.

Egypt has the largest drug –manufacturing base in the MENA region accounting for around 30% of the regional market. Local production covers around 93% of the market with 7% made up of highly specialized pharmaceuticals not produced locally.

Multinational corporations account for about 30% of local sales through domestic manufacturing, and about 35% through licensing agreements, while the remaining ratio represents generic medicines produced by local companies.

This industry has a good potential for the future with investments keep increasing. The number of pharmaceutical factories has increased from 90 factories in 2006 to 120 factories in 2010 with other 70 plants that are under construction.

Large multinationals as GlaxoSmithKline (GSK) is the leading company in the Egyptian market with 9% of the market share. Sanofi-Aventis and Novartis are also among the top multinational manufacturers in the market. Furthermore, multinationals like Pfizer, Servier, and Bristol- Myers are active players in the pharmaceutical industry in Egypt.

Holdipharma, the state owned producer, contributes with 1700 types of medicine, 42.1% of them are sold in cheap prices, with LE 1.3 billion as new investments every three years, bearing LE 0.5 bn. annual losses because of its low prices. The total capital of Holdipharma and its affiliates is about LE 2 billion, with a cumulative growth rate over the last five years 50% (Innovic, 2013).

PRICING

Before September 2009, the Pricing Committee in the Ministry of Health was determining the profit margin ceiling for different types of medicine through the "cost plus system." The profit margin ceiling was 15% for essential drugs, 25% for non-essential drugs and 40% for over-the-counter drugs. According to its new vision, the Ministry of Health has declared the decision 373 for the year 2009 that sets up two new pricing systems for the registration of new medicines in the market, one for branded pharmaceuticals and the other for generic drugs. The first system determines the price of branded drugs to be 10% lower than the cheapest retail price of the medicine in 36 countries in which the drug is available; however, this does not mean that the drug should be registered in all the 36 countries.

Second, the price of generic drugs will be decreased by a fixed percentage of branded drugs price, and therefore is expected to increase compared to its previous prices that were cheaper by 80% and 90% than branded drugs as follows:

- The price of generic drugs produced by companies licensed by the Ministry of Health and certified by international agencies would be decreased by 30%.
- The price of generic drugs produced by companies licensed by only the Ministry of Health, the license validity lasts till 2020 which is the due date to get international quality certifications for all plants, would be decreased by 40%.
- The price of generic drugs produced by companies do not possess plants but using other plants would be decreased by 60%.

However the court of administrative justice has stopped the implementation of the new decision on 27th of April 2010 enforcing the Ministry of Health to re-implement the cost plus system in pricing, and the Supreme Administrative Court will discuss the decision on 6th of December, 2010.

STRONG POLICY GUIDELINES

The Egyptian Drug Authority (EDA) is the pharmaceutical regulatory body of the Egyptian Ministry of Health (MOH) and it is committed to supporting initiatives which help promote its goals of protecting people's health by regulating safety and quality of pharmaceutical products, regulation & legislation of pharmacy practice, availability of high quality medicines at affordable prices, strategic planning & policy making for the sector, setting standards of pharmaceutical services for both hospital & community, cooperation with relevant international organizations (such as the WHO) in order to improve standards of pharmaceutical products and practices.

In January 2012 the Egyptian Ministry of Health and EDA announced the launch of new Pharmaco vigilance (PV) guidelines for Marketing Authorization Holders (MHAs). These laws make the reporting of adverse drug effects compulsory for firms and are part of a wider increase in focus on regulatory activity in the field of PV in Africa, which help combating soaring rates of drug counterfeiting.

BONDET CO. IN EGYPT

Bondet Company is a leading multinational company that has been operating in Egypt for more than 70 years. Currently, Bondet is ranking 3rd in the pharmaceutical market with MS 9% representing 250$ sales turnover, it has a huge factory for medical products' manufacturing with labor force slightly above 1000 employee, in addition Bondet Co. imports brands that are difficult to be produced in Egypt. It is well known for its quality brands and diversified portfolio in different disease areas. Bondet is dominating the chronic market, ranking first while they are lagging behind, 7th rank, in the acute market. So in order to grow, the company's strategy is to keep dominating the chronic market while expanding and penetrating the acute market.

The Company's vision is to be No.1 health care provider in the Egyptian Market by 2020, with a mission aiming at enhancing the health of the population through providing quality brands that helps treat different diseases. Bondet has been taking very good steps during the past 5 years towards achieving the ultimate vision of leading the pharmaceutical market in Egypt. It has been growing with double digit growth year after year surpassing the market growth and gaining market share resulting in rank improvement from 5th to 3rd in 2013 (see Figure 1).

Bondet Company wants to secure and increase its presence in the acute market through existence in the major categories where pain is one of them. It has been present in pain category for 30 years capturing MS 9% with 2 Brands.

Figure 1. Total market performance

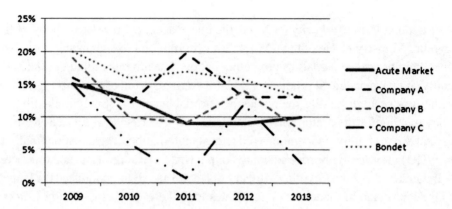

SONALFEN AND SONAGEN BRANDS[2]

Sonalfen, contributes with 8% MS, has been in the market for 30 years and has strong brand equity at consumer and pharmacist level and ranks 3rd in the market. While Sonagen has been launched 3 years back and has 1% MS. The issue is that Sonalfen is currently hurting the income statement bottom line due to increase in the cost of goods while the price hasn't changed since it was launched, 30 years back. On the other hand, Sonagen, does not have the strong brand equity nor the heritage of the old brand, it has not been gaining adequate market share despite the various marketing initiatives executed by Bondet targeting physicians and pharmacists using POS materials in pharmacies, flyers, samples and face to face detailing with physicians.

Sonalfen has huge volume turnover in order to reflect the value turnover and this is due to the low price of this brand. The volume turnover is mainly coming from the rural areas; Delta and Upper Egypt. It has been known in such places by its unique pill shape and is being dispensed mainly in these low SEC by pill not by pack. Consumers can recognize the pill and ask the pharmacist about the "fast pill" reflecting its fast pain relief. More than 80% of turnover comes from these classes where the role of physician is minimal while pharmacist role is almost 40%, and 55% is consumers' request. Bondet Co. cannot maintain Sonalfen as it has −ve business operating income and not expected to improve to the extent that all A&P (advertising and promotion) and Personal promotions to physicians has been completely stopped on this brand to try to decrease expenses and improve the BOI – Business operating income – yet it remains −ve (see Table 2).

The good thing is that without promotion Sonalfen kept growing relying on its equity, heritage and commercial advantage that has been offered to distributors and accordingly to pharmacists. However, it is extremely risky decision to discontinue

Table 2. Business operating income (2009-2013)

Description	Y9	Y10	Y11	Y12	Y13
Catalogue turnover	119.1%	119.6%	118.9%	118.9%	118.9%
Sales return	0.0%	0.0%	0.0%	0.0%	0.0%
Customer discounts	0.0%	0.0%	0.0%	0.0%	0.0%
Commercial advantages	-19.1%	-19.6%	-18.9%	-18.9%	-18.9%
Net Sales	**100.0%**	**100.0%**	**100.0%**	**100.0%**	**100.0%**
Royalties received	0.0%	0.0%	0.0%	0.0%	0.0%
Royalties paid	0.0%	0.0%	0.0%	0.0%	0.0%
ISC	-92.0%	-92.0%	-96.0%	-104.0%	-105.0%
Cost of Sales	**-92.0%**	**-92.0%**	**-96.0%**	**-104.0%**	**-105.0%**
Gross Margin	**8.0%**	**8.0%**	**4.0%**	**-4.0%**	**-5.0%**
Medical management	0.0%	0.0%	0.0%	0.0%	0.0%
Local clinical studies	0.0%	0.0%	0.0%	0.0%	0.0%
Research and Development	**0.0%**	**0.0%**	**0.0%**	**0.0%**	**0.0%**
Sales force	0.0%	0.0%	0.0%	0.0%	0.0%
Medical material advert	0.0%	0.0%	0.0%	0.0%	0.0%
Samples	0.0%	0.0%	0.0%	0.0%	0.0%
Upstream margin Marco	0.0%	0.0%	0.0%	0.0%	0.0%
Press/advertising expenses	0.0%	0.0%	0.0%	0.0%	0.0%
Specialised scientific information	0.0%	0.0%	0.0%	0.0%	0.0%
Advertising and Promotion	**0.0%**	**0.0%**	**0.0%**	**0.0%**	**0.0%**
Doubtful debts	0.0%	0.0%	0.0%	0.0%	0.0%
Cost of transferring receivable	0.0%	0.0%	0.0%	0.0%	0.0%
Pharma contrib	0.0%	0.0%	0.0%	0.0%	0.0%
Pharma Contrib/Bad Debt	**0.0%**	**0.0%**	**0.0%**	**0.0%**	**0.0%**
Marketing	**0.0%**	**0.0%**	**0.0%**	**0.0%**	**0.0%**
General exp	0.0%	0.0%	0.0%	0.0%	0.0%
Marketing and General Expenses	**0.0%**	**0.0%**	**0.0%**	**0.0%**	**0.0%**
Opex	**0.0%**	**0.0%**	**0.0%**	**0.0%**	**0.0%**
Other operating income	0.0%	0.0%	0.0%	0.0%	0.0%
Other minority interests	0.0%	0.0%	0.0%	0.0%	0.0%
BMS minority interests	0.0%	0.0%	0.0%	0.0%	0.0%
Total BMS Minority Interests	**0.0%**	**0.0%**	**0.0%**	**0.0%**	**0.0%**
Business Operating Income	**8.0%**	**8.0%**	**4.0%**	**-4.0%**	**-5.0%**

the production of this brand and any replacement might not be as fast and effective as this brand so consumers might not accept it.

Loosing high turnover and high presence in the pain market is at stake and actually jeopardizing the company's vision in penetrating and expanding in the acute market. Competitors will be taking over specially the top 2 strong competitors who has strong heritage as well, so switching to competitors brands is more liable than switching from Sonalfen to Sonagen, which is still new, still building its image at physicians and pharmacists level and almost not known to consumers, especially for these SEC. Sonagen is a different pain killer that has been proven effective in relieving pain yet not with the same strength as Sonalfen so it is positioned towards mild and moderate pain, it was priced relatively low so when Bondet launched Sonagen it had this plan in mind to switch users from Sonalfen to Sonagen, and that's why they choose the name of the new brand to be so close to the old brand. But considering the MOH regulations, that companies cannot communicate brand names to consumers, Bondet Co. couldn't communicate the link between both brands to consumers and the only open channel was pharmacists, distributors and physicians. In 2010, Bondet launched Sonagen with Pharmacists first and then a year later started to promote the brand to physicians however the brand remained anonymous with low turnover in the crowded pain market.

The distribution cycle in Bondet Co. is from the company factory to wholesales (distributors) and from distributors to pharmacies. In Egypt There are 7 big wholesalers and up to 60,000 pharmacies. Companies can communicate promotional offers by utilizing the distributor's telesales who call pharmacies and inform them about new brands launched, availability of certain brands or offers on existing brands. Bondet Co. has a sales team who covers around 5000 pharmacies especially those in premium places their role is to educate pharmacists about brands and communicate any commercial offers for brands.

Competition in this market is very aggressive as all companies understand the worth of this growing market which is growing by double digit growth +15% 3 years CAGR (compound average growth rate). Still dominating the acute market which is growing by CAGR 3 years ++9% and thus remains the most appealing market with the most aggressive competition and crowded brands. The major competitors have strong brand equity for their brands at consumer, pharmacist and physician level and they have allocated huge investment to support their brands and sustain their growth in this market to the extent that some brands have above the line advertising that is being aired from the gulf and of course have a very good spill over in Egypt. See Figure 2 for brands performance in acute market.

Figure 2. Brands' performance

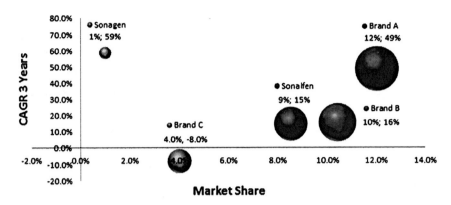

SUCCESS STORIES

VACSERA

VACSERA (Holding Company for Biological Products & Vaccines) is a vaccine producer, comprising five subsidiaries, and manufactures blood and biotech treatments as well as being the sole local producer of a variety of vaccines. The company also has a solid R&D infrastructure. BMI estimates its annual revenue to be in the region of USD 45-65 million (Vacsera, 2014).

Misr Pharmaceuticals

Originally established in 1939 as the first pharmaceuticals company in Egypt, Misr Pharmaceutical Industries is one of the government-owned pharmaceutical firms in Egypt, and part of Holdipharma. Misr exports to a number of countries in the region, as well as in Africa and Romania in Europe. The company employs around 1,750 individuals.

Misr is engaged in production and wholesale trade in pharmaceuticals, as well as some research and development of new drugs. The company mostly produces medicines in a powder, syrup, ampoule and tablet forms, although some of its output is generated as creams and vials. Most sales are in the human medicines segment, with animal health representing the remainder. In FY08/09, Misr posted EGP155.9 million in net revenue (Wahba, 2014).

Amoun Pharmaceutical Company (APC)

APC is one of the leading domestic drug makers in Egypt, with five branches in the country manufacturing human and veterinary pharmaceuticals products and nutritional supplements. Following the sale of two factories to GSK Egypt in the 1990s, Amoun was the first Egyptian drug firm to gain ISO 9001 certification, and now operates a large modern plant in El-Obour City. It was also the first private drug company founded in the country to import and distribute drugs.

APC was established as a drug import and distribution firm in 1976 and currently operates three facilities, which produce cardiovascular drugs, analgesics, vitamins, antihistamines, antirheumatics, gastrointestinal drugs and antipyretics, as well as food supplements. APC exports to 19 countries in Africa, Europe and the Middle East, and has sister companies in the US, Romania, Russia and Kenya. Amoun works as a contract manufacturer for German Merck and Rowa, and French Leurquin, as well as for Sanofi-Aventis (for some veterinary products) (Amoun, 2014).

Egyptian International Pharmaceutical Industries Co. (EIPICO)

EIPICO started production in 1985 and now claims to be the largest domestic drug manufacturer in Egypt, with a 10-12% total drug market share by volume and nine manufacturing plants in the country. It exports medicines around the world, accounting for 20% of Egypt's total pharmaceuticals exports. The company also owns majority shares in Egyptian International Ampoules Company (EIACO), which produces some 800mn units annually.

Additionally, EIPICO holds a 30% share in the Saudi Arabia-based 'Universal for Pharmaceutical Production', having invested EGP27.7 million. EIPICO has its own R&D laboratories, which are included under its 'Quality Sector' category of activities. This category also includes its chemical control and Biotechnology Centre. The Biotechnology Centre was inaugurated in 2001 to produce raw materials, extract useful compounds from natural sources, and to conduct preclinical and clinical trials for drug efficacy and bioequivalence as well as other detailed research using pharmacology. This centre is considered as separate to the operations of the main body of EIPICO, and has its own budget and staff. The drug production facilities are GMP certified, which adds respectability to the company's standing as an exporter to the EU.

EIPICO's 2010 financial results show revenue increasing from EGP1.0 billion (USD 180 million) in 2009 to EGP1.1bn (USD195 million) in 2010. In 2010 net income rose 14% to EGP326 million (USD 55 million). After the re-opening of the Egyptian stock market in March 2011, EIPICO's share price slumped to EGP33.24, though it has since recovered to EGP37.21 (EIPICO, 2014).

South Egyptian Drug Industries (SEDICO)

SEDICO started production in 1990 and its facilities are GMP certified. The company manufactures a variety of insulins, in addition to the non-traditional dosage forms such as the soft gelatin capsules, lyophilized products, gels, sprays and effervescent tablets. Products launched in the first quarter of 2007 include magnabiotic injections (amoxicillin and clavulanic), bromurex and ultracillin vials. The company focuses on generics, but also has three patented medicines – all skin treatments containing Jojoba oil as the active ingredient. The 24% share of SEDICO is owned by Akzo-Nobel's Organon, one of the companies for which SEDICO provides contract manufacturing services. SEDICO is engaged in the production of some biotechnology products, in partnership with foreign players. In 2009, the company posted EGP345.7 million in sales, as a result of higher production levels (which reached a record EGP398.8mn). Income before tax came in at EGP65.7million, with income after tax reaching EGP51.1 million. Exports were worth EGP15.2 million (SEDICO, 2014).

Medical Union Pharmaceuticals (MUP)

First established in 1984 through the cooperation of the medical professionals syndicates union data, MUP was listed on the Egyptian stock exchange in April 1997 and has since gone on to become one of the largest domestic drug makers in the country with a market share of 4.4% of the domestic market in value terms in 2010. It is believed to produce 60 million units of drugs in various pharmaceuticals forms.

The company predominantly produces generic and licensed drugs with its most important partners listed as Schering Plough and Kline Smith Beecham, although both of these two companies have since merged and no longer exist under these names. According to its 2010 annual report the company's biggest shareholder is the Arab Company for Drug Industries and Medical Devices (ACDIMA) which holds 40% of the company's shares. The next biggest shareholder is the Industrial Investment Company which holds around 10% of the company's equity.

MUP's sales grew from EGP456.5 million (USD 77.4 million) in 2005 to EGP780.9 million (USD 131.5 million) in 2010 at a CAGR of 11.3% in local currency terms. In the same time period, net profit doubled from EGP84.2 million (USD 14.3 million) to EGP167.1 million (USD 28.1 million). However, the company issued a sales guidance note in September 2010 that forecast sales of EGP700 million for 2011, down 10% on the previous year. The Egyptian financial year runs from July 1 to June 30 so the latter half of FY 2011 is also likely to have been impacted by the effects of the revolution (MUPEG, 2014).

GlaxoSmithKline (GSK)

GSK operates in Egypt through its 91%-owned subsidiary GSK Egypt, which employs around 1,500 staff. The subsidiary, established in 1990, principally manufactures ethical drugs, but also markets and distributes other pharmaceuticals products and toiletries. GSK was listed in Egypt in 1985 and has a market capitalization of EGP1.55 billion (USD 266.45 million).

The company has more than USD 100 million of investments in Egypt. According to IMS Health data for September 2009 MAT, GSK ranked first in Egypt, with an 8.7% value share of the market. GSK's main activities in Egypt are manufacturing, packaging, marketing, selling and distributing GSK products. GSK Egypt also imports and distributes a range of its parent company's products that are not manufactured in Egypt. In addition, GSK Egypt manufactures a range of products under license from other pharmaceuticals manufacturers. GSK's production capacity in Egypt equates to approximately 107 million medicine units per year. The factory, laboratories, warehouse and head office are in El-Salam City, Cairo. GSK Egypt also has scientific and sales offices in Mohandessin, Nasr City, Alexandria, Tanta, Mansoura and Souhag. Company officials claim that about 90% of the subsidiary's production is sold in Egypt, with the remaining 10% being exported to other MENA markets. This indicates the retention of a significant share of the local Egyptian market, despite profit slides suffered by the firm, resulting from turbulent market conditions, relating to currency devaluation and tight price controls.

During Q4 2008, GSK acquired BMS's mature products business in Egypt for USD 210 million, giving it a 9% market share in the country. The strategic move consolidated GSK's ambitions to increase its portfolio and presence in emerging markets such as Egypt. With GSK reporting revenue for its emerging markets division of US$4.2bn in 2008, the acquisition of a high-value portfolio from BMS will boost future sales.

In 2009, the proportion of its 'white pill/Western markets' sales to total sales fell from 36% to 30%, as the company aims to diversify its presence. Emerging markets represented GBP 66 million, or some 14% of the company's total sales in 2009 (GlaxoSmithKline, 2014).

Sanofi-Aventis

Sanofi-Aventis is among the five largest pharmaceuticals companies in Egypt. It operates in Egypt through its affiliate, Sanofi-Aventis Egypt, which operates a plant and four offices in the country, employing more than 800 people. The company's manufacturing capacity is 50 million boxes and 20 million packs per annum. The company markets the following medicines in Egypt: Plavix, Aprovel (irbesartan),

Tritace (ramipril), Actonel (risedronate), Depakine (sodium valproate), Amaryl (glimepiride), Lantus, Eloxatin (oxaliplatin), and Taxotere (docetaxel), among a number of other products. Sanofi- Aventis has also provided the vaccines used in mass polio immunization programmes in the country. In 2009, the company posted EUR 29.31 billion in global sales, up by 6.3% y-o-y. Markets other than those in Europe and the US accounted for around 26.7% of the company's total sales (Sanofi, 2014).

Pfizer

Pfizer, the world's largest pharmaceuticals company, operates in Egypt through its 100% owned subsidiary Pfizer Egypt. The company was established in 1961 and was one of the first foreign-owned companies to commence operations in Egypt. It now employs around 800 people. The company specializes in manufacturing and distributing chemicals, pharmaceuticals and animal health products. Its main pharmaceuticals product areas are antibiotics, cardiovascular preparations, anti-allergy treatments and anti-infectives. Pfizer recently acquired compatriot Wyeth, which also has operations in Egypt. The company deals in prescription and consumer health products (Pfizer, 2014).

Novartis

Novartis operates in Egypt through its subsidiary Novartis Pharma, established in 1962. It is based in Cairo and manufactures, markets and sells patented pharmaceuticals, OTCs, generics and animal healthcare products. Leading product areas are analgesics, cardiovascular treatments and ear, nose and throat preparations. Novartis employs approximately 1,120 individuals.

In 2009, Novartis posted USD 44.3 billion in global net sales, up from USD 41.5 billion achieved in the previous year. Sales of Voltaren (excluding OTC sales) reached USD 797 million, up by 1% y-o-y in local currency, driven by solid performance in emerging markets, including those in Africa. In 2009, net sales in Asia/Africa/Australasia rose to USD 8.09 billion, thus representing 18% of the total, up from 17% in the previous year (or USD 7.14 billion) (Novertis, 2014).

THE DILEMMA

Currently the company has decided to stop the production of Sonalfen on a medium term plan. However, there is no clear strategy what to do next, whether to focus on Sonagen and start building a new brand from scratch, or try to create the name resonance between the two brands as per the initial plan or may be maintain both brands and try to build a family or may be some other approach would be the optimum to secure profitability and minimize brand equity loss. Several pros and cons for each strategic decision yet an action should be taken.

"What alternatives do you have in mind?" Said Tamer

"Three years ago we launched Sonagen which has the same prefix as Sonalfen to create name resonance between the two brands and appeal to consumers. It wasn't a great success as Sonalfen consumers are of low socioeconomic class and we cannot communicate brand name change directly with them as per MOH regulations. Pharmacists responds to consumers request but we thought they would have influence on consumers choice so we need to think about pharmacists as gate keepers to start dispensing sonagen instead of Sonalfen. Still we cannot have a proper coverage for pharmacists in Egypt. I am thinking of a switching 360 campaign across the four stakeholders; physician, pharmacists, distributors and consumers. I believe we need to work in parallel on these four stakeholders and not in series as we did earlier." Amr replied.

Tamer looked back with passion and said "I will leave you to think about all alternatives and we can set meeting in presence of board members to discuss and challenge your plan to adopt the best strategic direction."

"Great, see you in the meeting then." Amr answered.

ACKNOWLEDGMENT

We would like to acknowledge all the help and support done by El-Khazindar Business Research and Case Center (KCC), Egypt, during the preparation and submission of this case.

REFERENCES

Amoun. (2014). *Amoun Pharmaceutical Co. S.A.E.* [Company Overview]. Retrieved on June 23, 2014 from http://www.amoun.com/about-amoun/company-overview.html

EIPICO. (2014). *Egyptian International Pharmaceutical Industries Co.* [History]. Retrieved June 25th 2014 from http://eipico.com.eg/index.php/about-us/our-history

ESPICOM. (2011). *The pharmacutical market: Egypt* [Data File]. Retrieved June 21st, 2014, from http://www.espicom.com/egypt-pharmaceutical-market.html

GlaxoSmithKline. (2014). *GlaxoSmithKline* [About us]. Retrieved 26th June 2014 from http://www.gsk.com/en-gb/about-us/

Innovic. (2013). *The pharmaceutical sector in Egypt* [Data File]. Retrieved June 21st, 2014, from http://innovicbusiness.blogspot.in/2013/05/the-pharmaceutical-sector-in-egypt.html

MUPEG. (2014). *Medical Union Pharmaceuticals* [About us]. Retrieved 26th June 2014 fromwww.mupeg.com

Novartis. (2014). *Novartis* [About us]. Retrieved 26th June 2014 from http://www.novartis.com.eg/aboutus/index.shtml

Pfizer. (2014). *Pfizer* [About us]. Retrieved 26th June 2014 from http://www.pfizer.com/about

Sanofi. (2014). *Sanofi in Egypt* [Index]. Retrieved 26th June 2014 from www.sanofi.com.eg/l/eg/en/index.jsp

SEDICO. (2014). *South Egyptian drug industries* [Project]. Retrieved June 25th, 2014 from www.ebm.com.eg/.../SedicoWebsiteProject_e.htm

Vacsera. (2014). *Vacsera* [Component Content]. Retrieved June 22nd, 2014 from http://www.vacsera.com/component/content/?view=featured&start=5

Wahba, M. N. (2014). *Holdi Pharma* [Home]. Retrieved June 22nd, 2014 from www.holdipharma.com/en/home/Pages/misr.aspx

KEY TERMS AND DEFINITIONS

Biologics and Biosimilars: Biological medicines are produced using biological processes and biosimilar medicines are copies of original biological medicines.

Generics: When the patency period is over, companies can start producing the same active ingredient and thus called generics to the parent original brand.

MOH: Ministry of health is concerned with all the legalization for drug industry and health care system.

OTC: Over the counter, OTC products are those products that can be dispensed without a prescription.

Patency: A privilege given to new innovation from the FDA to secure a high return from this innovation before any other entity can copy it. Usually it is a 10 years.

Pharma-Emerging Markets: 20 emerging markets in the pharmaceutical industry that have high growth rate and high potential in terms of size of the market.

RX: Products that need a prescription.

ENDNOTES

[1]   This is not the real name of the company.

[2]   Brand names are not real.

Chapter 12
Ariika Bean Bags:
A Successful Brand Capable of International Expansion?

Rania Hussein
The American University in Cairo, Egypt

Hend Mostafa
The American University in Cairo, Egypt

ABSTRACT

This case deals with Ariika, which produces a large variety of bean bags that have innovative designs. The company focuses on quality and aims at becoming the first branded bean bag in Egypt with high quality and reasonable prices. Over the years, Ariika was able to build a strong customer base, sell its products online, and maintain strong relationships with large retailers. The success of Ariika in the Egyptian market encouraged Attallah, the owner, to consider his next move. The key problems discussed in the case are, Should the company capitalize on possible opportunities by immediately expanding beyond Egypt? If they decide to expand abroad, how should the company strategically expand: in the two countries at the same time, sequentially one at a time, or only in one of them? Should they rely on simple exports or consider foreign direct investment?

DOI: 10.4018/978-1-4666-7393-9.ch012

ORGANIZATION BACKGROUND

Ariika is an Egyptian brand that started in 2011 by four students who attended the American University in Cairo. Its goal was to deliver high quality comfortable innovative products like bean bags, floating mattresses, or travel pillows with reasonable prices. Ariika now is the largest bean bag brand in the MENA Region. Ariika was founded by Hassan Arslan who majored in Business Administration with Marketing concentration, Shahir Arslan, Hassan's brother, Construction Engineering major; Khaled Attallah, Business administration and Mohamed Bahgat, Computer Science. In 2011 Ariika focused on bean bags and its launch was in AUC. Ariika expanded its portfolio by 2012 to comfortable products and acquired at large share of the market. The largest furniture stores in Egypt such as Istikbal, Taki, In and out, Home Center, and Divano sold Ariika's products. By 2013 Ariika was already selling bean bags for consumers and businesses alike. Companies like Pepsico, Coca Cola, Emaar, Palm Hills, Ahram beverages and many more were lining up to purchase consumers favorite product. Organizations either printed on bean bags and distributed them on beaches, or used them for giveaways. In 2014 Ariika launched 4 stores, 3 seasonal ones and 1 in Cairo.

ORGANIZATION STRUCTURE

Ariika has three main departments that are managed by one of the founders of the company. These departments are marketing, sales and production. The marketing department has two members; a manager and an assistant. This department is responsible for developing marketing campaigns for Ariika's products. They are also responsible for introducing Ariika at different universities and exhibitions. The marketing team is continuously searching for new opportunities to introduce Ariika by approaching online stores and furniture magazine. The marketing team also designs all promotional materials needed to promote Ariika. Finally the marketing team also manages the company's website. Although the department has only 2 members, the number is expected to increase in the future.

The sales department is considered to be the main pillar of Ariika. This department consists of 12 sales executives and one manager. The sales executives are responsible for all of the logistics required for each order. They take orders, send to the production, receive the order then deliver it to the client. The sales team is also responsible for finding new outlets to sell Ariika's products as well as approaching different cafes, hotels, and beaches, to introduce Ariika's products. The sales team is also responsible for the customer service and financials. The sales team set up a yearly target and sales executive are paid based on commissions. The number of sales executives is also expected to increase in the future.

The production department has a manager and an assistant. The production team is responsible for the production process of Ariika's products, the quality control and the customization required to satisfy customers' needs. They are also responsible to maintain the machines in the factory and ensure that the orders and supplies reach on time. The capacity of Ariika's production was very limited; accordingly introducing new products was very challenging. However through improving the production process, Ariika's production capacity improved.

The employees working at Ariika are young, mostly graduates of the American University in Cairo who share same passion and enthusiasm for what they are doing. Together they hope to help Ariika grow and expand locally and internationally.

ARIIKA'S MARKETING MIX

Marketing Mix is a particular combination of the product, its price, the methods used to promote it and the ways used to make the product available to the customer. Based upon its understanding of customers, a company develops its marketing mix of product, price, place and promotion. The elements of the marketing mix are interrelated. All the elements have to reinforce each other to enhance the experience of the customer. When a change is proposed to be made in one of the elements, it has to be checked if the changed element still fits with and reinforces other elements in order to ensure the effectiveness of the marketing mix. A company's marketing mix must satisfy customer needs better than the competition. A company implements its strategy through its marketing mix.

Product

Ariika aimed at developing high quality and innovative products to the Egyptian market. The products are made of leather or water proof with PVC coating. The bean bags are filled with Styrofoam that is developed specially for Ariika. These high quality Styrofoam are more durable than other ordinary Styrofoam available in the market. Ariika also sells Styrofoam for refilling and maintenance.

Ariika's products allow for customization, which differentiates it from other competitors. Customers can customize their order in terms of shape, color, images or writings, which requires additional charge. The degree of customization provided by Ariika differentiates it from other traditional competitors in the market.

Although Ariika started by only producing bean bags, it now has four different products; beans bags, floating bags, floating mats, and U pillow. The company has

8 different designs of beans bags, 5 floating bags, 3 floating mats and U pillows. Ariika provides six months warranty on its products. Within these six months, the product could be repaired or replaced.

Advertising and Promotion

Ariika's main goal was to build a strong brand name in the market that is linked to innovation and high quality. Accordingly, Attallah invested a lot of time and effort on developing Ariika's brand name and image. He started by associating Ariika's brand name with comfort, quality and customization. Attalah's strategy was to focus on these three attributes in promoting Ariika. However, he later amended his strategy and preferred to focus on comfort to differentiate the brand from future competitors. The company always highlighted the innovative designs and high quality of its products in its marketing campaigns to build a strong brand image.

Ariika implemented its marketing plans at different private universities in Egypt such as the American University in Cairo (AUC), the German university in Cairo (GUC) and the British University in Egypt (BUE). Ariika chose these destinations as it is targeting A-class youth who study in these universities. Through these campaigns the company introduced its brand and allowed customers to try its products.

Moreover, Ariika relied heavily on online marketing. The company developed its website where customers can customize, place and track their orders. Ariika also used other social media tools such as Facebook, Twitter and Instagram to promote its products. Through social media, customers can interact with Ariika, ask questions and add comments. On the other hand, Ariika could announce new offers, introduce new products or promote new events to its customers directly through social media.

Ariika also marketed its products on Enigma magazine, which has an online store that displays different furniture and clothing. In addition, Ariika sold its products on Nefsak.com, which is an E-commerce website. Through displaying its products on Nefsak.com, Ariika increased its sales by being exposed to a large customer base. Attallah introduced Ariika in two main furniture exhibitions in Egypt; Le Marche 2011, and La Casa. These exhibitions allowed the company to introduce its products to many visitors.

Pricing Strategy

Attalah wanted to position Ariika as a high quality innovative product. Accordingly the pricing of Ariika's products is aligned with this objective. Therefore Ariika's products were priced slightly higher than competitors. The price of Ariika's traditional beans bags is LE 540. While competitors such as Antakh and Cozy price their bean bags at LE 490 and LE 530 respectively. However in the B2B sales, the company provides discounts to its clients as they buy in large quantities.

Distribution Strategy

Ariika sold its products directly to consumers through the company's website. The customers can place an order online and Ariika sends it to them directly. Although buying through the website is very convenient to some customers, others are reluctant to buy a product they cannot see or touch. Accordingly Ariika allowed for 2 days return of the product to reduce customers' perceived risk and allow them to see the product. Moreover, Ariika started to introduce its products at different furniture outlets. These outlets buy Ariika's products at a discounted price and sell them to the clients. One of these outlets that sell Ariika products is In & Out. In & Out is a famous furniture outlet that has show rooms in many places in Egypt. The outlet sells both indoor and outdoor products. Ariika also managed to sell its products at other outlets including Taki, Sofa Home and Kare.

To increase its market presence, Ariika tried to reach other places outside Cairo, especially in Ain el Skhna, a beach destination for upper class Egyptians. Additionally, Ariika sold its products at Smart Home that has a showroom in Ain el Sokhna and Hurgada, another beach destination. Ariika also displayed its products in different gift shops such as Giftshop, Grab and Rape and Cow. Although the demand for Ariika's products is increasing, opening a standalone store is postponed for the time being due to the high cost associated with running such a store.

TARGET MARKETS

In evaluating different market segments, a firm must look at three factors:

1. Segment size and growth,
2. Segment structural attractiveness, and
3. Company objectives and resources.

The company must collect and analyze data on current segment sales, growth rates and expected profitability for various segments.

The companies also need to examine major structural factors that affect long-run segment attractiveness. For example, a segment is less attractive if it already contains many strong and aggressive competitors. The existence of many actual and potential substitute products may limit prices and affect profits earned in a segment. The relative power of buyers also affects segments' attractiveness.

Finally a segment may be less attractive if it contains powerful suppliers who can control prices or reduce the quality or quantity of ordered goods and services. Even if the segment has the right size and growth and is structurally attractive, the company must consider its own objectives and resources. A company may lack the skills and resources needed to succeed in an attractive segment.

Business to Consumer

Ariika started by targeting youth, mainly university students who are more likely to try new product. Attallah started to market Ariika at different universities such as AUC, GUC, and BUE. At this stage, few competitors started to enter the market. "The barriers to entry were low, any company with enough financial resources could present a threat to Ariika," explained Attallah. Attallah also targeted customers online through selling its products on the company's website. Customers could place, pay, and track the order online and the product will be delivered directly to the client. The company's sales were growing and it currently has 60% market share of the branded bean bags market in Egypt

Business to Business

In order to increase its sustainability in the market and build on its success, Ariika decided to take a step further and target B2B. Through contacting different furniture outlets, Ariika was able to display its products in different furniture outlets such as In & Out Furniture, Kare, etc. Moreover, Ariika sold large quantities of bean bags to beaches, cafes and compounds. Although the B2B sales represent 70% of the total company sales, Attallah believes that having strong B2C sales will guarantee the company's growth and expansion in the future. The company has many satisfied clients such as Vodafone, Coca Cola, Heinkien, Google, Bianchi Beach, Hilton, Mountain View compound, Palm Hills, and In & Out Furniture.

Competitors

After establishing its brand name in the Egyptian market, Ariika had a market share of 60% in the branded bean bags. The low barriers to entry encouraged some competitors to enter the market such as "Antakh" and "Cozy." These competitors, however, failed to meet the high demand of large retailers due to their limited capacity and limited time frame. Ariika, on the other hand, had a larger capacity than its competitors and was able to sustain a strong customer relationship management strategy with large retailers.

ARIIKA's Success at the Local Level

Although Ariika was launched in May 2011, the company's sales were increasing tremendously. During the first month of the launch, Arslan forecasted to sell 30 bean bags, however, the company sold 130. The demand for Ariika's bean bags increased further as corporations, such as Coca Cola, approached Ariika. By the end of 2011, the company supplied Coca Cola with 200 bean bags and started to contact different cafes, beaches and residential compounds. In 2013, Ariika introduced floating bags that were required by Pepsi and Coca Cola for their marketing campaigns. Through a bidding war, Pepsi won the bid and Ariika developed 7000 floating bags for Pepsi. By the end of 2013, Ariika was controlling 50% of the consumer market for branded bean bags in Egypt, 80% of the corporate market and 90% of the reseller market in Egypt. (See Table 1) indicates Ariika's sales and profits between 2011 and 2013. Building on its success in the Egyptian market, Arslan was considering future alternatives for Ariika. He believed that the success model of Ariika in Egypt could be invested in international expansion and accordingly was considering the UAE and SA.

UNITED ARAB EMIRATES (UAE): COUNTRY OVERVIEW

Macroeconomic Overview (World Fact Book: UAE, 2013)

The UAE is one of the oil-producing influential countries in the gulf region. Though the country depends mostly on oil, there are tremendous developments in different other sectors such as construction and trade. These developments allowed the UAE to become a distribution center and a trade hub. For more than three decades, the UAE depended on oil and global finance to improve the country's economy. The global financial crisis affected the UAE tremendously due to decline in oil prices and the collapse in real estate prices. However, the country's GDP started to increase and the GDP per capita reached $29,900 in 2013 with 4% real growth rate (See Table 2).

Table 1. Ariika's revenues and profits

	2011	2012	2013
Revenues	650,000	1,200,000	2,000,000
Costs	475,000	1,080,000	1,300,000
Profits	175,000	120,000	700,000

Table 2. Business environment analysis report (2013)

	United Arab Emirates	Saudi Arabia
Demographics		
Total Population	5.5 million	26.9 million
Population Growth Rate	2.87%	1.51%
Age Structure		
0-14 years:	20.6%	28.2%
15-24 years:	13.8%	19.6%
25-54	61.5%	44.8%
55-64	3.1%	4.3%
65 years and over	1%	3.1%
Urban/Rural Composition	Urban:84.4% Rural:%	Urban: 82.3% Rural:%
Government		
Economic Freedom*	71.4	62.2
FDI (home)	$103 billion	$240.6 billion
Ease of Doing Business**	23	26
Currency Convertibility	Convertible	Convertible
Physical Infrastructure		
Roads and Highways	4,080 km	221,372 km
Airports	43	214
Ports	8 main ports	6 main ports
Economics		
GDP Growth Rate	4%	3.6%
Per Capita GDP	$29,900	$31,300
Consumer Inflation Rate	1.3%	4.1%
Unemployment (2001)	2.4%	10.5%
Communications Infrastructure		
Fixed Telephone Market (2012)	2.0 million	4.8 million
Wireless Telephone Market	13.8 million	53 million
Internet Users (2009)	3.4 million	9.8 million

Trade Environment

The UAE was able to achieve economic diversification and reduce the portion of GDP that depends on oil and gas output to 25%. The UAE went through many transformations to become a modern state with high standard of living. The country's exports reached $368.9 billion in 2013, which ranked the UAE 18th compared to the world. The main exported products are crude oil, natural gas, dried fish and dates. The main exporting partners are Japan, India, Iran, Thailand, Singapore and South Korea. Regarding the imports, the UAE imports reached $249.6 billion in 2013. The main imported products are machinery, transport equipment, chemicals and food. The main import partners are India, China, US, Germany, and Japan.

Furniture Industry in the UAE

The furniture industry in UAE has been booming. In 2008, Siddarth Bhide, country operations and project manager of Swedish furniture giant IKEA, expected an annual 30% growth rate for the next 10 years. This was mainly due to the boom in construction of properties which is a complementary industry (Eljundi, 2008). The UAE has been a trading hub due to its strategic position in the gulf area which encouraged exports and imports. The contract furniture market was estimated to be half of all furniture sales in the country. The office furniture accounts for 27% of the UAE's contract furniture market (Center for Industrial Studies, 2009). In 2008, the furniture imports from the US increased by 32% reaching $40.8 million (Russell, 2009).

Competitors

The UAE market has different producers of bean bags, most of which are unbranded. These unbranded beanbags are sold through trading agencies to consumers. However, there are few branded bean bags that represent direct competition to Ariika, such as Fat Boy, Moon and Bag n Bean.

- **Fat Boy:** Fat Boy was introduced in the Dutch market in 2002. The company started by producing the perfect lounge chair that was designed for fashion and comfort. After its success, the company introduced a wider range of bean bags that were developed in a European style with creative designs. The company's philosophy is to "delete dull" by providing a unique experience to n its customers through the products it offers. The company aims at changing customers' perceptions and improving their lifestyle by introducing innovative and unique products. Currently the company sells its products to more than 60 countries worldwide ("Fat Boy," 2014).
- **Moon:** Moon is considered a local competitor that was based in Abu Dhabi, UAE. Moon produces a wide range of products such as soft play, adults and children's' furniture, and gifts. Most of these products are designed and produced exclusively by Moon. The company produces all its products in the

UAE. Moon collection includes gifts, furnishing as well as a variety of textiles. All of Moon's products are handmade with unique designs and have embroidery and/or appliqué that can be personalized based on customers' preferences. The company delivers its products within the UAE and to other countries such as Bahrain, Qatar, Kuwait and Saudi. The company also ships worldwide upon request ("Moon by Mazoon," 2014).

- **Bag n Bean:** Another local competitor is Bag n Bean that specializes in selling bean bags. The company is located in Sharjah, UAE and delivers its products to different areas in the UAE, Qatar and Oman. Bag n Bean produces variety of bean bags that are stylish and comfortable. The company is also consumer focused and is very keen to maintain the level of satisfaction of their customers. Bag n Bean uses high quality materials to develop durable products. The company produces different kinds of bean bags such as standard shapes, sofas and cupid chairs ("Bag' n' Bean,"2014).

Consumer Expenditure

The expenditure on housing increased tremendously between 1995 and 2009. In 1995 the expenditure on housing was estimated as $2573 and it increased to $8410 in 2009 ("The United Arab Emirates Consumer Behavior, Attitudes and Perceptions toward Food Products," 2010). The diversity in the employment, nationalities and cultures in the UAE created a range of consumption and expenditure patterns. The less affluent workers are usually foreigners who support their families in their home country. These workers try to minimize their costs through living together. They spend mostly on food and beverages, housing and transportation. On the other hand, the professional expatriates have a higher purchasing power and are more likely to buy U.S. or European based products. These expatriates live with their families and accordingly demand upscale housing, furniture, clothing and housing. Finally, nationals' expenditure is mainly on home, services and clothing ("The United Arab Emirates Consumer Behavior, Attitudes and Perceptions Toward Food Products," 2010).

Industries Related to Furniture: Construction Industry

The arrival of many foreign workers to the UAE increased the demand for housing. The government also changed the land ownership laws to allow foreigners to own houses in specific areas of the country. This created a large demand on housing and currently the housing projects are booked in advance, which creates a need for more projects in the future. The government also invested in national housing by donating houses or lands for building new residences ("The United Arab Emirates Consumer

Behavior, Attitudes and Perceptions Toward Food Products," 2010). However the demand for villas still outperforms that of the apartment sector. Regarding the retail sector, the demand for retail space in malls has been increasing. In 2012, the mall based retail space was estimated at 2.9 million square meters, and it is expected to increase by 243,000 square meters in 2014. Between January and September 2012, 1700 branded hotel rooms have been added to the hotel market. In 2011, the hotel supply of rooms in Dubai reached 53,400 and in 2012 it increased to 55,100 and is forecasted to reach 63,000 in 2014. In 2012, the office space increased by 1.5% reaching 6.9 million square meter. Most of the office space, 70%, is used for financial and professional services (Volpe, 2012).

Table 3. Business environment indicators in the UAE

	Value (From Table 2)	Rating	Weight	Weighted Rating	Justification
Demographics					
Total Population	5.5million	3	0.3	0.9	The UAE has a relatively small, which decreases the chances of reaching more diverse segments of people.
Population Growth Rate	2.87%	5	0.3	1.5	The UAE has high growth rate compared to other countries. Countries with a high growth rate range from 2% to 3% per year, while countries with a low growth rate are less than 1% per year.
Age Structure	0-14:20.6% 15-24:13.8% 25-54:61.5% 55-64: 3.1% 65 and over: 1%	5	0.25	1.25	The age structure of the UAE is highly adequate because it is normal for the majority of the population to fall between 15 and 54 years old. It also represents Ariika's target market.
Urban/Rural Composition	Urban: 84.4% Rural:15.6%	5	0.15	0.75	The UAE has very high urban population which is favorable to Ariika, as its target market is more likely to live in urban areas.
Category Rating				4.4	
Government					
Economic Freedom	71.4 (100-point scale)	5	0.3	1.5	The UAE's economic freedom score is 71.4, making its economy the 28th most free in the 2014 Index of Economic Freedom. Its score is 0.3 points higher than the previous year.

continued on following page

Table 3. Continued

	Value (From Table 2)	Rating	Weight	Weighted Rating	Justification
FDI (home)	$103 billion	4	0.2	0.8	The oil- production in the UAE has attracted many investors. Also the boom in the construction and trade industries has increased FDI inflows to the UAE.
Ease of Doing Business	23	4	0.3	1.2	The UAE ranked 23rd regarding ease of doing business. This is considered adequate forAriika if it decides to conduct business in the UAE.
Currency Convertibility	1 UAE Dirham = $0.27	4	0.2	0.8	The UAE has a strong convertible currency. This is shown in its value compared to the U.S. dollar.
Category Rating				4.3	
Physical Infrastructure					
Roads and Highways	4,080 km	3	0.4	1.2	The UAE ranks 157th worldwide, according to the CIA factbook. This is not adequate to Ariika as it could be difficult to transport its products through roads and highways.
Airports	43	3	0.2	0.6	The UAE ranks 100th worldwide, according to the CIA factbook, which is not considered adequate.
Ports	8 main ports	4	0.4	1.6	It has an adequate number of cities with ports, which would ease transportation for Ariika.
Category Rating				3.4	
Economics					
GDP Growth Rate	4%	4	0.3	1.2	The UAE ranks 75th worldwide, according to the CIA factbook, which is considered adequate and promising.
Per Capita GDP	$29,900	4	0.3	1.2	The UAE ranks 48th worldwide, according to the CIA factbook, which represent an opportunity to Ariika.
Consumer Inflation Rate	1.3%	5	0.2	1	The UAE ranks 33rd worldwide, according to the CIA factbook, which is a sign of low inflation.
Unemployment Rate	2.4%	4	0.2	0.8	The UAE ranks 16th in unemployment which indicated the low unemployment rate in the UAE.
Category Rating				4.2	

continued on following page

Table 3. Continued

	Value (From Table 2)	Rating	Weight	Weighted Rating	Justification
Communications					
Fixed Telephone Market	2.0 million	4	0.10	0.4	The UAE ranks 59th worldwide, according to the CIA factbook, which is highly adequate.
Wireless Telephone Market	13.8 million	5	0.40	2	The UAE ranks 61st worldwide, according to the CIA factbook, which reflects the high percentage of the population using wireless phones.
Internet Users	3.4 million	4	0.50	2	The number of Internet users is high as the UAE ranks 61st in usage of the Internet, according to the CIA factbook.(almost 62% of the population uses the Internet)
Category Rating				4.4	

Table 4. Weightage of variables

	Total Rating	Weight (Support Material)	Weighted Rating
Demographics	4.4	0.25	1.1
Government	4.3	0.20	0.86
Physical Infrastructure	3.4	0.15	0.51
Economics	4.2	0.25	1.05
Communications	4.4	0.15	0.66
Total		**1**	**4.18**

SAUDI ARABIA (SA): COUNTRY OVERVIEW

Macroeconomic Overview

Saudi Arabia is an influential country in the gulf region. The country posses around 16% of the world's petroleum reserves, is considered the largest exporter of petroleum and plays a leading role in OPEC. Although the petroleum sector accounted for 80% of the countries revenues, SA was encouraging the growth of the private sector in order to diversify its economy. The country was trying to diversify in different areas such as telecommunications, natural gas exploration and petrochemicals. Saudi Arabia has over 6 million expatriates working in the oil and service sectors. The government, however, is trying to reduce unemployment among nationals by providing training and education to its growing youth population who lack technical skills required in the private sector. In 2005, Saudi Arabia accepted the WTO and started developing six economic cities in different regions across the country to promote foreign investment. The government also spent $373 billion between 2010 and 2014 on social development and infrastructure to improve the country's economic development (World Fact Book: SA, 2014).

Trade Environment

The petroleum sector accounts for around 80% of the country's revenues. It accounts for 45% of the GDP and 90% of the export earnings. The government, aiming to diversify the economy, encouraged the private sector. The per capita GDP increased from $30,000 in 2011 to $31,300 in 2013 with a 3.6% growth in 2013. Saudi's exports reached $376.3 billion in 2013 which made the country rank 16th worldwide. The country's main exports are petroleum and petroleum products and the export partners are US, China, Japan, South Korea, India and Singapore. The country's imports reached $147 billion in 2013 ranking the country 31st worldwide. The major imported products are machinery and equipment, foodstuffs, chemicals, motor vehicles, and textiles. The major import partners are China, US, South Korea, Germany, India, and Japan (World Fact Book: SA, 2014).

Furniture Industry in KSA

The Saudi Arabian furniture market is considered to be one of the biggest markets in the Middle East. In 2001, the value of the furniture market was estimated at 3 billion Saudi riyals per annum and showed a high growth rate. There were around 156 furniture manufacturer operating in SA in 2001 with a capital investment of 1.8 billion Saudi Riyals. The local furniture industry supplied 30% of the market while the remaining 70% was supplied by imported furniture brands("Saudis spend 11 percent of income on furniture,"2001). Between 2000 and 2011, the manufacturing of furniture in SA increased by 7% annually as was expected to increase in the future. This was mainly due to the increase in population and the creation of new economic cities. The furniture sales increased between 2001 and 2011 reaching 9.8 billion Saudi Riyals ($1.28 billion) in 2011. 63% of the furniture sales were accounted for by households in 2011 ("Furniture in Saudi Arabia," 2011).

Competitors

Similar to the UAE market, the Saudi Arabian market has few branded bean bags. The unbranded bean bags are usually sold in large stores such as IKEA. The branded bean bags that represent a direct competition to Ariika are Lady D Bean Bag, Slack Life Style, and Fat Boy.

- **Lady D Bean Bag:** Lady D bean bag is considered a main competitor to Ariika. The company specializes in bean bags that are produced in Saudi Arabia. Their collection includes variety of indoors and outdoors, kids, medical and pets bean bags. The company also provides customized bean bags according to customers' preferences. Lady D Bean bags aims at manufacturing high quality bean bags with elegance and creativity. They differentiate themselves by offering high quality filling and specially designed cover materials such as leather, PVC and fur (Lady D Bean Bag, 2014).
- **Slack Life Style:** One of the international competitors to Ariika is Slack Life Style. Slack was founded in Hong Kong and is specialized in the production of bean bags. The company designs and manufactures different kinds of bean bags. The company is considered the world's first designer of branded bean bags that is dedicated to provide relaxation to customers. The company produces products that are designed to those who enjoy individuality. Their product range includes; outdoor, classic, kids and pets bean bags. The company exports its products to different countries such as France, Spain, Italy and Saudi Arabia. The company is expected to open showrooms soon in US, France and Dubai ("Slack Lifestyle," 2014).
- **Fat Boy:** Fat Boy is another international competitor to Ariika. As mentioned earlier, Fat Boy produces wider range of bean bags that are developed in a European style with creative designs. Although the company doesn't have showrooms in Saudi, it sells its products in the Saudi markets through distributors.

Consumer Buying Behavior

Saudi families usually renew their furniture, either partially or entirely, every 3 to 5 years. In 2001, it was estimated that Saudi families spent 120,000 Saudi Riyals annually on furniture purchases, which represents 11% of their annual income ("Saudi furniture market estimated at SR 4 million," 2001). On the other hand, non Saudi households spend 7% of their annual income on furniture ("Saudis spend 11 percent of income on furniture," 2001). The upper class families in Saudi usually buy class style furniture or a mixture of classic and modern. The most popular furniture materials bought are fine wood in dark colors, richly decorated with gold ornaments as well as metal and glass accessories (Troian, 2011).

The demand for furniture is increasing in Saudi Arabia. In 2001, the US exports of furniture to Saudi increased by 10% reaching $71,379 million ("Saudi Arabia:

Investment and Business Guide," 2011). US furniture was bought by middle and upper class Saudi families as well as young Saudis who lived or studied in the US. The increase in demand for US furniture as well as European furniture was due to the increase in population of Saudi (1.51% in 2013), where 50% of the population is under 21 years. Moreover, the expatriates living in Saudi prefer to buy US or European furniture. High income families in Saudi prefer to buy US or European furniture as it is more durable, comfortable and has more variety. Italy had the highest share of furniture imports at Saudi 22%, followed by US 16% ("Saudi Arabia: Investment and Business Guide," 2011).

Industries Related to Furniture: Construction Industry

The construction sector is Saudi Arabia has been booming for the past years. It was expected that by 2015 the construction market will be the fastest growing segment in the economy. In 2013, the government allocated $76 billion to the development of different construction projects. This budget is projected to exceed $3 trillion in 2020. The allocated budget is used in the development of mega projects that include six major economic cities that in total will cost more than $160 billion to develop. The government is also spending $40 billion on Sudair Industrial City, $15 billion on King Faisal University and $16 billion on Jeddah Kingdom Tower. The increase in population together with the increase in disposable income raised demand on housing in Saudi Arabia ("Saudi Construction Market Analysis," 2012).

Table 5. Business environment indicators in SA

	Value (From Table 2)	Rating	Weight	Weighted Rating	Justification
Demographics					
Total Population	26.9 million	4	0.3	1.2	The population very high population relative to UAE. The larger the population the better, as the probability of sales will be higher.
Population Growth Rate	1.51%	4	0.3	1.2	The growth rate is considered high.
Age Structure	0-14: 28.2% 15-24:19.6% 25-54: 44.8% 55-64: 4.3% 65 and over:3.1%	5	0.25	1.25	Most of the population falls between 15 and 54, which represents Ariika's target market.

continued on following page

Table 5. Continued

	Value (From Table 2)	Rating	Weight	Weighted Rating	Justification
Urban/Rural Composition	Urban: 82.3% Rural: 17.7%	5	0.15	0.75	The urban population is 82.3%, which is considered highly adequate as most of Ariika's target market live in Urban areas.
Category Rating				4.4	
Government					
Economic Freedom	62.2(100-point scale)	4	0.3	1.2	The SA's economic freedom score is 62.2, making its economy the 77th most free in the 2014 Index of Economic Freedom. Its score is 1.6 points higher than the previous year.
FDI (home)	$240.6 billion	5	0.2	1	The oil- production in SA as well as the boom in the construction sector attracted many investors and increased FDI inflows to SA.
Ease of Doing Business	26	4	0.3	1.2	SA ranked 26[d] regarding ease of doing business. This is considered adequate to Ariika if it decided to conduct business in SA.
Currency Convertibility	1 Saudi Riyal = $0.27	4	0.2	0.8	Saudi Riyal has a stable value against the dollar, which indicates SA's strong economy.
Category Rating				4.2	
Physical Infrastructure					
Roads and Highways	221,372 km	5	0.4	2	SA ranks 22nd worldwide, according to the CIA factbook. This is adequate to Ariika as it would ease road transport.
Airports	214	5	0.2	1	SA ranks 26th worldwide, according to the CIA factbook, which is considered adequate.
Ports	6 main ports	4	0.4	1.6	This is highly adequate, as it provides access to many other potential markets in neighboring countries.
Category Rating				4.6	
Economics					
GDP Growth Rate	3.6%	4	0.3	1.2	SA ranks 90th worldwide, according to the CIA factbook, which is considered adequate and promising.

continued on following page

Table 5. Continued

	Value (From Table 2)	Rating	Weight	Weighted Rating	Justification
Per Capita GDP	$31,300	4	0.3	1.2	SA ranks 44th worldwide, according to the CIA factbook, which is high and represent an opportunity to Ariika.
Consumer Inflation Rate	3.7%	3	0.2	0.6	SA ranks 122nd worldwide, according to the CIA factbook, which is a sign of high inflation.
Unemployment	10.5%	4	0.2	0.8	SA ranks 110th in unemployment which indicated the high unemployment rate in SA.
Category Rating				3.8	
Communications					
Fixed Telephone Market	4.8 million	5	0.1	0.5	SA ranks 31th worldwide, according to the CIA factbook, and is highly adequate.
Wireless Telephone Market	53 million	5	0.4	2	SA ranks 26th worldwide, according to the CIA factbook, which reflects the high percentage of the population using wireless phones.
Internet Users	9.8 million	5	0.5	2.5	SA ranks 30th in usage of the Internet, according to the CIA factbook, which is highly adequate.
Category Rating				5	
Total					

Table 6. Weightage of variables

	Total Rating	Weight (TN-1)	Weighted Rating
Demographics	4.4	0.25	1.1
Government	4.2	0.20	0.84
Physical Infrastructure	4.6	0.15	0.69
Economics	3.8	0.25	0.95
Communications	5	0.15	0.75
Total		**1**	**4.33**

ARIIKA MOVING FORWARD

Though Ariika is considered to be a new company, it was able to establish itself in the Egyptian market. Currently the company has 60% market share and has strong relationships with large retailers. Moreover, Ariika increased its B2B sales and was able to supply its products to different companies, compounds, cafes and universities. The success of Ariika in Egypt encouraged Attallah and Arslan to consider their next move. International expansion could present a great opportunity for Ariika to increase its sales and market share, however, fierce competition from international brands could have a negative impact on the company. Therefore, Attallah and Arslan are considering different alternatives. Should they expand internationally or focus more on the Egyptian market? If they decided to expand internationally, which country should they expand to first? Should they rely on simple exports or consider more involved modes of entry?

ACKNOWLEDGMENT

Special acknowledgement is to be provided to the following Business Students in The American University in Cairo for their project on Ariika Bean Bags that provided useful insights in the early phases of work on this case. Mina Ishkandar, Amin Atwa, John Hanna and Reema El Sisy.

REFERENCES

Agriculture and Agri-Food Canada. (2010). *United Arab Emirates consumer behavior, attitudes and perceptions toward food products*. Retrieved Feb 27, 2014, from http://www.ats-sea.agr.gc.ca/afr/5661-eng.htm

Center for Industrial Studies. (2009). Retrieved Feb 26, 2014, from http://www.worldfurnitureonline.com/showPage.php?template=reports&id=5743&masterPage=report.html

CIA. (2013). *UAE world fact book*. Retrieved March 2, 2014, from https://www.cia.gov/library/publications/the-world-factbook/geos/ae.html

CIA. (2013). *World fact book SA*. Retrieved Feb 25, 2014, from https://www.cia.gov/library/publications/the-world-factbook/geos/sa.html

Eljundi, R. (2008). Furniture Sector in UAE to have highest growth rate in world. *Emirates 24/7*. Retrieved Feb 25, 2014, from http://www.emirates247.com/eb247/companies-markets/retail/furniture-sector-in-uae-to-have-highest-growth-rate-in-world-2008-10-02-1.56620

Fat Boy. (2014). Retrieved March 2, 2014, from http://fatboyusa.com/about/

Furniture in Saudi Arabia. (2011). *Industrial markets research*. Retrieved Feb 27, 2014, from http://www.euromonitor.com/furniture-in-saudi-arabia-isic-361/report

Lady D Bean Bag. (2014). Retrieved March 2, 2014, from http://ladydbeanbags.com/2014/en/Accessories.html

Moon by Mazoon. (2014). Retrieved March 2, 2014, from http://www.moonbymazoon.com/en/

Russell, T. (2009). Dubai market has a large export appeal. *Furniture Today*. Retrieved March 1, 2014, from http://www.furnituretoday.com/blogpost/12127-dubai-market-has-large-export-appeal

Saudi Arabia: Investment and Business Guide. (2011). Retrieved from http://books.google.com.eg/books?id=69zeEq4KA3gC&pg=PA182&lpg=PA182&dq=spending+on+furniture+in+Saudi&source=bl&ots=RceTBTSxx&sig=o3QWdjzIrExCLaYkPNt93986dEY&hl=en&sa=X&ei=OoIbU6n9O4HmywOinoCQDg&ved=0CDEQ6AEwBQ#v=onepage&q=spending%20on%20furniture%20in%20Saudi&f=false

Saudi Furniture Market Estimated at SR 4 Million. (2001). *Al Bawaba Business*. Retrieved Feb 24, 2014, from http://www.albawaba.com/business/saudi-furniture-market-estimated-sr-4-million

Saudis Spend 11 Percent of Income on Furniture. (2001). *Al Bawaba Business*. Retrieved Feb 27, 2014, from http://www.albawaba.com/business/saudis-spend-11-percent-income-furniture

Slack LifeStyle. (2014). Retrieved Feb 27, 2014, from http://www.slackbeanbags.com/e-store/index.php?main_page=page&id=8&chapter=0

Troian, D. (2011). *Furniture industry: The consumers furniture preferences in different markets*. University of Trento. Retrieved Feb 26, 2014, from http://www.academia.edu/1502656/The_consumer_perception_of_design.Case_study_furniture_sector

Volpe, A. (2012). Real estate in the gulf countries. *The World Luxury Market*. Retrieved Feb 24, 2014, from http://www.worldfurnitureonline.com/PDF/WFR-Magazine.pdf

KEY TERMS AND DEFINITIONS

Brand Image: The brand image is consumers' perception about the product whether it is real features or not. The brand image is developed over time through customers' experience with the product and the degree of their satisfaction.

Brand Name: The brand name is a name, symbol, or design that differentiates a product from its competitors in the market. The brand name is usually relevant to the product, easy to be pronounced and retrieved by customers.

Brand Strategy: The brand strategy is related to the goals set by the company for the brand. It is related to the products target market and the ability of the product to satisfy their needs.

Internationalization: Internationalization refers to the tendency of companies to maximize their sales and profits by selling their products to other countries abroad. Through studying the international markets, companies develop products that are designed to suit the needs of these markets.

Product Development: Product development occurs when the company adds new features to an existing product or develops a new product. The aim of product development is to satisfy customers' changing needs and increasing the company's target market.

Chapter 13
Semiotics of Brand Building:
Case of the Muthoot Group

Sudio Sudarśan
Hult International Management School, USA

ABSTRACT

Most theories in brand management, evolved from 20th century economics, rely on a convenient assumption of how consumers should make purchase decisions. In contradistinction, this chapter demonstrates a semiological tradition in the context of brand management using a 128-year-old brand, Muthoot Group, to expound upon the ways consumers prevalently perceive brands, which then drive their purchase decisions. Just as in marketing, where the focus changed from "economic exchange" to "social exchange," in brand management the focus needs to change from "symbols" to the way people use semiotic resources to produce both communicative artifacts and events to interpret them, which is also a form of semiotic production. Since social semiotics is not a self-contained field, the chapter historically plots the brand-building voyage of Muthoot Group, applying semiotic concepts and methods to establish a model of brand and extend the scientific understanding of differentiation, loyalty, and advocacy.

DOI: 10.4018/978-1-4666-7393-9.ch013

ELEPHANT IN THE ROOM

While several scholars and theorists of marketing as well as a myriad of brand practitioners and consultants irrefutably acknowledge the momentous role brands play in generating a company's value, the actual levers that ascertain how a successful brand is created have been unjustifiably advanced solely by neoclassical economics and social psychology.

Historians credit a Danish nobleman, Tycho Brahe as the first competent mind in modern astronomy who accurately cataloged the movements of celestial bodies in the sixteenth century. Brahe's assistant, Johannes Kepler along with a long list of brilliant physicists that includes Sir Isaac Newton later further advanced Brahe's empirical data to postulate laws of planetary motion. Charles Darwin, a pivotal thinker in establishing the fact of evolution, based his heretical theory upon empirical evidence and rational argumentation. Advancements in physical and biological sciences, like astronomy, obtain compelling evidence after assiduous observations that then lead to bases of theories or postulations.

The theory of consumer behavior under the canopy of marketing advanced by neoclassical economics, however, is not founded on any such empirical observation of how and/or why consumers make purchase decisions, develop strong sense of brand loyalty, or become fierce advocates for brands. The brand-building process has been fabricated on the convenient assumption that human beings are rational animals who make rational economic decisions. The entire body of work in branding is then constructed by elementary extrapolations from these specious assumptions. As if humans were equipped with unlimited knowledge, time, and power of information-processing, these theories in marketing assumed that humans made decisions involving rational Bayesian maximization of expected utility in products they bought or in services they hired. However, the imprudent assumption of *homo economicus* does not take into consideration any of the mental mechanisms underlying purchase decisions, loyalty formation, and other consumer actions that include symbolic, hedonic, and aesthetic nature of consumption (Hirschman &Holbrook 1981). Run-of-the-mill theories borrowed from social psychology which adhere to the neopositivistic perspectives of the hypothetico-deductive approach have also failed to address these significant phenomena in brand building methods and approaches.

To comprehend brand building as we are competent to describe it today, one requires a fairly wide background of interests and the meticulously cultivated tendencies favoring complexities of processes over simple provisional truths and temporarily adequate generalizations. The somewhat lofty goal of this paper is to develop a semiotic approach to brand building which finally overhauls the current obsolete model of branding that was anointed in the seventies, which has been the standard ever since. The semiotic approach to branding draws from the vibrant discipline of

Consumer Culture Theory, one which not only experientially elucidates how brands are built over time, but also offers a distinctive way to identify opportunity space for growth, as well as providing an invaluable construct to encourage more successful startups and/or reviving moribund brands. The paper uses the one-hundred-twenty-seven-year peregrinations of a representative corporate brand, the Muthoot Group, as a stanchion for understanding the web of meanings woven from signs and symbols ensconced in cultural space and time.

If nothing else, this paper illustrates that the semiotics of branding is pure semiotics; the neuroscience of branding is all neuroscience; the cultural anthropology of branding is all cultural anthropology; and so forth into the future expansion of brand as a science. Interspersed throughout are direct quotes from industry experts and consumers served by Muthoot.

DIFFERENT KETTLE OF FISH

On the continuum stretching from the cave paintings of *Homo Erectus* to present social media updates, via the postmodern man, the insatiable need to communicate identity has created an infinite sensory palette of both visual and verbal expression, together unfolding the mysterious and elusive power of symbols. As states of mind, the distinctive power of symbols lies in their ability to divulge myriad levels of reality, otherwise latent, as a means of stimulating the human mind to wider awareness; heightening a strong sense of belonging, in order to induce greater recall and memory.

The US-based trade group, American Marketing Association (AMA) recognizes the influence that symbols dispense that it defines a brand as a: "name, term, design, symbol, or any other feature that identifies one seller's good or service as distinct from those of other sellers."

In 1887 during the days of British-colonized India, Muthoot Ninan Mathai, patron founder of the Muthoot Group, established a business involved in the wholesale of food grains and timber in Kozhencherry, a small town in the Kingdom of Travancore (called Kerala today), supplying rations to large British-run plantations. Since mechanization of forest harvest such as power saw, skidder, and motorized tractor were absent back in the day, Mathai's business employed trained elephants to haul logs. The icon of two elephants standing trunk to trunk, inspired from the herd that Muthoot used to own to transport timber, was astutely used as the company logo in Muthoot's hauling business (George & George 2014).

Logos induces recognizability and consensually held meanings and expectations of a brand in consumers' mind. Social scientists of the 20th century evince that the structuralism of semiosis, the mental process by which understanding occurs, is germane to a dynamic account of import and tenor. Carved out of the semiosic ubiquity, semiotics explicates how a symbol (Muthoot twin-elephant logo) stands as a visual shortcut for a specific referent (financial product or service), which then culminates as cardinal instruments of interpersonal and/or group persuasion (trust, security).

Even though semiotics relies solely on philosophical and linguistic notions (Nöth, 1990), the synchronical model early semiotics proposes, under the influence of structuralism (Pinson, 1993), offer durable, systematic dyadic representation of the Muthoot two-elephant logo (sign), with which consumers associate the company's financial products and services.

To apply the sign-referent relationship popularly called the Signification Model, a theoretical basis for science of signs proposed by Ferdinand de Saussure, sign is fundamentally composed of the signifier, the form the sign takes; and the signified, the business concept the sign represents. The two-elephant icon, the sign, results

Figure 1. Application of Saussurean model of signs to the Muthoot brand

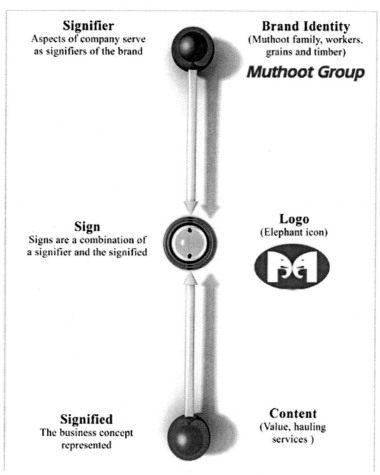

from the association of the signifier, the Muthoot family behind the running of the new business, and the signified, the related tangible value created by Muthoot Group.

In 1939, the business passed to George Muthoot, acknowledged as founder and chairman, who initially diversified the company into financial services by starting a chit fund; a home-grown savings system to help villagers in rural Kerala towns who did not have direct access to retail banks located in cities.

Since information to consumers should come more in the configurations of already established symbol-system, and preserve the description of communicative effects of identity elements, the venerable icon of two elephants standing trunk to trunk was continued as the company logo in Muthoot's newly diversified business.

Do symbols really unveil reality? Muthoot's retention of its logo is a case in point that brand iconography is merely the material markers entirely devoid of meaning. When branding is advanced from piffling material symbols to the deliberately conceive realm of symbolism, a collective understanding of metaphors, allegories, and extraneous symbolic representations that incite consumer associations perhaps begin to get defined. For instance, a wedding ring worn does not necessarily denote that a marriage has occurred. Substituting an entirely different object but nonetheless equally recognizable physical representation, brides from the Syrian Christian communities of Kerala wear *minnu* (a pendant) to signal marital union. Further, symbols connote disparate set of meanings in different cultural groups; the swastika is an ideogram signaling cosmic effervescence to the Hindus, but blazons Aryan racial purity in the historical context of Nazi-governed Germany. In Muthoot's instance, the symbol of twin elephants stood for trust more than for the core business service.

Furthermore, AMA's shorthand definition, fails to acknowledge nor does it even recognize the unavoidable mental association and emotional linkages which consumers deliberately create in order to intimately orient them with symbols. Perhaps reflecting an attitude of avoiding 'throwing out the baby with the bath water,' industry representatives and brand practitioners have adopted a second set of popular definitions to solely regard the indelible relationship between the signifier and the signified.

- **Walter Landor:** Products are made in the factory, but brands are created in the mind.
- **Marty Neumeier:** A brand is a person's gut feeling about a product, service, or company.

The concept of symbolism and symbolic process therefore hurls us into the postgraduate departments of sociology and anthropology in order to fathom the web of ideas and perceptions that symbol systems report them as "created in the mind" or "person's gut feeling."

To achieve a consummate understanding of the meanings that the identity markers have embodied for Muthoot's mission, relationships, and business, and to embrace practitioners' definition of brand, Peirce's (1958, 1931) semiotic model, which has long established roots in philosophy, examines how humans connote as well as denote (Short, 2009).

Unlike the Saussurean legacy derived from linguistic leanings, Charles Peirce, motivated by original pragmatism, described a sign as a triadic, dynamic, and irreducible constituent, and viewed semiosis as an active influence on human cognition. The three-part framework of signification:

1. **The Representamen:** Muthoot's brand name; what the brand stands for;
2. **The Object:** Finance services as a referent that the sign refers;
3. **The Interpretant:** Consumer's interpretation of trust, or the sense effect on the consumer.

The efficacious interaction among representamen, object, and interpretant referred as semiosis determines how a brand is built over time.

The Peircean Model includes academic definition of a brand as an iconic sign to signal the imitative source and explicit representation of the product. This framework also includes the practitioner's approach who view a brand as an indexical

Figure 2. The semiotic triangle

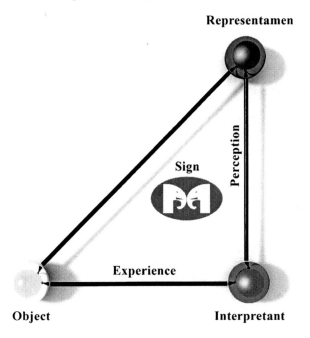

sign that involve cause-and-effect relationships; as an array of meanings, promises, and expectations of a consumer. Brands are also symbolic signs of meaning; that is, open to interpretation like language, which the paper explores in later sections using Muthoot as a prop.

Muthoot's service-related perceptions, designated as 'interpretant,' affords a foothold to understand three categories of sense made of sign:

1. Functional aspects of Muthoot's services as direct interpretant;
2. Attitudinal aspects of Muthoot's services as transitory interpretant;
3. Experiential aspects of Muthoot's services as absolute interpretant.

The evolution of the Muthoot's business with the retention of the twin elephant logo suggest the symbolic meaning seems the clearest logical route to confirm the supposition the cloud of mysticism and mystery that surrounds symbols.

TALKING TURKEY

In 1971, the refashioned Muthoot Bankers expanded its homegrown financial services to lending money by using gold jewelry as security, which proved a boon to the embarking Indians of lower economic class as state-owned retail banks believed it was risky business (George &George, 2014). Low-skilled workers from Kerala state in India migrated in large numbers in the seventies and eighties, referred as the Persian Gulf Boom; the timely and useful loan that Muthoot provided met their impending expenses toward visa and air passage and the starting of their new life. Though India's young men and women graduate high school with exceptionally high grades, the odds of getting admitted into a program of their choice are staggering due to intense competition. Many fled to universities abroad. Muthoot's loan came in handy to parents, enabling them to finance their children's education.

I am a retired banker living out of my pension. Without Muthoot's timely loan, I could not have financed my child's education expenses as medical school tuition is very high. I availed loan beginning of each academic year to pay my child's tuition fees; he is now in the final year. I am thankful to Muthoot for the timely help. – Usha (retired banker)

Muthoot Finance, as it was called in the nineties, grew to one-hundred-fifty branches all over India, under the current Chairman, M. G. George who joined the family business in 1979 to aggressively lead Muthoot's market expansion.

Though the core business evolved from homegrown chit fund to gold-lending business, the twin elephant symbol and the Muthoot brand name remained as identity markers for consumers thereby transferring positive perceptions into Muthoot's newly established service offerings. The universal semantization of symbol usage of the new business service, referred as object in semiotics parlance, was favorably converted through the continued possession of positive interpretants. Cultural theorist, Jean Baudrillard (1968) contends that objects lose their material and functional status by their integration into object systems; amply evidenced in Muthoot's brand voyage from a proprietary organization to a partnership, Muthoot Bankers, to a non-banking financial corporation in the new millennium to a public limited company today.

To effectively fuse multifaceted semiotic inquiry of changing objects to produce a comprehensive model of brand building in Muthoot's context, Morris' (1946) definition of semiotics is invaluable:

The science of signs. Its main subdivisions are syntactics, semantics, and pragmatics. Each of these and so semiotics as a whole, can be applied, descriptive, or pure. Pure semiotics elaborates a language to talk about signs, descriptive semiotics studies actual signs, and applied semiotics utilizes knowledge about signs for the accomplishment of various purposes.

From the three correlates, Morris deduces three dimensions:

1. Syntactics studies the relation of given sign vehicle to another;
2. Semantics examines the relationship of sign vehicles to their designata;
3. Pragmatics inquires relationship between sign and its interpretants.

Applying Morris' triadic relation of semiosis, on the syntactic level of sign-sign relationship, elephants have been subject of a broad spectrum of cultural depictions in Indian culture, religious traditions, mythology, and symbolism. One of the popular gods of the Hindu pantheon, deity Ganesh, is portrayed as a human with elephant head. Lord Indra rode on an elephant. In Islamic tradition, Muhammad was born in the Year of the Elephant; medieval artists depict the killing of Eleazar the Maccabee and a war elephant in the Judeo-Christian tradition.

In a personal conversation, Alexander George, Director of Muthoot Group, who belongs to the fourth generation of leaders in the Muthoot family, passionately described how the elephant embodies the company. The two large ears that keep Muthoot alert to consumer feedback or grievance; the small mouth to talk less, but work more; the long trunk signaling Muthoot's curiosity to understand customer's needs better and deliver more value; the mighty head underscoring a long and accurate memory. The Executive Director of Muthoot Group, G. M. George, affirmed the slow movement of the behemoth guides Muthoot to maintain balance despite its immense strength. This semantic self-dialogue, the most enduring aspect of Muthoot's semiotic legacy can be applied into descriptive metalanguage to be understood as codes within the consumer ecosystem in a wider social context.

Unlike vision or mission statements, brand strategy cannot just be hung on the wall. Strategy can only be known through the interconnected string of decisions a brand takes over a period of time. Muthoot has always emphasized its 'generations of trust'; commitment to trustworthiness, ethics, values, reliability, dependability, integrity, and goodwill in every business decision it takes (Muthoot, 2014). As Morris would contend, brand strategy is an observational normative doctrine; knowledge internal to Muthoot derived by abductive reasoning from external meanings that the brand projects.

Considering Muthoot's rich and varied history in financial services as its main object of signs, the brand as a symbol is a static vision of a banking sign structure semantically. Even if gold-pawning is deemed a hoary trade, a century and quarter years of trust built on customer relationships, paraded by the twin elephant symbol, consecrated the brand with respectability. To operationalize the vast reserves of household gold, Muthoot needed to create a craft-like process that enabled it to look reputable with customer-friendly branches reaching out the rural India. Because the gold loan process can so easily project the appearance of a shady pawn broker, so did transparency in the loaning process create a powerful halo effect on other dimensions of brand value.

I came to know about Muthoot from my neighbors; my relatives also utilized their services a few years ago. Based on their feedback, I decided to pledge gold with Muthoot. Being a working woman, I always had a dream to own a penthouse in Delhi, but I was never able to figure how to materialize my dream with my salary. Once I knew about Muthoot Gold Loan from my relatives in Bhopal and my neighbors here in Delhi, I decided to take a home loan. I can't be a happier woman. I am fully satisfied with the services. I had a positive experience with them; their staff was helpful. – Romsha Srivatsava (works at a private company in Delhi)

On the pragmatic level, the third correlate of Morris' triadic relation of semiosis, Muthoot sign can be taxonomized as intrapersonal, interpersonal, and societal. As culturally-determined activity, symbolism unfolds ideological aspects of symbolic perceptions that point one's feet in the direction of the philosopher's stone. Direct experience of brand is concrete, while described experience of a brand is abstract. In branding, the object of symbolism is the enhancement of what is symbolized. This enrichment to symbolic meaning occurs when brand stories are recited by

Figure 3. Semiotic trichotomy of brand model

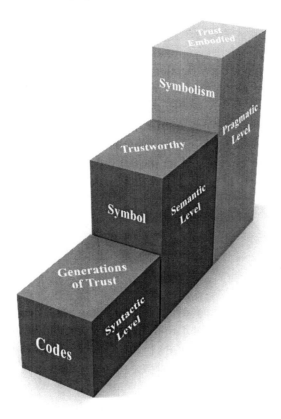

various authors: company, culture intermediaries, critics, retail sales personnel, and customers. Symbolism, the tenacious glue which consumer groups invent to conscientiously apply to sense-markers, then yields a subtle logic of social nature to consumption, though they may very well be non product/service-related perceptions. In all, evaluating the brand image of a brand identity is of great import; that is, the pragmatic component of semiotics. It is often the case of not what the brand stands for, but what consumers think the brand stands for.

Consequently, this new brand model, a modification of Nauta's semiotic framework (1972), offers adequate explanations of the consumer's behavior, which go far beyond brand's functional aspects; brands must be understood as a linking value given the status of that of a partner in the manufacturer-consumer relations. Whether through fierce advocacy or genuine loyalty to brands, brand meanings are transferred to the self through purchase and consumption rituals (McCracken, 1993). This relational and symbiotic perspective where both brand and symbolism live and grow with one another, akin to symbiosis in biology, can be defined as the 'living together of two or more entities to their mutual benefit' (Cooper, 1979). This symbiotic process of aligning identity with image which unifies consumers and brands occurs through various customer touch points: brand awareness, product contact, transaction, consumption, and communication.

This tripartite semiotic classification of syntactics-semantics-pragmatics identifies the Muthoot sign as the fundamental vehicle connecting its financial service as an object to trigger positive consumer perceptions and reactions. To translate and transfer the insights from our multi-cultural, global consumer ecosystem to the branding world, this semiotics-inspired new model of brand, which includes key elements of consumer culture and its impact on collective consumer perceptions and behavior, can amply help marketers and brand owners to weigh how symbolism impacts product or company perception than focusing on mere symbols which represent them.

THE DUCKS IN A ROW

Not only are the Indians compulsive about hoarding gold, there is also the matter of emotional value attached to the gold they possess. Gold is an appreciable asset commanding long term value, a tag for being a safe haven. More importantly, gold is a symbol of status and wealth to man across many cultures and geographies. To the Indians, it is carries a higher perceived value for the great religious significance gold imports and high emotional quotient; it is an auspicious metal bought and gifted for various purposes on different occasions and religious festivals. Hence, Indians typically have a sense of personal belonging to the gold they own, be it in the form of ornamental jewelry, coins, or bars. Jewelry made of the metal is an essential part of the Indian dowry system that bride's parents give to their daughters at weddings to help them embark on their new lives.

Because of the high emotional value gold exerts, many Indians decide against the idea of pawning. Some who do pledge gold for quick access to money are extremely cautious because Indian pawn brokers and pawn shops have a somewhat seedy reputation. Privately owned businesses and mom-and-pop owned pawn shops have a long history of shady practices of deceiving their customers while making loans in exchange for gold as collateral. They are notorious for deluding loaners through faulty assessment of the metal and then defrauding them with high interest rates.

On the other spectrum of the consumer ecosystem where security or cheating was not a concern, people required to pledge something that represents so much to them simply don't feel comfortable. Gold is weighted with meaning. Gold is their ancestral treasure saddled with sentimental and emotional value.

If one part of the brand tapestry was how the brand wants its customers to perceive it, the other part, equally vital, was what the brand does for identity to be transmitted and impressions to be created. The heavy responsibility rested on Muthoot to create and maintain right perceptions to operationalize the all-powerful yellow metal.

Finally, it is consequential to discuss perception in the context of Muthoot, especially when one of their competitors shares the same brand name. Muthoot Pappachan, brother of George Muthoot, recognized as founder, established Muthoot Pappachan Group, which today is a diversified conglomerate with a presence in multiple industries cannibalizing customers from the Muthoot Group, focal brand of the case study presented. Muthoot Fincorp, a finance company, caters to the financial needs of retail and institutional customers, stylizing itself with products such as Express Gold Loan.

The study of perception - building blocks that are essential to the consumer's inquiry into aspects of branding - takes us to an area of discourse beyond the productive application of behaviorism in psychology for a number of reasons. First, perception is not merely a behavior; it is an intricate process defined physically, mentally, and culturally. Second, the physical aspects of perception center heuristically in the realm of neuroscience, which is still an arcane subject of conjecture and experiments utilizing noninvasive, surgery-free EEG or fMRI brain scan techniques.

Which of the two circles in the center is bigger? The one on the right? Herman Ebbinghaus, a German psychologist, who pioneered the experimental study of memory, has been credited with devising this illusion (sometimes called Titchener Illusion). The two circles in the center are of the same size; we cannot undo this illusion by will.

Figure 4. Ebbinghaus Illusion

The Ebbinghaus Illusion reveals a quintessential feature of the human neural system: relative perception. The cognitive contrast due the apparent differences in sizes of circles between the adjacent or surrounding elements creates distortions in behavioral responses (Coren et al., 1976). Human brain cannot perceive in absolute terms; objects influence us by their surrounding and how consumers have seen them in the past. A handbag at the price of $50 in an upscale fashion store may seem cheap, if it is surrounded by more expensive bags. The same bag at the same price will be overpriced if sold at a typical department store, when surrounded by inexpensive bags. Any familiar product has a prototypic price, which is different for each consumer, depending on their past experience with the product (Posner & Keele, 1968). Similarly, the prototypic price for a bottle of wine can be $10 or $100. Brand managers familiar with visual after-effects and prototypes can make use of this knowledge from basic perceptual neuroscience. It is fascinating that this contrast principle remains, even if the perceptual distortion is well-known.

Just as with images, all symbols are polysemous. During the development of brain, even words, the foundational molecules of language, seem as symbols, and language itself experienced as a nomenclature because its existence precedes brain's understanding. Research today has established brand identity designs connote symbolic meanings. Visual properties and marketing communications influence brand perceptions: typeface design or lettering style affected brand meaning (Childers & Jass, 2002); relative height impacted brand personality recognition (Van Rompay et al., 2005); and logo shape influenced consumer-brand relationship (Zhang et al., 2006). For instance, Walmart recently rounded (perceived harmonious) its sharp (perceived dominant) uppercase letters of its typeface to signal the emotional benefits of shopping there, and how it helps customers to live a better life.

Moving into the consideration of symbolic perception, which by the way has taken many of hours of culture-specific sensorial experience before gyropilot cognition takes place, our concern with fields, organizations, situations, and relationships (constantly in motion) shifts the framework of discourse. Consider the stimulus of freshly brewed coffee. It's almost instinctual to visualize mothers brewing coffee in the kitchen or think of a favorite coffee shop. Since humans grow up with the concept of association of family gathering with the flavorful smell of coffee, the brain sets itself in an autopilot mode to form an indelible frame of reference; this symbolical framing effect is paramount to branding products and services. The mental processes of selective perception, which integrates attention, intuition, and retention, determines how consumers make decisions and behave almost as if human brains were on a self-steering, rapid cognition mode (Kahneman & Frederick, 2001). After reading this sentence, you will realize that the the brain did not recognize the second 'the.' The specialized structures in the human brain, developed over years of reading, sets itself in this autopilot mode. Perhaps this also explains why it can be very challenging to many to proof-read their own writing.

When brands are thought as frames, sensory adaptations and symbolic perceptions can be created, controlled, maintained, or altered. The prototype theory expounds many effects of this adaptation; it proposes brain mechanisms governing visual learning are based on perceptual averages or prototypes (Posner & Keele, 1968). A number of Americans who live in the New England area give pine tree as response when asked for an example of a tree; those in India would rather mention coconut or mango trees. Prototypes are very culture specific and depends on the individual's past experiences that form 'cultural codes' in their selective perception of their physical environment.

Taking the discourse back to the focal brand in discussion, little argument denies that first, consumers perceive the gold loan environment precariously though a grave need of quick money exists. Second, consumers are set against a framework of previous impressions of shady pawn brokers, their fallacious estimation of gold or their extortion of unreasonably high interest rates. And finally, Muthoot's own competition from the sharing of brand name by Muthoot Pappachan Group.

Muthoot did things differently and did different things to repair consumer perceptions of the gold-pawning business. In order to revolutionize gold banking, Muthoot went where its consumers existed in remote rural geographies of India to serve a large populace who were in dire need of funds but who did not have access to scheduled banks to issue formal credit. By processing loans to the commoner who could not associate with organized banking, Muthoot fashioned itself as a bank. The

Figure 5. Muthoot strongroom

integrity of a bank is its safety. Muthoot provided a secure environment to safeguard the gold deposited by building armored vaults and strong rooms in every location it served to claim protection from thefts, fire, natural disasters, unauthorized use, and other threats. Every branch is installed with CCTV and a surveillance system.

Significant aspects of superior financial service are the ease and pace to perform its basic function, the ability of the front-line personnel to actively listen to a customer, demonstrate a sizable measure of empathy and concern. In the human-focused business, service quality is derived from the interaction of Muthoot's employees and its customers. In order to create customer satisfaction, every Muthoot frontline employee needed to be satisfied with his/her job (Herzberg, 1987, Heskett, et al., 2008) and adapt service offering to fit specific customer needs (Gwinner et al., 2005). In order to make the customer satisfied, Muthoot strives to make the employees satisfied, thereby driving their productivity and Muthoot's external service value to its customers.

Seven years ago, I came to know Muthoot through an advertisement I saw on cable television. The advertisement said that cash seekers can get loan in under five minutes. I used to run a declining leather goods business then. I was eager to know more that I went to nearby branch in Nehru Place. I availed the loan against gold to change my line of business. Today, I own a fleet of automobiles. I have also pledged gold with Muthoot's competitors, because I was getting a higher value, but I have always come back to Muthoot because of the trust I have with them over time. I have been dealing with Muthoot for seven years now. I have dealt with a few of Muthoot's branches, and my experiences with them have always been good. – Vinod Kumar (owner of small business in Delhi)

Employees at all levels undergo rigorous training in the multi-step gold quality appraisal process, which involves chemical and sound tests. Extensive indoctrination to customer interaction and etiquette, service sensitivity, and customer grievance are built into the standardized employee training module. In a world where every corporation talks about corporate governance, Muthoot implants self governance. It advises its customer-facing and management staff to exercise necessary functions of power without the intervention of supervisors, thus empowering Muthoot staff to swiftly take decisions on routine matters independently. Today, Muthoot boasts of their five-minute gold sanction process and service quality that truly demonstrates their service delivery, which has aptly served as a brand differentiation. Muthoot's billboards gloat about their loan transaction speed.

The greatest challenge, however, was the brand name confusion among customers seeking fast cash. One customer quite astutely stated that her friends who suggested Muthoot reminded her of the Muthoot with red elephants. Color red activates

Figure 6. Customer-centricity via employee-centricity

pituitary gland; the visceral response makes red attention-grabbing, energetic, and provocative (Attrill et al., 2008). On the other hand, Muthoot Pappachan Group has a weak "P" emphasizing on Pappachan than Muthoot as brand logo in forbidding turquoise colors. Color semiotics draws upon emotional and visceral impact of colors, and meanings of colors are dictated by culture. The influence of color on psychological functioning, such as attitude formation, mood, etc. is as pervasive as it is subtle and provocative. In color semiotics, turquoise stands for emotional balance that heightens levels of creativity and enhances inner healing through its ability to enhance empathy and caring. None of which bode well in the customers' perception of creating an urgency, dynamism, (Hill &Barton, 2005) or promisingly differentiating it with the Muthoot Group.

From babies to barroom brawlers, humans advance from a static level of thinking based on inceptive imprints to symbols to a kinetic level of thinking where they create meaningful thoughts surrounding symbols. Research has shown in infinite detail the way people, regardless of their age and/or experience, are fully capable of shifting from a passive state of mind to a much more complex pattern of thinking; one where they are shown to be fully capable of creating meaningful symbols and thoughts. Symbols and pictures without emotion, or affect – that is, without meaning - create memories without meaning, like the "P" symbol of Muthoot Pappachan Group. To create a meaningful symbol, like the vibrant, red, twin-elephant symbol the image must be invested with consistent repetition, meaning, and emotion. Meaningful symbols invest the consumers with affect the same way impersonal objects, such as the golden arches symbolizing McDonald's or concepts, such as the sixteenth-century Norse woodcut of the twin-tailed mermaid (or Siren) personifying Starbucks, require emotional investment if they are to become relevant and speaking symbols. The second condition observed in the case of Muthoot's symbol provides evidence that perception should be divorced from the company's service or action. The developmental process that enables a consumer to separate perception from action provides the missing link in understanding symbol formation and higher levels of consciousness, thinking, and self-reflection.

GUNSHOT STARTLES A HEARD OF ANTELOPE

India's deep association with former U.S.S.R. and its fanciful predilection for a socialist state decelerated economic growth with absolutely no market-reforms, and thereby India insulated itself with economic progression. For forty-four years India, like the former Soviet Union, was a centrally planned industrialization of an agrarian, fragmented land, a confluence of Jawaharlal Nehru's industrialization dreams with Mohandas Gandhi's rural ideology. A political and economic earthquake rocked India in 1991 when it elected the first non-Nehru clan Prime Minister, P. V. Narasimha Rao to lead Congress and India. He then boldly dismantled its socialist-inspired framework under the auspices of International Monetary Fund. As India diligently pursued economic reforms, a new segment of customers of potential entrepreneurs opened up to Muthoot. Liberalization may have proceeded in fits and starts in the 90s, but Muthoot infused large capital, demonstrated value, and increased the intensity of entrepreneurial spirit in India. In all, Muthoot responded well at India's second independence.

Independent research into how Muthoot's gold loan helped entrepreneurs corroborated how Muthoot went about targeting the segment of entrepreneurs.

For small business owners like me, Muthoot became an easy source of credit. I use gold as an instant credit tool. I run my business successfully, but always face liquidity issues and need to purchase parts that go out of stock. With loan from Muthoot, I can keep a good amount of inventory and do not face stockout of the auto spare items in my business. – Sanjay Sethi (owner of auto parts business)

In fact, Muthoot has a book in the planning stage entitled 'One Hundred Tales of Hope'. It contains pertinent examples of both entrepreneurs and its own customers who validate the core values of confidence and trust Muthoot has championed throughout its business history.

Though classified as non banking financial company, Muthoot rapidly evolved from a mere adjunct to monetary and credit policies to an active participant in the mainstream financial sector in the new millennium. Launching from the gold lending platform, Muthoot expanded into other financial segments ranging from money and foreign exchange to shares and commodity trading.

Recognizing that consumers prefer a brick-and-mortar institution with a wide national presence, Muthoot rapidly increased its locations in the length and breadth of India, thereby successfully transforming consumers' perception of gold loan from a distressed product to a lifestyle product.

Brand image is an intangible asset that generates value for corporations. Research on marketing advantages yielded by robust brand building efforts and related constructs has been substantially extensive (for reviews, see Albert, Merunka & Valette-Florence, 2008), finding brands to be associated with advocacy and positive word of marketing (Keller, 2007), consumer loyalty (Carroll & Ahuvia, 2006; Thomson et al., 2005), brand trust (Delgado-Ballester et al., 2003), brand attachment (McAlexander et al.2002), willingness to pay price premium (Steenkamp et al., 2010), and forgiveness of product failure (Bauer et al., 2009), among other coveted outcomes. G. M. George and Alexander George, Directors from the fourth generation of Muthoot family, believe the true branding advantage was an outgrowth of their trusted interaction with customers. From this interaction that made customers feel valued, inspired loyalty and incited advocacy to the Muthoot brand. It's the Muthoot's customers who then transcend as sales people for the brand through word of mouth marketing. (George & George 2014).

Figure 7. Growth of Muthoot branch locations (2005-2014)

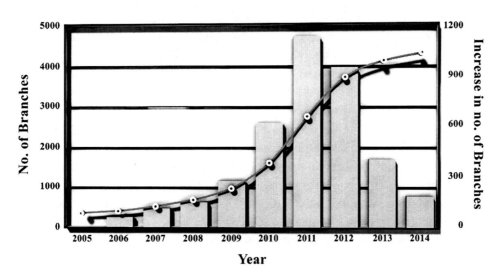

I did not care to check with Muthoot's competition. My neighbors had a positive loan experience that they recommended me to pawn my gold with them. It was the trust created through word of mouth that I preferred Muthoot. Muthoot rendered excellent customer service; my own experience with Muthoot has been positive. The loan helped me maintain a proper stock of all the models of air coolers in my warehouse. I was able to purchase these coolers on cash from suppliers, because of which I was able to negotiate a great price that in turn increased my profitability. Since air conditioning is a seasonal business, I've always faced cash liquidity issues and could not maintain a proper stock before I went to Muthoot for help. – Shafiq Ahmed (owner of Air Cooler business in Delhi)

Dominating influence of economics and psychology rooted in share of wallet and share of mind can inhibit the brand building process to the denotative and personal connotative levels. Brand building models has had an intense focus on the essence of the brand and its strength of mental association between the product and its benefits and brand persona. Until the dawn of the new millennium, Muthoot brand, though successful, was confined to the lower rungs of the brand pyramid delineated in Figure 8. In order to climb to the status of reputable brand, Muthoot shifted its focus to broader and deeper issues surrounding sustainability, account-ability, and governance for doing societal good. Muthoot addressed areas such as, financial inclusion, medical assistance to the lesser privileged, education for poor, and marriage assistance among others to transform rural and semi-urban communi-ties of India in its triumphant march of the corporate social responsibility (CSR) movement. The Muthoot Group catalyzed rural and urban economies through timely, adequate, and affordable credit; with outstanding loan accounts of over six million and additions through financial inclusion in new geographies as well as existing locations, business per branch increased, enhancing profits, dividend payout, and shareholder wealth (George & George, 2014). Muthoot provided financial support to the economically weaker sections of the society through free medical treatment at their hospitals, marriage assistance to girls, educational facilities to disadvantaged children many of whom were the first generation in their families to be educated, public-interest projects, environmental preservation through tree plantation drive in collaboration with the Department of Environment, and green school program promoted by Center for Science and Environment, and post-disaster relief manage-ment. For Muthoot's efforts to integrate India's marginalized into the mainstream and pro bono activities aimed at causes of benefitting the rural poor, women, and children, Muthoot was presented with the Golden Peacock award, regarded as a benchmark for corporate excellence.

Muthoot entered the world of society to compete for culture share. Brands rise to iconic stature when they compete with other popular culture products, namely:

Figure 8. Brand pyramid

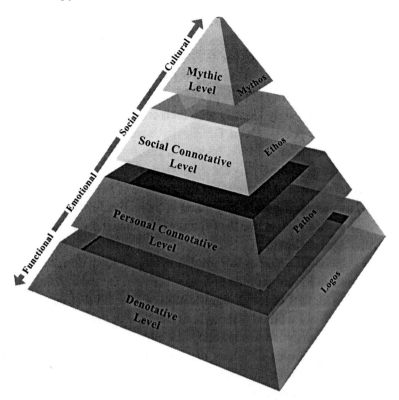

movies, sports, music, television, video games (Holt, 2004). To create memorable stories in the collective nation's culture, the augmented definition of brand embeds the extremely successful microanalysis of individual consumption of brand into a new analysis of cultural interaction.

Adding to the accumulation of evidence, Indians love for cricket, a quintessentially British sport, is inevitable. When cricket went through an overhaul in the new millennium, truncated to twenty overs a side from a game played five days long for over one hundred fifty years, the new, ostentatiously glitzy version of the game not only brought the game closer to the timespan of other popular team sports of the world, but it rightly fit the bill of three-hour evening's family entertainment. Muthoot's meteoric growth and climb to iconic status came in the noughties, when Muthoot sponsored a bright red jersey-wearing cricket franchise, Delhi Daredevils, in the Indian Premier League (IPL), riding on the novelty of this unmatchable icon-building. By immersing the Muthoot brand into the populist world, source materials in the realm of social connotation began to pinpoint in emerging cultural opportunities.

As chief sponsors, Muthoot received sizable coverage in stadia on advertising billboards; their symbol emblazoned on the red jerseys that cricketers wore. Muthoot underwent an image make-over; a thunderous call to attention on interview back-drops, on tickets and hospitality passes, in cricket match programs, and in hospitality areas. Muthoot received exposure not only via the global telecast of the IPL event, but also by earning exclusivity of their products and services in commercial airtime.

Indian consumers strongly identify with their cricket icons who serve as India's foundational compass points. Delhi Daredevils' captain and Indian cricket team opening batsman, Virender Sehwag, became a compelling representative symbol of the Muthoot Group, intensifying the collective consumers' perceptions. Today, Muthoot is a chief sponsor of Junior Pitch, an initiative of Sehwag Cricket Academy to nurture and mentor young cricketing talent in India. Established in memoriam of one of Muthoot's late directors, the Paul George tournament promotes sports among the lesser privileged children.

Myth has stupendous value as it transmits symbolic load; dominant ideologies of a culture provides a constant hide-and-seek between factual and fanciful, which defines myth, the highest order of signification of a brand that perhaps Muthoot strives to achieve. When a brand is thought as a culture of the product, one can borrow principles from the dynamic marketing discipline of Consumer Culture Theory to understand the numerous nebulous epithets characterizing brands as cultural artifacts (Arnould & Thompson, 2005). Myths can be seen as extended metaphors to help consumers make sense of brand experiences within a culture. The acquired meanings - connotations - then circulate in the society to become conventional, widely accepted truths about a brand. At a mythic level the Chanel brand, for instance, activates the myth of Hollywood: the dream factory that produces glamor in the form of stars. Harley Davidson loyalists don't care about the torque generated by the engine; rather, it is Harley's mythic brand values espoused by socio-cultural, symbolic, and ideological aspects that transform the casual biker into a Harley loyalist. In fact, many car buyers ignore and/or are completely ignorant of product attributes and technical specifications, such as a multi-point fuel injection system, the engine compression ratio, etc. The goal for marketers and brand owners is to transfer qualities into creating metaphorical identity, derived from physical, social, and cultural experiences that will offer consumers meaning. It is imperative that we not under-appreciate the significance of metaphors in the science of Branding. They are not to be dismissed as mere rhetorical flourish; while they may reflect the characteristic of ordinary language, they are equally pervasive in impelling a higher level of cognizance which in turn furthers a developmental mode of action in our everyday conceptual system of what we perceive and how we relate with people or brands.

RISE LIKE A PHOENIX

Semiotic meanings can be viewed either as use value (denotation), the direct, literal purport or symbolic value (connotation), the referential meaning of a brand permeated with value judgment of product or service. Denotation is the definitional, most literal relation between signifier and signified. Historical analysis of brand like Muthoot uncovers metaphoric associations based on how consumers interpret them. Connotation, on the other hand, calls attention to the socio-cultural, ideological dimensions how consumers interpret a brand through beliefs, prior product usage experiences, and emblematic meaning (Bignell, 2002; Aiello, 2006). Connotation builds secondary mental associations by turning a sign into the signifier of another sign. In semiotics, denotation and connotation describe the relationship between the signifier and its signified. Though both denotation and connotation can both be used to describe imagery of form or function of a brand, they have different contexts and orders of signification represented in a semiotic 2x2 framework (Murray, 2013).

Semiotic summary of Muthoot delineated in Figure 9. The cultural interpretation of Muthoot symbol of financial inclusion, IPL cricket belongs to the connotative, experiential function of Muthoot sign systems, in contrast to the denotive functions of discourse that simply indicates their business concept of getting loans against gold or role of technology and mobile apps which enable their customers to conveniently transact and operationalize their gold. Connotative function of brand discourse endows signs with nuances of meaning and interpretations that are subjective and culturally dependent. The application of this framework instantly offers brand owners and marketers conceptual crowbars to deconstruct or construct codes, meanings in consumption practices.

Some of the most effective insights into how brands are engineered in today's entropic, consumption-driven world - whether involving strategists, celebrities, czars, or saints - are achieved accidentally or refracted from events that apparently have nothing to do with branding. Under these circumstances, therefore, much of what is interpreted as brand building is fancifully considered by many as simple commercial advertising, propaganda, or the mere transmission of one or another insignificant aspect of culture from consumer group to another. Books on branding by the industry's self-anointed 'experts' abound in their outmoded and overly simplistic cookie-cutter sameness. They either ignore or conveniently bypass the intrinsic emotional connection that enables and empowers consumers of Nike to mark themselves with the swoosh tattoo in permanent ink to proclaim their membership in the 'just do it' tribe; just as today's youth sprinkle the rim of their Corona beer bottle with sea salt and push a lime wedge to flavor the beer and show that they, indeed, are of the chosen membership of an almost secret society. Several successful brands in post-war US business history from Marlboro to Coca Cola aptly describe

Figure 9. Semiotic brand chassis

CONNOTATION

Core values
Post-colonial growth
IPL cricket
CSR Activities

Customer stories
Realizing personal goals

EXPERIENCE

PRODUCT

Technology
Simplicity

Loan/repayment
Operationalizing gold
Perception of ubiquity

DENOTATION

how all four quadrants of the semiotic brand chassis are important on abstracting the brands from the functional, emotional, social, and cultural contexts that give them wallet-share, mind-share, and culture-share.

CART AFTER THE HORSE

A symbol refers to a brand; a brand refers to a symbol amongst myriad other realizable mental associations and germane abstractions. Broad currents of brand engineering evidently have influenced ways of life, made brand names verbs, aroused desire to treasure, and incited consumers to stand in a line for hours to purchase the next version of the mobile phone or post-PC. Syntactics, semantics, and pragmatics, the skeletons taken from semiotics vastly help in refurbishing a model of brand and in constructing the brand building process. The overarching goal of this new semiotic approach to brand building is to socialize marketers and practitioners into the genealogical mind-set to inspect brand identity value that evoke memorable perceptions and emotion through cultural lens of myth, symbolism, and ethos.

Not mere symbols, but symbolic meaning provides marketers and practitioners with a new and exciting opportunity to influence consumer behavior. To create these semantic meanings and manage the meanings is the art and science of brand building. Brand signifiers participate in a complex semiotic system connecting brand symbolism to culture providing meaning and relevancy in a given market. A brand must already possess the supreme integrity that amply corroborates its fidelity to advancing those brand values espoused by socio-cultural, symbolic, and ideological aspects of its consumption.

The theoretical apparatus of semiotics has a central place in the analysis of building brands both synchronically and diachronically. True understanding of the brand building process must include knowledge of a brand's historicity; it is equivocal to accept theories, however scientific it may be, without knowing the brand's voyage - of how the brand got where it is. Regrettably, existing theories of brand building neglect this invaluable maxim that has so often led to convenient assumptions and thus a misleading core of propositions.

The aim of this paper has been not only to integrate the doctrine of structural semiotics, but also to increase understanding and appreciation of the innate power of structural semiotics. Profiling a century-old brand, Muthoot Group, has generated deep insights into the way brand identity can be aligned with brand image for differentiation, loyalty, growth, and profitability among other significant assets that breed meaningful overall corporate value. Marketing signs become incorporated into the culture itself over time, as with the generic association of trust with Muthoot's twin elephants. Several studies based on semiotics

1.   Journal articles (Arnould et al., 2001; Sherry & Camargo 1987);
2.   Books or chapters in books (Schroeder, 2002) investigate logos from a general perspective or evolution of logos (Cowin &Matusitz, 2011) in a period of time.

As a secondary objective, this paper also examines precise meanings consumers attach to brand symbols in the context of semiotics when even the core business service of Muthoot changed in its business history.

Symbolic ability is a central component to human nature, and therefore, an important characteristic of consumer behavior. The human species are driven by a deep desire to make meanings. Peirce asserts that *homo significans* (meaning makers) think in terms of signs (Peirce, 1931, 1958). Signs in the form of brand logos, images, acts, etc. may have no intrinsic meaning, but they metamorphose as signs with meaning when customers create, evoke, or interpret meaning to them. Perhaps semiotics is not a panacea, but it can unmistakably help brand owners, managers, practitioners, and consultants to build stronger and more relevant brands. Brands are what they say they do and what they do. This performed action shifts our framework of brand discourse to approach brands as vessels of symbolic meanings that then evoke personalities and emotion, which has regrettably been ignored thus far. It's about time that additional brand building approaches that literally and metaphorically analyze how consumers process visual-verbal information of brands are researched. After all, brands win competitive battles when they forge an intimate fusion with culture and myth market. And, semiotics can amply help.

REFERENCES

Aiello, G. (2006). Theoretical advances in critical visual analysis: Perception, ideology, mythologies, and social semiotics. *Journal of Visual Literacy, 26*(2), 89–102.

Albert, N., Merunka, D., & Valette-Florence, P. (2008). When consumers love their brands: Exploring the concept and its dimensions. *Journal of Business Research, 61*(10), 1062–1075. doi:10.1016/j.jbusres.2007.09.014

Arnold, E. J., Kozinets, R. V., & Handelman, J. M. (2001). Hometown ideology and retailer legitimation: The institutional semiotics of Wal-Mart flyers. *Journal of Retailing, 77*(2), 43–271. doi:10.1016/S0022-4359(01)00046-X

Arnould, E. J., & Thompson, C. J. (2005). Consumer culture theory (CCT): Twenty years of research. *The Journal of Consumer Research, 31*(4), 868–882. doi:10.1086/426626

Attrill, M. J., Gresty, K. A., Hill, R. A., & Barton, R. A. (2008). Red shirt color is associated with long-term team success in English football. *Journal of Sports Sciences, 26*(6), 577–582. doi:10.1080/02640410701736244 PMID:18344128

Baudrillard, J. (1968). *Le système des objets*. Paris, France: Gallimard.

Bauer, H., Heinrich, D., & Albrecht, C. (2009). All you need is love: Assessing consumers' brand love. In *Proceedings of the American Marketing Association Summer Educators Conference*, (pp. 252-253). Chicago, IL: American Marketing Association.

Bignell, J. (2002). *Media semiotics: An introduction*. Manchester, UK: Manchester University Press.

Carroll, B. A., & Ahuvia, A. C. (2006). Some antecedents and outcomes of brand love. *Marketing Letters, 17*(2), 79–90. doi:10.1007/s11002-006-4219-2

Childers, T. L., & Jass, J. (2002). All dressed up with something to say: Effects of typeface semantic associations on brand perceptions and consumer memory. *Journal of Consumer Psychology*, *12*(2), 93–106. doi:10.1207/S15327663JCP1202_03

Cooper, P. (1979). Symbiosis: The consumer psychology of branding. *ADMAP*, *15*, 578–586.

Coren, S., Girgus, J. S., Erlichman, H., & Hakstian, A. R. (1976). An empirical taxonomy of visual illusions. *Perception & Psychophysics*, *20*(2), 129–137. doi:10.3758/BF03199444

Cowin, E., & Matusitz, J. (2011). The ongoing transformation of the McDonald's logo: A semiotic perspective. *Journal of Visual Literacy*, *30*(2), 20–39.

Delgado-Ballester, E., Munuera-Alemán, J. L., & Yagüe-Guillén, M. J. (2003). Development and validation of a brand trust scale. *International Journal of Market Research*, *45*(1), 35–53.

Gwinner, K. P., Bitner, M. J., Brown, S. W., & Kumar, A. (2005). Service customization through employee adaptiveness. *Journal of Service Research*, *8*(2), 131–148. doi:10.1177/1094670505279699

Herzberg, F. (1987). One more time: How do you motivate employees? *Harvard Business Review*, *65*(5), 109–120. PMID:12545925

Heskett, J. L., Jones, T. O., Loveman, G. W., Sasser, W. E., & Schlesinger, L. A. (1994). Putting the service-profit chain to work. *Harvard Business Review*, (March-April), 164–174.

Hill, R. A., & Barton, R. A. (2005). Red enhances human performance in contests. *Nature*, *435*(7040), 293. doi:10.1038/435293a PMID:15902246

Hirschman, E. C., & Holbrook, M. B. (1981). *Symbolic consumer behavior*. Ann Arbor, MI: Association of Consumer Research.

Holt, D. B. (2004). *How brands become icons: The principles of cultural branding*. Boston, MA: Harvard Business School Publishing Corporation.

Kahneman, D., & Frederick, S. (2002). Representativeness revisited: Attribute substitution in intuitive judgment. In T. Gilovich, D. Griffin, & D. Kahneman (Eds.), *Heuristics of intuitive judgments: Extensions and applications* (pp. 67–83). New York, NY: Cambridge University Press. doi:10.1017/CBO9780511808098.004

Keller, K. L. (2007). Unleashing the power of word of mouth: Creating brand advocacy to drive growth. *Journal of Advertising Research*, *47*(4), 448–452. doi:10.2501/S0021849907070468

McAlexander, J. H., Schouten, J. W., & Koenig, H. F. (2002). Building brand community. *Journal of Marketing*, *66*(January), 38–54. doi:10.1509/jmkg.66.1.38.18451

McCracken, G. (1993). The value of the brand: An anthropological perspective. In D. Aaker & A. Biel (Eds.), *Brand equity and advertising* (pp. 235–245). Hillsdale, NJ: Lawrence Erlbaum.

Morris, C. W. (1946). *Signs, language, and behavior*. New York, NY: Prentice-Hall. doi:10.1037/14607-000

Murray, J. B. (2013). *The semiotics of brand management*. Retrieved April 22, 2014, from http://jeffbmurray.files.wordpress.com/2013/06/the-semiotics-of-brand-management.pdf

Muthoot Group. (2014). *The Muthoot Group corporate brochure*. Author.

Nauta, D. (1972). *The meaning of information*. The Hague, The Netherlands: Mouton Publishers.

Nöth, W. (1990). *Handbook of semiotics*. Bloomington, IN: Indiana University Press.

Peirce, C. S. (1958). The collected papers of Charles Sanders Peirce. In C. Hartshorne & P. Weiss (Eds.), *Peirce* (Vols. 1-6). Cambridge, MA: Harvard University Press. (Original work published 1931)

Pinson, C. (1993). Marketing: Semiotics. In R. E. Asher & J. M. Y. Simpson (Eds.), *The encyclopedia of language and linguistics* (pp. 2384–2388). New York: Pergamon.

Posner, M. I., & Keele, S. W. (1968). On the genesis of abstract ideas. *Journal of Experimental Psychology*, *77*(3), 353–363. doi:10.1037/h0025953 PMID:5665566

Schroeder, J. E. (2002). *Visual consumption*. London: Routledge.

Sherry, J. F. Jr, & Camargo, E. G. (1987). May your life be marvelous: English language labeling and the semiotics of Japanese promotion. *The Journal of Consumer Research*, *14*(2), 174–188. doi:10.1086/209104

Short, T. L. (2009). *Peirce's theory of signs*. Cambridge, MA: Cambridge University Press.

Steenkamp, E. M., Van Heerde, H. J., & Geyskens, I. (2010). What makes consumers willing to pay a price a premium for national brands over private labels? *JMR, Journal of Marketing Research*, *47*(6), 1011–1024. doi:10.1509/jmkr.47.6.1011

Thomson, M., MacInnis, D. J., & Park, C. W. (2005). The ties that bind: Measuring the strength of consumers' emotional attachments to brands. *Journal of Consumer Psychology*, *15*(1), 77–91. doi:10.1207/s15327663jcp1501_10

Van Rompay, T. J. L., Pruyn, A. T. H., & Tieke, P. (2005). Symbolic meaning integration in design and its influence on product and brand evaluation. *International Journal of Design*, *3*(2), 19–26.

Zhang, Y., Feick, L., & Price, L. J. (2006). The impact of self-construal on aesthetic preference for angular versus rounded shapes. *Personality and Social Psychology Bulletin*, *32*(6), 794–805. doi:10.1177/0146167206286626 PMID:16648204

KEY TERMS AND DEFINITIONS

Brand Advocacy: Active championship of a brand through positive word-of-mouth messages to other prospective consumers thereby influencing their purchase decision.

Brand Loyalty: Harboring true devotion of a brand that causes high relative attitude exhibited through repurchase behavior or willingness to defray higher prices.

Brand Meaning: Implied or explicit significance of a brand that define consumers and the environments they inhabit.

Connotation: Emblematic relation usually comprising of socio-cultural meaning, between signifier and signified.

Consumer Behavior: Interdisciplinary field within the discipline of marketing that aims to study of individuals, groups, or organizations in the context of consumption.

Consumer Culture Theory: Family of theoretical approaches in consumer behavior that examines consumption and involved behavioral choices and practices from an anthropological lens and cultural phenomena.

Denotation: Literal relation between signifier and signified.

Metaphor: Two incongruous words or phrases presented as a relationship to one another such that the source term or idea helps transfer relevant properties or aspects to the targeted word or phrase.

Peircean Model: Triadic model of sign consisting of representamen, object, and interpretant.

Semantics: Study of meaning denoted by signs and symbols.

Semiology: Saussurean school of sign study that studies life of sign systems within societies.

Semiotic Brand Chassis: Analytical tool that plots use values and symbolic values of a brand.

Semiotics: Formal study of the functioning of sign systems.

Sign: An object, quality, or event whose presence or occurrence indicates the probable presence or occurrence of another.

Signification Model: Dyadic model composed of signifier and signified devised by Ferdinand de Saussure.

Signified: Meaning, idea expressed by a sign distinct from its physical form.

Signifier: Material or physical form or aspect of a sign.

Symbol: Visual image that evokes or conveys an idea, belief, or action.

Symbolism: Collective cultural face of a brand that dynamically integrates modular units of social aggregation to the symbol.

Chapter 14
Sensory Branding:
Branding with Senses

Surabhi Mukherjee Chakravarty
CMR – Institute of Management Studies, Bangalore, India & Alliance University, India

ABSTRACT

This chapter presents sensorial branding approaches in practice and theory. Senses play a vital role in human life. We understand almost everything in life through senses. Sensory branding is an approach through which marketers create better experience of brands. Our senses are our link to memory, which can tap right into emotion. Using senses and their effect on understanding the consumer paves the way for an enriching experience of brand, discriminating their personality, creating a core competence, more interest, preference, and customer loyalty. Sensory branding is the marketing strategy that is investigating the emotional relationships between consumer and the brand through senses. Two cases presented in the chapter are on Starbucks and Apple Inc., which highlight their sensorial strategies for stimulating consumers' relationships and fostering a lasting emotional connection that retains brand loyalty.

INTRODUCTION

In the branding literature, the concept of brand identity is defined as a unique set of brand associations that a firm can create or maintain. It may involve a value-proposition with functional, emotional or self-expressive benefits. It does not matter whether the associations are tangible or emotional/symbolic or both (Anselm &

DOI: 10.4018/978-1-4666-7393-9.ch014

Kostelijk, 2008). The sensorial and emotional linkage between brand and consumer has been proposed as important in building strong brands. It has also been confirmed in research that consumers look for and buy emotional experiences around what has been bought and no longer buy products and services alone (Brembeck & Ekstro"m, 2004; Ratneshwar & Mick, 2005).

ORGANIZATION BACKGROUND

Starbucks

Starbucks Coffee Company, founded in 1971 is headquartered in Seattle, WA and operates in 37 countries around the world. The backbone of Starbuck's business is its company-operated retail stores. Starbucks has employed a strong differentiation strategy in order to turn a traditional $.50 commodity into a $4 experience. Starbucks' governing principles are based on three strategic stances: the third place experience, creating a human connection, and providing a quality everyday experience for customers.

Today, Starbucks welcome millions of customers through their doors every day, in more than 17,000 locations in over 50 countries.

History of the Organization

1971: Starbucks opens first store in Seattle's Pike Place Market.

1982: Howard Schultz joins Starbucks as director of retail operations and marketing. Starbucks begins providing coffee to fine restaurants and espresso bars.

1983: Howard travels to Italy, where he's impressed with the popularity of espresso bars in Milan. He sees the potential to develop a similar coffeehouse culture in Seattle.

1984: Howard convinces the founders of Starbucks to test the coffeehouse concept in downtown Seattle, where the first Starbucks Caffè Latte is served. This successful experiment is the genesis for a company that Schultz founds in 1985.

1985: Howard founds Il Giornale, offering brewed coffee and espresso beverages made from Starbucks coffee beans.

1987: Il Giornale acquires Starbucks assets with the backing of local investors and changes its name to Starbucks Corporation. Opens in Chicago and Vancouver, Canada.

1988: Offers full health benefits to eligible full- and part-time employees

1989: Total stores: 55

1990: Starbucks expands headquarters in Seattle

1991: Becomes the first privately owned U.S. Company to offer a stock option program that includes part-time employees.

Opens first licensed airport store at Seattle's Sea-Tac International Airport

1992: Completes initial public offering (IPO), with common stock being traded on the NASDAQ National Market under the trading symbol SBUX.

1993: Opens roasting plant in Kent, Wash. Announces first two-for-one stock split.

1994: Total stores: 425

1995: Begins serving Frappuccino blended beverages

Introduces Starbucks super-premium ice cream.

Announces second two-for-one stock split.

Opens roasting facility in York, Pa.

1996: Begins selling bottled Frappuccino coffee drink through North American Coffee Partnership (Starbucks and Pepsi-Cola North America).

Opens stores in: Japan (first store outside of North America) and Singapore.

1997: Establishes The Starbucks Foundation, benefiting local literacy programs.

Opens stores in: the Philippines.

1998: Acquires Tazo, a tea company based in Portland, Ore.

Extends the Starbucks brand into grocery channels across the U.S.

Launches Starbucks.com.

Opens stores in: Malaysia, New Zealand, Taiwan, Thailand and U.K.

1999: Partners with Conservation International to promote sustainable coffee-growing practices.

Acquires Hear Music, a San Francisco–based music company.

Announces third two-for-one stock split.

Opens stores in: China, Kuwait, Lebanon and South Korea.

2000: Howard Schultz transitions to chairman and chief global strategist, Orin Smith promoted to president and chief executive officer.

Establishes licensing agreement with TransFair USA to sell Fairtrade certified coffee in U.S. and Canada.

Opens stores in: Australia, Bahrain, Hong Kong, Qatar, Saudi Arabia and United Arab Emirates.

Total stores: 3,501

2001: Introduces ethical coffee-sourcing guidelines developed in partnership with Conservation International. Introduces the Starbucks Card, an innovative stored-value card for customers to use and reload. Announces fourth two-for-one stock split.

Opens stores in: Austria and Switzerland.

Total stores: 4,709

2002: Starbucks enters into licensing agreements with national Fair Trade organizations to sell Fairtrade certified coffee in the countries where Starbucks does business.

Establishes Starbucks Coffee Trading Company (SCTC) in Lausanne, Switzerland.

Opens stores in: Germany, Greece, Indonesia, Mexico Oman, Puerto Rico and Spain.

Total stores: 5,886

2003: Acquires Seattle Coffee Company, which includes Seattle's Best Coffee and Torrefazione Italia coffee brands. Opens roasting facility in Carson Valley, Nev., and Amsterdam, Netherlands.

Opens stores in: Chile, Cyprus, Peru and Turkey.

Total stores: 7,225

2004: Opens first Farmer Support Center in San Jose, Costa Rica.

Releases Ray Charles, Genius Loves Company CD through collaboration with Concord Records. Introduces Starbucks Coffee Master Program.

Opens stores in: France.

Total stores: 8,569

2005: Jim Donald becomes president and chief executive officer to replace retiring Orin Smith. Acquires Ethos Water. Announces fifth two-for-one stock split.

Opens stores in: Bahamas, Ireland and Jordan.

Total stores: 10,241

2006: Launches the industry's first paper beverage cup containing post-consumer recycled fiber, saving more than 75,000 trees each year.

Opens stores in: Brazil and Egypt.

Total stores: 12,440

2007: Eliminates all artificial trans-fat and makes 2 percent milk the new standard for espresso beverages in all U.S. stores as part of commitment to health and wellness.

Opens stores in: Romania and Russia.

Total stores: 15,011

2008: Chairman Howard Schultz returns as chief executive officer.

Acquires Coffee Equipment Company and its Clover brewing system.

Launches My Starbucks Idea, Starbucks first online community. Announces Starbucks™ Shared Planet™, the company's long-term commitment to conducting business responsibly. Expands partnership with Conservation International for work on ethical sourcing and climate change.

Launches Pike Place Roast, which quickly becomes Starbucks top-selling coffee.

Opens stores in: Argentina, Bulgaria, Czech Republic and Portugal.

Total stores: 16,680

2009: Launches Starbucks VIA Ready Brew Coffee.

Opens East Africa Farmer Support Center in Kigali, Rwanda.

Starbucks partners with (RED) to help save lives in Africa.

Launches my Starbucks and Starbucks Card iPhone apps and Starbucks Card Mobile payment. Opens stores in: Poland and Aruba.

Total stores: 16,635

2010: Expands digital offerings for customers with free unlimited Wi-Fi, Starbucks Digital Network in U.S. stores. Seattle's Best Coffee reinvents business strategy to extend brand's reach. Expands coffee offerings with ultra-premium Starbucks Reserve line and Starbucks Natural Fusions, the first nationally-branded naturally-flavored packaged coffee. Announces first Asia Farmer Support Center in Yunnan Province, China.

Opens stores in: Hungary and El Salvador.

Total stores: 16,858

Type of Business

The mission of Starbucks is "To Inspire and nurture the human spirit– one person, one cup and one neighborhood at a time". Their logo is inspired by sea- featuring a twin-tailed siren from Greek Mythology. The company believes in serving the best coffee possible. The coffee used by Starbucks is grown under the highest standards of quality, using ethical sourcing practices. Their coffee buyers personally travel to coffee farms in Latin America, Africa and Asia to select the highest quality Arabica beans. Once these quality beans arrive to their roasting plants, Starbucks experts bring out the balance and rich flavor of the beans through the signature Starbucks Roast. The stores of Starbucks always have a welcoming third place for meeting friends and family, enjoying a quiet moment alone with a book or simply finding a familiar place in a new city.

Starbucks have total stores of 17009 (as of January2, 2011) out of which 8870 are company owned and 8139 are licensed stores. Starbucks is operating in more than 50 countries which comprises of Argentina, Aruba, Australia, Austria, Bahamas, Bahrain, Belgium, Brazil, Bulgaria, Canada, Chile, China, Cyprus, Czech Republic, Denmark, Egypt, El Salvador, England, France, Germany, Greece, Hong Kong, Hungary, Indonesia, India, Ireland, Japan, Jordan, Kuwait, Lebanon, Malaysia, Mexico, New Zealand, Netherlands, Northern Ireland, Oman, Peru, Philippines, Poland, Portugal, Qatar, Romania, Russia, Saudi Arabia, Scotland, Singapore, South Korea, Spain, Sweden, Switzerland, Taiwan, Thailand, Turkey, United Arab Emirates, United States and Wales.

Products/Services Provided

Starbucks Portfolio comprises of

1. **Coffee:** More than 30 blends and single-origin premium Arabica coffees.
2. **Handcrafted Beverages:** Fresh-brewed coffee, hot and iced espresso beverages, coffee and non-coffee blended beverages, Vivanno smoothies and Tazo teas.
3. **Merchandise:** Coffee and tea brewing equipment, mugs and accessories, packaged goods, music, books, and gift items.
4. **Fresh Food:** Baked pastries, sandwiches, salads, oatmeal, yogurt, parfaits, and fruit cups.
5. **Ready-to-Drink (RTD):** Starbucks bottled Frappuccino coffee drinks, Starbucks Discoveries chilled cup coffees, Starbucks Doubleshot espresso drinks, Starbucks Doubleshot, Energy+ Coffee drinks; Seattle's Best Coffee® Iced Lattes, Tazo bottled iced and juiced teas.
6. **Starbucks Ice Cream:** Super-premium coffee and coffee-free flavors.

Financial Status (Including Annual Sales)

Few observations from last six year period ratio & growth analysis of Starbucks's Financials from 2008 to 2013 are:

1. The revenue growth of the company has experience a drop of -5.9% during the 2008-09 recession but from then on, Starbucks posted a healthy revenue growth of from FY2010 to FY2013 with posting a great growth of 13.7% in FY2012 and currently posted revenues $14.9 billion for FY2013.
2. The operating income margins have increase substantially from 4.9% in FY2008 to a high of 15% in FY2012.
3. Starbucks ROE and ROA have been impressive with 29.2% and 17.8% respectively for FY2012.
4. Starbucks Boasts Good Financial Health with Low Debt/Leverage with a Debt/Equity Ratio of 0.29 for FY2013 and maintains decent current and quick ratios.

Strategic Planning

The Specific Strategies used by Starbucks include:

1. **Horizontal Integration:** Acquisitions of Seattle's Best, Torrefazione Italia and Coffee People.

2. **Market Penetration:** Differentiation and Product Placement Outside Of Retail Stores.
3. **Market Development:** Educating the Consumer about Specialty Coffee.
4. **Concentric Diversification:** Release of Bottled Drinks, Ice Creams, and Liqueur.
5. **Conglomerate Diversification:** Expansion into Music and Movies.
6. **Value Chain Development:** The Human Connection Gained By Business.

Since the beginning, Starbucks has been a different kind of company. It is always dedicated to inspiring and nurturing the human spirit which is committed to serving the finest coffee, creating an exceptional customer experience, and being a great place to work.

Starbucks is a proud recipient of the following awards and recognition:

- "No. 1 Best Coffee," Fast Food and Quick Refreshment categories, Zagat's Survey of National Chain Restaurants, 2009-2010.
- "No. 1 Most Popular Quick Refreshment Chain", Zagat's Survey of National Chain Restaurants, 2009-2010.
- One of the "World's Most Ethical Companies", Ethisphere, 2007-2010.
- "Most Ethical Company, European Coffee Industry", Allegra Strategies, 2009-2010.
- "Best Coffee House, Germany", Deutschland Institute for Service Quality, 2010.
- One of the "100 Best Corporate Citizens", Corporate Responsibility Officer/ Business Ethics, 2000-2010.
- One of the "Global 100 Most Sustainable Corporations in the World", Corporate Knights, 2010.
- One of "The 100 Best Companies to Work For", FORTUNE, 1998–2000, 2002–2010.
- One of the "Most Admired Companies in America", FORTUNE, 2003–2010.
- One of the "Best Places to Work for LGBT Equality", The Human Rights Campaign, 2009-2010.

Apple

History of the Organization

Apple was incorporated in 1977. It was co-founded by Steven Wozniak and Steven P. Jobs. They introduced the first Apple I computer in 1976. The Apple I was a failure but Apple II launched in 1980 was successful. The company offered its IPO in the year 1980. In the early eighties, competition from the PC market and internal difficulties led to critical management changes. By 1983, Apple faced stiff competition with the entry of IBM into the PC market, and the failure of its Apple III version computer. Apple introduced its first mouse driven PC, the Macintosh, in 1984.

By 1990, the market was flooded with cheap PC clones and Microsoft had launched Windows 3.0. In 1994, the company launched the PowerPC chip based PowerMac, which allowed Macs to compete with the speed of Intel's PC processors. Apple still had problems though and in 1995, the company had a $1 billion order backlog. These problems were compounded by the launch of Windows 95. The company's performance nosedived in 1995-96 when it lost $68 million. In 1996, Apple acquired NeXT, and by virtue of which, its operating system (OS), Rhapsody, became Apple's next-generation OS. By 1997, Apple had incurred huge losses running in millions of dollars. Mr. Jobs, the co-founder returned as interim CEO. Under his leadership, Apple reorganized to concentrate on its more profitable competencies, and divested its unsuccessful businesses as spin-offs, including Newton, its personal digital assistant line of products.

Soon after Mr. Jobs returned, an agreement was made with Microsoft, and was subsequently followed with the appearance of MS Office on Mac PCs. In 2001, the company acquired Power School, one of the providers of web-based student information systems for K-12 schools and school districts, and Spruce Technologies, a privately held company involved in developing and marketing DVD authoring products.

In the following year, Apple, Ericsson and Sun Microsystems formed an alliance to create a standard format for delivering multimedia content to wireless devices, such as smart phones and PDAs. The alliance combined Apple's QuickTime video creation software, Sun's content distribution software and hardware, and Ericsson's mobile infrastructure and services expertise. Apple pursued a number of acquisitions during 2002. The company acquired Prismo Graphics, Silicon Grail, certain assets of Zayante, and also acquired the German based specialist music software manufacturer, Emagic. Additionally, in 2002, the company acquired certain assets of Nothing Real, a privately held company engaged in the development of high performance tools designed for the digital image creation market. Apple launched its iTunes music store, an online store for downloading music tracks and albums, in 2003. In the following year, the company signed licensing agreements with three of the largest European independent music labels, Beggars Group, Sanctuary Records Group and V2, adding tens of thousands of additional independent tracks from leading artists to the iTunes music store in the UK, France and Germany. In the same year, Apple introduced its fourth generation iPod portable digital music player. In 2005, the company made an agreement to use Intel microprocessors in its Macintosh PCs. Later in the year, the company collaborated with Acura, Audi,

Honda and Volkswagen to deliver iPod with their car stereos for 2006 model lines, and also introduced mobile phone with iTunes in collaboration with Motorola and Cingular Wireless.

Chrysler, in association with Apple, integrated iPod option in the audio systems in its 2006 models. In the same year, Apple sold its student information systems (SIS) division, Power School, to Pearson. Later in the year, Ford, General Motors and Mazda teamed up with Apple to integrate iPod across their brand and models. In 2006, Apple teamed up with Air France, Continental, Delta, Emirates, KLM and United Airlines to integrate iPod with in-flight entertainment systems. The company changed its name from Apple Computer, Inc to Apple Inc in 2007, representing its expanding product portfolio and increasing focus on consumer electronics market. Apple resolved its 'iPhone' trademark issue with Cisco Systems by entering into an agreement in 2007. According to the agreement, both the companies acknowledged the ownership rights and will use the trademark in their products. In the same year, Apple launched its revolutionary product, iPhone, a smart phone device, and also launched iPod nano, featuring two inch display.

In 2008, Apple introduced Time Capsule, a backup appliance that automatically and wirelessly backs up everything on one or more Macs running Leopard. Subsequently, it also introduced Mac Pro with eight processor cores, and Mac Book Air, a thin notebook, which measures a maximum height of 0.76-inch. Apple introduced Xsan 2, the first major upgrade to its easy-to-use, high performance, enterprise class SAN file system for Mac OS X, in 2008. Subsequently, the company introduced MobileMe, a new internet service that offers push email, push contacts and push calendars to native applications on iPhone, iPod touch, Macs and PCs. Also in 2008, Apple announced iPod touch. In 2009, Apple introduced iWork '09, a new version of Apple's office productivity suite, and iLife '09, which features major upgrades to iPhoto, iMovie and Garage Band, and included iDVD and an updated version of iWeb. Subsequently, the company introduced the iPhone 3GS, Apple's third-generation smartphone with new features such as, longer battery life, high-quality 3 megapixel autofocus camera, easy to use video recording and hands free voice control.

Later in the year, Apple launched its iTunes Store in Mexico with a selection of Mexican and international music from all the major labels and independent labels. Subsequently, Apple launched its previously announced iPod touch lineup with features including Apple Multi-Touch user interface, 3.5-inch widescreen glass display, Wi-Fi, Bluetooth, and a built-in accelerometer and speaker. During the last quarter of 2009, the company updated its MacBook with LED-backlit display, Apple Multi-Touch trackpad and built-in seven-hour battery, and subsequently, introduced its wireless Magic Mouse, the world's first mouse to use Apple's Multi-Touch technology. Subsequently, Apple responded to a lawsuit brought against it by Nokia with a countersuit, claiming that Nokia infringed 13 Apple patents.

In January 2010, Apple announced iPad, a high-resolution, Multi-Touch display device for browsing the web, reading, sending email, and viewing entertainment content. In March 2010, Apple filed a lawsuit against HTC for infringing of 20 Apple patents related to the iPhone's user interface, underlying architecture and hardware. In the next month, the company's iPad, which was announced in January 2010, was made available in the US, Australia, Canada, France, Germany, Italy, Japan, Spain, Switzerland and the UK, and sold 300,000 units on the first day of its launch in the US. Subsequently in April 2010, the company previewed its iPhone OS 4 software and released a beta version of the software to iPhone Developer Program members.

The company launched iPad in nine more countries, including Australia, Canada, France, Germany, Italy, Japan, Spain, Switzerland and the UK in May 2010. In the following month, Apple introduced the new iPhone 4 featuring FaceTime, which allows video calling, and Apple's new Retina display for super crisp text, images and video. In July 2010, Apple released Safari 5.0.1 with extensions support allowing developers to create extensions with HTML5, CSS3 and JavaScript web standards. In the same month, the iPhone 4 was launched in 17 more countries. Also in the month, Apple updated its all-in-one iMac line, with the latest Intel Core i3, Core i5 and Core i7 processors and powerful new graphics.

Apple announced the new iPod touch in September 2010, with new features including Retina display, FaceTime video calling, HD video recording, Apple's A4 chip, 3-axis gyro, iOS 4.1 and Game Center. In the same month, Apple introduced iTunes 10 with Ping, a new music-oriented social network. Subsequently, Apple announced the new Apple TV which allows viewers to watch HD movies and

TV shows. In October 2010, Apple introduced the Apple Store in China (apple.com.cn) to shop online for Apple products. In the same month, Apple unveiled an all new MacBook Air. In the same month, Verizon

Wireless and Apple announced the availability of iPad at over 2,000 Verizon Wireless Stores in the US.

The company announced that iOS 4.2, the latest version of Apple's mobile operating system, is available for download for iPad, iPhone and iPod touch in November 2010. In the same month, Oracle and Apple launched the OpenJDK project for Mac OS X. Subsequently, Apple and The Dentsu Group formed a partnership to expand Apple's iAd mobile advertising network to Japan in early 2011. As part of the agreement, Dentsu will be responsible for the selling and creative execution of iAds in Japan, and Apple will host, target and deliver the iAds to its iPhone and iPod touch users. In January 2011, Verizon Wireless launched the iPhone on its network, ending the exclusivity of AT&T. In the same month, Apple launched the Mac App Store with more than 1,000 free and paid applications.

Apple updated its MacBook Pro family with next generation processors and graphics, high-speed Thunderbolt I/O technology and a new FaceTime HD camera in February 2011. In the same month,

Apple introduced iPad 2, featuring a new design that is 33% thinner and up to 15% lighter than the original iPad. In March 2011, Apple introduced IOS 4.3, the latest version of its mobile operating system, with faster Safari mobile browsing performance with the Nitro JavaScript engine; iTunes Home Sharing; enhancements to AirPlay; and the Personal Hotspot feature for sharing an iPhone 4 cellular data connection over Wi-Fi.

Type of Business

Apple is engaged in design, development and marketing of personal computers, media devices, and portable digital music players. The company also sells a variety of related software, services, peripherals, networking solutions, and third-party digital content and applications. The company's portfolio of offerings comprises Macintosh (Mac) Computing Systems, IPods Line of Portable digital music and video players, IPhone Handsets and IPad portable multimedia and computing devices.

Products/Services Provided

Apple designs, manufactures and markets a range of personal computers, mobile communication and media devices, and portable digital music players. The company sells a variety of related software, services, peripherals, networking solutions, and third-party digital content and applications.

In addition, the company sells a variety of third-party Mac, iPhone, iPad and iPod compatible products, including application software, printers, storage devices, speakers, headphones, and various other accessories and peripherals. The company sells its products worldwide through its retail stores, online stores, and direct sales force and third-party cellular network carriers, wholesalers, retailers, and value-added resellers.

Apple's products can be grouped under different product lines which are as follows: Mac Hardware Products, iTunes, iPhone, iPad, iPod, displays and peripheral products, software products and computer technologies, and internet software and services.

Management Structure

The Company Primarily Operates In The US. It Is Headquartered In Cupertino, California And Employs 46,600 Employees. The Company Manages Its Business Primarily On A Geographic Basis. It Operates Through Five Operating Segments:

Table 1. Management structure

Name	Title	Age
Timothy D. Cook	Chief Executive Officer And Director	53
Luca Maestri	Chief Financial Officer, Principal Accounting Officer And Senior Vice President	50
Jeffrey E. Williams	Senior Vice President Of Operations	50
Angela Ahrendts	Senior Vice President Of Retail and Online Stores	53
Eduardo H. Cue	Senior Vice President Of Internet Software & Services	49

Americas, Europe, Japan, Asia-Pacific And Retail. The Americas Segment Includes Both North And South America. The Europe Segment Includes European Countries As Well As The Middle East And Africa. The Asia-Pacific Segment Includes Australia and Asia, But Does Not Include Japan. The Retail Segment Operates Apple Retail Stores In 11 Countries, Including The US. Each Operating Segment Provides Similar Hardware And Software Products And Similar Services.

Financial Status (Including Annual Sales)

The company recorded revenues of $65,225 million during the financial year ended September 2010 (FY2010), an increase of 52% over 2009. The increase in revenues was mainly due to 93% growth in sales of iPhone and robust sales of the iPad. The operating profit of the company was $18,385 million in FY2010, an increase of 56.6% over 2009. Its net profit was $14,013 million in FY2010, an increase of 70.2% over 2009.

SWOT Analysis

Strengths
- Strong brand image provides an edge over competitors.
- Robust financial performance strengthens investors' confidence and provides capital for future growth avenues.
- Focused R&D driving innovation and consolidating its market position

Weaknesses
- Patent infringement lawsuit may affect financial condition and operating result.
- Product recalls may harm Apple's reputation and add significant warranty and other expenses

Opportunities

- Strong growth in smart phone and tablet markets to boost Apple's revenues
- Robust outlook for mobile advertising market provides growth opportunity

Threats

- Rising popularity of Google Android may affect its market share
- Intense competition may affect revenues and profitability
- Dependence on specific suppliers may affect its operations

Setting the Stage

Marketers use sensorial brand-experience in differentiating, distinguishing and positioning their brand in the human mind as an image. A sensorial experience is created through involvement of the five human senses which provides a brand's personal imprint to the customers. Marketers usually use sensorial strategies expressed through sensors, sensations and sensory expressions in relation to the five human senses in leaving imprints of a good or service. A multi-sensory brand-experience offers behavioral, emotional, cognitive, sensorial, or symbolic value at a deeper, more internal level than the Traditional Marketing and Relationship Marketing models. In this regard, a smell, sound, vision, taste or touch can reinforce a positive feeling, following the experiential logic which generates a certain value to the individual and, in particular, creates a brand image. Sensory Branding has its focus on the human mind and senses; hence managers identify emotional/psychological connections in differentiating and distinguishing their brand's identity.

CASE DESCRIPTION

Opening Case: Starbucks, a Sensory Experience

Starbucks is the world's largest chain of coffee shops, with around 40 million visitors per day. A visit to Starbucks is much more than a cup of coffee. By using a sensory marketing framework the company creates a deeper and more personal relationship with its customers. This is achieved by involving all five human senses to offer the customer a total sensory experience.

As early as the 1980s Starbucks developed a strategy for creating and delivering a sensory experience to consumers as a way to strengthen the brand. Giving the brand further aesthetics and emotional values and dimensions was seen as essential to creating a view of the chain as a third place outside of home and work. A visit to Starbucks should be an experience for the mind and the heart.

The inspiring environment makes it comfortable to read a book or talk with friends. The green and yellow of the interior, together with pleasant light, offer a soothing and restful visual experience. The relaxing music is selected with precision and care by the Starbucks Content Team to create the "Sound of Starbucks". Add to this the smell and taste of freshly ground coffee, as well as the comfortable texture, solidity and shape of the armchairs, and you have the characteristics of the sensory experience of the brand.

Starbucks uses a sensory marketing framework in creating an atmosphere where experience can be shaped, emotions can be expressed, and memories can be created.

SENSORY BRANDING: BRANDING WITH SENSES

Introduction

From the greatest to the smallest, The Law of Attraction is what holds every star in the universe and forms every atom and molecule. The force of Attraction of the sun holds the planets in our solar system, keeps them hurtling into space. The force of attraction in gravity holds us, each person, animal, plant and mineral on earth. This force is seen all around us; let that be a flower attracting the bees, the seeds attracting the nutrients from soil. This force holds together the cells of our body.

The Marketers are so much fascinated with the Law of Attraction that they try to imbibe in it in all their conceptions to lure the customers. The Law of Attraction has given birth to a new concept called "Sensory Marketing".

Sensory Branding: The Law of Attraction

Branding these days makes sense when the marketer uses the Law of Attraction to make its product/ brand more attractive and striking. The marketers have understood that to survive in the cut-throat competition conventional (traditional) marketing techniques are not going to help. The 'feel factor' should be associated with the emotional value of a product/ brand to give it a sharp edge over its competitors in the market.

By going beyond the traditional marketing media of sight and (sometimes) sound, brands can establish a stronger and longer-lasting emotional connection with consumers. 'Marketing that engages the consumers' senses and affects their perceptions, judgments and behavior', can be termed as Sensory Marketing. Sensory branding is based on the idea that consumers are most likely to form, retain and revisit memory when all five senses are engaged. It's about capitalizing on what one knows about their sensory links to recall emotion and leveraging that information to strengthen brands and increase sales.

From a managerial perspective, sensory marketing can be used to create sub-conscious triggers that characterize consumer perceptions of abstract notions of the product (e.g., its sophistication or quality). Given the gamut of explicit marketing appeals made to consumers every day, subconscious trigger/s which appeals to the basic senses may be a more efficient way to engage consumers.

Concept and Meaning of Sensory Branding

Sensory Marketing seems to be emerging business discipline that applies analytical techniques, to amalgamate the use of sensory stimuli such as Scent, Sound, Taste and Texture in order to develop strong brands that are more appealing for customers as compared to conventional - visual branding techniques alone.

Sensory Branding/Marketing
- Measures and Explains Consumer Emotions
- Recognize, Analyze and Capitalize New Market Opportunities
- Maximize Product Line/ Brand Profitability
- Ensure First time Purchase
- Ensures Repeated Purchase
- Increase Brand Loyalty
- Ensure Product Success.

Traditional Branding is based on the idea that as consumer is rational; his behavior is a result of logical reasoning, based upon his requirements and the product offerings. In contrast, Sensory Branding creates emotional, cognitive, behavioral and relational experiences through five senses so to enhance the chance of product purchase. In such a case, the consumer behaves according to his emotions more than his reasons and logic. By incorporating sensorial branding, brands create a stronger emotional connection with the consumers. Brands have started using Sensory Branding as an effective marketing communication tool.

These days for most of the consumers, affectivity, perception and pleasure stand more important than price. Since most of the products are technically similar, differentiation between the brands is on the basis of delight experienced during the purchase or post-purchase stage. Let's take an example of two bakeries in the colony. The good taste of pastries/ cake is not enough for a consumer, the ambience inside the bakery, the exotic smell of fresh bakery products; the sensation of pleasure/delight created by stimulating senses of the consumer will give competitive advantage to one bakery over the other.

Kotler (1973) had already mentioned the need for brands to position them differently that according to the price or the assortment. He started to explain the influence of the point of sales physical environment on the behavior of the customers and gave a definition of the atmosphere as "the creation of a consumption environment that produces specific emotional effects on the person, like pleasure or excitation that can increase his possibility of buying". He considered the creation of this atmosphere as the most important strategic way of differentiation for retailers. [1]

Sensory Branding: Gaining Competitive Advantage

Let's not forget that the little emotions are the great captains of our lives and we obey them without realizing it. – Vincent Van Gogh, 1889

Human senses have been ignored in the concepts of Traditional Marketing, despite of our awareness of their greater significance. The fundamental of sensory branding is to establish a connection between a consumer and a brand on an emotional level through an interaction of five human senses; sight, sound, smell, taste and touch in buying process. These five senses are of crucial importance for an individual's experience of purchase decision and consumption process. It is through these senses every individual possess an opinion about the brand and firm.

Volvo, the Sixth Sense

In 2006, Volvo, a Swedish Automobile brand and a part of Ford Motor Company broadcasted an Advertisement in Swedish channel TV4 under the theme, "The Sixth Sense".

When one drives a car, the human senses are activated: Sight, Sound, and Touch, sometimes smell. Volvo understood the importance of human senses and spread the message that Volvo car should be seen as "The Sixth Sense". The Car had automated system whereby when it is close to collision with other vehicle, it automatically slows down.

Volvo presented a car that should be pleasure to drive, offer safety and extraordinary driving experience.

These days, not only the T.V. / Print Ads or Social Media messages, but also the Malls, Superstores, Restaurants, Retail Outlets, and Shopping Centers are trying to build emotional linkages in addition to the rational ones to attract human senses through sensory experiences.

Sensory Branding is differentiated with Traditional (Mass) Marketing and Relationship Marketing Concepts. Sensory Branding has originated from the major five human sense organs which are assumed to have deeper emotional connection/bonds with the brands in contrast to the traditional approach. In Sensorial Branding approach, the brand is positioned not only on the basis of rationality and logic, but also on the emotional and value appeal.

EXPERIENCING BRANDS WITH FIVE SENSES

Let's consider an example. The images in Table 3 shall speak the whole story about the Five Senses which immediately connect with the consumers.

Visual Branding

Sight is the most relied upon and important sense for most humans and often drives a first impression. For this reason, creative directors have long worked to create images, messages, and calls to action that are appealing and easily understood by the consumers. Strong visual brand assets take advantage of a consumer's immediate connection with the brand.

The choice of colors and forms of a product, the layout of a point of sale, the realization of promotion campaign are key factors of success (or failure), well understood by marketers. Colors and shapes are the first way of identification and differentiation. Many brands are associated to a specific color, and then it is memorized more easily in the consumers' unconscious: Coca Cola is red, Kodak is yellow…

Table 2. From mass and relationship to sensory marketing

	Mass Marketing	**Relationship Marketing**	**Sensory Marketing**
Marketing	Goods Logic Exchange Perspective Transactional Marketing	Service Logic Relationship Perspective Relational Marketing	Experience Logic Brand Perspective Sensorial Marketing
Strategic Marketing	Product Focus Customer Acquisition Transactional Strategies	Customer Focus Customer Retention Relational Strategies	Sense Focus Customer Treatment Sensorial Strategies
Tactical Marketing	Persuasion and Promotion One-Way Communication Production Technology	Interaction and Interplay Two-Way Communication Information Technology	Dialogue and online interactivity Multi dimensional communication Digital Technology
Source: Developed from B.Hulten, N. Broweus, and M.van Dijk, *Sinnesmarknadsforing* (Malmo: Liber AB, 2008).			

Table 3. Examples of five sense which connects with the consumer

continued on following page

Table 3. Continued

Touch/Texture	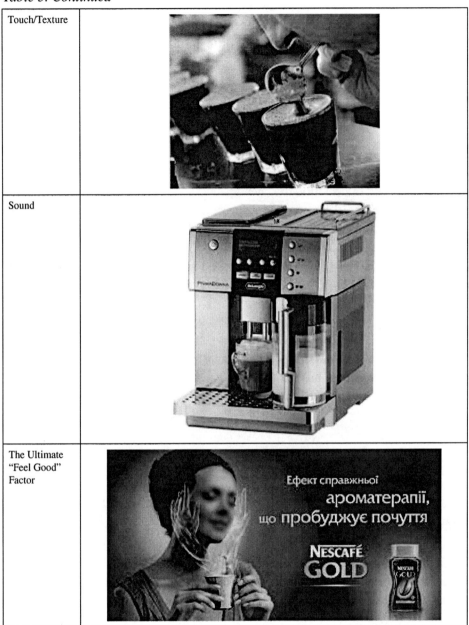
Sound	
The Ultimate "Feel Good" Factor	

According to memory retention studies, consumers are up to 78% more likely to remember a message printed in color that in black and white.[2] Visual aspect of a store must be considered to match four different functions, according to Roullet (in Rieunier 2009).

- **Alert Function:** The store should contrast with its surrounding to catch consumer attention even from far away.
- **Attracting Function:** The store must be able to make people willing to explore it, through its appearance.
- **Well-Being Function:** Meaning making easier for consumers to find the products and information they need.
- **The Coherence of the Visual Aspect:** With the offering and customer expectations (linked to the store positioning)[2] (Pantone Institute, 2000).

According to Kotler (1973), visual included layout, brightness and color. They are store environment cues that effect customers" mood and purchasing behaviors."

Layout

"Layout is the main visual design cue that influence customers" expectations of their efficient movement through a store". There are three perspectives in general that influence customer's perceptions and purchase behaviors.

These are

- Layout and "Information Rate",
- Layout and "Customers Moods",
- Layout and "Merchandise Evaluation".

Lighting

The light is also a major component of the environment. The lights in a store/ outlet/ restaurant can be either natural light, or softened artificial one. Artificial and Intense Lights will increase customers' dynamism. The vision gives the first impression of the quality, for the product as for the environment.

Literature about "in-store lighting" says:

- Kotler (1973) stated that consumer's perception of store image dependent on the conditions of in-store lighting.
- According to Mehrabian"s (1976) as cite from Areni and Kim (1994), a highly level of lighting will bring high arousal to people and make them

feel "stimulated, jittery and alert". On the other side, people in a non-arousing environment "will feel relaxed, calm, sluggish, or sleepy." Furthermore, highly aroused people will behave "increased heart rate, muscle tension, and lowered skin temperature". In this way, lighting is an extremely important determinant in the environment.

- Markin et al. (1976) suggested that retailers should implement soft lighting to reduce the arousal level of customer if they want the customers to pay more attention on products.
- Gorn (1982) used the example of a wine shop to indicate that the soft lighting was a clue in relating to merchandise quality evaluation: soft lighting may imply high quality.
- Steffy (1990) suggested that environments in which the "lighting is designed to harmonize with furniture and accessories are perceived as more pleasant than environments in which lighting does not harmonize with other elements of the room".
- On the opposite side, Areni and Kim (1994) found that shoppers have less interest in "visually oriented activities" (i.e. checking prices, reading labels, etc.) when in-store lighting levels are lower; i.e. consumers examined and handled more merchandise under brighter lighting.
- Summers and Hebert (2001) Were in view that consumers touched more items with an additional light display.

Colour

Colour, as a visual part of the physical environment, can bring "certain autonomic biological reaction, create certain emotional response, and obtain attention". The responses to colour are "immediate, direct and evoked rather than deliberated or mediated". For example, experiments show that warm colours such as red and yellow are "physically stimulating", whereas cool colours such as blue and green relax and calm. Table 4 sums up the characteristics of each colour and their impact on consumer behavior.

Auditory Branding

Sound is incredibly powerful in creating emotional connections and triggering memories. The auditory branding focus on creating a special sound, music etc. which touches heart of the customer, create emotional connections and also to enables him/her to imagine the attributes of the product. The recent Ads of Airtel, Jo Tera Hai, Wo Mera Hai and Har Ek Friend Jaroori Hota Hai are excellent examples of Branding through sounds. The Kaun Banega Crorepati music which is played before

Table 4.Color and its marketing implications

Color	Characteristics	Marketing Implications
Red	Highest stimulation hue: strong excitation power. Red increases the pulse and heart rate, as it raises blood pressure, and stimulates appetite	Really popular in restaurants as it increases appetite. However, due to its exciting properties, red is more likely to be used in bars.
Orange	Orange is friendlier than red, but still stimulate appetite and attract attention, especially among kids and teenagers.	Companies like Burger King or Dunkin Donuts use orange as main colour.
Pink	Sweet and appealing. The perfect color for sweets.	Mainly used by candies producers and sweet shops.
Yellow	Comforting color. It can also mean tangy, creamy or delicious connected to aliments.	Popular hue for tea houses or pastry shops. Ointment like Burnol.
Green	Meaning of refreshment and nature. Connected to vegetables, it is means healthiness for the consumer.	Green is a delicate color, as if not used in the right environment it is not appealing but can be repelling.
Blue	Associated with sea and sky calmness, suggest trust and serenity.	As blue icy hues refer to purity and coolness, this is the ideal colour for product like packaged water bottle.
White	Sign of purity, cleanness and coolness. White is the basic colour, as it brings out everything else.	In a restaurant, white is used everywhere the customer expects for cleanness (plates, kitchen…)
Black	On a packaging, black is symbol of top-of range, quality, and sobriety.	As it is the darkest colour, black is exclusively used to create a very specific environment.

the show starts and during break time also reflects the same. The consumers just by hearing the sound immediately recall the brand.

Music is in every point of sale or restaurant, and is an integrant part of the atmosphere, so are lightning or design, and whatever its place (discrete speakers or video-clips in a big flat TV) has a role to play in the customer perceptions. Background music is the cheapest and the easiest factor of atmosphere to manage (one button and it is off or a track is skipped, another one and sound is louder…), but it is definitely not the less powerful.

Studies about "music" say

- Music can also act on the "crowd management", by influencing the time spent inside by the customer. For example, according to two studies from Roballey & Ali (1985) and
- Milliman (1986), fast-tempo music will push the customer to leave earlier. In the other hand, a slow music played at low volume will increase the time and the money spends inside.

- Same studies revealed also that clients will eat faster and consume less with a loud volume and fast tempo music. Another research from Smith & Curnow (1966) revealed that in a point of sales, customer adopts his walk speed according to the tempo of the music. Music offers a wide range of possibility to the marketers to influence customers' behavior and complete the atmosphere to create a coherent sales environment.

The power of music is in its capacity to contextualize the different articles and support emotional states and poses. Music aims to put customer in a state of mind corresponding to the articles that are sold: play rock music in a guitar shop and the person will imagine himself playing with what could be his future purchase. Music can then, if connected to the product, be a way to act on the buying behavior of the customer. It is also proved in research that high volume music in a bar will increase the consumption of the customers.

Sound is used in Sensory Branding to evoke emotions and feelings to influence brand experiences and interpretations. Perhaps the second most used variable by marketing and advertising is the sense of hearing. Sound when matched with a message is a powerful way to make the customer remember it. Background music is an effective way to influence customer behavior at the point of purchase. If used properly, music can create a mood for the consumer that encourages them to buy. The potential for Auditory Branding is endless if used wisely by the marketers.

Table 5. The art of sound; popular auditory branding examples

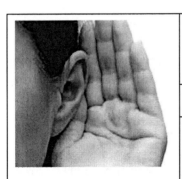

Harley Davidson: In 1994, Harley-Davidson attempted to register as a trademark the distinctive "chug" of a Harley-Davidson motorcycle engine. This "chug" has helped elevate the brand's perception, garner a cult-like following and command a higher price for its motorcycles.
McDonald's Corporation: "I'm lovin' it" is an international branding campaign used by McDonald's.
Volkswagen Beetle: High, front vowels are used in words that are small, quick and light. Hence the reason Volkswagen chose the name "Beetle" to brand its iconic, low-cost, miniature car. The name was quickly adopted by the public and was seamlessly integrated into pop culture (movies, songs, etc.)
Audi: associated the sounds of a steady heartbeat, a piano and a breath with its automobiles.
Mercedes Benz: assigned a team to create the most appealing sound for a closing card door.
In India, **Royal Enfield** uses the same sound to distinguish its motor cycles from the rest.

OLFACTORY BRANDING

Scent is one of the most memorable elements of sensory branding. It is an important mode of communication to guest experience. – Westin Hotels & Resorts (2009)

Recall your school days when new notebooks and copies for your new session spread its fragrance all over your study room. Our sense of smell is closely linked with memory and various researches have proved that school children increase performance when exposed to positive scents. Marketers have recognized the strength of smell and have started capitalizing the opportunity to use specific scents/ perfume/ aroma so that consumers may identify their brands.

Scientific studies have shown that 75% of our emotions are generated by the smell[4]. This is maybe the reason why the use of smells in a commercial way is increasing every day. Brown (2005) states smell stimulate certain areas of the brain which is responsible for creating emotions and memories. The most famous technique of olfactory marketing in the food industry is the use of artificial smells to appeal to customers in the street, subway or supermarkets.

Smell is one of the most powerful senses and directly linked to brain. Marketers are using Aroma Marketing strategies to leave an impression in the minds and hearts of the consumers. To quote a few of the strategies:

1. HUL aggressively communicates the special aroma of its Bru coffee brand. Coffee lovers associate high quality and purity (made from pure coffee beans) with nice aroma.
2. Another relevant example is "Arrey Hajoor…waah TAJ boliye" from the Taj Mahal Tea advertisement where the characters showcase mesmerising aroma of various flavours of Tea.
3. For quality-wise identical skin-care products, fragrance can be a great differentiator. Olfactory aspects of powders, sunscreen, fairness creams, moisturizing creams and body lotions, especially in case of "extract theme" products (like strawberry silk crème) speak about product ingredients and quality. However, the smell should not be too strong or repulsive to the consumer.

Smell, the language of scent, has been used throughout history and in all forms of propaganda, cultural divides and social distinctions of both class and education. It is now with such advanced research that scientists, sociologists and psychologists can use this information to construct bespoke scents, engineered to evoke response and relationship to brands.

Table 6. Sweet smell of victory: Some facts

 **Your Brand**	According to Spangenberg, Crowley & Henderson (1996), a pleasant smell influence positively the evaluation of the customer on a point of sale (and some of its products), the intent of walk-through, of buying, as on the time spent inside (real and perceived). But the precise olfactory characteristics that could be at the origin of these influences are not yet determined.
	Hirsch & Gay (1991) have noticed that women are more sensitive to smells than men. However, each gender doesn't have the reaction faced on the same smell: for instance, men stay longer than women in a shelf perfumed with spicy scent (Wall Street Journal, 1990), when women are more sensitive to shampoo smelling than men.
	The age of the customer modify his perception, as according to (Doty 1984, 1985), the sense of smell break up as the person gets older. In this way, there is also a difference between generations: persons born before 1930 are more likely to call up natural smells, when youngest report more food or artificial smell (Hirsh, 1992).

Research, points to the science of odour typing so that brands can create direct, emotional relationships with their customer in such a subverted way that the memory and limbic system drives the consumer loyalty.

The use of olfactory marketing can be interesting for a brand, provided that it knows how its target, to avoid a bad perception and then a negative impact.

GUSTATIVE BRANDING

Taste is one of the most difficult senses for marketers to use. Outside the realm of food and beverages companies, rarely brands use this strategy. Recall the advertisement of Taj Mahal Tea, where Zakir Hussain first smells and then taste the tea.

Do you know?

- ◦ People can detect 4 basic tastes – sweet, salty, sour, and bitter. But combined with our olfactory sense, we can perceive a variety of flavors and these flavors can be associated with a variety of feelings and emotions.
- ◦ Scientists now know that the 4 basic gustative sensations, sweet, sour, bitter and salty, are respectively linked by consumers to the red, green, blue and yellows colours (Célier, 2004). This might be important in the packaging design process of a product for instance.
- ◦ Chemical qualities of food pass through taste buds are then transmitted to brain. Smell and taste are closely linked together and referred as chemical sense (Korsmeyer, 2002).

The sensation of taste has an important role in human lives, like physical, social and emotional level. Since what we eat is closely linked to our survival, taste provides the most specific function of any of the five human senses. The first image that comes up to mind while talking about taste is the mouth. It is the organ which detects and identifies what we eat is called taste buds. There are many taste receptors called taste buds on the tongue. These buds are spread over the entire surface of the tongue.

A person can be exposed to aroma excluding the taste but it is almost impossible to taste something without smelling it (Lindstrom, 2005). The link between these senses is clear when people are asked to describe a brand involving both smell and taste. Brands like Dominos, Café Coffee Day, KFC, Pizza Hut, McDonalds, use this amalgamation very wisely. Here consumers tend to either like either both the smell and taste, or hate both the smell and taste. Even if a product is not directly linked to oral use, the taste aspect could still be included. In a promotional way, companies often use gustative marketing to convince consumers by making blind test or directly with sampling or free tasting promotional operations.

Our world is converging, and brands need to expand their experiential identities across multiple senses to enrich their brand, make it unique, and establish more emotional connections with customers.

Table 7. Taste success

Successful Stories of Brands Who Adopted Gustative Branding	
	In U.K.'s Royal Mail was experiencing a dramatic reduction in the volume of letters being sent, they sought to use sensory integration to enhance the affinity to their brand. Royal Mail sent its customers a personalized letter with a piece of chocolate. The results were fantastic. People began sending letters again, inspired by the experiential depth of the chocolate mailing.
	Charcoal companies choose to get associated with the smell or taste of barbecue.
	In 2007 Skoda Fabia baked a cake that looked exactly like the real car and they filmed this whole process. They wanted to project Fabia as a "sweet & tasty" car. During the first week of the campaign, sales went up by 160 percent.
	In a promotional way, companies often use gustative marketing to convince customers, by making blind-tests (trough comparatives advertisements for instance) or directly with sampling or free-tasting promotional operations.

TACTILE BRANDING

Touch is very important in marketing. Indeed often the clients need to touch the product in order to test its texture, its quality etc… that is why marketers try to take in considerations these elements during the conception of the product choosing appropriated materials but also during the commercialization by the selection of the packaging.

The power of touch can empower a brand identity and make it more attractive and captivating to the customers. A customer is forced to engage in psychological and physical interaction with the brand, the moment he touches a product. Touch creates a sort of intimacy between the consumer and the brand.

Recall an incident when you visited the famous Saree Shop in your town, and your mom shall "Touch and Feel" her favorite picks before deciding the final one. Yes, Touch Sense indirectly associates with the consumer's emotions.

Touch can tap into imaginations and emotions through newer technologies appearing across printing platforms, including dimensional printing, foil printing, embossing, and glitter application on press, as well as in lamination. Marketers try to take in account the emotions sparked off by this touch during the conception of the product (pen, clothes, car steering wheel…) or its conditioning (perfume bottle, crisps pack).

Table 8. Feel the difference

	Restaurants take into account the weight of the cutleries or the softness of the napkins, the comfort of a chair because these factors can have a repercussion on the customer's perception.
	An Apple store allows the audience to freely touch and test all the products.
	The bottle of the French mineral water brand *Valvert* evocates through its rough touching the natural origin of its source in the heart of the mountains.
	Microsoft invented a Keyboard and a mouse made in semi leather to create an extra sensation of softness and comfort for the consumer.
	Brands associated with Personal Care Products like soaps, shampoos, Face Wash, scrubs, Talcum Powder, Brush also pay considerable attention to the 'Touch' factor.
	The unique metallic surface of the iPhone can be associated with the brand even without seeing it.

Touch is one of the major determinants of the well-being sensation. Have a look around you; the marketers have tapped this unconquered zone with excellence. The touch screen mobile phones, laptops, tabs, palmtops and so on, uncountable examples and many more yet to approach in the coming years.

SENSORY BRANDING: IMPACT ON RESPONSE AND RETENTION

Sensory marketing is a deep and complex concept, as it deals with the sensorial/emotional attachment of the consumers: their perceptions, feelings, likings and tastes.

Advertising researchers have observed the sensorial effect for years; only the interesting bits of ads gets stick to consumers memory and get played back at ad recall questions. Therefore, when the brand and message are not intrinsically relevant (which will be most of the time), they must be integrated into the creative manner so that a consumer gets engaged with it. The "footprint" of engagement is advertising memorability. Because memorability is an inevitable by-product of engagement, when consumers remember advertising, we can safely assume that they engaged with it.

How brands impact our brain:

- Numerous research studies have demonstrated that brands can have significant impact on consumption experience. An experiment was conducted by the researchers, where consumers were asked to taste wine presented in a bottle of prestige brand label or a budget brand label. When tasting from the budget brand bottle, people rated the tasting experience quite poorly. And when tasting from the prestige brand bottle, they rated the wine quite positively. Of course, the researchers gave them the same wine in both the cases, so what they tasted was completely determined by their brand expectations.
- Using fMRI (Functional Magnetic Resonance Imaging) technique the same experiment was repeated while the consumers were enjoying their wine. The results were quite stunning: Participants actually experienced the taste of the wine differently when it was presented as a prestige brand instead of a budget brand.
- This powerful impact is sometimes called the placebo effect of branding, which means that the brand doesn't actually change the physical experience.
- Researchers have suggested this example as how people consume concepts rather than just physical products.

   ◦   In simple terms, you may attribute your satisfaction with a product to its physical consumption or usage, but in fact, the concept about the consumption experience represents is impacting your response the most.

Let's consider Figure 1 to understand the impact of sensory branding and emotional attachment on consumer's memory, retention and response.

BRANDING INITIATIVES BY FIRMS

Branding strategies helps the firms to establish a product within the market and to build a brand that will grow and mature in a saturated marketplace. Making smart branding decisions are really crucial since a company may have to live with the decision for a long time.

Figure 1. Model depicting the impact of sensorial involvement and emotional attachment on purchase decision and brand loyalty

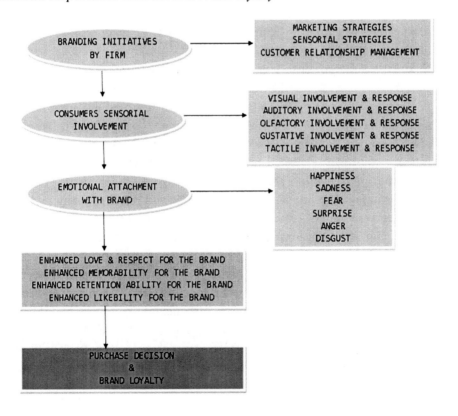

Marketing Strategies

Marketing Strategies can be:

1. Differentiating and positioning the market offering.
2. Developing new products.
3. Managing life-cycle strategies.
4. Designing appropriate competitive strategies (leader, challenger, follower, nicher).
5. Designing global marketing strategy.
6. Marketing mix strategies (product related, pricing decisions, marketing channel decisions, promotion decisions).

Sensorial Strategies

1. **Visual:** Synonymous to understanding and believing. It is a very effective sense that affects purchase decisions and hence targeted most by marketers. Arrangement, infrastructure, aesthetics and illumination of new Malls/Superstores are designed in such a way, just to attract the customers and make them visit again and again. Cloth stores use techniques like mannequins to display their best offerings. Supermarkets keep fresh fruits and vegetables on display to attract customers.

2. **Sound:** Has the power to impact one's mood and sway their buying habits. Researchers have found that the pace of background music affects customer perceptions of wait time, spending and turnover in stores and restaurants. As a marketing tool, sound is a messenger of sorts, often reaching us before we reach a product or even have a visual image. It can evoke a sense of quality, increase consumer relevance, boost recall, and impact purchase intent.

3. **Smells:** Stimulate certain areas of the brain responsible for creating emotions and memories. The human nose can identify and recall as many as 10,000 scents and as much as 75 percent of emotions are generated by what a human smells. Out of all the senses, smell is the only one with a direct link to the brain. Marketers have been leveraging the power of scent for decades. It can be divided into most common strategies into three categories: 1) product scenting (shampoos n candles) 2) environmental scenting (retail space, movie theatres) 3) advertising scenting (scented ink in print materials).

4. **Taste:** Linked to emotions. It can help an individual to change the brand perception and image. Brands/shops offer free sample of food products (especially new launches) in order to make better impact of product on customer mind.

Pizza Hut, pizza chain by Yum takes all efforts to maintain the taste of its pizzas same worldwide.

5. **Touch:** Proves an important link between our brains and the world. In fact, humans have more tactile receptors in their little fingers alone than their entire back. These receptors help in exploring objects in their surroundings. When a pleasant touch is encountered, the brain releases a hormone called oxytocin, leading to feelings of well-being and calm. Researchers have found that shoppers who touch a product are more likely to purchase, even as it relates to impulse buys.

Customer Relationship Management

Customer Relationship Management is a strategy used to learn more about customers' needs and behaviors in order to develop stronger relationships with them. Good customer relationships are at the heart of business success. CRM can be termed as a strategic process that helps the firms to better understand their customers' needs and how to meet those needs and enhance customer satisfaction. This strategy depends on bringing together lots of pieces of information about customers and market trends that a firm can sell and market their products and services more effectively.

CONSUMER'S SENSORIAL INVOLVEMENT

Given the gamut of explicit marketing appeals made to consumers every day, subconscious trigger/s which appeals to the basic senses may be a more efficient way to engage consumers.

The human brain uses multiple sources of sensory information derived from the modalities of vision, touch, hearing, smell and taste, by merging them efficiently to form a coherent and robust perception of the world. These multisensory signals originate simultaneously from a physical event like an in store experience

EMOTIONAL ATTACHMENT WITH BRAND

Emotion is like Everest. Emotions are psychological phenomena representing ways of adapting to certain environmental situations or one's particular state. Emotions are an interesting amalgamation of Biology (The Body), Psychology (The Mind), and Sociology (Our relationship with others).

Understanding Emotions

Emotions are a perfect example of how everything in our body works as an inter-related whole. When we experience an emotion, our body and our state of mind react at the same time, in a synchronized fashion. Emotions flood our whole being and make us reach as a whole. Emotions color our lives.

Six basic emotions
- **Happiness:** Positive Emotion, directly related to everything that makes us feel good at all levels.
- **Sadness:** Negative emotion, one wishes to avoid.
- **Fear:** It acts to protect the individual. Although negative valence yet it fulfills the survival function
- **Surprise:** The emotional reaction to an unanticipated or new situation. May be positive or negative, depending on the content.
- **Anger:** Negative reaction of a hostile/aggressive nature.
- **Disgust/ Aversion:** A negative emotional reaction, both physical & psychological when confronted with unpleasant objects/ situations.

Responses

1. **Enhanced Love and Respect:** Love and Respect are the most critical component in building and maintaining a strong, emotionally driven and enduring brand. This bond is wholly on strong emotional connections as a result of the perceived share values between the brand and the customer.
2. **Enhanced Memorability and Retention Ability:** Powerful emotional currents exist as part of the human conditions. Human beings are in fact the most complex emotional concepts that God has created. Great brands find relevant ways to tap the emotional drivers that already reside deep within all individuals.
3. **Enhanced Likeability:** Once the consumers are able to connect with the brand, the likeability automatically increases. Consumers are looking for brands that are visible and have potentiality, the one who not only promises but also 'delivers'.

Purchase Decision and Brand Loyalty

Enhanced Love, Trust and Respect shall contribute to enhanced memorability and retention of the brand, which in turn shall increase the likeability for the brand. All the factors shall contribute to the Purchase Decision and Brand Loyalty (repetitive purchase).

Role of Emotions in Purchase Decision

Emotions have a direct impact on consumer decision-making and purchase decision. Emotional thinking works much faster than rational/logical thinking. Our gut feeling directs very quick reactions.

Whenever consumers are confronted with a brand, they experience emotions. We do not only consume a product, we are also emotional consumers. We eat chocolates or drink warm drinks such as coffee when we feel sad. We drink tea to relax and take away our agitation. Because of our typical memory structures, our perceptions are constantly coloured by our emotions.

What the heart thinks, the mind speaks. People who experience an emotion tend to start a communication process to share this emotion with others. Research found that only 10 per cent of the emotional experiences are kept secret and never socially shared with anyone. The more disruptive the event, the sooner and more frequently it will be shared. Social sharing of emotions is also positively related to the intensity of emotions. Emotions do not only appear to be an important element in stimulating word-of-mouth but also in creating online buzz.

SENSORY BRANDING AND MARKETING STRATEGIES

Any assessment of brand strategies needs to measure the strength of a brand's associations in terms of Knowledge, Experience, and Emotion. Most marketers give due importance to Knowledge module. Emotion has enjoyed more prominence in recent years as marketers have paid increased attention to the emotional connections people form with brands. But in terms of Experience, rarely marketers attempt to deliver the same to the consumers. Sensory Branding techniques may allow the strategists to attempt an interesting amalgamation of Knowledge, Experience and Emotion.

CONCLUSION

Gone are the days when simple advertisements like "Swaad Bhare, Shakti Bhare Parle-G" used to create market shaking effects. Today the markets are more competitive and are buzzing with number of players. The conventional advertisements are not enough to make the impact on customer's mind. This is the time, to make consumers *feel* more intensely what additional functions and emotional value a product of a company has to offer for its customers, compared to its competitors.

Sensory branding is exploding. It stands to reason that as technology makes sensory integration more practical and affordable; marketers will be looking to it as the logical new frontier. As companies diversify their product offerings, new sensory marketing tactics will better allow consumers to trial a new product before purchasing. Likewise, sensory cues such as sound and smell will help companies develop greater emotional connections to their brands.

Sensory branding makes intuitive sense. The time is right to evaluate sensory branding. Early proponents of sensory branding are finding that its potential to strengthen their brands is making their initial efforts worthwhile. Whether it includes the customized scent in a new car or the sound track in a hotel lobby, the new emphasis on identity systems of sensory elements promises much more opportunity to connect with customers and to create lasting differentiation.

CLOSING CASE: APPLE USES SENSORY BRAND MARKETING

APPLE is one of the leading branding companies in the world. Marketing Experts like Marc Gobe argue that Apple's Brand is the key to the company success.

During the late 1980s and early 1990s it was a marketing executive from Pepsi, John Sculley, who turned Apple into the biggest single computer company in the world, with $11 billion in annual sales. Sculley marketed Apple like crazy, boosting the advertising budget from $15 million to $100 million."People talk about technology, but Apple was a marketing company," Sculley told the *Guardian* newspaper in 1997. "It was the marketing company of the decade."

The current CEO, Steve Jobs, spent $100 million marketing the iMac, which was a run-away hit. Apple continues to spend lots of money on high-profile ads like the "Switch" campaign, and it shows.

Apple is a really powerful brand. It was awarded as the "Brand of the Year" in 2001. The overwhelming presence of Apple comes through in everything they do. That's the magic.

Apple is the archetypal emotional brand. It's not just intimate with its customers; it is loved. Apple is about imagination, design and innovation. It goes beyond commerce.

The brand is all they've got. The power of their branding is all that keeps them alive. It's got nothing to do with products. Apple has established deep, lasting bonds with their customers.

Before Steve Jobs joined the company, the brand was pretty much gone. It was imperative that Apple should be rebranded – so as to rejuvenate the brand. Apple abandoned the old rainbow-hued Apple logo in favor of a minimalist monochrome one, gave its computers a funky, colorful look, and streamlined the messages in its advertising.

The sensory strategy appealed the customers. And results were wonderful. People's connections with Apple transcend commerce.

According to Marketer Marc Gobe, author of *Emotional Branding*, "Apple comes across as profoundly humanist. Its founding ethos was power to the people through technology, and it remains committed to computers in education. Apple has a unique visual and verbal vocabulary, expressed in product design and advertising is clearly recognizable. Apple's products are designed around people, consider the iPod, it brings an emotional, sensory experience to computing. Apple's design is people-driven. Apple has always projected a human touch -- from the charisma of Steve Jobs to the notion that its products are sold for a love of technology."

The human touch is expressed in product design. Apple's flat-screen iMac, for example, was marketed as though it were created personally by Steve Jobs and Jonathan Ive, not by factory workers in Asia.

Apple has established a "heartfelt connection" with its customers. It's like having a good friend. Somewhere they have created this really humanistic, beyond-business relationship with users and created a cult-like relationship with their brand. It's a big tribe, everyone is one of them. We all are part of the brand.

CURRENT CHALLENGES FACING THE ORGANIZATION

Starbucks

1. **Increased Competition:** This is by far the biggest threat that Starbucks faces with the market being at a mature stage, there is increased pressure on Starbucks from its competitors like Dunkin Brands, McDonalds, Costa Coffee, Pete's Coffee, mom and pop specialty coffee stores. Dunkin Brands had at its main threat in the US market by trailing Starbucks with a 24.6% share.
2. **Price Volatility in the Global Coffee Market:** There has been a significant fluctuation in the market prices of high quality coffee beans, which Starbucks can't control.
3. **Changing Consumer Tastes and Lifestyle Choices:** The shift of consumers toward more healthy products and the risk of coffee culture being just a fad represent a threat for Starbucks going into the future.

Apple

1. **Intense Competition:** The biggest challenge for Apple Inc. is competition. Apple is competing against big brands like Google Inc., Dell, IBM, Microsoft, etc.
2. **Continuous Research and Development:** Apple is successfully growing because of its rigorous R & D and risk taking ability. Apple should continue the same momentum for more innovative products in the market.

SOLUTIONS AND RECOMMENDATIONS

The basic challenge that both the companies are facing, i.e. Starbucks and Apple is Intense Competition and changing customer preferences. The only solution for combating with these two issues is to create a core competence which shall retain the customers and handle the competition. Sensory Branding can be an answer to address the issues, which both of these brands have already identified and are working on it.

Buyers of Apple computers, iPhones and other products know it all too well, the smell of a new device. This very specific smell is rumored to come from inside the devices, but some have suggested that the packaging is responsible. The plastic iPhone has the same smell as the aluminum MacBook, so the scent is probably not added to the plastic.

Starbucks' philosophy is to give satisfaction to consumers not only in realms of taste, but also olfactory, visual, tactile, and auditory sense. In order to purse such goals, Starbucks is making an effort to consistently create a sound, perfume, font, and taste that can appeal to consumers. From this, consumers are able to enjoy coffee at a refreshing and comfortable environment. Regardless of countries and places, consumers share the similar experience at atmosphere at Starbucks.

REFERENCES

Aitamer, G., & Zhou, Q. (2011). *Motives and guidance for the use of sensory marketing in retailing*. (Master's Thesis). Karlstad Business School.

Alba, J. W., & Chattopadhyay, A. (1986). Salience effects in brand recall. *JMR, Journal of Marketing Research*, 23(4), 363–369. doi:10.2307/3151812

Alba, J. W., & Hutchinson, J. W. (1987). Dimensions of consumer expertise. *The Journal of Consumer Research*, 13(March), 411–454. doi:10.1086/209080

Andrade, E. B. (2005). Behavioral conseuqences of affect: Combining evaluative and regulatory mechanisms. *The Journal of Consumer Research, 32*(December), 355–362. doi:10.1086/497546

Batra, R., Aaron, A., & Bagozzi, P. (2012). Brand love. *Journal of Marketing, 76*(March), 1–16. doi:10.1509/jm.09.0339

Block, L. G., & Keller, P. A. (1998). Beyong protection motivation: An integrative theory of health appeals. *Journal of Applied Social Psychology, 28*(September), 1584–1608. doi:10.1111/j.1559-1816.1998.tb01691.x

Brody, L. R., & Hall, J. A. (2000). Gender, emotion, and expression. In *Handbook of emotions* (2nd ed.). New York: Guilford.

Broniarczyk, S. M., & Alba, J. W. (1994). The importance of the brand in brand extension. *JMR, Journal of Marketing Research, 31*(May), 214–228. doi:10.2307/3152195

Chattopadhyay, A. (1998). When does comparative advertising influence brand attitude? The role of delay and market position. *Psychology and Marketing, 15*(5), 461–475. doi:10.1002/(SICI)1520-6793(199808)15:5<461::AID-MAR4>3.0.CO;2-5

Chattopadhyay, A., & Nedungadi, P. (1992). Does attitude toward the ad endure? The effects of delay and attention. *The Journal of Consumer Research, 19*(1), 26–33. doi:10.1086/209283

Domenico, C. (2010). A new concept of marketing: The emotional marketing. *Broad Research in Accounting, Negotiation, and Distribution, 1*(1).

Eiseman, L. (2000). *Pantone guide to communicating with color*. Sarasota, FL: Grafix Press, Ltd.

Eriksson, E. (2001). *A multi-sensory brand experience- Sensorial interplay and its impact on consumers' touch behavior*. (Master's Thesis). School of Business and Economics, Linnaeus University.

Keller, A., & Block, L. G. (1996). Increasing the persuasiveness of fear appeals: The effect of arousal and elaboration. *The Journal of Consumer Research, 22*(March), 448–459. doi:10.1086/209461

Kotler, P. (1973/74). Atmospherics as a marketing tool. *Journal of Retailing, 49*(4), 4–64.

Lange, F., & DahleAn, M. (2003). Let's be strange: Brand familiarity and ad-brand incongruency. *Journal of Product and Brand Management, 12*(72003), 449–46.

Lee, Y. H., & Mason, C. (1999). Responses to information incongruency in advertising: The role of expectancy, relevancy, and humor. *The Journal of Consumer Research*, *26*(September), 156–169. doi:10.1086/209557

Loken, B., & Roedder-John, D. (1993). Diluting brand beliefs: When do brand extensions have a negative impact? *Journal of Marketing*, *57*, 71–84.

Loken, B., & Ward, J. (1990). Alternative approaches to understanding the determinants of typicality. *The Journal of Consumer Research*, *17*(September), 111–126. doi:10.1086/208542

Low, G. S., & Lamb, C. W. Jr. (2000). The measurement and dimensionality of brand associations. *Journal of Product and Brand Management*, *9*(6), 350–368. doi:10.1108/10610420010356966

Martin, L. (2005). Broad sensory branding. *Journal of Product and Brand Management*, *14*(2), 84–87.

Pechmann, C., & Stewart, D. W. (1990). The effects of comparative advertising on affection, memory, and purchase intentions. *The Journal of Consumer Research*, *17*(September), 180–191. doi:10.1086/208548

Travis, D. (2000). *Emotional branding: How successful brands gain the irrational edge*. Roseville, CA: Prima Publishing.

Valenti, C., & Riviere, J. (2008). *The concept of sensory marketing*. (Marketing Dissertation). Hogskolan I Halmstad.

KEY TERMS AND DEFINITIONS

Auditory Branding: Sound helps to communicate the tone of a brand and encourage an emotional reaction. For example soft, relaxing music is played at beauty spas in an effort to help consumers unwind and escape, while upbeat music is often used in TV commercials or clothing stores to communicate the fun attitude of the brand.

Customer Relationship Management: A strategy used to learn more about customers' needs and behaviors in order to develop stronger relationships with them.

Emotional Branding: A creative strategy in developing, building, and managing the brand to build loyalty, drive perceived quality, provide differentiation, and create credibility through a relational and story-driven approach to forging deep and enduring affective bonds between consumers and brands. The term was coined by Marc Gobe.

Gustative Branding: Taste is an individual experience that differs greatly between people. Subconsciously taste is assumed, so if the colour, texture and smell of food are appealing it is assumed that the taste will be pleasing.

Olfactory Branding: The strongest sense for evoking memories, the smell of a product or its surrounding environment reaches us on an emotional level. For example the smell of a lightly fragranced department store can subconsciously lead us to stay longer and enjoy the experience, developing a lasting positive memory associated with the fragrance and store.

Sensory Branding: Based on the idea that consumers are most likely to form, retain and revisit memory when all five senses are engaged. It creates emotional, cognitive, behavioral and relational experiences through five senses so to enhance the chance of product purchase. In such a case, the consumer behaves according to his emotions more than his reasons and logic.

Tactile Branding: Weight, texture, form, and finish all have an impact on our evaluation of a product. For example top end, expensive goods are associated with a smooth, silky feel, while environmentally friendly products generally have a rougher texture. Customers will subconsciously make purchase decisions and judgments on brands based on initial touch.

Visual Branding: Brand identities are built on strong visual design foundations. Logos, colors and fonts should be carefully selected to evoke different emotions and encourage a particular response or thought process. The lighting of a store is also crucial at presenting a product and conveying an environment as being warm and inviting, dark and dingy or as stark and clinical.

Conclusion

CASE 1

"A Scheme for Identifying Branding Strategies with Case-Based Identification of Internal and External Issues," by Abu Sayeed Mondal and Dilip Roy of India talks about a strategic platform to pinpoint the variables for developing branding strategies. The case describes the concept of branding as described by Philip Kotler "the name, associated with one or more items in the product line, which is used to identify the source of character of the item(s)." Branding is all about making the products and services equipped with the power of the brand. Brand enables consumers aware of product's meaning and benefits and the reasons for consumers' craving for the products and service.

Brand makes the consumers identify the source of the product. As branded goods are perceived by the consumers are of quality products, they do not have to spend much time to make brand purchase decisions. Thus, brand reduces the perceived risk of the consumers and save their valuable time. The consumers also develop relationship with the manufacturers due to brand awareness and associations.

There are five branding eras: identification oriented, generic branding, image oriented, communication oriented and innate value oriented- in this chapter. In identification branding era branding means making the consumers identify the goods and services. Generic branding involves offering commodity like products in the form of brands. Image oriented branding era seeks to create favorable image of the brand to attract the consumers. To communicate effectively with consumers is the basic practice in communication oriented branding era, where as innate value oriented branding era recognizes brand as an asset.

Branding efforts to ensure brand's specific mode of communication and its adjustments to the external environment is called internal effort. External realization is the brand's external effect realized by the consumers. These two dimensions – internal effort and external realization- vary from low to high and their interplay gives rise to a four-cell strategy matrix known as C_4 strategy matrix.

There are four types of branding strategies recommended in C_4 strategy matrix. These four strategies are continuity, caution, change and correction. These strategies are known as the C_4 strategy.

Conclusion

The authors analyze the branding problem of Shahnaz Herbals in the light of C_4 strategy matrix, Shahnaz Hussain brand falls in the 1st cell of C_4 strategy matrix. In this cell the strategy recommended is the continuity strategy. So, the most suitable strategy here is continuity strategy.

Brand managers must strategically manage brands to ensure brands' success and long term sustainability. This strategic approach is required to enable brand communicate and compete effectively and to adjust to the changes in its external environment. This chapter seeks to develop a strategic premise on the basis of these issues and offer a strategic approach to brand management. The prime task in this work is to identify the internal and external aspects of a brand and develop an approach matching these two aspects. Internal and external aspects of a brand have been identified in the backdrop of existing literature and a case analysis. A conceptual model has been suggested for decision making to make the proposed concept operational.

The authors have done extensive survey of literature on branding and have offered adequate knowledge on the understanding of brands and different dominating branding concepts in various industrial eras. The readers can be the authors aware of the importance of branding and branding strategies. A thorough guide line to initiate and improve the thoughts of the brand planners setting out to formulate branding strategies is also available. Furthermore, the strategic tool proposed herein will be of general appeal to the brand planners irrespective of product field and market.

CASE 2

"Promoting Bucovina's Tourism Brand," by Prof. Alexandru NEDELEA talks about place branding. Bucovina area is among the most popular cultural destinations in Romania, together with Transylvania and Maramures. What Bucovina stands out for centuries is its Orthodox-Christian religion. Also, 'hosting' the UNESCO (United Nations Educational, Scientific, and Cultural Organisation) World Heritage Sites on its territory makes it a unique place in the world. Bucovina attracts wide range of tourists, from backpackers to businessmen, who come to 'gaze' upon the frescos and experience a mixture of heritage, cultural and religious tourism.

Most of the tourists are coming by organized tours which are mainly focused at the monasteries. Religious built heritage is a particular strength for Bucovina. Today's traveller is mainly interested in the tourist circuits, which includes the famous monasteries, Arbore, Humor, Moldovita, Sucevita, Suceava, Patrauti, Probota and Voronet, with their painted frescoes on the exterior walls. The value and the density of the historical monuments, such as monasteries, some of them unique in the whole world, ranked and listed in the "Protected Universal Heritage" by UNESCO in 1972, situates Bucovina on the first position in the country, in what the cultural and historical resources are concerned.

Amongst the strengths of Bucovina region there are: the multitude of types of tourism practiced in Bucovina: itinerant tourism with cultural valences, the balneary tourism, rural tourism, ecotourism, transit tourism, hunting and fishing tourism, riding tourism, winter sports tourism, congresses and reunions tourism, leisure and recreational tourism; hospitality of the inhabitants; the diversity of tourism resources, natural and anthropogenic easily accessible and harmoniously distributed; water quality and a great variety of mineral waters; diversity of organic food, at very low prices; traditional kitchen and specialties regional; pollution very low; temperate continental climate favorable to the practice of tourism throughout the year; the variety of folklore and traditions inherited well preserved and practiced and now (New Eve's customs, masks, traditional music/dances); rich calendar of trade fairs and folk events throughout the year and all areas. In order to create Bucovina touristic brand it is necessary to create a customized unitary offer of Bucovina. Creating a Bucovina touristic brand must take into account the fact that it is necessary that this product be a complete one which includes: the cultural attraction visiting (monasteries, museums, churches, citadels etc.), sports tourism (hunting and fishing, mountain-biking, trekking, river-rafting) relaxation tourism, rural tourism which is included in more optional programs.

The promotion of Bucovina tourism brand can bring numerous economic and social advantages to the area: the differentiation of the tourism product of Bucovina form the other similar products, granting it an extra value; growing the perception of the global product, triggering and favoring the selling price of the private tourism products related to Bucovina; the possibility of launching new products much faster and more efficiently; the creation of the conditions of collaboration with the greatest international tour-operators.

The promotion program of the brand of Bucovina must take into account objectives such as: the presentation in a more attractive way of the advantages the tourists will have by visiting the region and the creation of a very good reputation of the tourism services provided in this area; creation of the adequate organizational frame – partnership type – between the public organisms of the central and local administration, economic agents, professional associations and organizations, having their own organization and operating statute; creation of a slogan for Bucovina tourism.

The promotion program of the brand of Bucovina must include also: the increase of the quality of the services provided to tourists by the operators; the increase in the number of tourists in Bucovina; the increase of the incomes obtained from tourism; the creation and permanent updating of a database comprising the objectives and the tourism companies in Bucovina; the identification of the main attractions; the performance of an inventory of all information centers for tourists on the county's territory; the establishment of tourist's information points/centers in the communes which represent the limits of the county, the border localities and in the localities having a great tourism potential; the elaboration and the promotion of the yearly calendar of events: festivals, fairs; the elaboration of marketing and business plans for the local entrepreneurs; the creation of a tourist trademark of Bucovina.

The lessons learnt from this case are enumerated below:

1. **Motivation of the Tourists Visiting Bucovina Region:** Since years, the core motivation for travelling to Bucovina was culture and nature. Tourists may visit because they have an educational interest in learning more about the history of Bucovina or understanding Christianity religious faith and its culture and beliefs, rather than being motivated purely by pleasure-seeking or spiritual growth. cultural and heritage tourism is a form of tourism in which participants seek to learn about and experience the past and present cultures of themselves and of others.

2. **Importance of Promoting Bucovina's Tourism Brand:** Tourism has a strategic importance for the Bucovina region. It is one of the few sectors where Bucovina has clear competitive advantages. Brand Bucovina should be urgently prioritized and within it there is a need to promote Bucovina's diverse and tourist unique attractions. A promotion program of the Bucovina brand it is compulsory because there is a fierce competition on Western European markets and other foreign markets, while the competing destinations offer a wide range of facilities for all kind of tourists.

3. **Requirements of an Efficient Promotion of Bucovina Brand:** Before starting a marketing campaign for promoting Bucovina's tourism brand it is necessary a better segmentation of the offer, of value proposals and an increasing of quality. In the effort of developing and promoting the tourism in this region, the actions of policy makers in tourism and of the local entrepreneurs must be focused not to offer "all for everyone", but to elaborate a coherent marketing strategy at the level of entire tourist region of Bucovina. Better event data collection and dissemination is required in order to promote efficiently the Bucovina tourism brand.

CASE 3

"Branding and Brand Management: Case of Amul," by Dr. Anupam Sharma talks about the one of India's most beloved brand AMUL. Amul (Anand Milk-producers Union Limited), formed on December 14, 1946, is a dairy cooperative organization of India. It is a brand name managed by cooperative organisation, Gujarat Cooperative Milk Marketing Federation Ltd. (GCMMF), which today is jointly owned by some 2.41 million milk producers in Gujarat, India. It is situated in Anand town of Gujarat and has been a true example of a co-operative business organization's success. The Amul Pattern has established itself as a completely suitable model for rural expansion and growth.

The brand name Amul, has been originated from the Sanskrit word *Amoolya*, it means *priceless*. So Amul means priceless.

In 1946, initiative of milk production was taken by Sardar Vallabhai Patel. Patel has developed innovative ideas and thoughts adjacent to the privately owned Polson dairy and established as the first cooperative society known as Kaira District Cooperative Milk Producers' Union Limited (KDCMPUL). The motto behind establishment of cooperative society was "No Cooperation, No Progress!" spreader very fast and milk was used as a sign to object against British hegemony, throughout a 15-day farmers' strike.

Initially Amul started with 2 village societies and collected 247 liters of milk per day. The society grew and, in 1973, the Gujarat Cooperative Milk Marketing Federation (GCMMF) was established in the state of Gujarat for marketing the milk and milk products of cooperative unions. In the year 1980s the word Amul was transformed into a brand. At present, in the state of Gujarat, Amul manufactures 10.16 million liters of milk daily, that is collected from 2.7 million farmers, further processed by30 dairy plants, and circulated through 500,000 retail outlets.

Starting with a single common plant at Anand and two village cooperative societies for milk procurement, the dairy cooperative movement of State of Gujarat had developed into a network of 2.12 million milk producers (i.e., farmers) who are organized in 10,411 milk collection cooperatives (called Village Societies). These Village Societies (VS) further supply milk to thirteen independent dairy cooperatives (called Unions).

Amul Butter: Pricing Strategy

Today GCMMF is India's largest exporter of Dairy Products. It has been known as a "Trading House" status. GCMMF has received the APEDA Award from Government of India for Excellence in Dairy Product Exports continuously for the last 9 years.

Despite of high competition in the dairy product segment from firms such as Hindustan Lever, Nestle and Britannia, GCMMF guarantees that the product mix and the series in which Amul launch its products is reliable with the core values of delivering butter at a basic, reasonable price to plea the common masses. This price strategy initially helped AMUL BUTTER to create its brand image in the domestic sector of the society.

Conclusion

Effective implementation of pricing strategy of Amul resulted that, at present Amul has 2.41 million milk producer members with average milk collection of 5.08 million litres/day. Moreover India, Amul has penetrated overseas markets such as Mauritius, UAE, USA, Bangladesh, China, Singapore, Australia, Hong Kong and a few South African countries.

Many researchers believe that the charm of Amul publicity and popularity lies in the catchy lines followed by them in the advertisements. Because the humor created by adds was enjoyed by all. They don't mention on anyone's nationality or hurt people's sentiments. These ads are pure and simple, everyday fun.

In 1966, Sylvester daCunha, joined ad agency of Amul. At that time, situation of India was like one couldn't afford to have food and food products. Sylvester daCunha decided it was time to change the image. Scott Bradbury, the marketing genius behind success of Nike and Starbucks, once said "A giant brand is a legend that is never completely told. A brand is a symbolic story that's developing all the time. Stories create the exciting context that people need to locate themselves in the larger practices".

Since the Sixties to the Nineties, the Amul ads have come a long way. whereas most citizens agree that the Amul ads were at their peak in the Eighties they still continue that the Amul ads continue to rag a laughter out of them The Amul ads are one of the greatest running ads based on a theme, now vying for the Guinness proceedings for being the fastest running ad movement ever.

Amul has opened Scooping Parlors across the country including cities like Mumbai, Chennai, Delhi, Bangaluru, Thane, Pune, Kolkata, Nagpur, Ahmedabad and Coimbatore. Apart from these cities, Amul is planning to open up Amul Scooping Parlors in different parts of the country too.

These Parlors have been well welcomed by customers and are doing cheerful business. Some of the recipes offered at these Parlors include:

- Simply Delicious Ice Cream Scoops.
- Double and Triple Sundaes.
- Double Swirl/Magic Swirl.
- Thick Shakes.
- Amul Kool Drinks.

Amul also offers a brilliant business prospect to entrepreneurs who want to open up franchisees of the Amul Scooping Parlors and can become part of the rising ice cream industry with India's most admired brand.

In the ever changing globalized world modern technology and various e-initiatives taken up by Amul also contributed in the success of the brand. GCMMF's technology strategy is composed of four distinctive components i.e., new products, process technology, and complementary assets to enhance milk production and e-commerce.

Automation in processing and packaging areas is regular, as is HACCP certification. Amul aggressively follow progress in embryo transfer and cattle breeding to regulate and to improve cattle quality and to increases in milk yields.

GCMMF was among one of the first FMCG (fast-moving consumer goods) firm in India to utilize Internet expertise to execute B2C commerce.

Today customers can select a diversity of products through the Internet and be secure of timely delivery with cash on payment option.

Emergence of globalization and liberalization has given confinement to numerous key proposals into Indian economy. Forces and factors enforced by globalization into Indian economy are quality conscious movement, conscious consumer and corporate social responsibility.

Corporate social responsibility (CSR) has been defined as a "assurance of business and firms to contribute for sustainable economic growth by working with employees, workers their families, serving the local community, and society at large to improve the quality of life, in a way that both society and business get the development."

As fact natural resources are depicting at a faster pace, and Gujarat is not an exception, over the time, demanding agriculture and dairying a variety of natural resources are getting consumed on daily basis at a faster pace in Gujarat state of India too. On this serious note the state level apex body of dairy farmers of Gujarat has taken a serious consideration in this direction and discovered a novel scheme of giving back to the nature, so that momentum should be maintained.

A shocking earthquake (7.9-Richter scale 9) strike Gujarat on 26th January 2001. The epicenter of the shake was positioned in Kutch district. It caused death of thousands of citizens, tens of thousands were offended, hundreds of thousands were turn into homeless and harm of billions of Rupees was made.

Amul put step forward to help the needy ones and in 2001 GCMMF created a particular association named "Amul Relief Trust" (ART) under the supervision of Dr. V. Kurien.

This chapter is focusing upon brand AMUL with major attention on how its emerged as a brand from the local co-operative society further it dproceeds with branding strategies used by the firm to popularize the brand, technological e-initiatives taken up by the firm, how the local milk dealer expanded from small town to the cities and finally now Amul's products are available across the nation too. Amul is been primarily accountable, through its inventive market and product practices and adaptive to market changes, for India to become world's largest producer of milk. In state of Gujarat Amul is a state level head body of milk cooperatives which aim to endow with remunerative returns to the farmers and also gratify the interests of customers by continuously providing quality products according to varying needs of customers also by providing good value for money. Amul's product range consist of milk, milk powders, ghee, butter, cheese, curd, chocolate, ice cream, cream, shrikhand, paneer, gulab jamuns, basundi, Nutramul brand and others

The brand name Amul, has been originated from the Sanskrit word *Amoolya*, it means *priceless*. It is a brand name managed by cooperative organisation, Gujarat Co-operative Milk Marketing Federation Ltd. (GCMMF), which today is jointly owned by some 2.41 million milk producers in Gujarat, India. The Amul Pattern has established itself as a completely suitable model for rural expansion and growth. Amul has promoted the White Revolution of India, which has contributed in making India the largest producer of milk and milk products in the world. Gujarat Cooperative Milk Marketing Federation (GCMMF) is India's leading food goods marketing organisation. Finally a local Indian frim gained lots of competion from global palyers like Nestle, cadboury, and have given them tough compettion in all respects that is popularity, branding, advertising, and initiating CSR practices etc.

CASE 4

"Service Branding through Quality Practices in Public and Private Telecommunication Organization," by Ms.Archana Krishnan talks about branding of telecommunications services. The private sector telecommunication industry seems to be better in the implementation of quality practices and therein building a better brand image. The public sector organizations compromise on quality by awarding management and technical contracts to the lowest bidder which neither satisfies neither the customer nor the employees thereby earning them a poor reputation. Also, the management does not study the lacunae in the management practices through which it learn and compete with the private players. Such practices lead to stagnation and hence questioning the survival of the public sector organizations. There are several challenges faced by both public and private sector organizations. The public sector is embroiled in various bureaucratic hurdles, social obligations, lack of training, incentives and lack of thrust by the senior management in understanding that quality is indeed the need of the hour, for a long time survival. On the other hand, the private sector faces its own challenges in terms of lack of communication, the leader's orientation and empathy towards the subordinates, procedural delays due to hierarchical structure and lack of recognition of employee issues by the management.

Lack of implementation of quality practices could have a serious impact on the survival of organizations in both the sectors. Quality practices facilitate the organizations to survive the fierce market conditions through their good products and services. The quality management programme also encourages the participation of all organizational members and encouraging their feedback thereby making the employees more committed to quality programme.

The public sector the management must focus on good HR practices, Human Resource Information System (HRIS), MIS (Management Information System), IP-based Multimedia Services (IMS), training and feedback. There should be a greater sense of ownership by employees as well as senior managers, stronger and faster grievance redressal and better communication mechanism. On the other hand, the private sector must focus on leaders involvement in the processes and more employee centric attitude, developing a strong bond with the employees, bringing slow and steady changes to the organization service orientation service orientation that employees are prepared to take up new challenges.

The case highlights the service branding efforts of telecommunication organizations in the public and the private sector through quality initiatives such as benchmarking, leadership, service orientation, continuous improvement and knowledge management. The case brings about the perceptions of employees towards the implementation of various quality initiatives and also the challenges faced by the management in implementing these quality programs. The case could act a style guide for young managers who are trying to improve their service branding through implementation of quality practices in an unfavorable environment in their organisations. It further throws light on how the implementation of various quality practices could lead to the development of organization culture and organization effectiveness and subsequently contribute towards organization service branding. The case also stresses on the importance of 'employee reaction' to the change initiatives which if harnessed properly, could be a major determinant in the development of organization culture and organization effectiveness.

The case highlights the service branding efforts of telecommunication organizations in the public and the private sector through quality initiatives such as benchmarking, leadership, service orientation, continuous improvement and knowledge management. The case brings about the perceptions of employees towards the implementation of various quality initiatives and also the challenges faced by the management in implementing these quality programs. The case could act a style guide for young managers who are trying to improve their service branding through implementation of quality practices in an unfavorable environment in their organisations. It further throws light on how the implementation of various quality practices could lead to the development of organisation culture and organisation effectiveness and subsequently contribute towards organisation service branding. The case also stresses on the importance of 'employee reaction' to the change initiatives which if harnessed properly, could be a major determinant in the development of organisation culture and organisation effectiveness.

CASE 5

"The Importance of Supply Chain Management in Positioning and Creating Brands of Agro-Based Products" is written by Mr. Aroop Mukherjee and Dr. Nitty Hirawaty Kamarulzaman. The company is facing major challenges of globalization, economic uncertainty increase in demands of palm oil, and reducing cost of the products. There is an increase in pressure to make the right decision for better supply chain to have better performance.

The market environment will be highly challenging and competitive for effective and smart supply chain to create its product position in the market. Better supply chain management and its strategy will be good to manage and tackle the situation and to enforce better chain for better brand value of the product. As the market will be having turbulent environment and higher uncertainty on decision-making. It would require the companies to have strong supply chain management practices to facilitate the implementation of marketing strategy to capture the maximum market.

RSPO makes sure to implement better management agricultural practices, environmental, social risk, management tools, and to verify the credibility of the plantation and production process through certification and be sustainable.

The MPOI major role is make sure that during the process from harvesting to work-in-progress and final products is to reduce waste, reduce costs, and increase efficiency in lean systems, to build customer brand loyalty and optimize the supply chain process. It will result in the improvements of operational efficiency and reduction of costs with continuous improvements for long-term economic viability and create a brand image.

Normally, business people think that the brand image created by the relationship between brand and customers. However, the importance of company's brand is developed by having effective relationships through the complete supply chain, which enhance the organization brand equity. The business professional should not believe that it is because of marketing strategies have an impact on brand equity on downstream and also in upstream activities. The conclusion made from Joseph Benson and Bret Kinsella in their study "How Your Supply Chain Can Build or Destroy Your Brand" in 2004, that the supply chain capabilities can make or break companies' ability to fulfill promises made to all supply chain players. As a result, the supply chain can powerfully influence the brand equity, positively or negatively. Thus, supply chain plays an important role in positioning and creating brand equity, if it is carried out in an effective and efficient manner regardless of the market potential and customer preferences. Thus, it will help to create an attitude towards the brand among the customers.

This case study is done on agro-based company in Malaysia palm oil industry. To understand the importance of having an effective and efficient supply chain in a complex environment to position or reposition of the products. Since, it is as agro-based company the issue of sustainability is also taken into consideration to have sustainable supply chain management.

CASE 6

"Building and Development of Dairy 'Dana' Brand," by Boris Milović, deals with the branding processes of an agricultural company called "Sava Kovacevic" in Serbia. Problem that is presented in this research is brand creation, redesign and its role as a carrier of company's prosperity. Through case study question has appeared on how should brand become a driving force of development and strategic advantage of company. In order to achieve success in branding customers and market needs and desires must be understood. This is achieved with integration of brand strategy through company on each contact point with the public. Brand dwells in mind and heart of the customers, clients and market. It is the overall sum of all their experiences and perception, of which some can be influenced on and some can't.

Modern literature and business practice shows that the brand is created by long-term, persistent, patient and dedicated work on company's own offer. Each company or entrepreneur can, already during its foundation, create a brand, which is quite logical and in business terms necessary. All brands do not become "brands" as same as not all competitors are equal. Market of dairy products was not segmented. It was dominated by basic products focused on basic nutritional needs. Specialized products and value-added products that meet the specific needs of the customers are undeveloped or very modestly present, with specific characteristics that are not communicated. Arrival of significant foreign competition is expected.

The first step could be a measurement of brand equity in the market, which is calculated as follows: brand sales / sales within the category = brand share. This will show the position in relation to other players in the market and can be used for portfolio analysis of the brand, like the matrix of market development - market share. Primarily these techniques concern constructing the customer-brand relations and the recommendation is to use information technology through web sites, on-line communication in social networks and through telephone lines, etc. in order to achieve long-term relationships with customers and creation of their loyalty.

Dairy "Dana" should be transformed from a traditional company into a modern company with a strong and recognized regional brand. The main driving force of both transformation and future development are the needs and desires of consumers that are primarily reflected in the quality food, and then in the health and general welfare through the simultaneous differentiation of competition. Importance of creating a strong brand, although not a new concept, is currently attracting a lot of attention in the business world. More and more companies realize that if they want to diversify in a highly competitive market, they need a strong brand that will create a specific image of the company to potential customers. It takes much more than a cute name and logo in order to create long-term customer loyalty. Brand should reflect the vision of the company, values and philosophy of the organization. It requires a lot of strategic thinking.

Product and brand are important elements of the marketing program. Although, it is a big difference between the product and the brand. The product is all that is offered on the market and has the ability to meet the needs of consumers. Brand is an efficient and effective mean with which marketing oriented company distinguishes its own offer from competitors' bids. Brand management represents a special challenge in the implementation of marketing activities. These challenges relate to the adoption of the necessary decisions throughout the lifecycle of the brand, then the decision-making regarding the planning and development of new products, innovation of products, building manufacturers brand and private brands, making decisions on the extension and expansion of the brand, but also the realization of co-branding, and finally a decision to build a regional or global brand.

Brand benefits in marketing are realized by the producers and consumers. Effects of developed brand are resulting from the valuable, but intangible assets that marketing managers more and more carefully manage. Modern marketing practice clearly shows that there are significant differences in the realization of market performance of products and developed brand, which further implies the existence of real market value of the brand. Successful brand positioning depends on all instruments of the marketing mix.

In the process of branding marketing oriented company decides which elements of the brand are applied to the offer of a particular product. If in the offer of a marketing-oriented company is present portfolio of products and brands, marketing managers make decisions about the ways how to cover certain segments of the market, protect intellectual property on the market, build the image and market positioning. In the end, the product and brand marketers create certain ethical issues, especially in terms of protecting the rights of consumers and taking social responsibility. Basic ethical questions are related to the safety of products and brands during the use, planned obsolescence, the consumer's right to free choice, the consumer's right to full information, etc.

CASE 7

"Simply Food: The Crossroads in Front of A New-Born Food Brand," by Mr. Hakim Meshreki and Ms. Maha Mourad. This case deals with the branding of a food chain named simply foods a brand launched by "Orange International Company". The main purpose of launching simply food that originally was planned by Orange international board members was to create a strong food and beverage brand upon which brand extension could be possible. The first vehicle that was used to launch this brand was Simply Pasta and Simply Potatoes restaurants. The initial aim was the success of these two restaurants in order to create a strong brand buzz upon which many other restaurants could be launched in addition to other on-the-shelf food items that could be sold in supermarkets could be presented. The two sub-brands that were launched faced some technical problems in the operations as well as some challenges in terms of launching other Simply Food sub-brands and their geographical distribution. The main cause of the lack of success of the first two brands relate to some technical shortcomings such as the main chef and his assistants leaving the company without previous notice which resulted in a decline in the food quality which constitutes a very important ingredient in the success of the food and beverage business. Moreover, the management of operations was also lacking since the operation manager did not perform very well and the management hence depended on the board members availability which was not enough. Moreover, Orange International board members did not have a clear strategy of expansion and hence their steps in strengthening brand presence were not fast to capitalize on the successful launch of the first two sub-brands.

Simply organizational structure was lacking many important ingredients most important of which is the management representative intended to dedicate all the time to SIMPLY. Instead, this job was carried out by the board members who were not full-timers in simply and hence many shortcomings occurred in terms of the foods quality, proper communication with prospective customers and personnel management. Furthermore, the lack of lauching a professional call-center hindered delivery to pick-up which therefore decreased sales figures.

Simply team used information management in a very good way since they relied in their communication on social media which is a very efficient communication tool nowadays used by a lot of Egyptians and youth. Furthermore the store was managed through an integrated POS system which was used in stores and its reports were further used to analyze sales and the most prominent selling menu items.

Firstly, In terms of marketing simply foods has the option to remain communicating using social media, an alternative that is still important but did not so far prove its effectiveness. Otherwise simply team could use other communication tools such as billboards, booths in clubs (community based outlets) something that could foster brand awareness but needs on the other hand a strong and efficient management of operations to assure food quality, staff experience and friendliness.

Secondly, in terms of expansion, the decision to launch more stores having simply brand name is another important challenge facing management. From one side, it represents a big investment required which creates a financial burden on the investors, and from the other side it is crucial for brand equity building whereby more brand awareness is required and further emphasis on building the right image in consumers 'mind. Simply management can refrain from launching more stores or brands until properly mastering operations which is a safe avenue to follow however, this could slow down the brand buzz. On the other hand simply team can launch further brands which could be a burden on shareholders but and another failure could tarnish the brand image, however it can still be a good opportunity to increase brand awareness and expand the brand perspective.

A good approach or remedy to the current problem is for simply team to refrain from launching further stores since they incur a lot of initial cost and operations are still not mastered by the simply team. Instead they can launch quick community-based stores that could be a good opportunity to create more brand awareness and involves a lower investment than founding a big store. To support this, a strong management representative carrying out all the operational tasks of the board members should be hired in order to properly manage this expansion and to be able to rectify the current operational problems currently existing in stores. Furthermore, diversifying simply promotional mix is a must besides social media since it will allow for more brand awareness and should help in further shaping simply brand image to support expansion in community-based activities.

This case is useful for students starting topics such as marketing management, marketing strategy and branding. It provides a hand-on experience on brand building activities and tools to increase brand equity for a newly launched brand. Furthermore, it opens avenues for students to understand tools of brand extension and various promotional tools that could be used to foster brand building activities. In addition, it sheds the light on the importance of digital marketing including social media and other tools. Finally, it could be also used to provide some insights on the operational and financial challenges that face entrepreneurial endeavors for newly launched brands.

Overall some lessons could be learned from this case. First, launching a new food brand involves many activities and challenges most important of which are product quality sustainability and the creation of a strong brand image through the use of several promotional tools most important of which is digital marketing which represents a new and effective avenue for reaching young, fast paced and modern youth market segment. Second, marketing budgets should be managed with care for newly launched brands since in most of the cases, budgets are limited and reaching the appropriate market segment requires a lot of research in order to choose the most effective promotional mix. Third, operational excellence must be considered as a marketing tool since it is part of the market offering and a value added to the customer.

CASE 8

"Branding and New Product Development: A Case of Glemma," is written by Mr. Dennis Damen, Mr. Tim Wijnhoven of Glemma Netherlands, and Ms. Miao Wang. This case describe how a startup company trying to entre Dutch market. As a small business organization, Glemma doesn't have enough experience and capital. Branding is quite difficult for a company, which doesn't really have a brand. Glemma combined their experience and knowledge and has a special way of working. For example, they are using remote working style and MVP methods for the new product. These factors affect their branding strategy. Discuss managerial, organizational, and technological issues and resources related to this case. Managerial: It's a small company. They are work as team. No legal specification to control staff. The team contribute their work depends on their passion. Organizational: In the future, they would like to find the most talented co-workers to join their team. However it is very difficult to find. Technological: This related to remote working style. They have to make sure the technology supports them every time they have a meeting. There are only three people in the company. Different people has different role. They make decision together. The possible alternative is that they work together in one location. The advantage is that they don't have to suffer time difference and technology problem will disappear. The disadvantage is that they can't find the talented people without location restrictions. There are some very useful Applications can help the team share files and centralized communication tools so everybody is up-to-date. Some other technology like Google Drive can help them share resources, and make files accessible. Glemma has very good plan of approach, and knowing well of their brand. The important thing is to actually implement it and engage with real customers. They need to find the very first customer, and work for it. Then the first customer will bring more customers.

CASE 9

"Factors Influencing the Buying Behavior of Female Consumers with Reference to Top Three Brands of Make-Up Cosmetics in Pune City," by Ms. Mukta Srivastava talks about the case of influence of brands on the buying behavior of Cosmetics at

Conclusion

Indian city of Pune. A unique case in itself that describes the interplay between the concepts of branding and consumer behavior . The case is intended to obtain the answers of the following problems:

1. What factors are influencing the buying behavior of female consumers with reference to make-up cosmetics?
2. Has there been a relationship existing between the demographical factors and other influencing factors?
3. How the female consumers take decision for buying a particular brand of make-up cosmetics and what factors affect the decision?

The various factors are number of years of marriage, annual family income, skin type, purchase of other products from the same brand, reading reviews, purchase of cosmetics based on commercial, quality, durability & brand name of product.

Stiff competition, unpredictable behavior of consumers, brand switching, unpredictable decision making process of female consumers etc. are some major challenges faced by today's cosmetic marketers.

Customers are the end beneficiary of all marketing activities. No matter what type of cosmetics a marketer is dealing with, finally, he has to satisfy the needs of the customers. Therefore, the marketers need to understand the psyche of the end users. They have to study the buying behavior of consumers, the factors influencing this behavior and the decision making process of female consumers in detail.

Since factors like number of years of marriage, annual family income, skin type, purchase of other products from the same brand, reading reviews & purchase of cosmetics based on commercial have significant impact on the brand preference of consumers, the marketers need to focus on these factors while designing their strategies. As per the study quality is the most influencing product feature in the purchase of cosmetics, followed by durability and brand name. Hence, the marketers should focus on these factors accordingly. Most of the respondents purchase cosmetics from Retails (General Stores), followed by Super Markets and Premium Groceries. Therefore, the marketers need to make their products available at these places without fail. Last but not the least, the marketers should focus more on TV advertisement as per the study, respondents have ranked TV advertisement as the most influencing promotional factor in the purchase of cosmetics.

The Indian cosmetic market has a lot to offer in terms of penetration of new brands. The customers are becoming more aware with the willingness to try new brands and products. This is for a variety of reasons. Firstly, there is greater consciousness among the well-travelled, prosperous middle-class about international brands before they even enter the Indian market. Hence as they enter into the Indian market, they find ready reception. Secondly, it is also to do with changing retail environment, especially with more number of departmental stores coming up in the last decade. The new international brands see potential in the market and hence lots of brands are coming and launching in departmental stores. Thirdly, increased advertising has created and captured the imagination and awareness of the people. Today, not just youths but people of all ages use cosmetics - and think over the importance of grooming and being fashionable. Definitely the future seems to be brighter for the industry.

CASE 10

"A Case Study on Pitfalls in Branding of Boroline," is written by Mr. Pawan Kumar and Ms. Padma R. from India. Boroline is a one of the major products of GD Pharmaceuticals. The company was established in the year 1929 by Mr Gourmohon Dutta, a merchant from Calcutta, over the years Boroline is seen as a well trusted brand. In the initial stage, word of mouth helped Boroline in becoming the market leader. The brand identity the logo of the product was developed carefully. Elephant was chosen has the Boroline's logo as it had a enormous significance to all Indian's as it symbolises lord Ganesha (elephant god). The logo caught the attention on the customers even those who were not able to read. Boroline was known as the "Hathiwala Cream" (cream with elephant logo).

The overall problem of Boroline is that with the passing time they did not change their marketing or to be precise their advertising strategies because of which boroline seen more of a septic cream than a cosmetic cream and it resulted in no connect with present generation. Boroplus is the product of Emami. Leader in the antiseptic cream market with a 74% market share. It was launched in the year 1977 and it is the biggest competitors of boroline. Boroline branded themselves as cosmetic cream and they constantly come up with advertisements with stars such as Amitabh Bacchan, Kareena Kapoor and Bipasha Basu. Emami also Launched brand extension – Body Lotion and Healthy and Fair winter cream. The product has grown at a healthy CAGR of 12% in last three year.

Brand revitalization can be done for solving Boroline current issues. Brand revitalization gives new life to the existing brand. Strategies should be made to change the product, the packaging, the logo, and the advertisement. Many companies such as Nescafe, Horlicks or the Boroline's biggest competitor Boroplus keep updating their product.

Boroline was the market leader so it has the entire recipe for again becoming the market leader such as distribution channel, manufacturing units, established brand name, small segment but loyal customers. So acknowledging the strength and opportunities Boroline should work on its threats and weakness which is upgrading the product and updating marketing strategies.

Conclusion

It has been learnt from the case that even market leader can suffer in the same market if customer is not the focus. Every company has to keep customers need, want and demand on their priority list then only they can survive in the market. If Boroline would have understood they would have changed the product. Marketing should be not treated as step child. For a customer a good quality product is important but how a company convince him that the product is of good quality is in the hand of company and it can be done by a good marketing strategy only. One of the biggest reason of Boroline downfall was communication gap between them and customer. Competitors should also be given importance. It's very important to watch your competitors move step by step not to copy them but to learn from them. If Boroline would have analyzed how Boroplus is taking their market percent by percent they would have learned and could have updated themselves.

CASE 11

"Managing Brand Portfolio in a Crisis: The Case of a Pharmaceutical Company in Egypt," is written by Mr Rafic Khalil and Dr. Ahmed Tolba. This case tackles a real challenge that one of the leading pharmaceutical companies in Egypt is facing. The main problem is how to manage portfolio branding, when to start consolidating, divesting, and switching brands. External factors like the MOH, price regulations, and devaluation of the Egyptian pounds. This increased the cost of active ingredients. Internal factors as cannot improve the gross margin. There should be a strong communication between different stakeholders at the company as several decision makers are involved including, marketing, finance, factory, supply chain, business development and the top management committee.

To switch the brand to a new brand with the same mode of action and quality yet with a new dossier that could be granted a better price from MOH, with a name resonance between the current brand and the new one and start communicating the new brand from the makers of the old strong brand yet with a different strong molecule to treat pain. Students will learn from this case that companies always look for profitability so even when there is strong presence and high market share in certain market, still the brand profitability is the key factor in determining the brand potential and future. In addition they will try to think of different scenarios of a real life case and get to understand the pros and cons of each scenario whether it is portfolio branding or brand building from scratch, when to associate and link between brands and when to detach completely any relation between different brands.

CASE 12

"Ariika Bean Bags: A Successful Brand Capable of International Expansion?" is authored by Dr. Rania Hussein and a group of her students. The case deals with the brand expansion strategy followed by Ariika Bean Bags a popular company in Egypt. After analyzing the different PEST factors that affect the attractiveness of the countries, students need to bear in mind that some variables are likely to change. Accordingly, students should recommend monitoring these variables as it may affect the company either positively or negatively.

United Arab Emirates

Economic freedom is one of the factors that Ariika needs to monitor. Although the UAE ranked high on economic freedom, the country was directly affected by global economic changes Through further research, students could indicate that the UAE suffered tremendously during the global financial crisis. Accordingly any changes in the global environment will have a direct effect on the UAE.

Students could also extract from the case the importance of the construction industry and its effects on Ariika's sales. As mentioned in the case, there was a huge increase in the number of apartments, hotel rooms, and retail space. Accordingly, students could recommend monitoring the changes in the construction sector as it represents a great opportunity for Ariika.

Finally students could also extract from the case that the UAE has a large number of expats . These expats are more likely to buy Ariika's products as they have high disposable income and prefer European style products. Therefore students could recommend Ariika to consider the changes in the expat population as it will have a great impact on the company.

Saudi Arabia

Similar to the UAE, students could indicate that the construction industry in SA is a very important factor to be monitored. Students could extract from the case that the construction sector in SA has been booming and that three new economic cities are being built. The boom in the construction industry would increase demand on furniture and accordingly represents an opportunity for Ariika.

Another factor that students could indicate is the consumer buying behavior in SA. Students could extract from the case that Saudis change their furniture partially or completely every 3 to 5 years and spend 11% of their annual income on furniture. These figures are very attractive to Ariika, accordingly students need to recommend Ariika to continually monitor changes in spending patterns of Saudis

CASE 13

"Semiotics of Brand Building: Case of the Muthoot Group" is written by Prof. Sudio Sudarśan. The ultimate goal of branding programs is to build an iconic brand. The portage trail most corporations conform in the momentous navigation of the iconic goal is regrettably a cul-de-sac. Academicians, researchers, marketers, and practitioners misunderstand how brand building work, because, for over four decades, they have been taught to assume marketing theories advanced by neoclassical economics or social psychology builds strong brands. This chapter showcasing the Muthoot brand boldly abandons obsolete one-size-fits-all models of aspirational identity and taken-for-granted principles of mind share, to construct a new model at the intersection of cultural anthropology, perception science, and semiotics to extend the discourse of engineering brands beyond contemporary branding processes. To demonstrate culture-share of branding, the paper plots the one-hundred-twenty-seven year journey of the Muthoot Group to explicate structural semiotic concepts, approaches, and methods to establish scientific understanding of brand differentiation, true loyalty formation, and brand advocacy.

The case attacks the existing, incomplete or inadequate definitions of a brand to refurbish a comprehensive model of brand and to reconstruct the brand building process that will amply socialize academicians and practitioners into a genealogical mind-set to inspect brand building through a cultural lens for long-term profitability.

As a concept, brand relevancy has won a decisive foothold in the debate on how brands are shaped for future. Yet, there is still a conspicuous lack of critical scientific insight; concrete answers are few and far between. The case provides ample examples in the context of the focal Muthoot brand to explicate universal semantization of symbol usage in its journey of continued possession of positive interpretants and consumer perceptions to keep the brand fresh and relevant. Semiotic Brand Chassis and a 2x2 matrix introduced in the chapter describes imagery of form and function and how brands have different orders of signification.

If one half of Muthoot's consumers perceived the gold loaning business was downright risky,the other half had deep emotional attachment to the gold metal to relinquish as collateral. Muthoot serves as a shining example of definitive turnaround in the perceptions of its target consumers. Despite a competing company sharing brand name resulting in possible brand cannibalization, the case expounds what the Muthoot Group did in the domain of brand building that neutralized dilution and thwarted competition. The case ties these problems to semiotics to reinforce the significance of symbolic activity in consumer behavior. The case is as unique as the brand. Despite changes and diversifications of the core business, the case of Muthoot casts light how precise meanings attach to brand symbols. Though founded as a timber-hauling company in the 19th century, Muthoot craftily diversified into financial services by starting a homegrown chit fund on 1939. Throughout the 20th century, Muthoot expanded its financial services, almost changing the core to gold-lending business. During these years, Muthoot also targeted different market segments from low-skilled workers who needed loans to meet their impending expenses toward visa and air passage at the helm of the Persian Gulf boom to entrepreneurs in the liberalized, new India.

Gold is an appreciable asset, but to Indians the yellow metal carries a higher perceived value and greater emotional quotient. The onerous responsibility to convince customers to pawn against gold was on Muthoot's shoulders. Another mighty challenge was that scores of Indians were extremely heedful because of the seedy reputation of brokers and pawn shops. The greatest challenge, however, was the sharing of brand name that could potentially create brand name confusion in the consumer ecosystem, resulting in disastrous side effects: cannibalization of customers, identity ambiguity, transfer of both positive and negative brand associations. Markets change; brands do not. If brand is a covenant between the brand and its consumers, the Muthoot DNA encoded with 'generations of trust' reflects the web of mental associations that stem from myriad attributes with this long-term orientation despite diversifications, transformations, and changes to target market segments. Structuralist semiotic approach of Muthoot's brand equity profusely addresses in the delineation of the morphology of its brand discourse and in the syntax of rigorously monitoring the fundamental tenet of trust in the one-hundred-and-twenty-six years of its existence. Through long-term consistency, brand coherence enriches the Muthoot brand code. The strength of the brand code transmits continually the impressions of trust that Muthoot reinforces itself and its customers. To summarize operationalizing of Muthoot brand, the case examines various initiatives from denotative level to mythic level: brand integrity, customer-centric service offering, internal branding, CSR activities, and culture share. As is true with human beings, all brands are also born equal. The challenge then is to demonstrate that one brand is differentiated and a cut above the rest. Branding is the art and science of identifying and fulfilling human physical and emotional needs by capturing attention, stimulating imagination, and arousing emotion long enough to underscore that difference and make a profit from it. Consequently, building strong brands, the necessary lubricant that reduces marketing superfluous, has occupied a peculiar corner of consumer behavior since the world progressed from production-based economy toward consumption-driven economy. Since 1988 after the Economist called it the Year of the Brand, firms awoke to the financial value in brands. Brand building has since attracted massive interest amongst brand custodians and marketing researchers in the past twenty-five years. Because brand building in the 21st century has rapidly evolved as a diverting topic, concerning with myriad fields but not directly connecting with any, it is futile by virtue of the justifications to which camps in identity development and image research and management go to construe contemporary branding as something which it is not. Justifications and techniques of behavioral sciences, in one camp, are met by excess and irrelevant aesthetic and artistic rhetoric, in the other. In all, brand building does call for a tall order; the description of the entire dinosaur, including the various horns, crests, hoses, and tails of which the leviathan is fabricated in limited real estate. Structural semiotics offers a good deal of intelligent and responsible examination of every part of the branding anatomy with different degrees of success to uncover the underlying machinations that drive consumer motivations and develop memorable identity elements. The Muthoot brand demonstrates how a brand maintains its structural coherence and revitalizes itself throughout its varying and meandering journey. Marketers could also meaningfully apply knowledge from semiosis, which ingeniously provides a blueprint to better position brands in the minds of the target consumers, and also examine how consumers form distinctive brand perceptions to grow loyalty and advocacy for the brands they build and manage. Semiotics can provide robust brand-consumer structure as all brand custodians and owners strive to build iconic brands to get etched in the culture of the society.

CASE 14

"Sensory Branding: Branding with Senses" is by Ms. Surabhi Mukherjee Chakravarty. Starbucks is the world's largest chain of coffee shops, with around 40 million visitors per day. A visit to Starbucks is much more than a cup of coffee. By using a sensory marketing framework the company creates a deeper and more personal relationship with its customers. This is achieved by involving all five human senses to offer the customer a total sensory experience.

As early as the 1980s Starbucks developed a strategy for creating and delivering a sensory experience to consumers as a way to strengthen the brand. Giving the brand further aesthetics and emotional values and dimensions was seen as essential to creating a view of the chain as a third place outside of home and work. A visit to Starbucks should be an experience for the mind and the heart.

The inspiring environment makes it comfortable to read a book or talk with friends. The green and yellow of the interior, together with pleasant light, offer a soothing and restful visual experience. The relaxing music is selected with precision and care by the Starbucks Content Team to create the "Sound of Starbucks". Add to this the smell and taste of freshly ground coffee, as well as the comfortable texture, solidity and shape of the armchairs, and you have the characteristics of the sensory experience of the brand.

Starbucks uses a sensory marketing framework in creating an atmosphere where experience can be shaped, emotions can be expressed, and memories can be created. The green and yellow colour interior, together with pleasant light, offer a soothing and restful visual experience. The relaxing music is selected with precision and care by the Starbucks Content Team to create the "Sound of Starbucks". The smell and taste of freshly ground coffee, as well as the comfortable texture, solidity and shape of the armchairs, add up to the sensory experience of the brand. Starbucks provide a congenial environment for their customers to enjoy the entire experience. Sensorial Marketing Framework for Starbucks is achieved by involving all five human senses of the guests. The Guests get emotional connection with the brand as the pleasing ambience for them seems to be like the second home. The emotional values and sensorial experiences captivate the mind and heart of the customers, thence creating a personal relationship with the brand. Core competencies for Starbucks can be defined as high quality coffee and products are available at accessible locations and affordable prices, provided a community to share in the coffee drinking experience, and variety of choices. Starbucks also value ethics and good business practices and they are a leader being voted one of 2010's most ethical businesses by Ethisphere magazine for the 4th year running.

APPLE is one of the leading branding companies in the world. Marketing Experts like Marc Gobe argue that Apple's Brand is the key to the company success. During the late 1980s and early 1990s it was a marketing executive from Pepsi, John Sculley, who turned Apple into the biggest single computer company in the world, with $11 billion in annual sales. Sculley marketed Apple like crazy, boosting the advertising budget from $15 million to $100 million."People talk about technology, but Apple was a marketing company," Sculley told the *Guardian* newspaper in 1997. "It was the marketing company of the decade." The current CEO, Steve Jobs, spent $100 million marketing the iMac, which was a run-away hit. Apple continues to spend lots of money on high-profile ads like the "Switch" campaign, and it shows. Apple is a really powerful brand. It was awarded as the "Brand of the Year" in 2001. The overwhelming presence of Apple comes through in everything they do. That's the magic.Apple is the archetypal emotional brand. It's not just intimate with its customers; it is loved. Apple is about imagination, design and innovation. It goes beyond commerce. The brand is all they've got. The power of their branding is all that keeps them alive. It's got nothing to do with products. Apple has established deep, lasting bonds with their customers.

Conclusion

Before Steve Jobs joined the company, the brand was pretty much gone. It was imperative that Apple should be rebranded – so as to rejuvenate the brand. Apple abandoned the old rainbow-hued Apple logo in favor of a minimalist monochrome one, gave its computers a funky, colorful look, and streamlined the messages in its advertising. The sensory strategy appealed the customers. And results were wonderful. People's connections with Apple transcend commerce. According to Marketer Marc Gobe, author of *Emotional Branding*, "Apple comes across as profoundly humanist. Its founding ethos was power to the people through technology, and it remains committed to computers in education. Apple has a unique visual and verbal vocabulary, expressed in product design and advertising is clearly recognizable. Apple's products are designed around people, consider the iPod, it brings an emotional, sensory experience to computing. Apple's design is people-driven. Apple has always projected a human touch -- from the charisma of Steve Jobs to the notion that its products are sold for a love of technology."

The human touch is expressed in product design. Apple's flat-screen iMac, for example, was marketed as though it were created personally by Steve Jobs and Jonathan Ive, not by factory workers in Asia. Apple has established a "heartfelt connection" with its customers. It's like having a good friend. Somewhere they have created this really humanistic, beyond-business relationship with users and created a cult-like relationship with their brand. It's a big tribe, everyone is one of them. We all are part of the brand.

Apple knows the power of a sensory experience. Their product design and the architecture of their stores have built an emotional connection with people that is unprecedented in the history of branding. Apple is famous for creating a unique brand experience using all the senses. A customer can "experience" the brand in its full form in any Apple concept store. In any of these stores customer can see, touch, listen and even smell Apple.

An artistic collaborative group has created the scent of Apple's Mac Book Pro to recreate the aroma of an Apple product being opened for the first time. Greatest Hits claims a distinctive scent is created when unwrapping a new Apple product and claims Apple will recognize the smell. The scent recreates the smell of the plastic wrap covering the box, printed ink on the cardboard, the smell of paper and plastic components inside the box and the smell of the aluminium laptop. Apple almost went under in the 1990's but a marvelous brand rejuvenation strategy propelled it to 21st century super-brand status. Apple has succeeded in giving its product a humanized touch in an ever-evolving technical world. Responding to consumer anxiety about technology's evolutionary speed, Apple managed to make its customers feel like part of its brand by making it clear the brand understands their needs. Apple has always projected a human touch -- from the charisma of Steve Jobs to the notion that its products are sold for a love of technology. According to Marketer Marc Gobe, author of *Emotional Branding*, "It's like having a good friend," That's what's interesting about this brand. Apple have created this really humanistic, beyond-business relationship with users and created a cult-like relationship with their brand. It's a big tribe, everyone is one of them. All users are the part of the brand."

Sarmistha Sarma
Institute of Innovation in Technology and Management, Guru Gobind Singh Indraprashtha University, India

Sukhvinder Singh
Institute of Innovation in Technology and Management, Guru Gobind Singh Indraprashtha University, India

Compilation of References

(2006). Bulletin 372 - Origin-based products. Invan de Kop, P., Sautier, D., & Gerz, A. (Eds.), *Lessons for pro-poor market development*. Amsterdam: KIT Publishers.

Aaker, D. A. (1991). What is brand equity and why is it valuable? *Managing Brand Equity*. Retrieved from http://www.prophet.com/blog/aakeronbrands/156-what-is-brand-equity-and-why-is-it-valuable

Aaker, D. (1991). *Managing brand equity: Capitalizing on the value of a brand name*. New York: The Free Press.

Aaker, D. (2006). *Brand portfolio strategy*. Bucharest, Romania: Brandbuiders Group.

Aaker, D. (2006). *Capital managenment brand*. Bucharest, Romania: Brandbuilders Group.

Aaker, D. (2007). Innovation: Brand it or lose it. *California Management Review*, *50*(1), 12. doi:10.2307/41166414

Aaker, D. A. (1991). Foreword. In *Managing brand equity* (p. ix). New York: The Free Press.

Aaker, D. A. (1992). Managing the most important asset: Brand equity. *Strategy and Leadership*, *20*(5), 56–59. doi:10.1108/eb054384

Aaker, D. A. (1996). *Building strong brands*. New York: The Free Press.

Aaker, D. A., & Joachimsthaler, E. (2000). *Brand leadership*. New York: Free Press.

Aaker, D. A., & Keller, K. L. (1990). Consumer evaluations of brand extensions. *Journal of Marketing*, *54*(1), 27–41. doi:10.2307/1252171

Aaker, J. L. (1999). The malleable self: The role of self-expression in persuasion. *JMR, Journal of Marketing Research*, *36*(2), 45–57. doi:10.2307/3151914

Adnan, H. (2010). Dealers unsung heroes in palm oil supply chain. *The Star Online*. Retrieved May 27, 2014, from http://www.thestar.com.my/Story/?file=/2010/12/21/business/7656951&

Agriculture and Agri-Food Canada. (2010). *United Arab Emirates consumer behavior, attitudes and perceptions toward food products*. Retrieved Feb 27, 2014, from http://www.ats-sea.agr.gc.ca/afr/5661-eng.htm

Aiello, G. (2006). Theoretical advances in critical visual analysis: Perception, ideology, mythologies, and social semiotics. *Journal of Visual Literacy*, *26*(2), 89–102.

Aimin, H. (2011). A research on the supply chain management of brand agricultural products. In *Proceedings of Internet Technology and Applications (iTAP)*. Academic Press. doi:10.1109/ITAP.2011.6006258

Aitamer, G., & Zhou, Q. (2011). *Motives and guidance for the use of sensory marketing in retailing*. (Master's Thesis). Karlstad Business School.

Akoorie, M., & Scott-Kennel, J. (1999). The new zeal and dairy board: A case of group-internalization or a monopolistic anomaly in a deregulated free market economy? *Asia Pacific Journal of Management, 16*(1), 127–156. doi:10.1023/A:1015466304266

Alba, J. W., & Chattopadhyay, A. (1986). Salience effects in brand recall. *JMR, Journal of Marketing Research, 23*(4), 363–369. doi:10.2307/3151812

Alba, J. W., & Hutchinson, J. W. (1987). Dimensions of consumer expertise. *The Journal of Consumer Research, 13*(March), 411–454. doi:10.1086/209080

Albert, N., Merunka, D., & Valette-Florence, P. (2008). When consumers love their brands: Exploring the concept and its dimensions. *Journal of Business Research, 61*(10), 1062–1075. doi:10.1016/j.jbusres.2007.09.014

Alessandri, S. W., & Alessandri, T. (2004). Promoting and protecting corporate identity: The importance of organizational and industry context. *Corporate Reputation Review, 7*(3), 252–268. doi:10.1057/palgrave.crr.1540224

Altshuler, L., & Tarnovskaya, V. V. (2010). Branding capability of technology born globals. *Brand Management, 18*(3), 212–227. doi:10.1057/bm.2010.47

Ambler, T. (1992). *Need-to-know-marketing*. London: Century Business.

American Marketing Association. (1960). *Marketing definitions: A glossary of marketing terms*. Chicago: IL AMA.

Amoun. (2014). *Amoun Pharmaceutical Co. S.A.E.* [Company Overview]. Retrieved on June 23, 2014 from http://www.amoun.com/about-amoun/company-overview.html

Andrade, E. B. (2005). Behavioral conseuqences of affect: Combining evaluative and regulatory mechanisms. *The Journal of Consumer Research, 32*(December), 355–362. doi:10.1086/497546

Anholt, S. (2003). *Brand new justice: How branding places and products can help the developing world*. Oxford, UK: Butterworth-Heinemann.

Arnold, D. (1992). *The handbook of brand management*. The Economist Books.

Arnold, E. J., Kozinets, R. V., & Handelman, J. M. (2001). Hometown ideology and retailer legitimation: The institutional semiotics of Wal-Mart flyers. *Journal of Retailing, 77*(2), 43–271. doi:10.1016/S0022-4359(01)00046-X

Arnould, E. J., & Thompson, C. J. (2005). Consumer culture theory (CCT): Twenty years of research. *The Journal of Consumer Research, 31*(4), 868–882. doi:10.1086/426626

Aronczyk, M. (2008). "Living the brand": Nationality, globality and the identity strategies of nation branding consultants. *International Journal of Communication, 2*, 41–65.

ASSOCHAM. (2013). *Youths spend big on cosmetics, apparel & mobile: ASSOCHAM survey: Delhiites ahead of their counterparts on cosmetics, apparel & mobile!*. Retrieved from http://www.assocham.org/prels/shownews-archive.php?id=4128&month=&year=

Attrill, M. J., Gresty, K. A., Hill, R. A., & Barton, R. A. (2008). Red shirt color is associated with long-term team success in English football. *Journal of Sports Sciences*, *26*(6), 577–582. doi:10.1080/02640410701736244 PMID:18344128

Azoulay, A., & Kapferer, J.-N. (2003). Do brand personality scales really measure brand personality? *Journal of Brand Management*, *11*(2), 143–155. doi:10.1057/palgrave. bm.2540162

Baker, W., Hutchinson, J. W., Moore, D., & Nedungadi, P. (1986). Brand familiarity and advertising: Effects on the evoked set and brand preferences. *Advances in Consumer Research. Association for Consumer Research (U. S.)*, *13*, 146–147.

Barone, M., & Romeo, J. B. (2000). The influence of positive mood on brand extension evaluations. *The Journal of Consumer Research*, *26*(4), 386–400. doi:10.1086/209570

Bastos, W., & Levy, S. J. (2012). A history of the concept of branding: Practice and theory. *Journal of Historical Research in Marketing*, *4*(3), 347–368. doi:10.1108/17557501211252934

Batra, R., Aaron, A., & Bagozzi, P. (2012). Brand love. *Journal of Marketing*, *76*(March), 1–16. doi:10.1509/jm.09.0339

Batra, R., Mayers, J. G., & Aaker, D. A. (2006). *Advertising management*. Delhi: Pearson Education.

Baudrillard, J. (1968). *Le système des objets*. Paris, France: Gallimard.

Bauer, H., Heinrich, D., & Albrecht, C. (2009). All you need is love: Assessing consumers' brand love. In *Proceedings of the American Marketing Association Summer Educators Conference*, (pp. 252-253). Chicago, IL: American Marketing Association.

Benson, J. P., & Kinsella, B. (2004). How your supply chain can build or destroy your brand. *SSRN Electronic Journal*. doi:10.2139/ssrn.611543

Beverla, M. (2005). Brand management and the challenge of authenticity. *Journal of Product and Brand Management*, *14*(7), 460–465. doi:10.1108/10610420510633413

Bignell, J. (2002). *Media semiotics: An introduction*. Manchester, UK: Manchester University Press.

Blank, S., & Dorf, B. (2012). *Start-up owners' manual*. K&S Ranch Inc.

Block, L. G., & Keller, P. A. (1998). Beyong protection motivation: An integrative theory of health appeals. *Journal of Applied Social Psychology*, *28*(September), 1584–1608. doi:10.1111/j.1559-1816.1998.tb01691.x

Boer, H. (2000). *Changes from suggestion box to organisational learning: Continuous improvement in Europe and Australia*. Aldershot, UK: Ashgate.

Bowonder, B., Dambal, A., Kumar, S., & Shirodkar, A. (2010, May-June). Innovation strategies for creating competitive advantage. *Research Technology Management*, 19-32.

Brodie, R. J., Ilic, A., Juric, B., & Hollebeek, L. (2013). Consumer engagement in a virtual brand community: An exploratory analysis. *Journal of Business Research*, *66*, 105–114. doi:10.1016/j.jbusres.2011.07.029

Brody, L. R., & Hall, J. A. (2000). Gender, emotion, and expression. In *Handbook of emotions* (2nd ed.). New York: Guilford.

Broniarczyk, S. M., & Alba, J. W. (1994). The importance of the brand in brand extension. *JMR, Journal of Marketing Research, 31*(May), 214–228. doi:10.2307/3152195

Brown, G. (1992). *People, brands and advertising*. Warwick, UK: Millward Brown International.

Buzzell, R. D., & Gale, B. T. (1987). *The PIMS principle- Linking strategy to performance*. New York: Free Press.

Camp, R. (1989). *Benchmarking: The search for industry best practices that led to superior performance*. New York, NY: ASQC Quality Press.

Carroll, B. A., & Ahuvia, A. C. (2006). Some antecedents and outcomes of brand love. *Marketing Letters, 17*(2), 79–90. doi:10.1007/s11002-006-4219-2

Center for Industrial Studies. (2009). Retrieved Feb 26, 2014, from http://www.worldfurnitureonline.com/showPage.php?template=reports&id=5743&masterPage=report.html

Chaffey, D., Mayer, R., Johnston, K., & Ellis-Chadwick, F. (2000). *Internet marketing*. Harlow, MA: Pearson.

Chang, C. C., & Chen, H. Y. (2009). I want products my own way, but which way? The effects of different product categories and cues on customer responses to web-based customizations. *Cyberpsychology & Behavior, 12*(1), 7–14. doi:10.1089/cpb.2008.0111 PMID:19113951

Chattopadhyay, A. (1998). When does comparative advertising influence brand attitude? The role of delay and market position. *Psychology and Marketing, 15*(5), 461–475. doi:10.1002/(SICI)1520-6793(199808)15:5<461::AID-MAR4>3.0.CO;2-5

Chattopadhyay, A., & Nedungadi, P. (1992). Does attitude toward the ad endure? The effects of delay and attention. *The Journal of Consumer Research, 19*(1), 26–33. doi:10.1086/209283

Chernatony, L. D., & Riley, F. D. (1998). Defining a "brand": Beyond the literature with the experts' interpretations. *Journal of Marketing Management, 14*(5), 417–443. doi:10.1362/026725798784867798

Childers, T. L., & Jass, J. (2002). All dressed up with something to say: Effects of typeface semantic associations on brand perceptions and consumer memory. *Journal of Consumer Psychology, 12*(2), 93–106. doi:10.1207/S15327663JCP1202_03

Choi, W. J., & Winterich, K. P. (2013). Can brands move in from outside? How moral identity enhances out-group brand attitudes. *Journal of Marketing, 77*(2), 96–111. doi:10.1509/jm.11.0544

CIA. (2013). *UAE world fact book*. Retrieved March 2, 2014, from https://www.cia.gov/library/publications/the-world-factbook/geos/ae.html

CIA. (2013). *World fact book SA*. Retrieved Feb 25, 2014, from https://www.cia.gov/library/publications/the-world-factbook/geos/sa.html

Cobb-Walgren, C. J., Ruble, C. A., & Donthu, N. (1995). Brand equity, brand preference, and purchase intent. *Journal of Advertising, 24*(3), 25–40. doi:10.1080/00913367.1995.10673481

Colchester, M., & Jiwan, N. (2009). *RSPO principles and criteria for sustainable palm oil production.* RSPO. Retrieved March 15, 2014, from http://rspo.org

Cong, X. M., & Pandya, K. V. (2003). Issues of knowledge management in the public sector. *Electronic Journal of Knowledge Management, 1*(2), 25–33.

Cooper, P. (1979). Symbiosis: The consumer psychology of branding. *ADMAP, 15,* 578–586.

Coren, S., Girgus, J. S., Erlichman, H., & Hakstian, A. R. (1976). An empirical taxonomy of visual illusions. *Perception & Psychophysics, 20*(2), 129–137. doi:10.3758/BF03199444

Cowin, E., & Matusitz, J. (2011). The ongoing transformation of the McDonald's logo: A semiotic perspective. *Journal of Visual Literacy, 30*(2), 20–39.

Crainer, S. (1995). *The real power of brands: Making brands work for competitive advantage.* London: Pitman Publishing.

Cravens, D. W., & Piercy, N. F. (2006). *Strategic marketing.* New York: The McGraw Hill.

Crosby, P. (1979). *Quality is free.* New York: McGraw-Hill.

Czellar, S. (2003). Consumer attitude toward brand extensions: An integrative model and research propositions. *International Journal of Research in Marketing, 20*(1), 97–115.

Daniels, C. (2013). *Shahnaz Husain: The free spirit of an entrepreneur.* Retrieved February 17, 2014 http://news.in.msn.com/her_courage/shahnaz-husain-the-free-spirit-of-an-entrepreneur

Danta, H. (1999). Destination branding, niche marketing and national image projection in Central and Eastern Europe. *Journal of Vacation Marketing, 3*(5).

Davenport, T. H., & Prusak, L. (1998). *Working knowledge: How organizations manage what they know.* Boston: Harvard Business School Press.

Davis, D. F. (2003). The effect of brand equity in supply chain relationships. Knoxville, TN: University of Tennessee. Retrieved from http://trace.tennessee.edu/utk_graddiss/1996

Davis, S. (2002). Brand asset management: How businesses can profit from the power of brand. *Journal of Consumer Marketing, 19*(4), 351–358. doi:10.1108/07363760210433654

Daye, D. (2006). History of branding. *Branding Strategy Insider.* Retrieved 18th May 2014 from http://www.brandingstrategyinsider.com/2006/08/history_of_bran.html#.URzi-YaWDhSQ2013-04-05

De Chernatony, L. (1998). Criteria to assess brand success. *Journal of Marketing Management, 14*(7), 765–781. doi:10.1362/026725798784867608

De Chernatony, L. (2001). A model for strategically building brands. *Brand Management, 1*(9), 32–44. doi:10.1057/palgrave.bm.2540050

De Chernatony, L., & McDonald, M. (1998). *Creating powerful brands in consumer, service and industrial markets.* Oxford, UK: Butterworth-Heinemann.

Delazaro Filho, J. (1998). *Gestão da qualidade no Brasil: Setor de services.* São Paulo: Núcleo de Pesquisas e Publicações, Fundação Getúlio Vargas.

Delgado-Ballester, E., & Munuera-Alema, J. L. (2005). Does brand trust matter to brand equity? *Journal of Product and Brand Management, 14*(3), 187–196. doi:10.1108/10610420510601058

Delgado-Ballester, E., Munuera-Alemán, J. L., & Yagüe-Guillén, M. J. (2003). Development and validation of a brand trust scale. *International Journal of Market Research, 45*(1), 35–53.

Demarest, M. (1997). Understanding knowledge management. *Long Range Planning, 30*(3), 374–384. doi:10.1016/S0024-6301(97)90250-8

Dibb, S., Simkin, L., Pride, W. M., & Ferrell, O. C. (1994). *Marketing: Concepts and strategies* (2nd ed.). Boston: Houghton Mifflin.

DiMingo, E. (1988). The fine art of positioning. *The Journal of Business Strategy, 9*(2), 34–38. doi:10.1108/eb039211 PMID:10303386

Dollase, S., Joyner-Payne, S., Small, R., Milligan, R., Schneitler, G., Weavil, M., ... Asher, R. (2014). *Brand protection and supply chain integrity: Methods for counterfeit detection, prevention and deterrence a best practices guide.* Grocery Manufacturers Association. Retrieved from www.gmaonline.org

Domenico, C. (2010). A new concept of marketing: The emotional marketing. *Broad Research in Accounting, Negotiation, and Distribution, 1*(1).

Douglas, S. P., Craig, C. S., & Nijssen, E. J. (2001). Integrating branding strategy across markets: Building international brand architecture. *Journal of International Marketing, 2*(9), 97–114. doi:10.1509/jimk.9.2.97.19882

Duncan, T. (2005). *Advertising & IMC.* New York: McGraw-Hill.

Duncan, T., & Moriarty, S. E. (1998). A communication-based marketing model for managing relationships. *Journal of Marketing, 2*(62), 1–13. doi:10.2307/1252157

EIPICO. (2014). *Egyptian International Pharmaceutical Industries Co.* [History]. Retrieved June 25th 2014 from http://eipico.com.eg/index.php/about-us/our-history

Eiseman, L. (2000). *Pantone guide to communicating with color.* Sarasota, FL: Grafix Press, Ltd.

Eljundi, R. (2008). Furniture Sector in UAE to have highest growth rate in world. *Emirates 24/7.* Retrieved Feb 25, 2014, from http://www.emirates247.com/eb247/companies-markets/retail/furniture-sector-in-uae-to-have-highest-growth-rate-in-world-2008-10-02-1.56620

Eriksson, E. (2001). *A multi-sensory brand experience- Sensorial interplay and its impact on consumers' touch behavior.* (Master's Thesis). School of Business and Economics, Linnaeus University.

ESPICOM. (2011). *The pharmacutical market: Egypt* [Data File]. Retrieved June 21st, 2014, from http://www.espicom.com/egypt-pharmaceutical-market.html

EUROMONITOR. (2013, November). *EUROMONITOR international.* Retrieved from http://www.euromonitor.com/fast-food-in-egypt/report

Evans, P. (2014). Unilever commits to sustainable palm oil by end of 2014. *European Business News*. Retrieved April 5, 2014, from http://online.wsj.com/news/articles/SB10001424052702304644045791

Fan, Y. (2006). Branding the nation: What is being branded? *Journal of Vacation Marketing*, *1*(12), 5–14. doi:10.1177/1356766706056633

Fat Boy. (2014). Retrieved March 2, 2014, from http://fatboyusa.com/about/

Feigenbaum, A. V. (1961). *Total quality control*. New York: Mc Graw Hill.

Fetscherin, M. (2010). The determinants and measurement of a country brand: The country brand strength index. *International Marketing Review*, *4*(27), 466–479.

Fieldwick, P. (1996). What is brand equity anyway, and how do you measure it? *Journal of the Market Research Society*, *38*(2), 85–104.

Flint, D. J. (2004). Strategic marketing in global supply chains : Four challenges. *Industrial Marketing Management*, *33*(1), 45–50. doi:10.1016/j.indmarman.2003.08.009

Flock, E. (2009). *If it bears my name: It catches on*. Retrieved February 19, 2014 http://forbesindia.com/printcontent/4702

Fried, J., & Hansson, H. (2013). *Remote: Office not required*. New York: Crown Publishing Group.

Furniture in Saudi Arabia. (2011). *Industrial markets research*. Retrieved Feb 27, 2014, from http://www.euromonitor.com/furniture-in-saudi-arabia-isic-361/report

Gardner, B. B., & Levy, S. J. (1955). The product and the brand. *Harvard Business Review*, *33*, 33–39.

Ghodeswar, B. M. (2008). Building brand identity in competitive markets: A conceptual model. *Journal of Product and Brand Management*, *1*(17), 4–12. doi:10.1108/10610420810856468

Gilmore, F. (2002). A country – Can it be positioned? Spain – The success story of country branding. *Journal of Brand Management*, *4*(9), 281–293. doi:10.1057/palgrave.bm.2540078

GlaxoSmithKline. (2014). *GlaxoSmithKline [About us]*. Retrieved 26th June 2014 from http://www.gsk.com/en-gb/about-us/

Grayson, J., & Stampe, J. (2012). *Palm oil investor review: Investor guidance on palm oil the role of investors in supporting the development of a sustainable palm oil industry*. RSPO. Retrieved from http://panda.org

Gupta, S. (1988). Impact of sales promotion when, what and how much to buy. *JMR, Journal of Marketing Research*, (Nov), 25.

Gwinner, K. P., Bitner, M. J., Brown, S. W., & Kumar, A. (2005). Service customization through employee adaptiveness. *Journal of Service Research*, *8*(2), 131–148. doi:10.1177/1094670505279699

Hammer, M. (1997). Beyond the end of management. In *Rethinking the future*. London: Nicholas Barely Publishing.

Hanna, S., & Rowley, J. (2010). Towards a strategic place brand management model. *Journal of Marketing Management*, *27*, 5–6.

Harper, B. J. (2008). *Continuous improvement attitudes and behaviors- Assessing faculty practices in academic programs*. Paper presented at the Annual Meeting of the American Educational Research Association, New York, NY.

Harris, F., & de Chernatony, L. (2001). Corporate branding and corporate brand performance. *European Journal of Marketing*, *35*(3/4), 441–456. doi:10.1108/03090560110382101

Hasan, M., & Kerr, R. M. (2003). The relationship between total quality management practices and organisational performance in service organisations. *The TQM Magazine*, *15*(4), 286–291. doi:10.1108/09544780310486191

Hatch, M. J., & Schultz, M. (2008). *Taking brand initiative*. San Francisco: Jossey-Bass Inc.

Hennig-Thurau, T., & Thurau, C. (2003). Customer orientation of service employees—Toward a conceptual framework of a key relationship marketing construct. *Journal of Relationship Marketing*, *2*(1-2), 23–41. doi:10.1300/J366v02n01_03

Herzberg, F. (1987). One more time: How do you motivate employees? *Harvard Business Review*, *65*(5), 109–120. PMID:12545925

Heskett, J. L., Jones, T. O., Loveman, G. W., Sasser, W. E., & Schlesinger, L. A. (1994). Putting the service-profit chain to work. *Harvard Business Review*, (March-April), 164–174.

Hill, R. A., & Barton, R. A. (2005). Red enhances human performance in contests. *Nature*, *435*(7040), 293. doi:10.1038/435293a PMID:15902246

Hirschman, E. C., & Holbrook, M. B. (1981). *Symbolic consumer behavior*. Ann Arbor, MI: Association of Consumer Research.

Hislop, M. (2001). *Branding 101: An overview of branding and brand measurement for online marketers*. Dynamic Logic.

Hoeffler, S., & Keller, K. L. (2003). The marketing advantages of strong brands. *Journal of Brand Management*, *6*(10), 421–445. doi:10.1057/palgrave.bm.2540139

Holt, D. B. (2004). *How brands become icons: The principles of cultural branding*. Boston, MA: Harvard Business School Publishing Corporation.

Howard, J., & Sheth, J. (1969). *The theory of buyer behavior*. New York, NY: John Wiley & Sons.

Huang, Y., & Huddleston, P. (2009). Retailer premium own-brands: Creating customer loyalty through own-brand products advantage. *International Journal of Retail & Distribution Management*, *37*(11), 981.

Innovic. (2013). *The pharmaceutical sector in Egypt* [Data File]. Retrieved June 21st, 2014, from http://innovicbusiness.blogspot.in/2013/05/the-pharmaceutical-sector-in-egypt.html

Jenster, P. V., Hayes, H. M., & Smith, D. E. (2005). *Managing business marketing and sales- An international perspective*. Copenhagen Business School Press.

Jones, J. P. (1986). *What's in a name?* Aldershot, UK: Gower.

Joyce, T. (1963). Techniques of brand image measurement. In *New developments in research* (pp. 45–63). London: Market Research Society.

Kahneman, D., & Frederick, S. (2002). Representativeness revisited: Attribute substitution in intuitive judgment. In T. Gilovich, D. Griffin, & D. Kahneman (Eds.), *Heuristics of intuitive judgments: Extensions and applications* (pp. 67–83). New York, NY: Cambridge University Press. doi:10.1017/CBO9780511808098.004

Kapferer, J.-N. (1986), "Beyond positioning, retailer's identity", paper presented at Esomar Seminar, 4-6 June, Brussels.

Kapferer, J. N. (2008). *New strategic brand management* (4th ed.). London: Les Editions d'Organisation.

Kapferer, J.-N. (1992). *Strategic brand management*. London: Kogan Page.

Kaplan, A. M., & Haenlein, M. (2012). The Britney Spears universe: Social media and viral marketing at its best. *Business Horizons*, *55*(1), 27–31. doi:10.1016/j.bushor.2011.08.009

Kavaratzis, M. (2005). Place branding: A review of trends and conceptual models. *The Marketing Review*, *5*(4), 329–342. doi:10.1362/146934705775186854

Keeble, G. (1991). Creativity and the brand. In *Understanding brands by 10 people who do* (pp. 167–182). London: Kogan Page.

Keller, A., & Block, L. G. (1996). Increasing the persuasiveness of fear appeals: The effect of arousal and elaboration. *The Journal of Consumer Research*, *22*(March), 448–459. doi:10.1086/209461

Keller, K. L. (1993). Conceptualizing, measuring, and managing customer-based brand equity. *Journal of Marketing*, *57*(1), 1–22. doi:10.2307/1252054

Keller, K. L. (2001). *Building customer based brand equity: A blue print for creating strong brands*. Cambridge, MA: Marketing Science Institute.

Keller, K. L. (2001). Mastering the marketing communications mix: Micro and macro perspectives on integrated marketing communication programs. *Journal of Marketing Management*, *17*(7-8), 819–847. doi:10.1362/026725701323366836

Keller, K. L. (2003). *Strategic brand management: Building, measuring, and managing brand equity* (2nd ed.). Upper Saddle River, NJ: Prentice Hall.

Keller, K. L. (2004). *Brands and branding: Research findings and future priorities*. Academic Press.

Keller, K. L. (2007). Unleashing the power of word of mouth: Creating brand advocacy to drive growth. *Journal of Advertising Research*, *47*(4), 448–452. doi:10.2501/S0021849907070468

Keller, K. L. (2009). Building strong brands in a modern marketing communications environment. *Journal of Marketing Communications*, *15*(2–3), 139–155. doi:10.1080/13527260902757530

Kenney, J. (1998). Meeting the challenge of supply chain management. In *Competing through supply chain management* (pp. 1–6). Academic Press.

Kerin, R., & Sethuraman, R. (1998). Exploring the brand value shareholder value nexus for consumer goods companies. *Journal of the Academy of Marketing Science*, *26*(4), 260–274. doi:10.1177/0092070398264001

Klink, R. R., & Smith, D. C. (2001). Threats to external validity of brand extension research. *JMR, Journal of Marketing Research*, *38*(3), 326–335. doi:10.1509/jmkr.38.3.326.18864

Kniberg, H. (2007). Scrum and xp from the trenches. InfoQ.com.

Kotler, P. (1973/74). Atmospherics as a marketing tool. *Journal of Retailing*, *49*(4), 4–64.

Kotler, P. (1999). *Marketing management: Millennium edition* (10th ed.). Prentice-Hall.

Kotler, P., Armstrong, G., Saunders, J., & Wong, V. (1996). *Principles of marketing.* Hemel Hempstead, UK: Prentice Hall Europe.

Kotler, P., & Gertner, D. (2002). Country as brand, product, and beyond: A place marketing and brand management perspective. *Journal of Brand Management, 9*(4/5), 249–261. doi:10.1057/palgrave.bm.2540076

Kotler, P., Haider, D. H., & Rein, I. (1993). *Marketing places.* New York: The Free Press.

Kouzmin, A., Loffler, E., Klages, H., & Kakabadse, N. K. (1999). Benchmarking and performance measurement in public sectors: Towards learning for agency effectiveness. *International Journal of Public Sector Management, 12*(2), 121–144. doi:10.1108/09513559910263462

Krishnan, A. (2013). Effectiveness as an outcome of quality initiatives. In *Proceedings of International Conference on Technology and Business Management* (pp. 701-706). Dubai, UAE: Academic Press.

Kumar, V., Choisne, F., Grosbois, D., & Kumar, U. (2009). Impact of TQM on company's performance. *International Journal of Quality & Reliability Management, 26*(1), 23–37. doi:10.1108/02656710910924152

Lady D Bean Bag. (2014). Retrieved March 2, 2014, from http://ladydbeanbags.com/2014/en/Accessories.html

Lagergren, H. (1998). *Varumärkets inre värden.* Göteborg: ICT Education.

Lange, F., & DahleAn, M. (2003). Let's be strange: Brand familiarity and ad-brand incongruency. *Journal of Product and Brand Management, 12*(72003), 449–46.

Lee, H. L. (2004). The triple-A supply chain. *Harvard Business Review,* 102–112. PMID:15559579

Lee, Y. H., & Mason, C. (1999). Responses to information incongruency in advertising: The role of expectancy, relevancy, and humor. *The Journal of Consumer Research, 26*(September), 156–169. doi:10.1086/209557

Leif, M. H., De Chernatony, L., & Iversen, N. M. (2001). *Factors influencing successful brand extensions* (Working Paper). Birmingham, UK: Birmingham University Business School.

Leonard-Barton, D. (1995). *Wellsprings of knowledge: Building and sustaining the sources of innovation.* Boston: Havard Business School Press.

Levin, J. (2012). *Profitability and sustainability in palm oil production - Analysis of incremental financial costs and benefits of RSPO compliance.* WWF, FMO, and CDC. Retrieved from http://panda.org/finance

Levy, S. J. (1999). *Brands, consumers, symbols and research: Sydney J. Levy on marketing.* Thousand Oaks, CA: Sage publications.

Lindemann, J., & Valuation, B. (2004). Brand valuation, a chapter from brands and branding. In *An economist book.* New York: Interbrand.

Ljungstrom, M., & Klefsjo, B. (2002). Implementation obstacles for a work development-oriented TQM strategy. *Total Quality Management, 13*(5), 621–634.

Loken, B., & Roedder-John, D. (1993). Diluting brand beliefs: When do brand extensions have a negative impact? *Journal of Marketing, 57,* 71–84.

Loken, B., & Ward, J. (1990). Alternative approaches to understanding the determinants of typicality. *The Journal of Consumer Research, 17*(September), 111–126. doi:10.1086/208542

Low, G. S., & Lamb, C. W. Jr. (2000). The measurement and dimensionality of brand associations. *Journal of Product and Brand Management, 9*(6), 350–368. doi:10.1108/10610420010356966

Lytle, R. S., Hom, P. W., & Mokwa, M. P. (1998). SERV*OR: A managerial measure of organizational service-orientation. *Journal of Retailing, 74*(4), 455–489. doi:10.1016/S0022-4359(99)80104-3

Martineau, P. (1958). The personality of a retail store. *Harvard Business Review, 36,* 47–55.

Martineau, P. (1959). Sharper focus for the corporate image. *Harvard Business Review, 36*(1), 49–58.

Martin, L. (2005). Broad sensory branding. *Journal of Product and Brand Management, 14*(2), 84–87.

McAlexander, J. H., Schouten, J. W., & Koenig, H. F. (2002). Building brand community. *Journal of Marketing, 66*(January), 38–54. doi:10.1509/jmkg.66.1.38.18451

McCarthy, E. J., & Perreault, W. D. Jr. (1984). *Basic marketing* (8th ed.). Homewood, IL: Irwin.

McConnell, C. R., & Brue, S. L. (1999). *Economics* (14th ed.). New York, NY: Irwin-McGraw-Hill.

McCracken, G. (1993). The value of the brand: An anthropological perspective. In D. Aaker & A. Biel (Eds.), *Brand equity and advertising* (pp. 235–245). Hillsdale, NJ: Lawrence Erlbaum.

McWilliam, G. (1993). A tale of two gurus: Aaker and Kapferer on brands. *International Journal of Research in Marketing, 10,* 105–111.

Mielke, T. (2011). Global supply and demand outlook of palm and lauric oils - Trends and future prospects. *MPOC.* Retrieved April 28, 2014, from http://www.pointers.org.my/report_details

Milisavljevic, M. (2004). *Strategijski marketing.* Beograd: Centar za izdavačku delatnost Ekonomskog fakulteta u Beogradu.

Mohammad, M., & Mann, R. (2010, January 9-13). *National quality / business excellence awards in different countries.* Retrieved February 6, 2014, from NIST: http://www.nist.gov/baldrige/community/upload/National_Quality_Business_Excellence_Awards_in_Different_Countries.xls

Moilanen, T., & Rainisto, S. (2009). *How to brand nations, cities and destinations: A planning book for place branding.* New York: Palgrave Macmillan.

Moon by Mazoon. (2014). Retrieved March 2, 2014, from http://www.moonbymazoon.com/en/

Moreau, P., Lehmann, D. R., & Markman, A. B. (2001). Entrenched knowledge structures and consumer response to new products. *JMR, Journal of Marketing Research, 38*(1), 14–29. doi:10.1509/jmkr.38.1.14.18836

Morris, C. W. (1946). *Signs, language, and behavior.* New York, NY: Prentice-Hall. doi:10.1037/14607-000

MPOB. (2014). *The official portal of Malaysian palm oil board.* MPOB. Retrieved February 15, 2014, from http://www.mpob.gov.my

MUPEG. (2014). *Medical Union Pharmaceuticals* [About us]. Retrieved 26th June 2014 fromwww.mupeg.com

Murray, J. B. (2013). *The semiotics of brand management*. Retrieved April 22, 2014, from http://jeffbmurray.files.wordpress.com/2013/06/the-semiotics-of-brand-management.pdf

Muthoot Group. (2014). *The Muthoot Group corporate brochure*. Author.

Nandan, S. (2004). An exploration of the brand identity-brand image linkage: Communications perspective. *Brand Management, 12*(4), 264–278. doi:10.1057/palgrave.bm.2540222

Nauta, D. (1972). *The meaning of information*. The Hague, The Netherlands: Mouton Publishers.

Nedelea, A. M. (2003). *Tourism marketing policy*. Bucharest, Romania: Economica.

Nedelea, A. M. (2009). *Marketing in exercises*. Bucharest, Romania: Economica.

Newman, W. (2013). Focused brand management via supply chain visibility. *Supply Chain Management (SAP SCM)*. Retrieved January 20, 2014, from http://scn.sap.com/community/scm/blog/2013/05/15/focused-brand-management-via-supply-chain-visibility

Nijssen, E. J. (1999). Success factors of line extensions of fast-moving consumer goods. *European Journal of Marketing, 33*(5), 450–469. doi:10.1108/03090569910262044

Nilson, T. H. (1998). Competitive branding. New York, NY: John Wiley & Sons.

Nöth, W. (1990). *Handbook of semiotics*. Bloomington, IN: Indiana University Press.

Novartis. (2014). *Novartis* [About us]. Retrieved 26th June 2014 from http://www.novartis.com.eg/aboutus/index.shtml

Ohnemus, L., & Jenster, P. V. (2009). Corporate brand thrust and financial performance. *International Studies of Management & Organization, 7*(4), 84–107.

Olabode, A. J. (2003). The impact of total quality management on banks performance in Nigeria. *Advances in Management, 3*(1), 79–85.

Olins, W. (1989). *Corporate identity: Making business strategy visible through design*. London: Thames and Hudson.

Olins, W. (1990). *The Wolff Olins guide to corporate identity*. Ashgate Publishing.

Oliver, R. (1997). *Satisfaction: A behavioral perspective on the consumer*. New York: McGraw-Hill.

Onkvisit, S., & Shaw, J. J. (1994). *Consumer behavior: Strategy and analysis*. New York, NY: Macmillan.

Osterwalder, A., Pigneur, Y., & Clark, T. (2010). *Business model generation: A handbook for visionaries, game changers, and challengers*. Hoboken, NJ: Wiley.

Oxenfeldt, A. R., & Swann, C. (1964). *Management of the advertising function*. Belmont, CA: Wadsworth.

Palmoilworld. (2014). *Palmoil world*. Retrieved March 28, 2014, from http://www.palmoilworld.org

Papadopoulos, N., & Heslop, L. (2002). Country equity and country branding: Problems and prospects. *Brand Management, 9*(4-5), 294–314. doi:10.1057/palgrave.bm.2540079

Park, C. W., Jaworski, B. J., & MacInnis, D. J. (1986). Strategic brand concept-image management. *Journal of Marketing*, *50*(4), 135–145. doi:10.2307/1251291

Park, C. W., Milberg, S., & Lawson, R. (1991). Evaluation of brand extensions: The role of product feature similarity and brand concept consistency. *The Journal of Consumer Research*, *18*(2), 185–193. doi:10.1086/209251

Patel, S. (2013, July 18). Outline of production: Palm fruit to product. *Bloomberg Business Week*. Retrieved from http://www.schusterinstituteinvestigations.org/#!palm-oil-supply-chain/c1q1d

Patel, A. S. (1988). Co-operative dairying and rural development: A case study of AMUL. In *Who shares? Cooperatives and rural development* (pp. 362–377). Oxford University Press.

Paula, E., Chaves, S., & Moura Engracia Giraldi, J. (2014). Financial and economical value od country brand: Concept, conceptual definition and operational definition. *Asian Journal of Business and Management Sciences*, *3*(05), 42–55.

Pechmann, C., & Stewart, D. W. (1990). The effects of comparative advertising on affection, memory, and purchase intentions. *The Journal of Consumer Research*, *17*(September), 180–191. doi:10.1086/208548

Peirce, C. S. (1958). The collected papers of Charles Sanders Peirce. In C. Hartshorne & P. Weiss (Eds.), *Peirce* (Vols. 1-6). Cambridge, MA: Harvard University Press. (Original work published 1931)

Performance Management and Delivery Unit. (2010). Deepening Malaysia's palm oil advantage. In *Economic transformation programme: A roadmap for Malaysia* (pp. 281–314). Academic Press; doi:10.1002/047167849X.bio071

Peter, J. P., & Olson, J. C. (1990). *Consumer behavior and marketing strategy* (2nd ed.). Homewood, IL: Irwin.

Peters, T., & Austin, N. (1985). *A passion for excellence: The leadership difference*. New York: Random House.

Pfizer. (2014). *Pfizer* [About us]. Retrieved 26th June 2014 from http://www.pfizer.com/about

Pike, S. (2005). Tourism destination branding complexity. *Journal of Product and Brand Management*, *14*(4), 258–259. doi:10.1108/10610420510609267

Pinson, C. (1993). Marketing: Semiotics. In R. E. Asher & J. M. Y. Simpson (Eds.), *The encyclopedia of language and linguistics* (pp. 2384–2388). New York: Pergamon.

Pitcher, A. E. (1985). The role of branding in International advertising. *International Journal of Advertising*, *4*, 241–246.

Posner, M. I., & Keele, S. W. (1968). On the genesis of abstract ideas. *Journal of Experimental Psychology*, *77*(3), 353–363. doi:10.1037/h0025953 PMID:5665566

Probst, G., Raub, S., & Romhardt, K. (2001). *Managing knowledge: Building blocks for success*. Chichester, UK: John Wiley.

Randall, G. (2000). *Branding: A practical guide to planning your strategy* (2nd ed.). London: Kogan Page Limited.

Raturi, P. (2013). *An interview with Shahnaz Husain: You can be what you will yourself to be*. Academic Press.

Reddy, S. K., Holak, S. L., & Bhat, S. (1994). To extend or not to extend: Success determinants of line extensions. *JMR, Journal of Marketing Research*, *31*(2), 243–262. doi:10.2307/3152197

Reynolds, T. J., & Gutman, J. (1984). Advertising as image management. *Journal of Advertising Research, 24*, 27–38.

Richard, B. (2011). The new leadership paradigm. Raleigh, NC: lulu.com.

Richards, I., Foster, D., & Morgan, R. (1998). Brand knowledge management: Growing brand equit. *Journal of Knowledge Management, 2*(1), 47–54. doi:10.1108/13673279810800762

Ries, A., & Trout, J. (1982). *Positioning: The battle for your mind.* New York: Warner Books.

Ries, E. (2011). *The lean startup: How today's entrepreneurs use continuous innovation to create radically successful businesses.* New York: Crown Business.

Risitano, M. (2006). The role of destination branding in the tourism stakeholders system: *The Campi Flegrei case.* Paper presented at The XV Simposio Internacional de Turismo Y Ocio Esade – Fira, Barcelona, Spain.

Ritchie, R. J. B. (2000). The branding of tourism destinations. In *Tourism: Principles, practices and philosophies.* New York: John Wiley.

Roth, M. S. (1995). The effects of culture and socioeconomics on the performance of global brand image strategies. *JMR, Journal of Marketing Research, 32*(2), 163–175. doi:10.2307/3152045

Roy, D. (2006). *Discourses on strategic management.* New Delhi: Asian Books Private Ltd.

Roy, D., & Banerjee, S. (2007). CARE-ing strategy for integration of brand identity with brand image. *International Journal of Commerce and Management, 17*(1), 140–148.

RSPO. (2014). *Roundtable sustainable palm oil.* Retrieved March 28, 2014, from http://rspo.org

Russell, T. (2009). Dubai market has a large export appeal. *Furniture Today.* Retrieved March 1, 2014, from http://www.furniture-today.com/blogpost/12127-dubai-market-has-large-export-appeal

Sanchez, R. (2004). Conceptual analysis of brand architecture and relationship within product categories. *Journal of Brand Management, 3*(11), 233–247.

Sanofi. (2014). *Sanofi in Egypt* [Index]. Retrieved 26th June 2014 from www.sanofi.com.eg/l/eg/en/index.jsp

Saudi Arabia: Investment and Business Guide. (2011). Retrieved from http://books.google.com.eg/books?id=69zeEq4KA3gC&pg=PA182&lpg=PA182&dq=spending+on+furniture+in+Saudi&source=bl&ots=RceTBTSxx&sig=o3QWdjzIrExCLaYkPNt93986dEY&hl=en&sa=X&ei=OoIbU6n9O4HmywOinoCQDg&ved=0CDEQ6AEwBQ#v=onepage&q=spending%20on%20furniture%20in%20Saudi&f=false

Saudi Furniture Market Estimated at SR 4 Million. (2001). *Al Bawaba Business.* Retrieved Feb 24, 2014, from http://www.albawaba.com/business/saudi-furniture-market-estimated-sr-4-million

Saudis Spend 11 Percent of Income on Furniture. (2001). *Al Bawaba Business.* Retrieved Feb 27, 2014, from http://www.albawaba.com/business/saudis-spend-11-percent-income-furniture

Schiffman, L. G., & Kanuk, L. L. (2000). *Comportamento do consumidor.* Rio de Janeiro: LTC.

Schroeder, J. E. (2002). *Visual consumption.* London: Routledge.

Schultz, M., & Hatch, M. J. (2003). The cycles of corporate branding: The case of the LEGO company. *California Management Review*, *46*(1), 6–26. doi:10.2307/41166229

SEDICO. (2014). *South Egyptian drug industries* [Project]. Retrieved June 25th, 2014 from www.ebm.com.eg/.../SedicoWebsiteProject_e.htm

Sherry, J. F. Jr, & Camargo, E. G. (1987). May your life be marvelous: English language labeling and the semiotics of Japanese promotion. *The Journal of Consumer Research*, *14*(2), 174–188. doi:10.1086/209104

Shewchuk, J. P. (1998). Agile manufacturing : One size does not fit all. In U. S. Bititci & A. S. Carrie (Eds.), Strategic management of the manufacture value chain (vol. 2, pp. 143–150). Springer US. doi:10.1007/978-0-387-35321-0_16

Short, T. L. (2009). *Peirce's theory of signs.* Cambridge, MA: Cambridge University Press.

Siddiqui, J., & Rahman, Z. (2007). TQM principles' application on information systems for empirical goals: A study of Indian organizations. *The TQM Magazine*, *19*(1), 76–87. doi:10.1108/09544780710720853

Simon, C. J., & Sullivan, M. W. (1993). The measurement and determinants of brand equity: A financial approach. *Marketing Science*, *12*(1), 28–52. doi:10.1287/mksc.12.1.28

Sinclair, M. T. (1998). Tourism and economic development: A survey. *The Journal of Development Studies*, *5*(34), 1–51. doi:10.1080/00220389808422535

Singh, K. J. D. (2011). *National biomass strategy 2020: New wealth creation for Malaysia's palm oil industry.* Academic Press.

Slack LifeStyle. (2014). Retrieved Feb 27, 2014, from http://www.slackbeanbags.com/e-store/index.php?main_page=page&id=8&chapter=0

Solomon, M., Bamossy, G., Askegaard, S., & Hogg, M. K. (2006). *Consumer behaviour.* Harlow, MA: Pearson.

Steenkamp, E. M., Van Heerde, H. J., & Geyskens, I. (2010). What makes consumers willing to pay a price a premium for national brands over private labels? *JMR, Journal of Marketing Research*, *47*(6), 1011–1024. doi:10.1509/jmkr.47.6.1011

Steinecke, A. (2001). *Keynote presentation.* Paper presented at the Conference on Cultural Tourism at the ITB, Berlin, Germany.

Stine, G. (n.d.). *Supplemental information for the branding essentials workshop.* Retrieved from www.polaris-inc.com/assets / pdfs/9_Principles_of_branding.pdf

Suceava County Council. (n.d.). *Strategy development and promotion of tourism in Suceava.* Retrieved from www.tourisminbucovina.ro

Swaminathan, F., Fox, R. J., & Reddy, S. K. (2001). The impact of brand extension introduction on choice. *Journal of Marketing*, *65*(4), 1–15. doi:10.1509/jmkg.65.4.1.18388

Taylor, F. W. (1910). *The principles of scientific management.* Retrieved February 6, 2014, from http://nationalhumanitiescenter.org/pds/gilded/progress/text3/taylor.pdf

Taylor, V. A., & Bearden, W. O. (2002). The effect of price on brand extension evaluations: The moderating role of extension similarity. *Journal of the Academy of Marketing Science, 30*(2), 131–140. doi:10.1177/03079459994380

Teece, D. J. (2011, March/April). Dynamic capabilities: A guide for managers. *Ivey Business Journal, 1*.

Terry, G. R. (1968). *Principles of management*. Ricard D. Irwin.

TGI-Serbia. (2014, january 5). *Superbrands*. Retrieved August 4, 2014, from http://www.superbrands.rs/images/bible/60-61imlek.pdf

The Centre. (n.d.). Getting your organisation's branding right. *The Centre for all Your Training Needs*. Retrieved April 17, 2014, from www.the-centre.co.uk/documents/A_short_guide_to_branding.pdf

Thomson, M., MacInnis, D. J., & Park, C. W. (2005). The ties that bind: Measuring the strength of consumers' emotional attachments to brands. *Journal of Consumer Psychology, 15*(1), 77–91. doi:10.1207/s15327663jcp1501_10

Times of India. (2013). *India's cosmetics industry may treble by 2020*. Retrieved from http://articles.timesofindia.indiatimes.com/2013-12-24/beauty/45539514_1_cosmetics-indian-spa-creams

Travis, D. (2000). *Emotional branding: How successful brands gain the irrational edge*. Roseville, CA: Prima Publishing.

Troian, D. (2011). *Furniture industry: The consumers furniture preferences in different markets*. University of Trento. Retrieved Feb 26, 2014, from http://www.academia.edu/1502656/The_consumer_perception_of_design.Case_study_furniture_sector

Trout, J., & Ries, A. (n.d.). Positioning cuts through chaos in marketplace. *Advertising Age*.

Vacsera. (2014). *Vacsera* [Component Content]. Retrieved June 22nd, 2014 from http://www.vacsera.com/component/content/?view=featured&start=5

Valenti, C., & Riviere, J. (2008). *The concept of sensory marketing*. (Marketing Dissertation). Hogskolan I Halmstad.

Van den Heever, J. (2000). *Brands and branding in South Africa*. Johannesburg, South Africa: Affinity.

Van Rompay, T. J. L., Pruyn, A. T. H., & Tieke, P. (2005). Symbolic meaning integration in design and its influence on product and brand evaluation. *International Journal of Design, 3*(2), 19–26.

Veljković, S., & Đorđević, A. (2010). Vrednost brenda za potrošače i preduzeća. *Marketing, 41*(1), 3–16.

Völckner, F., & Sattler, H. (2006). Drivers of brand extension success. *Journal of Marketing, 70*(2), 18–34. doi:10.1509/jmkg.70.2.18

Volpe, A. (2012). Real estate in the gulf countries. *The World Luxury Market*. Retrieved Feb 24, 2014, from http://www.worldfurnitureonline.com/PDF/WFR-Magazine.pdf

von Reusner, L. (2014). How investors are changing the palm oil supply chain. *greencentury.com*. Retrieved April 28, 2014, from http://greencentury.com/how-investors-are-changing-the-palm-oil-supply

Vračar, D. (2010). *Strategije tržišnog komuniciranja*. Beograd: Ekonomski fakultet Univerziteta u Beogradu.

Wahba, M. N. (2014). *Holdi Pharma* [Home]. Retrieved June 22nd, 2014 from www.holdi-pharma.com/en/home/Pages/misr.aspx

Watkins, T. (1986). *The economics of the brand*. McGraw Hill Book Company.

Webster, F. E., & Keller, K. L. (2004). *A roadmap for branding in industrial markets*. Academic Press.

Welcker, J. W. (1949). The community relations problem of industrial companies. *Harvard Business Review*, *49*(6), 771–780.

White, I. S. (1959). The functions of advertising in our culture. *Journal of Marketing*, *23*(1), 8–14. doi:10.2307/1249358

Willsgire, J. (2014). *Empathy mapping with Lego figures*. Retrieved June 22, 2014, from http://smithery.co/random-inspiration-2/empathy-mapping-with-lego-figures/

Wong, H. Y., & Merrilees, B. (2007). Closing the marketing strategy to performance gap: The role of brand orientation. *Journal of Strategic Marketing*, *15*(5), 390. doi:10.1080/09652540701726942

WTO. (n.d.). Retrieved from http://www.wto.org/english/tratop_e/devel_e/d1who_e.htm

WTTC. (n.d.). Retrieved from http://www.wttc.org/research/economic-impact-research

WWF-Malaysia. (2012). *WWF-Malaysia strategy 2012-2020*. WWF-Malaysia. Retrieved May 8, 2014, from www.panda.org

Yoo, B., & Donthu, N. (2001). Developing and validating a multidimensional consumer-based brand equity scale. *Journal of Business Research*, *52*(1), 1–14. doi:10.1016/S01482963(99)00098-3

Zhang, Y., Feick, L., & Price, L. J. (2006). The impact of self-construal on aesthetic preference for angular versus rounded shapes. *Personality and Social Psychology Bulletin*, *32*(6), 794–805. doi:10.1177/0146167206286626 PMID:16648204

About the Contributors

Sarmistha Sarma is an Associate Professor at the Institute of Innovation in Technology and Management (affiliated to Guru Gobind Singh Indraprastha University, Delhi (India)) in the Department of Business Management. She has a PhD in Management from Fakir Mohan University, Balasore, Orissa, (India) along with a Master of Business Administration (M.B.A) from Gauhati University Assam (India). She likes to analyze the various factors leading to purchase decisions. Her research focuses on the ways lifestyle, culture, and ethnicity impact buying decisions. She is a founding member of the Center for Promotion of Multidisciplinary Research (CPMR), a society dedicated to the promotion of applied research in various disciplines.

Sukhvinder Singh is an Assistant Professor at the Institute of Innovation in Technology and Management (affiliated to Guru Gobind Singh Indraprastha University, Delhi (India)) in the Department of Business Management. He earned his MBA (Marketing & HR) from Guru Gobind Singh Indraprastha University, Delhi (India) and his BE (Computer Science and Engineering) from M .J P Rohillkhand University Bareilley (India). He has five years of industry experience at managerial level in MNC and private sectors banks such as Standard Chartered Bank, Axis Bank Ltd, and HDFC Bank Ltd. He has successfully achieved certifications such as NCFM (National Stock Exchange certification in Financial Markets) and AMFI (Association of Mutual Funds in India). He is the author of two books titled 'Sales And Distribution Management' and 'Services Marketing' published by Sun India Publications. His research interests include marketing management, sales and distribution management, services marketing, consumer behavior, and brand management.

***

Surabhi Mukherjee Chakravarty is an Assistant Professor in the Department of Management and Commerce with the CMR Institute of Management Studies (CMRIMS), a leading institution in Bangalore. She is currently pursuing her Ph.D from Alliance University, Bangalore. She earned her PGDBM from the Institute of Productivity & Management, Lucknow and her M.A. (Economics) from Lucknow University. She has presented papers in national and international conferences through reputed institutions such as IIM-Bangalore, IIM-Lucknow, and IIM-Indore. Her research is focused on marketing, consumer behavior, advertising, sensory branding, and emotional branding.

Dennis Damen is a co-founder of Glemma and a student at Fontys University of Applied Sciences. He has worked on several projects for a wide variety of companies, focusing on Front-End Development and Interaction Design for web applications. He has designed numerous web applications, including a virtual symposium for an Ecovillage in Brabant, Netherlands. His research specializes in workflow automation for small to medium-sized development companies.

Rania Hussein is an Assistant Professor of Marketing with the School of Business at The American University in Cairo. She earned her MBA from Georgia State University, USA in 2001 and her PhD from Nottingham University, UK in 2010. Her research interests include branding, innovation, and social media. Her research appears in journals such as the Journal of Business and Industrial Marketing and the International Journal of Marketing and Management Research.

Nitty Hirawaty Kamarulzaman (corresponding author) is a senior lecturer in the Department of Agribusiness and Information Systems, Universiti Putra Malaysia. Her research interests include supply chain management, sustainable logistics, reverse logistics, agribusiness marketing, and consumer purchasing behavior.

Rafic Khalil is an MBA student majoring in Marketing at the American University in Cairo. He worked in pharmaceutical sales for 8 years before expanding his career to marketing and brand management. He has since developed a variety of marketing campaigns for leading intercontinental brands.

Archana Krishnan is a Senior Research Fellow and Faculty of Management Studies (FMS) through the University of Delhi, Delhi, India. The author has a B.E in Computer Science Engineering (2006, Anna University, Chennai, India) and an MBA in Human Resource and Systems (2008, Anna University, Chennai, India). The author's interests include Total Quality Management, Organisational Behaviour, and Human Resource Management.

Hakim Meshreki is a visiting Assistant Professor of Marketing at the American University in Cairo, Egypt. He completed his PhD degree in Marketing from Nottingham University Business School, UK in 2012. His main research interests include international marketing, consumer behaviour, and branding with special emphasis on country of origin research, value research and brand equity. Since 1999, Dr. Hakim has worked as Partner and Commercial Director in Menatec, a Mena Company For Adhesives Technology. Since joining the company, he has contributed to a major business turnaround, defining and managing its strategic growth through key internal projects and partnerships with international organizations. He has also managed the transformation of Menatec from a product-oriented company to a service-oriented company, providing integrated solutions to current and potential customers. Additionally, he has project-managed the automation of internal company systems during the assessment, implementation, and running of a company-wide, fully integrated ERP system. Dr. Hakim is also an active board member in Orange International Company, a newly founded international food and beverage business. Through this company, Meshreki aims to create and manage high-quality food brands for consumers from Egypt through the MENA region.

Boris Milovic was born in 1969 in Vrbas. He earned his degree in Economics from Subotica in 1994 and his Postgraduate Studies Certificate – MS in Economics in 2005. In 2010, he completed his Phd in Economics and Customer Relationship Management through the University of Novi Sad. Milovec previously worked as an Executive Manager with Dana Sava Kovacevic, and currently works as Commercial and Financial Manager and Assistant General Manager for Sava Kovacevic. His areas of interest are internet marketing, market research, customer relationship management (CRM), customer behaviour, CRM in sales, branding, social networks, and brand management. He is also interested in applications of information communication technologies to various business areas, including agriculture, the hospitality industry, sports, education, and medicine.

Abu Sayeed Mondal is an Assistant Professor in the Department of Business Administration at Swami Vivekananda Institute of Science and Technology in Kolkata, India. He completed his Master of Business Administration (MBA) from the University of Burdwan, where he is also pursuing his PhD. He has worked as an Assistant Manager with reputed Indian banking organizations such as Axis Bank Ltd. He has also served as a faculty member for JIS College of Engineering and Mayfair Business School. His research interests include branding, strategic management, and services marketing.

Hend Mostafa is a Case Writer at the American University in Cairo. She graduated from the American University in Cairo in 2005 with a major in Business Administration, a Marketing concentration, and a minor in Psychology. In 2011, she completed her MBA from the American University in Cairo with a Marketing concentration. Since 2010, she has published numerous business cases through the Richard Ivey School of Business, the University of Western Ontario, McGraw-Hill Education, and "Innovations: Entrepreneurship, Values, and Development" a journal published by MIT Press. Her case, "Privatization of Madinat Nasr Housing and Development", was distributed at the Global Entrepreneurship Summit in Istanbul, Turkey in Dec 2011. She also developed and presented the business case "Azza Fahmy Jewelry: From a Local Bazaar to a Fashion Runway" at the Academy of International Business (AIB) MENA conference, "East Meets West", in 2013.

Maha Mourad is an Associate Professor of Marketing at the Department of Management and Director of El-Khazindar Business Research and Case Center-School of Business at the American University in Cairo (AUC). She was awarded a Fulbright Post Doctoral research grant at George Washington University, USA as well an Erasmus Munds Post Doctoral research grant at Warsaw School of Economics, Poland. Her research interests include: Brand Equity, Service Marketing, Innovation Marketing and Higher Education Marketing. Dr. Mourad has won numerous awards for her research, including the 2012 "Faculty Excellence in Research" award and the 2014 "Excellence in Research and Creative Endeavors" award through AUC. In 2012, her essay was selected as a Highly Commended Paper at the Literati Network Awards for Excellence. As an Instructor, she has taught a variety of marketing courses at AUC for both undergraduate and MBA levels. As a professional, she has provided consulting services for several regional and national organizations.

Aroop Mukherjee is a PhD candidate in the Department of Agribusiness and Information Systems at the Universiti Putra, Malaysia. His research interests include agribusiness, supply chain management, supply chain strategies, sustainability, innovation, knowledge management, and agri-informatics.

Alexandru Nedelea, Ph.D., is an Associate Professor of Marketing at the University Stefan cel Mare of Suceava, Romania. He has written extensively for a wide range of academic and professional audiences. Previous publications include *Small and Medium Enterprises in Contemporary Society* (KMV, Germany), *International Tourism: World Geography and Developmental Perspectives* (Abhijeet Publications, New Delhi, India), *Tourism Marketing* (Derc Publishing House, Tewksbury, USA), and *Knowledge Management Practices*, *Comparative Tourism Marketing Case Studies* (Abhijeet Publications, New Delhi, India). He is editor-in-chief of the journals

Ecoforum and Revista de Turism (Journal of Tourism: Studies and Research in Tourism) and a member of the editorial board for the journals Amfiteatru Economic, International Journal of Leisure and Tourism Marketing, Journal of Tourism: An International Research Journal, Tourism Today, *Asia-Pacific Journal of Innovation in Hospitality and Tourism, Enlightening Tourism. A Pathmaking Journal, International Journal of Qualitative Research in Services, Journal of Tourism Security, International Journal of Safety and Security in Tourism, Ekonomika, Ekonomika, Journal for Economic Theory and Practice and Social Issuses, Journal of Tourism Research, Service Management, The Journal Anuario de Turismo y Sociedad, Tourism Issues, European Journal of Tourism Research, Environmental Economics, The USV Annals of Economics and Public Administration.* He is a member of numerous scientific associations including the International Association of Scientific Experts in Tourism, International Association on Public and Non-Profit Marketing, Romanian Marketing Association, International Network for Research in Consumer Behaviour Studies, Regional Science Association International, World Research Club (WRC), European Association of Research on Services (RESER), Marketing and Tourism Research Interest Committees - EuroMed Research Business Institute (EMRBI), and the Centre International de Recherche et d'Etudes Touristiques (CIRET). He is coordinator of Asian Studies Club, Romania-, Voyage Club, Bucovina Tourism Marketing Center, Volunteer Order, and Marketing Club.

R. Padma teaches undergraduate courses with the Jain Group of Institution in Bangalore. She earned a Masters in Philosophy from Jain University and a Masters in Commerce with specialization in Finance from Christ University, Bangalore. She has written and presented various research articles in national and international conferences, focusing on human resources, finance, and marketing.

Dilip Roy is a fellow of the Indian Institute of Management, Calcutta (IIM-C) and a former Professor of Business Administration through the University of Burdwan. He received his MSc (with a Gold Medal) and PhD in Statistics from Calcutta University before pursuing his post-doctoral work with Dalhousie University, Canada. Dr Roy has contributed to more than one hundred and seventy five papers published in both international and Indian journals. His research has appeared in IEEE Transactions on Reliability, the Journal of Multivariate Analysis, the Journal of Applied Probability International, the Journal of Commerce and Management, and the European Journal of Marketing. He possesses over twenty five years of teaching experience at the postgraduate level.

Anupam Sharma has a Bachelors of Technology degree in Computer Science, a Masters in Business Management, and a PhD. In Corporate Social Responsibility from Thapar University, Patiala. She has published numerous research papers in international journals, three of which are listed in the Social Sciences Citation Index. Sharma has presented her research through both national and international conferences. She has contributed one book chapter on Organizations in the new millennium: Challenges and Opportunities with McMillan Publications. She has also published a book entitled, 'A Strategic Framework for Corporate Social Responsibility Practices: A Study of India', with LAMBERT (LAP Publications) Germany.

Pawan Kumar Sharma is currently pursuing his Masters in Philosophy and Management with the Jain Group of Institutions, where he teaches both undergraduate and post-graduate courses. As a professional, he has worked for an Advertising Consulting Firm in Hyderabad, gaining a comprehensive understanding of commerce and industry. He has written three management books and presented research papers in various national and international conferences.

Mukta Srivastava is a NET Qualified Post-Graduate Teacher through the University of Pune as well as a 2006 MBA Gold Medalist. She has presented papers in conferences through IIM Lucknow, IIM Kozhikode, and Symbiosis. She has previously published two books and thirteen articles in various national and international journals. Her teaching specialties include Business Research Methods, Marketing Management, Consumer and Organizational Buying Behavior, Distribution and Retail Management, and Brand Management. She is the recipient of a research grant through the BCUD Research Grant Scheme of the University of Pune.

Sudio Sudarsan has enjoyed a successful career as a Consumer Behaviorist and Brand Strategist. He has helped numerous companies drive demand through more effective use of their brand, marketing, design, and innovation assets. He is well-recognized for his unique approach for building brand strategies, integrating a practitioner's perspective with a profound knowledge of cognitive psychology, neuroscience, and cultural anthropology. Though he currently resides in New York City, Sudarsan travels globally for consulting, speaking, and teaching engagements.

Ahmed Tolba is an Associate Professor of Marketing and Department Chair with the School of Business at the American University in Cairo. He is also the founder of El-Khazindar Business Research and Case Center (KCC), the first center in the Middle East and North Africa region that focuses on developing world-class refereed case studies. He was awarded his Ph.D. from George Washington University in 2006; his MBA & B.Sc. from AUC in 1997 & 2001 respectively. He taught a variety of courses at the undergraduate and graduate levels. He received the Teaching Excellence Award (June 2010) and the School of Business Teaching Award (May 2009) from the American University in Cairo. His research focuses on Brand Equity, Innovation Marketing, Online Marketing, Nation Branding, Social Marketing and Entrepreneurship. He published in leading academic journals and conferences, and co-authored the leading textbook "Principles of Marketing: Arab World Edition" with marketing gurus Philip Kotler and Gary Armstrong.

Miao Wang is an International Business Management student of Fontys University of Applied Science in the Netherlands. During her bachelor study, she chose Academic Oration as her minor. Her research in market advertising contributed to her graduation thesis, *Dutch Consumers' Response towards Mobile Advertising --An exploratory study of what factors influence consumers' responses towards mobile advertising.* She has worked on several international marketing projects, including cases with Nike, Inc, Lely and BMW. She currently volunteers with the United Nations and UNICEF.

Tim Wijnhoven is a co-founder of Glemma and a graduate student at Fontys University of Applied Sciences. He has worked on several projects for a wide variety of companies, specializing in design complimented by storytelling. He has designed multiple web applications with a focus on creativity and effective communication. He proudly utilizes the GTD principle to manage his own company.

Index

A

Amul 47-68, 70-77, 242
antiseptic 239, 242-248, 250-251
Apple 187-188, 327, 333-339, 360-362
Ariika 277-283, 285, 291, 295
Auditory Branding 327, 348-350, 365

B

Benchmarking 79, 82, 87-90, 96, 98-101
Biologics and Biosimilars 256, 275
boric power 239, 245
Boroline 239-241, 243-251
Brand Advocacy 324-325
Brand Buzz 173, 175-177
Brand Elements 2, 253
Brand Equity 10-11, 18-21, 23, 103, 121,
    126-130, 162, 176-177, 237, 251-255,
    266, 268, 274, 324
Brand Identity 1, 3, 9-10, 12, 22-23, 30,
    32, 43, 151, 153, 165, 167, 172, 175,
    177, 245-246, 307, 310, 321, 327, 352
Brand Image 3, 8-10, 12, 20, 22, 28, 46,
    52, 82, 123, 125, 128, 132-133, 161,
    173-176, 178, 188, 240, 245, 250-251,
    277, 280, 297, 307, 315, 321, 338-339
Brand Loyalty 2, 5, 11, 97, 124, 126-127,
    199, 238, 248, 299, 325, 327, 341,
    355, 359
Brand Management 3, 19-21, 30-31, 43-44,
    47, 75, 80, 127, 129, 134, 147, 151,
    153-154, 160-163, 178, 252, 298,
    324, 364
Brand Meaning 310, 325

Brand Name 3-4, 13-14, 18, 47, 49-50, 52,
    56, 76-77, 103, 120, 164, 176-177,
    232, 237, 274, 280, 282, 297, 303,
    305, 309, 311, 313
Brand Personality 8, 10-11, 19, 165, 172,
    177, 310
Brand Positioning 1, 9-10, 12, 23, 56, 125,
    141, 164, 174
Brand Preference 19, 194, 198-230, 232-
    233, 235-238
Brand Promotion 239, 242, 253
Brand Strength 5, 43, 163
Bucovina 24-28, 31, 33-42
Buying Behavior 194, 196-197, 199, 238,
    291, 349

C

C4 Strategy Matrix 1, 12-13, 18, 23
Connotation 318-319, 325
Conscious Consumer 47, 67, 71, 77-78
Consumer Behavior 159, 238, 286, 295,
    299, 321-323, 325, 347
Consumer Culture Theory 298, 300, 318,
    322, 325
Continuous Improvement 65, 79, 82, 87,
    93-94, 97-100, 102, 123, 171
Cosmetics 15-16, 126, 194-195, 197-200,
    202-220, 222, 224-232, 234-238, 244,
    257
CSR (Corporate Social Responsibility) 47,
    77
Customer Relationship Management 282,
    357, 365
Customer Satisfaction 80-81, 86, 94, 132,
    163, 311, 357

D

Dairy farm 133, 135, 137, 139-145, 147, 149-150, 152-153, 155-161
Denotation 5, 319, 325
Destination Branding 24, 29, 33, 42, 44-45
Destination Marketing 24, 46

E

Egypt 5, 165-166, 170, 172, 176, 254, 256-266, 268-270, 272-275, 277-278, 280-283, 295, 330-331
Emotional Branding 327, 361, 364-365
External Realization 12-14, 18, 23

F

FMCG 15, 64, 67, 239-244, 250, 253

G

Generics 254, 256-257, 271, 273, 275
Glemma 178-186, 190-191
Globalization 47, 67, 71, 77-78, 125, 134, 147
gold loan 306, 309, 311, 314-315
Gustative Branding 351, 365

H

human resource 81, 85, 93, 97

I

India 1, 15-17, 21, 47-51, 53, 56-60, 62-63, 67, 70, 73, 75-76, 78-80, 82, 84, 86, 112, 114, 119-120, 194-195, 200, 238-249, 257, 260, 285, 290, 300, 304-306, 311, 314-318, 327, 331
Internal Effort 12-14, 18, 23
Internationalization 277, 297

K

Kaira District 48-50
Knowledge Management 79, 82, 87, 94-95, 98-100, 102, 253

L

Leadership 18, 42, 79, 82, 85, 87, 90-91, 96, 98-99, 101-102, 128, 151, 171, 334
Logo 3-4, 7, 13, 18, 32, 37, 86, 150, 171, 173, 177, 180, 239, 245-246, 250, 253, 300-302, 304, 310, 313, 323, 331, 361

M

Malaysian Palm Oil Industry (MPOI) 107, 118, 124, 126, 130
Marketing Mix 81, 136, 138, 140, 142-145, 148, 156, 194-195, 199, 238, 279, 356
Market Leader 86, 239, 246, 249, 253
Market Segmentation 132, 135-140, 147, 163, 243
MENA region 166, 261-263, 278
Metaphor 326
Milk 47, 49, 51, 53, 56, 59-60, 64-68, 70-72, 74-75, 133, 135-136, 139-141, 144, 146-149, 155, 157, 159, 330
MOH 254, 259, 265, 268, 274-275
MPOI 103, 107, 109, 111, 118, 124, 126, 130
Muthoot 298, 300-304, 306, 308-309, 311-319, 321-322, 324

N

New Product Development 178, 193

O

Oil Industry 104, 107, 109, 115, 117-118, 124, 126, 128-130
Olfactory Branding 327, 350, 365
Ordering Hub 165, 170, 177
Organisational Culture 79, 82, 86-93, 95, 99, 102
Organisational Effectiveness 79, 82, 87-91, 94-95, 99, 102
Over the counter 244, 248, 254-255, 258-259, 273, 275

P

Packaging and Labeling 164
Palm Oil 103-107, 109-115, 117-124, 126-131
Pasta 167-170, 172-176
Patency 254, 256, 275-276
Peircean Model 298, 304, 326
Pharma-Emerging Markets 256, 276
Place Branding 24, 29, 43-44, 46
Product Development 110, 125, 178, 193, 277, 297
Public and Private Sector 82-83, 87, 99, 102

Q

Quality Initiative 79, 82, 87-88, 96, 98, 100, 102

R

remote control 190-192
Roundtable on Sustainable Palm Oil (RSPO) 103, 120, 122-123, 127, 129-131
RX 258-259, 276

S

Semantics 305, 321, 326
Semiotic Brand Chassis 320, 326
Semiotics 298, 301, 305, 308, 313, 319, 321-326

Service Branding 79, 82-83, 85, 87-88, 91, 93-95, 99, 102
Service Orientation 79, 82, 87, 92-93, 97-98, 102
Signification Model 301, 326
Signifier 301-302, 319, 325-326
Skin care 16, 239, 241-243, 248-250
Slogan 32, 35-37, 132, 159, 164, 173, 245
Small Business Management 178, 193
Social Media 165, 173-175, 177, 185, 191, 252, 280, 300, 343
Spill-Over 176-177
Startup Company 178, 190, 193
Strategic Business Plan 193
Supply Chain Management 103, 109-110, 120-121, 124-126, 128-129, 131
Supply Chain Strategies 131
Sustainability 74, 117, 123-124, 126-127, 129-131, 154, 282, 316
Symbolism 302, 305-308, 321, 326

T

Tactile Branding 352, 365
Technology-Based Company 178, 193
Tele-Communication Industry 87, 91, 102
Tourism Brand 24-25, 32-34, 36, 40-41, 46
Tourism Marketing 28, 44, 46

V

Visual Branding 327, 341, 343, 365

CPSIA information can be obtained at www.ICGtesting.com
Printed in the USA
BVOW06*0849160215

387415BV00008B/22/P